Other Works of Irving Fineman

NOVELS

THIS PURE YOUNG MAN
LOVERS MUST LEARN
HEAR, YE SONS
DOCTOR ADDAMS
JACOB: AN AUTOBIOGRAPHICAL NOVEL
RUTH

PLAYS

FIG TREE MADONNA
AKIBA: A CHILD'S PLAY

The Life of Henrietta Szold 1860–1945

Woman of Valor

by IRVING FINEMAN

A woman of valor who can find?
For her worth is far above rubies.
PROVERBS 31:10

Simon and Schuster • New York • 1961

PUBLISHED BY SIMON AND SCHUSTER, INC.
ROCKEFELLER CENTER, 630 FIFTH AVENUE
NEW YORK 20, N. Y.

Second Printing

LIBRARY OF CONGRESS CATALOG CARD NUMBER: 61-15119
MANUFACTURED IN THE UNITED STATES OF AMERICA
BY H. WOLFF BOOK MFG. CO., INC., NEW YORK

To Hadassah

CONTENTS

On biography:

Alexander Pope: "The proper study of mankind is man."

Dr. Johnson: ". . . if nothing but the bright side of characters should be shown, we should sit in despondency and think it utterly impossible to imitate them in *anything*."

Thomas Carlyle: "How delicate, how decent is English biography, bless its mealy mouth!"

Walt Whitman, to his friend and biographer, Horace Traubel: "Whatever you do, do not prettify me. Include all the hells and damns."

William Dean Howells: "I wonder why we hate the past so!"
Mark Twain: "It's so damned humiliating!"

E. M. Forster: "The true history of the human race is the story of human affections. In comparison with it, all histories—even economic history—are false."

Sigmund Freud: ". . . a distinction must be made between greatness of achievement and greatness of personality."

Where one so manifold in deeds and obviously so complex yet so positive in sentiments and convictions passes beyond our physical vision, it is a duty to wrest from his record the secret of his vivid personality for our guidance. What is the ultimate meaning of the values that invest his acts and grow out of his character roots? For our consolation as well we crave to know the lesson. Death having rounded out life, the sting of separation is blunted, in a measure at least, if we possess the sweet or strong secret of the completed, precious life.

—Henrietta Szold 1931 *

* In Memoriam Nathan Straus, *Hadassah Newsletter*.

Why This *Life?*

But biography should be more than chronicle. It should stimulate thought, influence action, lead to introspection and creation.

—HENRIETTA SZOLD 1942 *

One must, in order to be truthful, sincere and instructive, and in order to control, stimulate, one must present the shortcomings as well as virtues, the defects as well as the positive qualities.

—HENRIETTA SZOLD 1936 †

* Letter to Mrs. David de Sola Pool
† Address to New York Regional Conference of Hadassah

IN HER OWN WORDS, vivid and lucid, Henrietta Szold has left us an unambiguous mandate for the writing of her biography.

She herself maintained that her life was not biographical material despite its remarkable length and background, spanning, as it did, the period from mid-nineteenth to the mid-twentieth century, with all its literally world-shaking events and developments, political and social upheavals. She was born December 21, 1860, the year after Darwin published *The Origin of Species* and Marx his *Critique,* the month after Abraham Lincoln was elected President of the United States; and she was a four-month-old baby in her cradle in a house on South Eutaw Street in Baltimore when Fort Sumter was bombarded and the Civil War began. When she died in Hadassah Hospital on Mount Scopus in Jerusalem, February 13, 1945, the atom bomb was being developed behind the squash courts of the University of Chicago—the atom bomb which would, with the destruction of Hiroshima six months later, put an end to the Second World War.

Chronicles of the convulsive history which was made in the course of that life of more than fourscore years, and of the alterations in the mores of mankind which Henrietta Szold witnessed between the age of Victoria and the age of Franklin D. Roosevelt, fill countless library shelves. And as she herself contributed in a number of ways to both the history and the social change of her long time, some attention must necessarily be given to such chronicles in the story of her life. Before John Dewey she preached and practiced progressive methods in education. Like Jane Addams she inaugurated social services; and like Florence Nightingale she introduced modern medical care in a backward area. In the United States she founded Hadassah, a women's organization which is, among other things, a successful demonstration of the emancipation of her sex; and in Palestine she played an important part in the revival of the nation of Israel. But, as she herself insisted, "biography should be more than chronicle"; and the primary intention here, if her challenge is to be met, will be the revelation of a "vivid personality for our guidance." For, despite her disclaimer of being a fit subject for biography, everyone who ever knew Henrietta Szold will insist that she, who gave guidance to so many in the course of her life, is now, by her own definition of biography, an eminently suitable subject for that purpose.

Unforgettably "vivid" she was, they recall, although so slight in stature and usually so gentle in mien and manner that the memory is not so much of herself as of her moving effect on themselves. "Manifold in deeds" and "complex" she was, as her innumerable works and the variety of her talents attest: she had the sensibility and expressiveness of an artist and the organizational powers of an executive; she had the penetrating insight of a psychologist and the analytical introspection of a philosopher. "Positive in sentiments and convictions" she was, as will testify those who had occasion to rouse either her affection or her opposition. All agree, even those to whom at times she was a thorn in the flesh, that she was great, a designation which is rarely unanimous. Of the greatness of her achievement there can be no doubt; and as for her personality, although she was a lifelong spinster, men who knew her when she was decades older than themselves still look misty-eyed at mention of her name and say: She was a great woman!

Now it is characteristic of the great that they do not seek praise. Mighty Moses, we are told, was the meekest of men; and Abraham Lincoln, in his most eminent position, remained a humble man. The simple fact is that the truly great, who are aware of their inherent gifts and worth, are so psychologically fortified that they have no need of that approval and fame which others avidly pursue, and which come to them unbidden. Henrietta Szold lived to see "her works praise her in the gates," but it was not for the honors heaped upon her in her latter years that she strove. The truly great are not ambitious.

But great people are impassioned people. And the passion which possesses them manifests itself in the energy of feeling and action to which they are moved. All her long life, until long after the age when most men and women retire from daily labors, Henrietta Szold passionately devoted herself, with unflagging, as if inexhaustible energy, to the onerous tasks she felt called upon to undertake for the good of her fellowmen. But although she was ordinarily undemonstrative, there is evidence that her passion was not entirely expended in thought and action; at one point at least in her life it expressed itself in emotion so powerful that it, too, can justly be designated as great.

It is regrettable that the word "passion" has in our time lost some of its pristine significance, which was not merely that of a powerful love but of all intense emotion or feeling involving suffering. Passion was considered synonymous with suffering by the ancient Latins who invented the word, and which, as a matter of plain fact, it still actually is. For even the passionate creation of greatly gifted genius—the music of a Beethoven, the painting of a Rembrandt, the writing of a Flaubert—is accompanied by labors and pangs as painful as those of childbirth. It is in this sense that the passion of Jesus is referred to in the New Testament; and, in the very beginning of the Old Testament, the story of Adam and Eve may be properly understood as a Hebraic parable expressing the inevitability of suffering as a concomitant of the passion of man and woman for each other.

This passion came to Henrietta Szold later in her life than it comes, if ever, to most women; and because she was even then innately a great woman, and hence a greatly impassioned one, it expressed itself in an intensity and a fervor of emotion rarely vouchsafed to ordinary women—or to men, for that matter. Whether so great a passion, which inevitably involves great suffering, is an enviable experience is a moot question, which each man and woman will answer according to his temperament. Henrietta Szold herself, as we shall see, tried at one point to renounce that passion and failed.

And here it may be well to raise another moot question regarding biography in general and this one in particular: Is there actually any justification beyond the gossip's prurient and envious inquisitiveness for our prying into the secret places of the hearts of the renowned, to discover those failings and frustrations of great men and women which make them akin to ourselves? Need we know about the struggles of a Kafka and an Elizabeth Barrett with their autocratic fathers? Need we know that a Proust and an Emily Dickinson had to retreat with their talents from the stresses of daily life and intercourse with their fellow men—the one to his cork-lined Paris apartment, the other to her prim white house in New England?

In the case of Henrietta Szold we have available a great accumulation of personal papers—letters to her family, friends and colleagues, diaries and journals kept in periods of particular interest and stress. And as she was remarkably articulate, observant, self-searching and self-revealing, it is possible for us now to know not only what she saw and did but what she thought and felt at significant times in her life. Her life can, therefore, be reconstructed without recourse to conjecture or fiction. We are fortunate, also, in having the reassurance of Henrietta Szold herself, who loathed senseless, sensational publicity but who said: "It is a duty to wrest from his record the secret of his vivid personality for our guidance," and bade us seek and possess "the sweet or strong secret of the completed, precious life."

She said this, of course, of another; but of no one could it be better said than of herself. For the life of Henrietta Szold was and is to this day precious indeed to countless men and women. Let us therefore seek for our guidance, as she bids us, the secret of that life, which was both sweet and strong.

PART ONE

Her Father's Daughter

So far as I personally am concerned, I am my father's daughter . . .

—HENRIETTA SZOLD 1891 *

* Letter to Rachel Szold Jastrow

1860s: THE CHILD

FRIDAY, APRIL 21, 1865, was a day Henrietta would never forget.

It rained in the early morning and the sky remained overcast. The shops did not open that day; the schools were closed; crowds grew and waited in the streets. All Baltimore was in mourning, its buildings draped with black, its flags at half mast. Since dawn, guns had boomed, church bells tolled. And at ten o'clock, from the Camden Street Depot came the mournful hooting of the train which had borne the body of the martyred President from Washington, on the first stage of its long journey across the shocked and grieving land to his last resting place in Springfield, Illinois.

A group of family friends had gathered in the front parlor of the Szold home on South Eutaw Street, through which the funeral procession would pass on its way to the Exchange Building. There the body was to lie in state so that tens of thousands of citizens might come and pay their respects. And bright, inquisitive little Henrietta, then in the spring of her fifth year, was lost among the tight pantaloons and the voluminous skirts of the excited grown-ups standing before the parlor windows.

Of course she had heard much of the War Between the States and how Abe Lincoln had freed the Negro slaves. Papa and everyone had talked about it almost every day, ever since she could remember. She had looked with childish horror at the slave block

Mamma pointed out to her with indignation at the corner of Eutaw and Camden streets; and though she never actually saw a black slave being sold there, she used to think about it when she went to play at the Warners', the Negro family who lived in a cottage in the alley that ran from Eutaw to Paca streets. She had heard the tramp of soldiers in the streets on the way to battle, and had seen some of the wounded who returned, bandaged, blinded, crippled. She had learned from Papa's impassioned talk what a dreadful thing war was; and on winter afternoons she had sat on the floor by the warm round stove in the back parlor helping Mamma and the neighboring women pick lint for the army from the heap of linens they had collected.

Because her birthday in December came during the *Ḥanukkah* holiday, the week in which Jews celebrate the heroic resistance of the Maccabees to Syrian-Greek tyranny, she had learned that dreadful war was sometimes unavoidable; and this war of liberation, also, good Abe Lincoln had found unavoidable.

Finally the war ended. Just two weeks before, there had been a great celebration of the Union victory. Baltimore was gay with bunting and flying flags, and loud with clanging bells and roaring guns. All day the streets were filled with people cheering and singing; brass bands brayed; and at night the city was bright with lights and fireworks.

That was in the week before the Passover which, this year, Papa and Mamma made more memorable than ever; for was not the Passover also a celebration of the freeing of the Israelite slaves from bondage in Egypt? So Henrietta helped Mamma bring out the shining Passover dishes and silver which were used just that one week in all the year, and prepare the symbolic viands, the *matzah* and the delicacies for the *seder* meal—that resplendent feast of liberty which Jews had celebrated year after year for ages. At the head of the extended dining-room table, Papa, leaning upon a cushion, presided with his "Henriettchen" beside him; at the proper time in the proceedings she raised her childish voice and asked, in Hebrew, as he had taught her, the four questions about the nature of that festival. Then he and the guests ranged around the gleaming white-clad table answered her with the history of that ancient liberation, which they all read from the quaintly illustrated texts of the *Haggadah,* provided for that occasion. And Papa could not fail, in a pause in the recital, to point out the parallel between great Moses, the liberator of the ancient Israelites, and Lincoln, whom he revered, and who in their own day had liberated so many of his fellow men from oppressive bondage.

Then, in the midst of the Passover week, came the news that someone had shot and killed good Abe Lincoln! Baltimore was filled with fearful dismay. That Easter Sunday there was little display of gay spring finery on the way to the churches of the city. Police and soldiers patrolled the silent streets.

And now they were bringing the dead President into Baltimore; and though the thought surely frightened her, Henrietta wanted to see him too. But Papa wasn't there to help her, as he always did. Papa had gone out, and she could hear the approaching tread of many feet marching to mournful music. So she pushed her way in among the grownups until someone picked her up—it must have been Uncle Eduard—and hoisted her up on his shoulder so she could look over the heads of all of them, standing hushed now before the dread, approaching mystery of death, which had by now aroused her childish curiosity. And there were many blue-clad soldiers marching row after row, bearing shrouded banners; and then came gray guns drawn by horses; and then rows of sailors in dark blue with their boyish, round, beribboned hats and fluttering ties; and then the glittering brass band in bright red uniforms, playing the slow somber march and ruffling their muffled drums; and then four jet-black horses hauling the long black-plumed hearse, with the flag-draped coffin visible through its shining, curved glass windows. It was surrounded by dashing officers mounted on rearing and curvetting horses, and was followed by a group of pallbearers and clergymen. And there among them was Papa! The Reverend Rabbi Benjamin Szold—her adorable Papa—looking different, distinguished from all the others, his handsome face darker, his black hair longer, curling down to his collar in back from under his wide, black felt hat, his black beard set off by the stiff white cravat which only Mamma herself could launder and tie for him. There was Papa, grasping his gold-headed cane and walking with all those dignified gentlemen, followed by group after group of men and women bearing the banners of their organizations: the Liederkranz, the Germania Männerchor, the Baltimore Gesangverein . . . the Hebrew Literary Association, the Mendelssohn Society . . . then dignitaries in carriages, and finally a thick river of people filling the street, thousands of mourning men and women . . . until the music and the marching died away, and she was set down, and the visitors left. And the house on Eutaw Street was again the most pleasant place in the world, where wonderful Papa petted her and taught her so many marvelous things, and loving Mamma made her such good things to eat and such pretty things to wear, like the new pink dress she would put on for the Sabbath, for supper that Friday evening and for services in the synagogue on Saturday morning. She was then their one child.

Papa, when he returned from the funeral, went himself to Oheb Shalom Synagogue on Hanover Street to conduct the Friday evening service which was generally attended only by the men and boys of the congregation, while the women prepared for the Sabbath evening meal which followed the service. Mamma, aided by Henrietta, got everything ready in the kitchen and set the dining-room table with gleaming china and glass and silver, the dark red wine and the *ḥallah*—the fragrant plaited loaf Mamma herself had baked. Then they dressed for the Sabbath—Mamma in rustling black and Henrietta in frilly pink—and Mamma lit the Sabbath candles in the shining brass candlesticks she had got from her mother in Hungary and brought with her when she and Papa were married and came to America, the year before Henrietta was born.

Every Friday at sundown Henrietta watched Mamma put a silken shawl over her wavy brown hair, light the candles and murmur the Hebrew benediction: "Blessed art Thou, O Lord, our God, Ruler of the Universe, who has hallowed us and commanded us to kindle the Sabbath light," her blue eyes bright and her rosy cheeks aglow in the light shining through her outspread hands and gleaming from her golden wedding ring.

And when Papa came from the synagogue they would join with him in singing: *Le-ḥo dody le-kras kahlo* . . . ("Come, my beloved, to meet the Bride; let us greet the presence of the Sabbath . . .") in which the joyful beauty of God's Sabbath and of a bride became one to little Henrietta. Then they would sit down to table, joined by Uncle Eduard Schaar, Mamma's brother, and Cousin Mary Szold, Papa's cousin, both of whom had come to America with them and lived with them for a while on Eutaw Street. Then Papa would say the *kiddush* over the sweet wine and fill their glasses and, with another blessing, would cut the *ḥallah* and distribute the fragrant slices. And they would eat the good Sabbath food—the golden soup, the spicy fish, the sweet compote—all prepared as they had been by Mamma's Mamma in Hungary and by generations of Jewish mothers in many other lands for countless Sabbaths and holidays. Always it was eaten between Papa's blessing before the meal and a grace afterward, in an aura of sanctified gratitude for the gift of life and Sabbath peace to which the calmly burning candles testified. And Henrietta could see those gentle lights reflected in Mamma's blue eyes and in the dark eyes of Papa as they conversed with each other and with their guests and herself, as they always did at table, about the events of the day.

Their conversation was in the purest German, since Papa, besides his rabbinical studies at the Presburg *Yeshiva,* had been educated at the Universities of Vienna and Breslau, and Mamma, as Sophie Schaar, the daughter of a prosperous Hungarian brewer and landowner, had been well tutored at home. Indeed it was as one of the teachers in the school established by strong-minded, capable Grandmother Schaar—then a widow—for her own ten children and others in the neighborhood of their estate near Presburg, that Papa, while completing his studies, had first met Mamma. So they had been conversing with each other in German for quite some time, although they were not very old now—he being thirty-five and she twenty-five.

On this Sabbath eve in Baltimore there could be, of course, only one thing for them to talk about: the tragic death of the President. Lincoln's words and deeds had found a kindred spirit in Papa, who had, while still a student in Vienna, taken part in the revolution of 1848, fighting for freedom on the ramparts, and had been banished from Vienna with other liberal students when the revolution failed. It was then that he had returned to Presburg and fallen in love with Mamma, the youngest of four beautiful sisters. Henrietta, who loved to hear him tell of those days in the old country, had seen pictures of Papa taken then, when his thick-flowing, coal-black hair and Byronic collar gave him an unrabbinical, romantic air, and his dark young eyes had an almost fiercely impassioned look, a look such as she imagined the prophets had of whom he had told her, but the like of which she no longer saw in the benign loving eyes Papa bent upon her through his gold-rimmed glasses when he talked to her.

She saw that prophetic look only on occasions when he spoke from his pulpit on the Sabbath or holidays. On these mornings Mamma and she would go to the synagogue later than Papa. After they had prepared for the Sabbath dinner they would dress—Mamma in her black, lace-trimmed, full-skirted basque with leg-o'-mutton sleeves, and a bonnet, and Henrietta carrying a diminutive, frilly brown parasol which went so well with the pink dress and her white straw hat. Henrietta would sit with Mamma up in the front row of the balcony which was reserved for the women, who sat apart from the men below, arrayed in their fringed and striped white prayer shawls.

By that time the service would be under way, and handsome Papa, looking majestic in his black robe and square clerical hat, would be sitting on the dais to one side of the velvet-curtained ark containing the sacred scrolls of the Torah, the Five Books of Moses, while the white-robed cantor intoned a prayer at the lectern before it, his rich ringing voice framing the noble Hebrew phrases in golden arabesques of traditional melody. Or Papa himself would be at the lectern, reading alternate lines of a psalm in his sonorous, cultivated German, to which the congregation of German, Austrian and Hungarian Jews would respond as with one voice, although there were many accents among them—Suabian, Hessian, Bavarian and Plattdeutsch, which bright little Henrietta was beginning to distinguish, because Mamma was rather critical, not to say snobbish, about the way people spoke German.

It was after the reading of a passage from one of the scrolls taken from the ark and divested of its embroidered velvet sheath and tinkling silver ornaments, and after the scroll had been replaced in the ark with resounding praises from the congregation, that Papa would go to the lectern and deliver his sermon, his mobile face animated by the beauty of his thoughts. Usually he would take a slight thread, a sentence or even a phrase drawn from the day's Scripture reading and, skillfully weaving it into the texture of his discourse with lovely metaphor and apt analogy, find new ethical light and moral meaning for modern times in the ancient tale from which it was taken. And even when it was not yet entirely understandable to little Henrietta, it was a pleasure to listen to his flowery phrases.

She could easily believe the story that was told about his Day of Atonement sermon the year before she was born. It was one of his first sermons. The synagogue was crowded with worshipers at the solemn penitential service in the afternoon, when the Book of Jonah is read; and, the day being warm, a door was left open. The scroll had been replaced and Papa had started his sermon based on the story of Jonah—and Jonah in Hebrew means dove—when a white dove flew in and alighted on the ark, then flew up to the choir loft and down again to circle Papa's head as he spoke, and then flew away.

Papa's spirit was benign even when concerned for the sinfulness of humanity; for had not God, after Jonah's preaching, forgiven the repentant sinners of Nineveh? But once in a while came those times when his dark eyes burned with a prophetic fire which made her quiver, even as he quivered whenever he was so moved as to speak, not, as was his wont, calmly and thoughtfully, but with emotion.

Such a time was the first of June, two days after Decoration Day, which the new President Johnson had proclaimed a Memorial Day for Abraham Lincoln. It was the Jewish holiday *Shavuot,* and Papa began his sermon, which he called *"Vaterland und Freiheit"* ("Fatherland and Freedom"), by saying that, this being a doubly joyful occasion for the Jews—the first harvest festival, when the story of Ruth was read, as well as the celebration of the giving of the Commandments from Sinai—it was not his wish to move them to tears for the loss of their great leader, but to glorify his spirit. For the spirit of Lincoln exemplified the fifth of the Commandments—Honor thy father and thy mother—not merely in the love he bore his parents, but in his devotion to his ailing Fatherland, and to that Freedom which is the tender mother of all mankind. And then, embroidering his theme with Talmudic allusions, which were still a mystery to little Henrietta, Papa, his voice vibrant, eyes fervently flashing, reminded his congregation how the Israelites, having lost their Fatherland long ago, had found many foster Fatherlands; but how, after much persecution and suffering in many countries, only in this land had they found that mother Freedom, for whose preservation Abraham Lincoln had given all his strength and service, his peace and happiness, and had come to his untimely death. . . .

With the idea of untimely death Henrietta, young as she was, was already familiar. It was then just a few months since a baby sister, Rebecca, only four months old, had died and been taken away; and in Henrietta's third year a first baby sister, Estella, had died after living a scant half year.

The advent of those babies was fixed in Henrietta's mind by the *Holegreisch,* the delightful naming ceremony to which children were invited and which took place in the bedroom of Papa and Mamma—a large bright room draped with the whitest of starched lace hangings. Each time, in the center of the room had stood the cradle, also daintily draped in lacy white, harboring in its snowy depths the pink-and-white baby whose advent was being celebrated by the encircling crowd of eager curious children, themselves having arrived not so very long ago. Mamma guarding the infant from their clutching hands quieted them; and Papa came and lifted up the cradle and called out the newcomer's name, which the children gleefully repeated as he set it back on its frame. Just so had Henrietta herself been given, besides her English name, the Hebrew name *Ḥaya,* which means "Life," and she had thrived. But Estella and Rebecca had each soon sickened and gone; and however lovingly Papa and Mamma must have softened those losses for her, observant little Henrietta could not have been unimpressed by the precariousness of motherhood.

But cheerful, buxom, rosy-cheeked Mamma was so fearless of the dread mystery that she sometimes performed the pious service of washing the dead for burial; and she was so devoted to children that she had suckled the babe of a less robust neighbor along with one of her own. The loss of those two infants made Henrietta more precious to her parents, of course, especially to Papa, who was already intent on making her his spiritual heir. Mamma, however, soon burgeoned again, and less than a month before Henrietta's fifth birthday sister Rachel was born and thrived. Henrietta now, happily, had someone on whom she could spend that budding maternal affection which had once been sadly misplaced upon some newborn chicks she found in the back yard and hugged to death.

Life in her sixth year changed markedly for Henrietta. She had more serious things to do than to wander down the alley to watch the black Warner man whitewashing the back fence for Papa, or to the cooper's shop where a heap of curly wood shavings supplied her with long blond ringlets to attach to her own brown hair, or to Mr. Rose's grocery to help him arrange piles of scented soap in his window. Now she went daily to the parochial school connected with Papa's synagogue. There she was taught both secular and religious subjects: the secular in English and the religious in German. This was customary among the German-Jewish immigrants, for their religious teachers were also immigrants who had got their training, like Rabbi Szold, in German. Indeed, a Jewish child was apt to think that besides the sacred Hebrew, God was more likely to speak German than English. And Henrietta's first letter to Papa when he was away on one of his trips to preach in another city, expressing her delight in being able to write to him, was written in neatly shaded copybook German.

So secure and confident did she feel in her German-Jewish world there in Baltimore that it was with astonishment she heard one day on Pratt Street, on her way to school, some children chanting:

Take a piece of pork; stick it on a fork
And give it to the curly-headed Jew, Jew, Jew.

Of course, she knew that the Jews were forbidden pork by the Torah, but this was her first lesson that there were people to whom this was ridiculous.

At home and in school a profound regard for Judaism had been instilled in her.

God's words—the sacred Torah—were not taught but learned. A Jew never said he studied the Torah; he learned it. The process was one of self-instruction by familiarization, and the teacher was there to keep the process going.

Henrietta's teacher in the synagogue school was Jonas Goldschmitt, a tall, lanky, long-faced graybeard shuffling around the two rooms—the one for classes in English, the other for classes in German—in slippers and houserobe, a long pipe with a china bowl hanging from his lips, one hand behind his back clasping a rattan which he would bring down sharply on a culprit's fingers, which had to be held clustered and pointed up to him. Even Henrietta, the rabbi's daughter and a paragon among pupils, did not escape that painful discipline. *"Und du, du, du Szold!"* he would say in pained surprise when she was caught with her mates in some childish prank: "And you, you, you Szold! You, too? Aren't you ashamed of yourself?" bringing the stick down hard on her tapering finger tips, thus teaching her early the painful price sometimes paid for any distinction.

She had had an equally unforgettable lesson to that effect the year before. The German immigrant community of Baltimore—one fifth of the city's population at that time, of which the German Jews were an integral part—had not only their *Turnverein,* their singing societies, their *Greisenheim* for the aged, of which Mamma was an officer, their Concordia Club where Papa stopped afternoons for coffee, and Schutzen Park where everyone went for picnics, but also a theatrical stock company which gave daily performances of German plays. And when Henrietta heard that Mamma and Papa, who particularly enjoyed the theater for which they had season tickets, were going to see the famous actor Dawisohn, who had arrived from abroad to give his repertoire of plays, she took it into her little head that she would like to see him too, and particularly in Gutzkow's *Uriel Acosta* of which Papa spoke so glowingly. In her then unabashed and forthright manner she spoke up and said so. Then dear Papa, who never denied her anything without giving her some good reason, put her off with the explanation that he had spent all their theater money for the tickets they had. For Henrietta, who had already been taught the lifetime virtue of German thrift and budgeting, this would have sufficed. But Papa, playfully adding with a regretful smile that, of course, he would have had no objection to her seeing the play if only there were a ticket for her, or if she could get one, had not reckoned on the determination of his little daughter. She said no more, but waited until the afternoon of the Sabbath when Papa and Mamma were entertaining visitors—and visitors constantly came and went at the hospitable and widely known Szolds'

—and she was arrayed in that pink dress. It matched the color of the excitement in her cheeks as she put on her white straw hat, unfurled the frilly brown parasol that matched her bright brown eyes, and proceeded down Eutaw Street to the Eutaw House where, she had heard, Dawisohn was staying, to call upon the surprised actor. He listened with interest to the explanation of her errand in impeccable German, and when she referred to her father's statement he asked, "Who is your father?" Then Henrietta, surprised, said, "You don't know my father, Rabbi Szold! He sits in the front row and has black curly hair." Whereupon she got not one but two tickets for *Uriel Acosta,* with the proviso that she let him have her opinion of his playing. But when she danced into the parlor with them crying, "Now I can go to the theater!" Mamma cried, "*Gott,* what has the child done?" and Papa was berated for his pleasantry which had sent her on this improper errand. He was advised to return the tickets, but it was too late, so Henrietta went to the play. The very next day, when Dawisohn appeared at the Szolds' for Henrietta's verdict, she said, with an admonishing forefinger which had become her habit, "Didn't your mother teach you that it is bad to curse?"

No harm would have come of the forthright sincerity of her lively nature were it not that the story, being such good publicity for an actor, was given to *Der Deutsche Correspondent,* one of the German newspapers published in Baltimore, and was thus broadcast, so that strangers stopped Henrietta on the street with their blunt curiosity: "Aren't you the little girl who went to see Dawisohn?" Thus she was made aware of the fact that an unself-conscious act prompted by an irrepressible good feeling can become a vain, audacious exploit in the eyes of others; and she came to loathe that prying publicity which seeks sensation without significance. She became shy and reserved with people in public, apparently cool and undemonstrative, for fear of exposing to the uncomprehending the passionate spirit that burned within her.

The grade-school teacher who told her she could not sing in key although she loved group singing never knew the anguish his curt discouragement caused her. Nor did anyone know that whenever she watched a beautiful dancer she wished and felt sure she could be one too.

Only within the circle of her loving family did she feel free to expend the energetic warmth of her nature. She felt free with incomparable Papa, who in his talks at table or in his booklined study upstairs where they read together Goethe's *Hermann und Dorothea*—which was not only classic German poetry but a picture of the plight of political refugees—opened to her so many vistas not to be attained in any school of learning, nourishing her avid mind with so many stimulating thoughts and exciting ideas. She felt secure with lovely little Mamma, scarcely five feet tall but capable in every department of her growing household, who taught Henrietta all the varied competences with which she helped and maintained her distinguished, scholarly husband—cooking and housekeeping, sewing, finances, the care and training of children. And on her younger sisters Henrietta could pour out her love—on Rachel, on Sadie, who was born when Henrietta was eight years old, and especially on little Johanna, who came when she was eleven.

By this time Henrietta would have been justified in no longer thinking of herself as a little girl. Mamma and Papa had decided that she should be transferred from the confines of the congregational school to the wider world of the public schools; and after a year in Grammar School No. 1 Henrietta was graduated into the Western Female High School on West Fayette Street where she was introduced to new fields of learning. There was "Mental Philosophy" which used such terms as "metaphysics" and "cognition," "objective and subjective," "tangible and intangible," "deduction and induction," and which dealt with such matters as human memory and association of ideas, the mechanism of the senses, ethics, and the problem of right and wrong—a mélange of philosophy and psychology. There was "parsing"—the dissection of language which could turn Milton's *Paradise Lost* from a moving work of art into a mutilated and repulsive mass of words. There was "Elocution"—the art of declamation—accompanied by suitable gestures—of such harrowing, breath-stopping, or blood-curdling poesy as "Casabianca," "The Charge of the Light Brigade," "Paul Revere's Ride," "How They Brought the Good News from Ghent to Aix," and (in breathless German) *"Der Erlkönig."* Neither Papa nor Mamma, products of their optimistically progressive age, were critical of the curriculum of the Baltimore high schools, nor was Henrietta herself at that time. Regardless of the subject, she applied that agile mind which Papa had exercised and developed precociously with such an intensity of will and conscience that, despite some difficulty with arithmetic and geography, she brought home reports of work so flawless that her record was never surpassed. In language and literature, which were her particular delights, she was quite remarkable.

At home she was equally diligent, intellectually and physically. At twelve she was helping Papa read proof of the German portions of the new synagogue prayer book he was preparing for publication. This was a result of a campaign for conservative reform of ritual he had waged ever since he first arrived in Baltimore in 1859 to serve the young congregation which called itself Oheb Shalom—"Love of Peace." It was then only six years old. His inaugural sermon based on Deuteronomy 29—"The secret things belong unto the Lord our God, but the things which are revealed belong unto us and to our children forever . . ."—which he interpreted in a conservative spirit, was contemptuously attacked by the rabbi of another, more radically reform congregation. On the other hand his insistence on reforming the ritual in Oheb Shalom Synagogue precipitated a conflict with the more orthodox part of his own congregation which brought him to the point of resigning —just as he had resigned from the Baltimore Ministers' Association when it refused to admit a Negro pastor. He was a peace-loving man, yet fearless of opposition. He won his way with his congregation; and his prayer book was adopted in other cities where he was called to preach. Henrietta was learning from Papa the difficult position of the liberal conservative between the radical reformer and the orthodox; and she was learning to have the courage of her convictions. She was also continuing under his guidance in Hebraic studies of Torah and Talmud which would make her before long the most erudite young Jewess of her time, while she helped Mamma with the house and the other three children, who all looked up to Henrietta. The baby Johanna became practically hers when yet another child was on the way.

Thus, by the time of her confirmation at thirteen, when Papa presented her with a small gold brooch watch enameled with tiny blue flowers, Henrietta had left her own childhood behind, and was a high-spirited, intelligent girl, competent, busy and happy.

1870s: THE GIRL

IN THE SPRING of Henrietta's thirteenth year, the growing family needed more room, although Uncle Eduard and Cousin Mary were no longer staying with them, and the Szolds moved from Eutaw to Lombard Street—to a more spacious house in a better, more picturesque part of the city which still expressed something of the indolent graciousness of the Old South. High bicycles, pony carts, carriages rolled along the red brick pavements. There were hitching posts in front of the houses, and iron fountains at the street corners for the refreshment of man and beast.

On the day they left Eutaw Street, when the moment came to follow the vans which had been loaded under Mamma's supervision, Papa was nowhere to be found, inside or outside the house. He had vanished! It was April first; was this one of Papa's little jokes? The burdened vans, drawn by huge horses, went off, and there was nothing to do but proceed after them on foot, Mamma carrying the baby, Johanna, and Henrietta leading the two little girls, Rachel and Sadie, each of them bearing some treasured possession too delicate to entrust to the burly moving men.

And there at 702 West Lombard Street, in the garden behind the house, they found Papa, happily bringing to pass that ancient Hebraic dream of every man of sitting "under his vine and his fig tree." While others were concerned with more immediate matters, he was planting for the future. By the back gate he had set a sapling which would furnish them figs every year just in time for the blessing of the first fruits at *Rosh Hashanah*—the Jewish New Year; and by the arbor he set a vine which would in time make a leafy roof bearing bunches of purple grapes under which they would celebrate in the fall the feast of *Sukkot*—of those booths which the children of Israel lived in when they were brought out of the land of Egypt.

The house itself was one of the more modest homes on the block, but like most of them it was of red brick with a short flight of white marble steps at the front door. Next door lived the Rosenfelds in a somewhat bigger house separated from the Szolds' by a narrow shady passageway, a delivery entrance with a wooden gate, which the Szold children envied the Rosenfelds because it was the best place to air their dolls on hot, humid summer days in Baltimore. Farther along the street were more stately mansions with taller windows curtained with fine Belgian lace. One of them, the Pritchards', had a grilled iron balcony across the wide front, and Henrietta, who had got from Papa and Mamma their European passion for plants and flowers, could look from their own pleasant little garden across two other back yards to the Pritchards' superbly landscaped formal flower beds. Afternoons, General and Mrs Pritchard, gray and stiff and cold-looking, as unlike lively Papa and Mamma as two human beings could possibly be, stepped out of their house and into their victoria, drawn by two lustrous chestnut mares in glittering harness and with a colored coachman on the box. The difference between such people—*goyim* ("strangers") they were called even by the immigrant Jews—and her own folk was something to be wondered at. Papa had made her proud to be a Jew, but there were proud *goyim,* too.

On the other side of the street was an even more manorial house than the Pritchards', set in a broad garden. A stately breed of men and women by the name of Cone inhabited this mansion, which had a flight of brown stone steps with iron railings to give it further distinction. A colorful picture of the seven male members of that family, the father and six sons, decorated the lids of the cigar boxes containing the fine cigars Papa enjoyed smoking when they were presented to him on festive occasions by wealthier members of his congregation. The Cones may have been Jews, but Henrietta did not know; they were not members of Oheb Shalom. She had heard of people who did not take pride in being Jews like Papa and Mamma and herself, but that was still incomprehensible to her. Like others on Lombard Street, the Pritchards and the Cones lived as if in another world, veiled from inquisitive young eyes. When you were grown up too, maybe the veil to that other world would be lifted. In the meantime you watched and wondered.

But not far away were other fine houses Henrietta loved and could enter; she often did with Papa and Mamma when they became close friends of the Friedenwalds, a large family, longer settled in Baltimore than the Szolds, warmhearted people, unpretentious, kind and affable like Papa and Mamma. There were Dr. and Mrs. Aaron Friedenwald and their two sons, Harry and Julius, who became interested in medicine like their father, a distinguished ophthalmologist. Harry and Henrietta became very good friends, and he came to her for lessons in botany, which was one of her favorite subjects. And there were the families of two brothers of Aaron Friedenwald, one of whom had a daughter, Racie, who became Henrietta's dear friend. She liked Dr. Aaron best, a genial man who enjoyed swapping stories with Papa. When a recovered patient complained that his bill was too high, he pointed out that it was far less than the cost of a decent funeral. It was funny when he told it; but the way grown people could joke about the dread mystery of death was also food for wonder.

The Friedenwalds had a coachhouse and a stable with horses; and sometimes when the doctor and his boys drove down to Chesapeake Bay to fish they would take a couple of the Szold girls along in the phaeton. Henrietta's world widened to include the great sea; in the summer they went to Cape May on the New Jersey coast and swam in the surf. The Friedenwalds and the Szolds took long walks, as all Europeans did, most often in Druid Hill Park, where they also went rowing on Boat Lake and skating in winter. They would stop for the view from Prospect Hill, the panorama of great Baltimore and its harbor, circling with its green woodlands and red brick streets about the axis of the tall white Washington Monument. Henrietta grew to love the old city.

The longer they lived on Lombard Street the more she found

there to excite the senses and engage the spirit. Next to the Friedenwalds' house, in front of the Lutheran church where the German gentiles worshiped, there was a whole row of ailanthus trees. The fragrance from their pendant clusters of blossoms would delight Henrietta in the spring; and in the fall the stripped spines of their compound leaves, when they dropped to the pavement, supplied all the children with toy switches. And still farther down the street there was a whole row of flowering linden trees in front of the Quaker meeting house. The garb of the Quaker women, their poke bonnets and gray or light-brown dresses, their long full skirts and plain snug bodices with a touch of white at the throat, made her wish that when she grew up she could dress like them, instead of in the overdressed fashions of the day, with bustles and ruffles and puffs. They looked so peaceful, so calm, without seeming coldly ascetic. Like Papa, they were warm and friendly yet controlled. When she thought of growing old, she imagined herself living serenely like those Quaker women.

In the other direction, beyond the Szold house, was an old neglected cemetery surrounded by a rough stone wall running half a block along Lombard Street, around the corner and down Fremont, and around the next corner along German Street. Unkempt vines trailed over the wall from the rank growth within, which was like a "bosky dell" of the sad poems one read, exhaling the damp green smell of nature's triumph over death. Henrietta and her sisters used to find four-leaf clovers at the foot of the cemetery wall.

Within their home, with its square high-ceilinged rooms, although it was not so elegantly furnished as those richer houses on Lombard Street, there was an aura of security and well-being which Papa, wise and benign, and Mamma, firm and competent, created between them. Solid walnut furnished the wainscoted dining room with its polished ornamental iron stove; the warm fire, glowing through its isinglass door in winter, reflected from shining Old World silver and brass. The hard-worn mahogany parlor chairs and sofas were covered with durable rep and horsehair; on the marble-topped tables there were plush-covered albums full of pictures of European relatives. Mamma filled the three sunny windows of the upstairs sitting room with flowers; and there she set the square piano at which Henrietta practiced assiduously—although it was plainly not her talent—the lessons she took at Peabody Institute; and by the window was Henrietta's desk at which she worked undisturbed by the children in the nursery, always leaving it neatly closed when not in use.

At that desk, like Papa at his desk downstairs, Henrietta began in her fourteenth year to exercise the gift of a fertile mind expressing itself in artful language. She wrote "A DIALOGUE: Between Two Schoolgirls the Day after Washington's Birthday," in which, after suitably piquing the curiosity of her colleague and her reader about how she had spent the holiday, she divulged that she had been visited by the shade of the Father of Our Country whom she recognized at a glance. "I thought, at first, his portrait had descended from the wall. You know Papa considers it the duty of a cultivated person, besides reading the lives of great men, to have continually before his eyes their pictures. This, he says, shields us against vicious dispositions, and incites us to noble deeds . . ." Then after a fanciful description of the great Presence she explained that he is resurrected every year in the hearts of all good citizens, but particularly in the breast of every true Israelite: "We had no home and no fatherland. Like orphans, who are mercilessly pushed out in the cold world and made to suffer, so were we. A whole nation, driven from place to place, persecuted and oppressed by everyone whom we happened to meet. So we suffered until Washington, with a mighty hand, reared this temple of freedom, a refuge for all persecuted. Then we, the forlorn, found a fatherland and home; a land flowing with milk and honey—the milk of liberty and the honey of humanity."

Whereupon her patient, presumably gentile interlocutor was permitted to break the flow of undeniably inspired eloquence with: "Oh, how dreadful! What a shame for the whole human race to persecute a whole nation for the sake of its belief."

Then Henrietta continued: "I cannot depict to you all we have to endure. The world is beginning to find out how barbarous such things are, and soon the light will dawn over all, and we will not hear of such persecutions any more . . ." at which point she reverted to her conversation with George Washington. "I asked W. how his wife, Martha, was . . ."

For her tragic but hopeful vision of anti-Semitism Henrietta was also indebted to Papa's sermons and the Jewish history he taught her. The most recent manifestation of such "persecutions" she had heard of was in a story Papa had told of how, when he was a boy of nine, he and his elder brother Solomon, returning from the *Yeshiva* on the eve of the Sabbath, were beset on the outskirts of their village by peasant boys who made them "Jump!" and "Jump higher!" until their fine Sabbath hats fell off and rolled in the dust. Papa told how he would weep with vexation, but fifteen-year-old Solomon, practically a man, would console him with, "Never mind. When Messiah comes, *they* will try to cross the river into the Garden of Eden on a bridge of iron, but it will break and they will drown; but *we* shall cross over even on a bridge of paper and live forever in glory."

But nothing like that ever happened in these days in Baltimore in the land of Washington and Lincoln, and even when Papa told it, it was like part of a fabulous history far removed in time and space from the security of life in the house on Lombard Street. Mamma stocked its cool stone-walled cellar with her preserves and provisions. Under the ladderlike stairway leading down from the kitchen was a well of cold spring water; and in it stood her tall earthenware jars of dill pickles. On shelves nearby were ranged inexhaustible rows of good homemade things the children loved—glasses of jellies, marmalade, chow-chow, catsup, gherkins, pickled beets, horseradish . . . and under the shelves stood a barrel of fragrant sauerkraut and a barrel of pickled meat. On a wine rack suspended from the ceiling reposed straw-encased bottles of Hochheimer, Liebfraumilch, Tokay, Kümmel, laid away by Papa for the days when children were born or confirmed or, "God willing," got married, or when parents had reached some important birthday or a celebration of their own marriage.

Mamma did her own marketing twice a week. In Lombard Street even women of means were seen bearing their baskets to Lexington Market. In the big kitchen Mamma presided over Maggie and Lizzie, the cook and maid, German sisters, who had become part of the family; and there was a summer kitchen in back where an extra laundress came to work on special occasions, a Negress wearing a bright bandanna, who smoked a pipe like Papa!

Papa had his study in back of the parlor on the ground floor. The bowed window lined with potted plants looked out on the small paved back yard and the bright garden beyond, which he cultivated in the early morning before setting to work. When you were out there at play or keeping an eye on the new baby—for sister Bertha, chubby pink-and-white "Betsy," was born the first winter in Lombard Street—you could see Papa writing at his red-leather-covered table. There he would sit in the middle of the room, under the three twisted brass branches bearing candle-shaped gas lights, or in his comfortable Morris chair, reading or sitting in scholarly meditation, plucking at his curly black beard. Then his study seemed a remote place, unapproachable, although never was a child forbidden to enter it. But when you went inside, it welcomed you like a warmhearted friend. Papa was always ready for a good talk, about books or events, present or out of the ancient past, or about whatever was troubling you. He would offer you the comfortable old cushioned rocking chair to sit in and read by the gas fire—Henrietta devoured there, one after the other, his big volumes of *Weltgeschichte*—while he went on writing. He was preparing for publication his Commentary on Proverbs, and he might read you what he thought about that last section which begins: "A woman of valor who can find, for her worth is far above rubies . . ." which Henrietta loved—it was so like a description of busy Mamma. Sometimes you didn't even read—just sat there and stared at the three white busts of philosophers on the mirrored mantel over the fireplace, or at the flowery arabesques endlessly repeated in the wallpaper above the tall oak bookcases, or at the rows and rows of books, in Hebrew, Latin, Greek, German, Hungarian, French, English, lining the walls and heaped on the desk around his pipe rack; and you marveled at how he could reach out and put his hand on just the book he needed among the many hundreds he had; and you let all sorts of thoughts run through your mind, but mostly about how wonderful was Papa, who could read and translate for you with ease from the Latin of Horace or recite by heart long passages from the Greek Homer, or the Hebrew Bible with its singsong cantillation, so that you would sit there and forget whatever it was that troubled you.

Yet, at the end of their second year in that pleasant house came a calamity that even Papa could not prevent or assuage, and that Henrietta found it dreadfully hard to forget. In the early spring, dear little Johanna, just three and a half years old, was stricken with scarlet fever, died, and was buried. This was not like the deaths of those two short-lived and vaguely remembered infants. This was as if she herself, as much as Mamma, had lost a child; and Henrietta in the spring of her own young womanhood saw for the first time how triumphant death really can be; and no longer could she go by the old cemetery down the street without a shudder. Indeed she found herself shuddering, quivering, twitching uncontrollably at other times too, now in the hand or the shoulder on which poor Johanna had so often rested, now in her face so that it grimaced as if it wanted to cry, even when she had ceased crying.

She was taken to the doctor who said it was a not uncommon affliction of children during puberty. Chorea, from the Greek word for dance, it was called by physicians, or St. Vitus's dance, because in the Middle Ages when there had been a mass dancing mania in Germany people had been cured of it by praying to St. Vitus. It often came on as a result of a child's having been frightened, said the doctor, and it usually passed in a month or two; but the child should be watched and strengthened lest—like rheumatic fever, to which it was not unrelated—it leave its mark on the heart. Fresh air and tonics were prescribed, and iron which one took through a bent glass tube lest it corrode the teeth. And it passed.

But had she been frightened? What was there to be frightened of? Greatly moved she had been; and did not Papa and everyone quiver when greatly moved? And had not Papa explained how we were all in the hand of God, how we all must die sooner or later and go on to another life for our just desserts—as he had said even of great Abraham Lincoln in that memorial sermon. So, for Henrietta, it was as shameful to be afraid as to be uncontrolled, and the uncontrollable quiver, the chorea, passed. Only once in a while, when she was very weary, would a slight twitch in the shoulder return.

Had it left its mark on the tender young heart? Who knew? Life must leave many unsuspected marks on the hidden heart, which is more tough and enduring than the heartbroken think—as Henrietta had learned. The soft and quivering heart, harboring some dreadful, ineradicable fear, covers it with the pearl of courage and goes on beating, beating. . . .

Yet how is it, a shocked and frightened child might well wonder, that all-knowing grownups like Papa, who so often officiated at funerals, do not shudder and twitch? Jews call a cemetery *Bet Ḥayim* ("House of Life"), and their mourners' *kaddish* makes no mention of death.

Papa from his pulpit still spoke wonderful words as inspiring and heartening as ever; although at his desk he was engaged in writing a new Commentary on the Book of Job, expounding his thesis that one cannot expect from Job any answer to that eternal question of the justice of the virtuous and faithful man's affliction; one can get from Job only the wonderful expression of how such a man feels when afflicted by his inscrutable Creator. And in the face of Mamma—stouter now and as cheerfully busy as ever with her children, her home, and her community—appeared two lines of determination on either side of her strong upper lip, although her blue eyes were as tender and compassionate as ever.

In the fall of the year after Johanna died, when Henrietta was going on sixteen, sister Adele was born, who took the lost child's place in her heart; and she was the last of the brood. Five Szold girls grew up in the house on Lombard Street: Henrietta, Rachel, Sadie, Bertha, Adele.

But not without mishap. Little Adele, too, was stricken with scarlet fever and, some years later, Bertha with diphtheria; and Henrietta, apparently fortified by her bout with chorea, for she never again got sick, insisted on nursing her sisters to recovery, in order to keep Mamma from infecting the others and to free her for duties Henrietta could not perform. Besides, Adele, whom Henrietta had pampered, would have no one else; and Bertha took sick at a time when a Rabbinical Conference in Baltimore made it necessary for Papa and Mamma to entertain visiting rabbis. This meant isolation for Henrietta with the sick child in an upstairs bedroom, reading and rereading *Aladdin* and *Ali Baba*, and their favorite German story about an artist called "The Raphael of the Cats," which was so dismally tragic it provoked them to wild hilarity.

For her sisters were gay little girls, and Henrietta, for all her erudition, loved laughter as much as they did. They were all good mimics, and even Mamma, looking disdainfully down her patrician nose at someone offensive, or reduced to sputtering incoherence by their mischievousness, was not exempt from their caricature. Henrietta entertained and taught her sisters in the nursery, a room over the dining room, warmed in winter by heat rising through a register from the stove below. And there they all scurried mornings from their chilly bedrooms on the third floor to dress with her help and get their hair combed, curled, or plaited. She was like a third parent to them—a bridge between them and Mamma and Papa—American-born like themselves and, though old enough to be looked up to, still young enough to laugh and play with them. She taught them German and helped them to read *Armes Lämmschen* for Papa's approval when he came up from his study to relax in the afternoon.

If Mamma was there, too, she would have taken off her formal, black, high-necked street gown and put on a blue percale housedress; and Papa, who seemed indifferent to what women wore, would remark how prettily it matched her eyes. Sometimes he lay down to rest on the nursery sofa, and if he dozed Mamma would hush the noisy youngsters—they were noisier than a houseful of boys, she said—and Papa would say, "Let them be, Sophie. It bothers me more when they are too quiet."

Papa took no part in household matters; he left such things to the women. Not that he thought any the less of such matters or of the women. He had the utmost regard for little Mamma, who was the epitome of that *eshet ḥayil*—that versatile woman of valor and virtue celebrated in the paean at the end of the Proverbs: "The heart of her husband doth safely trust in her. . . ." Was not Abraham told by God: "In all that Sarah may say unto thee, hearken unto her voice"? And was it not said in the Talmud: "If thy wife is small, bow down to her"? If he asked some service from his wife, a daughter, or a maid, Papa was most courteous, even apologetic. He was never the domineering, autocratic father of some of the fiction and biography Henrietta had read. His was the gentle tyranny of love. Democratic, considerate, kindly, tolerant, he loved peace in his home as well as in his society.

With a twinkle in his eyes Papa used to tell of his boyhood embarrassment in the presence of marital conflict. In the years when he attended the *Yeshiva* in Presburg he boarded out on certain days with a mismated couple who frankly carried on their violent altercations in his presence. One day in mid-meal the man chased his wife out, and returned to the table where poor Benjamin still sat on a bench, with his back to the window. There the wife appeared, pleading with the "little student" to open the door, while the irate husband sternly commanded the "little student" not to leave his seat. This so unnerved the "little student" that he preferred fasting on the days he should have eaten with them.

Between Papa and Mamma a harmony prevailed in matters large and small that sprang from a genuine libertarian spirit which was not at odds with their sense of responsibility. Jewish scholars are not ascetic, and Rabbi Szold was a loving and beloved man, happily married; and as it is a Jewish duty, indeed the very first command in the Bible, to "be fruitful and multiply," it was natural that he should have a large family and that his daughters should adore their distinguished father, who looked like Lord Tennyson.

That he hadn't a son was apparently not a deplorable matter to Papa; certainly his Henriettchen was never made to feel that it was, but rather that she was to him, as Naomi said of Ruth, "better than seven sons"; and he gave her no reason ever to wish herself anything but the bright girl she was. And not bad-looking either, she had reason to think when she looked in her mirror and carefully brushed her wavy brown hair. She let it flow back from the curly bangs on her brow and down behind her well-shaped ears, where she wore pretty clusters of jewels set in gold; and though her brow was higher than most girls', and her complexion darker, like Papa's—alas, she had inherited none of Mamma's pretty fairness—yet the soft roundness of the face below the vivacious dark brown eyes was very feminine. And she did have pretty ankles.

In the Jewish Prayer Book there is, in the Morning Service, a point at which men and women say different benedictions. While the men say, "Blessed art Thou who hast not made me a woman," the women say, "Blessed art Thou who hast made me according to Thy will." To Henrietta it seemed that the difference in these prayers, far from evidencing any inferiority, indicated an admirable humility on the part of the women in the presence of their Creator, together with a positive satisfaction with His gift of womanhood which should justify any woman for feeling superior to her fellow man, who negatively boasts of his manhood.

To be sure there were times when the greater freedom of movement and opportunity of the male in the Victorian world she was born to aroused Henrietta's envy; but she couldn't blame that on Papa, who opened every door for her that he would have for a son.

Of course Henrietta was devoted to Papa; who wouldn't be? She had grown up beside him; he had taken her along on his intellectual excursions, not so much from a desire to mold her mind and her views as for the pleasure he got from the fact that she quickly saw eye to eye with him. His statements and attitudes were unquestionable to her. His erudition was famous; far beyond the confines of Baltimore he was known as a distinguished Hebraist and Talmudist. Always she sat beside him at meals, which were unhurried, *gemütlich,* accompanied by much talk. Papa discussed with Henrietta his development of some subject for a sermon or a paper—it might be on Biblical poetry, its rhythms, assonance, and parallelisms for cumulative effects; it might be on some great Jewish figure—Maimonides, Moses Mendelssohn, or some article on world affairs or American politics in the day's *Deutscher Correspondent* or *The America.* They both read these until the politics of *The America* became distasteful to them and they changed to the Baltimore "Sun-papers."

Papa had been a "War-Democrat"—one who espoused the abolition of slavery yet adhered to the tenets of Thomas Jefferson's party; and, having become a full-fledged American citizen in '71, he took an active interest in public affairs and encouraged Henrietta to do so. When he received an appeal for support from a group calling itself "The Baltimore Association for the Education and Moral Improvement of the Colored People" addressed to all ministers and commending itself to "every Christian man's humanity," he replied that he didn't see why only Christians, who had been so inhumane to the colored men, were invited, and sent them a generous contribution. When he told the family at table that he had been elected to the Board of the Association, and that he was being referred to by its opponents as the "Rabbi of Timbuktu," Henrietta was proud, and the youngsters were vastly amused. He tried, of course, to elevate the interests of the younger girls, too, but he smiled benevolently at their childish chatter and laughter and told them funny stories. Henrietta learned from him a tolerance for the young, which she exercised in playing piano duets with Bertha whose regard for accuracy was not as well developed as her own.

Henrietta was sixteen and a half when she was graduated from the Western Female High School with the distinction of being the first of the Ten Dollar Medal girls of her class; and she was certainly the girl with the most distinguished father. Papa sat on the platform with the Mayor, who opened the exercises; and Henrietta delivered an address on "Our Public Schools." It took a painful effort to rise from among the forty-eight white-clad girls on the stage and face the vast audience gathered in Ford's Grand Opera House that June day, but she had marshaled all her well-developed linguistic forces in the preparation of this piece. She lauded the public schools as the place where the rich varieties of cultures contributing to American life were assimilated, and produced the kind of democratic leadership this great country required, and ended with the optimistic statement that "Public education truly is the cause, either directly or indirectly, of all the prosperity and harmony of our nation. Numerous other benefits are bestowed, and many other ends attained by our public schools, impossible of being enumerated, but these are sufficient to show the importance —no, the necessity—of their existence, and their invincible power for the accomplishment of the good." And she was rewarded for her effort with hearty applause in the theater and in the press—*stürmisch* the *Correspondent* called it.

And already, so marked was her talent for teaching, even without formal training in the art, that because of the illness of Mr. Hollingshead, the high school principal, she was asked to take over his classes in English the following semester. She had indulged in dreams of going on to Vassar; but although a few of the brighter girls like herself had ventured even to talk about such dreams in the high school halls, it was with the awe with which one speaks of a remote object one has never seen and dares not hope to approach. It was quite extraordinary for any girl to go away to college, especially in the postwar impoverished South. There had been a business panic in '73 when Grant was President; and in '77, the year Henrietta was graduated, another depression came with strikes and riots and reports of soldiers firing on citizens.

The Szolds were at all times a thrifty family, except that charitable, generous Papa had the habit of inviting countless guests to his table—itinerant scholars, students, immigrants, the needy—without counting the cost; and Cardinal Gibbons once said of him at a meeting of ministers: "Here is the best Christian in the room." Nevertheless Mamma managed to save from their modest income enough to get some of his books and papers published. And Henrietta had learned, as a matter of course, to keep in her desk a daily account of every penny she spent—for carfare, a spool of thread, a hair ribbon . . . not because the Szolds were in want but because thrifty budgeting was one of the Victorian and German virtues.

Henrietta did not go to Vassar; and after the year of teaching in high school she was asked to teach at the Misses Adams' School, run for the daughters of genteel but impoverished Southern families by three Southern gentlewomen, whose fortunes had decayed in the war. Thus at seventeen Henrietta became a teacher and was embarked on her first career. She enjoyed it, brought to it her fresh enthusiasm and an eagerness to share with her pupils her own delight in learning; but while teaching she learned that not all minds were so accessible to learning as her own. There was the glib little girl whom she suspected of reciting what she had studied without real understanding, when, in a history class, she referred to the "Prince of Oranges"; and once when she was reciting on "the Minute Men" Henrietta interrupted to ask which side they were on. "Oh," she said, "in front, in back, on all sides!"—and set Henrietta thinking that there was something more to the process of education than the accumulation of information.

She taught languages, history, natural sciences, mathematics—almost everything in the curriculum. The wide-ranging interests which Papa had transmitted to her stood her in good stead. She also taught weekend classes in the religious school of Oheb Shalom

Synagogue. And despite that teaching load she found it possible to embark on another career for which she was also indebted to Papa's example. She began writing for publication—essays, sketches, news letters, for *The Jewish Messenger,* published in New York; and for this she took the pen name "Sulamith" from the passionate Song of Songs:

> *Return, return, O Shulamite . . .*
> *How beautiful are thy sandalled feet,*
> *O Prince's daughter!*

Her pieces ranged from news of the activities of the Jewish community in Baltimore to observations on national and international events, and accounts of the lives of Jewish notables, past and present. But never would she be content with mere reporting or exposition; her vivid observations were always accompanied by incisive commentaries on human character and behavior, examined in the light of the ancient Jewish wisdom drawn from Torah and Talmud which she had got from Papa. She could now discuss her own writings with him as well as his. She even began to dream of becoming a "writer," like Louisa May Alcott and George Eliot.

One of her pieces was about the Corbin affair, which was being widely and vigorously discussed. Corbin was the owner of a fashionable hotel at Manhattan Beach in New York which had closed its doors to Jews. Jews, naturally outraged, and liberal Christians, almost equally scandalized, expressed their strong opinions of this un-American, antidemocratic precedent in the press, from New York to San Francisco. Henrietta's piece was in the form of a round-table discussion at which various reactions to the incident were expressed in dialogues with the host, who was patently Papa. His opinion was that nothing could or should be done to the likes of Corbin (there had been an earlier, similar, somewhat less publicized incident at a Saratoga hotel, managed by a man named Hilton), who could be left to the twinges of conscience caused by the righteous indignation of their fellow Christians. But it behooved the Jews to study this phenomenon in the light of the parable presented in the Bible, in Genesis 26, which tells how Isaac settled in the land of the Philistines. When they saw how he prospered there "the Philistines envied him," and said, "Go away from us, for thou hast become much mightier than we. The moral was that if the Jews applied themselves less to the acquisition of material wealth and more to their spiritual elevation they would be less apt to arouse the hostility of the Philistines among their neighbors. "Sulamith," like Papa, did not hesitate to point to the materialistic mote in the Jewish eye, while reproving the gentile.

At nineteen she arrived at a definition of religion apart from church, which she expressed in rebuking a minister who wanted Jews to observe Christian Blue Sunday laws: "I myself would like our laws framed only by religious men; but *religious* men are not necessarily *Christian* men; they are such whose every action is prompted and ennobled by the religion of their heart, by the precepts taught by every creed, by the higher morality inculcated only by religion; in their public life they must know neither Christian, Jew, nor Mohammedan, while in their private life they should be either Christian, Jew or Mohammedan. Church and state must be kept separate, but religion and state should be unseparable. . . ."

And in one of her pieces she attacked with bitter sarcasm the scholarship of an interpreter of Maimonides at the Hebrew Union College, in a tone of voice which gentle Papa would never have ventured to use in public, although she had got much of her insight into the matter from him. She also expressed very forcibly that courage of conviction she had learned from him when a critic in California had the temerity to remind her that she was only a woman—"a pan and pot scourer." Her blistering reply not only evidenced her familiarity with such extra-housekeeping subjects as Kant, Hegel, Fichte, Mendelssohn, Schlegel and Spinoza, but was also a declaration that she did not "consider it a disgrace, or belonging to a lower sphere, to occupy myself with the various branches of domestic economy" and that she did not "neglect the peculiar privilege of woman to attend to the physical comfort of their more awkward fellow creatures."

This fearless forthrightness of a girl still in her teens who "castigates" venerable male scholars made her publisher, Dr. Isaacs, somewhat nervous, and he tried suggesting that she apply herself to less inflammable subjects, say, a handbook for young Jewesses—"a collection of short pithy chapters on moral, religious topics, a bright, helpful book . . . enriched with references to Jewish thought, association, inspiration and achievement," on which work her father would be helpful. This suggestion, however, did not tempt Henrietta, and Dr. Isaacs again admonished her gently for "the punishment you have inflicted" with a "scathing letter," although he continued to print what she wrote and helped her improve her writing: "I have watched with much interest the growth of your style since you began to contribute to *The Messenger*. You have about wholly overcome what at first was a defect (natural to young writers). I refer to overexuberance in the use of epithets, and a fondness for amplification almost bordering on pleonasm. . . ." He then suggested that she do a piece on Sara Copia Sullam, a seventeenth-century Venetian Jewess she had never heard of, and shrewdly knowing how to engage her interest, added: "Pray forgive me for taxing you with fresh work; but I know you will enjoy it, and your father (to whom please give my best regards) will bubble over with satisfaction."

She wrote him a long piece on Sara Copia Sullam, and enjoyed, as he predicted, rescuing from oblivion the life of an extraordinary woman and setting off that life like a jewel against the dark history of her people—the Jews of the original Italian Ghetto.

She found a moral justification for the revival of this obscure personage: ". . . it is not from the acts and words of men who seem to exist in defiance of every law of being, or who are an epitome of centuries gone before and to come, that we derive the lessons for the conduct of life; but from men and women whose path of life greatly intersects our own, glorified only by their own rectitude and purity. If now, we find such gems . . . we dare not let them lie in the dust of ages." But Henrietta was drawn to this task by the romance and drama of Sara's life and by the discovery that the early development and character of this girl who had lived two and a half centuries ago were remarkably like her own. Sara Copia was not merely the eldest, she was the only child of her father who "lavished upon her education all the care and attention usually bestowed upon gifted sons who are to perpetuate the name of the father in an honorable and even distinguished manner"; and by the age of fifteen, "she was well versed in the Hebrew language and literature . . . she read Roman and Greek authors, and wrote Italian poetry."

Henrietta, moved by that empathy and love for her subject which is prerequisite for moving biography, proceeded to reweave the tapestry of Sara Sullam's short life—she lived less than forty-nine years—out of whatever threads she could find. The background began with the expulsion of the Jews from Spain just a century before Sara's birth and the establishment of the Italian Ghetto—not the somber isolated place that word suggests to the modern mind, but a sunny island set in the colorful congeries of medieval Venice —the place Shakespeare pictured, in part, in his *The Merchant of Venice*—where the Jews, although subjected to constant restrictions and occasional indignities, had a flourishing economic and cultural life and were not cut off from their gentile environment. Sara Copia, married at twenty-two to prosperous Jacob Sullam, was greatly gifted with grace and beauty as well as high intelligence; she was witty, composed music, and sang with a sweet voice. She was widely celebrated and beloved; and her fine home in the Ghetto became the gathering place of the learned, the witty, the beautiful—a salon to which flocked Christians as well as Jews, noble cavaliers as well as scholars.

Sara's drama began with her reading of an epic poem based on the Biblical Book of Esther, written by a Genoese monk, Ansaldo Ceba, by which she was so moved that she wrote him a letter of extravagant praise. It was not difficult for Henrietta to understand this impulsive act on the part of a virtuous young woman passionately devoted to the arts and to the history of her people; and Henrietta could condone Sara's ignorance of the potential evil consequence of a well-meaning, impulsive act—something she had herself learned in childhood. The fifty-three-year-old monk in Genoa, stirred by the praise of a young woman celebrated for her brilliance and beauty, responded with the fire of his poetry and engaged Sara's ardent spirit in a long correspondence which developed into a persistent effort on his part to convert her to Christianity. In this the impassioned monk failed, to his bitter disappointment; but not without bringing upon Sara, on the one hand, the condemnation of her Jewish community for her dangerous traffic with the monk, and, on the other hand, an attack by a Catholic priest which might have got her into fatal trouble with the Inquisition were it not that, with a fearless forthrightness Henrietta well understood, Sara published a masterly and scathing rebuttal of the priest's charges in a pamphlet dedicated to "her father, her leader in all the paths of mental and spiritual development." Henrietta's feeling of identity with Sara Sullam was crowned by her discovery of the coincidence that Sara's epitaph in the Jewish cemetery in Venice referred to her as "the Sulamite."

Into the texture of this tapestry of history and human drama, Henrietta, as every artist delights to do, wove strands of her own intuitive insights into human nature and—especially in the remarkable story of the attraction and conflict between two so disparate and fervent characters as this pair—into the relations of men and women: "In their relations, she was the giver and he the receiver, nay the demander. His feeling always exacted sacrifices from her. . . . One is so accustomed to think of men as the privileged who need but ask and receive, and women as submissive and yielding, that our sympathies are usually enlisted on the side of the man whose love is not returned, and we condemn the woman as a coquette. . . . The very firmness of her convictions and logical clearness of her arguments captivated and stimulated him to make greater efforts; usually, this is most exasperating to men, who expect every woman to verify their preconceived notions concerning her sex, and when she does not, immediately condemn her as eccentric and unwomanly. . . . She had the opportunity that few clever women can resist, of showing her superiority in argument over a man. . . . Women themselves have come to look upon matters in the same light as the outside world, and scarcely find any wrong in submitting to the importunities of a stronger will, even when their affections are withheld. . . . She was exposing herself to temptation which it is best to avoid where it can consistently be done. One who invites such trials of character is either foolhardy, overconfident or too simple and childlike in faith in mankind to see the danger. In any case but the last, such a course is sure to avenge itself upon the individual; the moral powers no more than the physical and mental, can bear overstraining. And, in the last case, a bitter disappointment but too often meets the confiding nature. . . ."

Henrietta was discovering in the process of writing, as the born writer does, not merely a channel for the discharge of accumulated information but a stimulus to the development of the creative powers of observation, insight and intuition.

Dr. Isaacs was so pleased with the quality of her biographical study of Sara Sullam that he considered submitting it to the *Century* Magazine or *Harper's* but he decided that its Jewish subject probably would not interest them and published it in *The Messenger,* "so our readers will be benefited instead." Under her father's influence it did not occur to Henrietta that she might write on subjects outside the Jewish field, but she did begin writing for other Anglo-Jewish papers and thus increased her output and her audience. And she wrote the libretto for an oratorio on the subject of Judas Maccabeus performed at the *Ḥanukkah* festival which came in December. By her eighteenth birthday her bent for writing was so evident that Papa and Mamma gave her a *Life of Dickens* as a spur to her aspiration.

Another source of intellectual stimulus was opened to her at that time by the founding of Johns Hopkins University within walking distance of home. It was established in a couple of buildings in the shopping district, with only a few professors, but all eminent men, and a few hundred eager students housed in nearby dwellings. In September '76 Thomas Huxley, Darwin's famous disciple, came from England to speak in a crowded auditorium at the formal opening of the University; and although it was a school for men only, it afforded Henrietta an opportunity to attend its public lectures.

In the following year her father undertook to give a course in Hebrew theology to Johns Hopkins students, and this brought to the Szold house a group of bright young Jews who had come to Baltimore to study, and who enjoyed being fed and mothered by Mamma and entertained by Henrietta and Rachel, who played and sang for them in the upstairs sitting room on Sunday evenings. From Philadelphia came Cyrus Adler and Joseph Jastrow. Adler, Judge Sulzberger's nephew, came to study Assyriology. A smart, shrewd and ambitious young man, well connected, and with a knack for getting in the good graces of important people, he was bound to go far. Joseph Jastrow, the younger son of the distinguished rabbi, Marcus Jastrow, was a friendly, round-faced fellow with a little mustache, whose field was psychology, and who was also a punster and a jolly tease. His father was a good friend of Rabbi Szold, and Joe lived with the Szolds for a while. Both these youths, who greatly admired Henrietta, were somewhat younger than she, as were also the neighboring Friedenwald boys, who were then studying medicine; and bright though they all were, they could not possibly compete for her interest with Papa, whose mind—although he never tried to dazzle or patronize lesser lights with it—naturally eclipsed theirs and made them seem to her even younger than they were. Besides, Miss Henrietta—as she was generally known since she had put up her hair with a chignon in the back—had little time to spare them from her teaching and writing; so Cyrus Adler became interested in her friend Racie Friedenwald, and Joe Jastrow—the only young man who when he wrote had the temerity to address her as Henrietta, and signed himself Joe—fell in love with pretty sister Rachel.

Henrietta, however, was at that time engaged in a lengthy correspondence with Joe's older and more serious brother, Morris, who was just about her own age and whom she had got to know well during trips to Philadelphia with Papa, when he substituted for Rabbi Jastrow at Rodeph Shalom Temple there during its Rabbi's absence in Europe. Young Morris, who, while attending the University of Pennsylvania, also taught and edited a paper, found time to write Henrietta twenty-page letters on everything that engaged his interest, from the acting of Sarah Bernhardt in Philadelphia to his reactions to the comments of "Sulamith" on the Jewish reform movement being promulgated by the Hebrew Union College in Cincinnati. Unlike his younger brother, Joe, he never presumed to address her more familiarly than as "My dear friend," although he praised and envied the elegance and purity of her style. And when he complained of the lack of time for all he wanted to do, Henrietta advised him to rise at five in the morning as she and Papa did.

One thing Papa had not taught Henrietta was how to handle a young man as high-spirited and opinionated as herself. She could not herself resist the opportunity "of showing her superiority in argument over a man" which she had remarked as one of the "feminine follies" of Sara Sullam; and in her forthright way, Henrietta, who in her story of Sara had indicated her own unwillingness "to think of men as the privileged" and "women as submissive and yielding," felt obliged to defend vigorously any statement of hers to which Morris Jastrow took the slightest exception—he objected to her stand on the Corbin affair, as well as on the radical reforms of Dr. Wise of Hebrew Union College—until once, in sheer desperation, he wrote that he had given up hope they would ever agree on anything. But that did not prevent him from writing more long letters, or from coming to spend his Christmas vacations with the hospitable, lively Szolds in their pleasant house on Lombard Street.

1880s: "LITTLE WOMEN"

"WE'VE GOT Father and Mother and each other . . ." said Beth on the first page of Louisa Alcott's *Little Women;* and, "I do think that families are the most beautiful things in all the world," burst out Jo some five hundred pages later in that popular story of the March family, which had first appeared when Henrietta was eight; and the Szold family, as it developed, bore a striking resemblance to the Marches.

Mr. March, like Benjamin Szold, was a clergyman, although of an indeterminate denomination; and "Marmee" March, like Sophie Szold, was the competent manager of her brood of girls, of whom the Marches had only four to the Szolds' five. But the March girls had their counterparts in the Szold girls. Henrietta could easily identify herself with Jo March, although Jo was not the eldest sister. Neither was Henrietta hoydenish like Jo, who frankly wished she were a boy and had deliberately shortened her name, which, like Henrietta's, was the feminine form of a boy's name. But both were high-spirited and vivacious, both had tempers to control, both loved languages, especially English and German, both were good teachers and wrote for publication. Each was her mother's assistant and confidante; and each stood out conspicuously in the family picture.

Bertha Szold was more like Meg, the eldest March girl, who "learned that a woman's happiest kingdom is home, her highest honor the art of ruling it, not as a queen, but a wise wife and mother." Bertha, blue-eyed like Mamma, was from the start her mother's daughter, destined for her mother's role in life. Sadie, like Beth March, suffered ill health—got rheumatic fever and had to be careful of her heart—but that never dampened her spirits. When her right hand was incapacitated by the rheumatism, Sadie learned to write with her left hand. She wrote gay plays about the girls for family entertainments, like "Oh, What Fun! A Comedy in Three Acts," in which, under "Personages," Henrietta appeared as "A Schoolmarm," and Bertha, who was only a trifle less brilliant in high school than Henrietta had been, appeared as *"Dummkopf."* Sadie studied piano; played Chopin in the "Soirée Musicale of Mr. Guthrie's Pupils"; and she recited "Hector's Farewell to Andromache" most movingly, to the special delight of Rabbi Jastrow at his home in Germantown near Philadelphia, where the Szold girls took turns visiting between the visits of the Jastrow boys at the Szolds' in Baltimore. Adele, like Amy, the youngest of the Marches, was the rebellious, mischievous, rather calculating and ambitious one. For Rachel, conceded to be the prettiest of the Szold girls—and she did make a pretty picture sitting in the grape-arbor strumming her guitar and singing in her silvery tones—there was no particular March counterpart; but both groups were so closely knit that despite individual differences the family life in both cases was remarkably similar in atmosphere if not entirely in content—the one being definitely Jewish and the other vaguely Christian.

The Szolds, like the Marches, enjoyed and loved living together, even in troubled times; and, as in the March home, any young man who called on the Szolds found himself confronted with a phalanx of femininity which made it rather difficult to direct his particular attention to any one of them. This included Mamma, jolly, generous, and pretty, with whom they all fell in love, just as Papa had first fallen in love with *her* Mamma before he chose her; and when a young man like Morris Jastrow had enjoyed the Szold hospitality, he felt obliged to send his respects and his gifts not merely to Henrietta, in whom he was really interested, but to all the Szold girls and Mamma. And just as "Laurie" Lawrence was first attracted to bright Jo March, who found him immature by her high standards, and then had to content himself with her younger sister Amy, so Joe Jastrow, who had also been writing Henrietta before he came to Johns Hopkins, had to content himself with her younger sister, pretty Rachel. And like Jo March, who saw her sisters Meg and Amy involved in "lovering" before herself, Henrietta saw her sisters Rachel and Sadie drawn outside their family circle by the attraction of suitors, Rachel by Joe Jastrow, and Sadie by Max Löbl, a young businessman who would write her romantic descriptions of his trips by steamboat down the Mississippi.

One marked difference, however, between the Szolds and the Marches was in their paterfamilias. For although both were gentle and lovable men, the influence of Mr. March on his girls, and especially on Jo, is not so apparent as was the influence of Papa on his girls, and particularly on Henrietta, a fact of which she was quite aware and quite happily accepted. Filial attachment was not uncommon, and not merely between daughters and fathers. The relation between Morris Jastrow and his father was as close as that between Henrietta and hers. And when Harry Friedenwald went to Germany for his postgraduate studies, he wrote his father regularly, long weekly letters which Dr. Friedenwald would read to the Szolds when they called. Harry wrote fairly often to Henrietta too.

Family ties among the Szolds were strong not only within the home on Lombard Street but even across the sea. When Henrietta was eighteen, dauntless Mamma had taken the three youngest children to visit her mother in Europe, leaving Henrietta and Rachel to keep house for Papa with the help of Maggie and Lizzie, who, like the Marches' Hannah, were considered more as friends than as servants of the family. And in the summer of Henrietta's twenty-first year, Papa took her abroad with him on a visit to his and Mamma's family.

They sailed the second week of June; and the fourteen-day trip across was, after a brief bout of seasickness, a wonderfully fresh experience for Henrietta—two weeks of *dolce far niente* between the ever changing beauty of sky and sea.

They disembarked at Bremerhaven, and rode by train through a lush green landscape dotted with thatched roofs on which storks nested, to Bremen, the old Hansa town with its narrow winding streets, flowery gardens, and fair blue-eyed folk.

There they were met by a friend of Papa's and, since it was Friday, went that evening and the next morning to the synagogue and celebrated the Sabbath with a small but fervent congregation. After sight-seeing and a visit to a *Rathauskeller* redolent of wine and beer, they went on to Hamburg, and were there taken by more of Papa's friends into a round of sight-seeing and social gaiety. In Berlin, Papa's relatives dined and entertained them, took them driving to parks and museums, theaters, cafés, and brought Henrietta flowers and bonbons; and they called on a relative of the Jastrows also. In Dresden, where they stayed at a hotel overlooking the picturesque Elbe River, they went to the Opera House for *Tannhäuser,* and sight-seeing with more of Papa's innumerable friends and relatives. There were Szolds and Schaars sprinkled all over Germany and Austria-Hungary. Of Mamma's nine brothers and sisters eight had married and seven had children, so Henrietta met many uncles and aunts and cousins. In Vienna a couple of cousins, students at the university, one in chemistry and the other in medicine, handsome, jolly, companionable fellows, gave Henrietta a very gay time. The cousins suggested that Henrietta stay there for a while and not go on with Papa. They would organize a trip of young people over the Alps into Italy. . . . It was tempting —and this was another one of those occasions when being a girl had its disadvantages—but Henrietta could not imagine doing something just because it would give her pleasure. Henrietta, like Jo March, had a duty-ridden conscience; she could not think of letting Papa return home without her, especially when he gently reminded her how much he would miss her assistance; and there was her own school work waiting, and Mamma and the girls expecting her. . . .

So she proceeded with Papa into Bohemia. In Prague they went to the Alt-Neu Shul, the oldest synagogue in Europe, where Jews had been praying for nine centuries. Even the ancient clock on its tower still turned with Hebraic stubbornness counterclockwise. High up in one wall she noticed a small round window through which no light came, and was told that it opened into the hidden women's gallery, and that during services one woman stood there and acted as the women's minister, relaying to them what was going on in the men's synagogue below. And it occurred to Henrietta that she might act in some such capacity, outside the synagogue, for modern Jewish women at home. All her life she had been absorbing Jewish learning which had had a great influence on her; perhaps she might relay to other Jewish women the ideas she had got from Papa. She remembered how, after Moses had led the Israelites safely through the Red Sea and they sang a song: "I will sing unto the Lord," his sister Miriam led the women, saying to them: "Sing ye to the Lord."

Both in Prague and in Hungarian Presburg, where they then went, Henrietta was pleased to meet women who, like herself, combined a knowledge of ancient Hebraic literature with their modern secular learning, a combination which was rare in American Jewry. Papa, remembering his days as a student at the *Yeshiva* in Presburg, piloted her through the tortuous streets of the town to its ancient ghetto. Though the iron gates of the ghetto, which used to be closed every night when Papa lived there, had since been removed, and Jews were now free to come and go as they wished, the thought of her people having been subjected to such humiliating restraint angered Henrietta, until they climbed the high Schlossberg to the ruined castle overlooking the beautiful Danube, and, as she wrote in her diary, she stood by the "battlemented ruins speaking of powerful nations that had come, lived a strong conquering active life, and disappeared from the world's theater, leaving scarcely 'footprints on the sands of time,' while Israel still survives and is successful enough in worldly matters to rouse the envy of the peoples among which it abides."

Everywhere they went Papa visited the important synagogues and outstanding members of the Jewish community, and Henrietta made notes which were to be the basis for a number of perceptive and lively articles to be published by "Sulamith" as "Reminiscences," "Thoughts on European Judaism," etc., in which she compared what she saw and heard abroad with the state of similar affairs in America. On their journey homeward they stopped in Paris, where she was enchanted by the decor of its great synagogue but was revolted by the mercenary way in which marriage ceremonies performed there were designed according to the fee charged: "from 500 francs up to 4000!"

Before sailing for home they went last to London, where Henrietta looked forward to meeting Morris Jastrow, who was coming over to pursue his postgraduate studies at Breslau. On a visit to the Jastrows before going abroad, Papa had told them of his intention to take Henrietta with him; and Morris, then about to be graduated from the University of Pennsylvania, wrote Henrietta that "your father did not surprise me," adding with a touch of boyish jealous teasing, "I felt satisfied that your father had positively determined to take his Baby along." He regretted that he could not accompany them, and immediately began planning for their meeting "somewhere between Liverpool and Cologne"; and when he was about to sail himself, he wrote Mamma that he would be in London just about the time Henrietta would be there with Papa and asked Mamma's help in arranging the meeting. He also wrote Henrietta in Vienna to that effect. But, alas, they did not meet in London. The sailing of Morris' steamer was somewhat delayed; Papa was by then anxious to return; and they missed Morris by just one day. It was a great pity. However, Henrietta and he continued to correspond during the three years he stayed abroad.

On the passenger list of the Norddeutscher Lloyd Postdampfers *Main,* which left Bremen September 4, 1881, after "Herr Dr. Szold," twenty-one-year-old Henrietta was erroneously listed as "Frau Dr. Szold"—a funny slip, coming at the end of what might possibly have been a honeymoon trip had Henrietta's heart moved her by then in that direction. Anyway, it had not moved her strongly enough toward young Morris Jastrow, who with his handsome heavy-lidded eyes and small Vandyke beard resembled Prince Edward of England, and whose letters were certainly interesting.

After three months abroad it was pleasant to be back home with Mamma and the girls, to sit in her accustomed place at table alongside Papa, which the others would no more think of taking in her absence than of sitting in Papa's chair. The table was almost always extended to its full length for the benefit of Papa's wayfaring friends, and the Johns Hopkins students who dropped in for one of Mamma's delicious meals or the girls' Sunday evenings—Harry and Julius Friedenwald, and Joe Jastrow, and Cyrus Adler with his talk of the brilliant fellow graduate students he was meeting—Josiah Royce, John Dewey, James Cattell. . . . It was stimulating to take part again in animated table talk about world and local affairs—the shooting and death of President Garfield, recalling the death of great Lincoln, and conjectures of what sort of President Arthur would make—with Mamma energetically carving the fragrant fowl Maggie and Lizzie brought in, and giving orders which everyone happily carried out.

Much of the talk at table at that time had to do with the controversy between Jewish orthodoxy and reform, which was developing into a bitter conflict among American rabbis. The storm center, Dr. Isaac M. Wise's Hebrew Union College in Cincinnati, was promulgating radical reforms in ritual and interpretation in response to the wave of scientific skepticism stirred up by Darwin, Huxley and others, disturbing to orthodox Judaism as well as fundamentalist Christianity. *The Origin of Species* was published in the fall of the year before Henrietta was born, just about the time Papa and Mamma arrived in Baltimore; and Rabbi Szold being a product not only of an orthodox European *yeshiva* but also of modern German universities, was in favor of a progressive organic development of Judaism such as flourished in Talmudic times. Had he lived then, he would have belonged to the school of Hillel, the liberal, rather than to that of Shammai, the orthodox.

Rabbi Szold, however, was never a radical, any more than he was a reactionary. He was in the best sense a conservative, a liberal and progressive conservative; and so were his friends, Rabbi Marcus Jastrow in Philadelphia and Rabbi Albert Bettelheim in San Francisco and Rabbi Alexander Kohut in New York, and others who had come from the same European background and training as his. But whereas they had no central organization and had no influence beyond their individual congregations, the radical reformers were training and sending out from Cincinnati an influential stream of young reform rabbis intent on changes which to the ultraorthodox were blasphemous, and to the conservative were dangerous.

The conflict, as it then developed, was not really between the reform and the orthodox, who merely went their unchanging way under the guidance of rabbis trained only in an Old World *yeshiva*, but between the radical reform and the enlightened conservative, who believed that reform was throwing out the baby with the bath water—was losing the essence of Judaism in an attempt to dispense with certain traditional forms, in which, to the conservative way of thinking, that essence inhered.

Rabbi Szold went to hear a debate at Temple Beth El in New York on "The Conflict Between Science and Religion" in which conservative Rabbi Kohut tried to stem the tide of extreme reform and was branded as an orthodox reactionary by Rabbi Kaufman Kohler of Beth El, who answered for reform. Rabbi Szold thereafter delivered a sermon at Oheb Shalom on "The Sabbath," in which he took his stand against radical reform in eloquently adjuring the unusually large congregation gathered to hear him to adhere to the traditional seventh day Sabbath instead of changing to Sunday observance, which the reformers were advocating.

Quivering with restrained emotion, he argued the point poetically and rationally: "The seventh day was the Sabbath in the beginning—when the whole of nature burst into a joyous anthem, when the stars of the dawn rang with the praise of their Creator. . . . God created the world according to a preconceived plan and for a predetermined purpose. These postulates, which also guarantee the son of man, created in the image of God, freedom of will and the privilege of self-chosen destiny, are the spontaneous gifts of nature; they gleam at the very dawn of conscious existence. Of that, the Sabbath among days, as later Israel among the nations, is witness. . . . Christianity, claiming to have found Jewish doctrine inadequate to secure the salvation of man, acted consistently with its own history in establishing the Sunday Sabbath; for with it is connected the dogma of redemption, which was not revealed spontaneously in nature itself, but in the fact of incarnation, believed by its adherents to have occurred in the later course of history. . . . The Sunday Sabbath is thus the emblem of a dogma contradictory to our religious system. Add to this the fact that a Jewish congregation can allege no other than material reasons for its introduction. . . . Such considerations go to stigmatize a celebration of that kind on the part of Jews as irreligious, immoral, and a disgrace to the Jewish name. . . ."

Rabbi Szold was urged to publish this sermon, which he did, with an introduction in which he said: "Far be it from me to send forth the word of contention, or to stir up religious strife. It is my sole intention to strengthen, in the hearts of those that agree with me, the conviction that it is treason to wrench from the traditional Sabbath the garland of blossoms woven about its brow by the hand of the Creator, in order to adorn its rival. . . . The conviction is firmly rooted in my mind that the Jewish tribe can ascend the luminous peaks of its priestly mission only by clinging to its peculiar tenets, and that a congregation by renouncing the Sabbath, is cutting asunder the most sacred bond that links it to the Israelitish community. . . ."

All this was grist to the mill of "Sulamith," who wholeheartedly concurred with Papa in his stand, which, as she understood it, was tolerant of difference in faith but not of change for expediency. She herself was in constant, active and amicable contact with her gentile environment, in which, daily, she functioned effectively and happily as an integral part; but she would not yield to it—and this right she considered an important part of American freedom for all—her observance of those Jewish rituals in each of which, to her mind as to Papa's, inhered some part of the spirit of Judaism. She would not work on Saturday; she would not eat food that was not *kasher*—not for the orthodox reason that it was sinful to do so but for the conservative reason that it was un-Jewish. And, like Papa, Henrietta felt and believed that being Jewish was something important, as important as being American.

This consciousness of being Jewish, far from limiting the family life of the Szolds, gave it a greater dimension. When Henrietta went abroad with Papa she got a sense of her relatedness not only to the Szolds and the Schaars but to the whole of world Jewry, going back to ancient times; and at home in Baltimore, being a Jew involved her actively in relation to other communities of Jews all over the continent—in Philadelphia and New York, Cincinnati and Chicago, San Francisco and Los Angeles . . . although the relationship, as is true in individual families, might sometimes not be perfectly amicable.

In connection with the conflict over adherence to old Jewish observances there was also to be considered the fact that some of them made good common sense, like the ritual cleansing of meat—making it *kasher*—with salt and water, and the ritual washing of hands before meals. And some of them, indeed, were undeniably more logical than the equivalent gentile mores: for example, that the Jewish Sabbath came on the last instead of the first day of the week; that *Rosh Hashanah,* the Jewish New Year, is celebrated in the fall when, after the summer holiday, communal activities are renewed, schools reopen, business takes a new lease on life, social activities are resumed . . . instead of in midwinter when only the calendar marks the change; and the Jewish tradition of inaugurating the new year with a period of penitence between *Rosh Hashanah* and *Yom Kippur* certainly seems more sensible than the gentile custom of celebrating New Year's Eve like a pagan orgy.

At the end of an article, "Thoughts on European Judaism," Henrietta wrote, "Judaism cannot die, its truth cannot be eradicated from the world, its nobility must become victorious." But Morris Jastrow, to whom she sent a copy, disagreed with her opinion that "the regeneration of Jewish fervor and piety will come, not, as we like to assert, from America but the more . . . intellectual European Jews." His observations in Germany with its strong assimilationist tendencies led him to believe that Judaism there was "destined to die."

As a result of her association with Papa, Henrietta had arrived at a certain conviction about religion: that religious organizations —churches—generally cohere on the basis of creed and have their uses on that basis, but that Jews differ from other religious groups in generally shrinking from the formulation of a creed. Apart from the dogmatic formulation of a creed, religiousness, she felt, was a personal, individual matter, not subject to organization, too subtle to be taught or talked; and when it ceased to be such a silent inner influence, it ceased to be religion. She felt impelled, however, to join a religious body—a congregation—as a means of giving public evidence of her Jewishness and adherence to the Jewish community. While she felt most comfortable in communion with a congregation expressing approximately her own attitude, the conservative, if she were living in a town which had only one synagogue, she would regard it her duty to attach herself to that congregation regardless of how little it might express her attitude; because attendance at a synagogue is the only way Jews have to declare publicly their Jewish association. The details of one's essential religion—one's theology—she felt, are between the individual and his Maker. Her personal concept of the Creator she had tried to express in part at one point in the Sara Sullam piece: "It is not in the violent convulsions of nature, in conflagrations, earthquakes, pestilences and inundations that God's power is greatest, His will most strongly manifest, His plan most wondrous; but in the silent changes of seasons, in the imperceptible motions of great bodies, in the endless, unceasing yet unobtrusive developments of organic life. . . ."

In the years following her return from abroad she was absorbed again in the rich routine of her preoccupations which, because there were so many exciting new things to do in Baltimore where "Miss Henrietta" was by then widely known, became augmented until the twenty-four-hour day could hardly contain them. Besides her "Baltimore Letters" for *The Messenger,* she contributed similar letters to *The Jewish Exponent* under the nom de plume "Miriam"; and her articles published in a number of Anglo-Jewish papers covered a wide range of subjects: a study of the relation of Moses Mendelssohn to the schools of philosophy; an essay on the history of Jewish literature; a criticism of *Herod and Mariamne,* a tragedy by Emilie Rives, in which Henrietta demonstrated her grasp of the essentials of dramatic art as well as of the historical background of the play; "Pauper Judaicus, Variety Americanus. Local Name: Schnorrer," a slyly humorous study, as if of a botanical specimen; a vivid retelling for children of the story of the heroic Maccabees.

She was overcoming her shyness in public speaking, having discovered that audiences were essentially friendly and eager for any interesting revelation. Her speaking voice, though small, was warm; it could on occasion, like Papa's, rise to emotional heights; and it carried the conviction of her well-stocked mind. She spoke to literary clubs in Baltimore on the history of the Jews in Maryland, on the poetess Emma Lazarus; and she was invited by the Young Men's Hebrew Association of Philadelphia to speak there on several occasions on Jewish historical subjects such as the return of the Jews to England in the seventeenth century.

All this in addition to her daily teaching at the Misses Adams' School, where she strove happily not only to inform her students

Illustrations

Papa and Mamma

"The Girl"

"The Spinster"

A rare time of tranquillity

With "her children"

On her eightieth birthday with Hans Beyth (right)

Photograph by Dr. Gidal

"... and turned Miss Szold into a beaming, cooing grandmother ..."

but to help them express themselves in writing as she herself was increasingly doing, with great effect and satisfaction. She trained them in letter writing, which for her was not merely a social grace but an important means of self-expression and communication. "Letter writing," she told them, "whether the letter be real or fictitious, is capital practice. . . . A fictitious letter should have exactly the tone and color of a genuine one. . . . A letter—remember this—is always a *talk*—what you would say to your correspondent if you were with him; and as he is abroad, you talk on paper instead of with your lips." Her sister Bertha attended the Misses Adams' School for a while and it was fun to set out mornings with her "twin" sister in tow—although thirteen years apart they had the same birthday—gaily talking, and instilling in "blue-eyed Betsy" her own love of literature and language. Together they read and wept over *Les Misérables,* laughed and cried with Dickens' characters, and loved George Eliot. Thackeray left them cold.

Despite the teaching, which took her out of the home a good part of the week, Henrietta managed to keep close to Mamma and the girls. The spring dressmaking for six females filled the house with bolts of materials, boxes of trimmings, and the great excitement of combined creative effort with frills, furbelows and feathers.

Summer Sundays, "The Five," as the girls called themselves, went on picnics laden with baskets of food. Marshaled by Mamma and Henrietta with her green tin botany can slung over her shoulder and armed with Gray's *Botany,* they set out for one of the parks, or the countryside of their summer resorts, where they gathered and studied plants and flowers. Proceeding along some woodland path or over verdant fields, botanically searching and sniffing the scene, they would call to each other at sight or scent of something new or delightful, halting to classify some small rare leaf with the help of Gray, or to revel in the loveliness of a whole hillside clad in wild June roses. Returning home, they would be laden with specimens for their collections, and with fragrance and beauty for room decoration or transplanting in the garden. And when Rachel and Henrietta joined the Baltimore Botany Club, Henrietta usually let one or two of her little sisters tag along after her on field trips, as no one else would.

Afternoons, when she was not working at her own desk upstairs, she would be in Papa's study working with him, acting as his librarian, or out in the garden reading proof of the Job book for him while he paced the graveled path, hands clasped behind his back, meditating on a sermon for the Sabbath, chanting a psalm, or stopping to examine the damage done to a rose bush by the caterpillars. Too tender-hearted himself to kill them, he offered to pay the children some pennies for every dozen they destroyed; but, either because they were too lazy or too squeamish, they never did, and they were never reproved for not doing it. Papa was gentler than ever; and his hair was getting gray so fast that Adele, sixteen years younger than Henrietta, could not believe it had ever been really black, so Henrietta had to lift it up in back to show her. He still let it grow long, and although he sometimes toyed with the shape of his beard he never shaved it off as the reform rabbis were doing; and it, too, was growing gray.

Henrietta was changing also; she was discovering in herself a streak of spirit which was more like Mamma's than Papa's. Mamma, less tolerant of childishness, stupidity or vulgarity than Papa, could be tart at times; and Henrietta could lose her temper too, although her disapproval was always politely, even primly, expressed. "I don't mind your using my ribbons or handkerchiefs," she would say to her sisters, who could never achieve the enviable exquisite perfection of Henrietta's tatting, embroidery and monograms, "but why must you make a mess of my bureau drawer!" And when they went off for a drive on a Friday afternoon with their visiting cousin, Miriam Schaar, the daughter of Uncle Eduard who had settled in Cincinnati, and failed to return before sundown, Henrietta met them on the doorstep, and, shaking an admonishing forefinger, had only to say "We observe the Sabbath here!" to make them feel her disapproval. Hers, like Mamma's, was the German-Jewish ideal of a beautiful order achieved by self-discipline. She trained the youngsters to care, each for her own belongings and to use no one else's without permission; and she taught them the esthetics of traditional ritual. And although these lessons might become irksome at times, she was beloved by them as their good teacher, always eager herself for more learning.

She joined a French conversation group and a Women's Literary Club. She frequented the new Pratt Library and studied pedagogy, to make up for her lack of formal teacher training. She resumed her attendance of lectures at Johns Hopkins, which in a few years had become a university known over the civilized world and acknowledged to stand in the highest rank. Its researches were watched attentively by scholars all over the globe, and its curriculum provided a liberal education in all branches of knowledge. There she developed a lively interest in the modern sciences and technology which were beginning to transform the face of the world: Roebling's remarkable suspension bridge had been constructed between New York and Brooklyn; they were talking of installing electric cars on the streets of Baltimore. And there she met other young women like herself, intent on widening the horizon of modern women and willing to work to that end, among them Miss M. Carey Thomas, who founded Bryn Mawr College, where Henrietta thought Bertha should go.

In the summer vacation of '87, enticed by the cheap fare and board offered by the State Teachers' Association of Maryland for their convention at Old Point Comfort, Henrietta, who had been asked to speak there, took Sadie and Bertha with her. They enjoyed the sea and the bathing—which Henrietta found inferior, however, to the surf bathing at Cape May—the beach walks, the colorful military exercises at nearby Fortress Monroe, the Indian School at Hampton; but the people she met there were depressing. The hotel was crowded with shoddy Virginia aristocracy flaunting their pride of purse or of blood, and with provincial teachers of a type that made her wish heartily never to become known as a Teacher.

The prospect of having to get up on a platform and deliver a talk in public still made her nervous. It might be considered rather presumptuous for a young teacher of twenty-six without formal training in the art to instruct graduate educators, most of them much older than herself; and she knew that the paper she had brought to read them would put her, from its opening sentence, in the class of the prophet crying in a wilderness.

She called it "Elementary Schools—Training Schools," and into it went everything she had learned about learning from her own childhood and her observation of her young sisters and the children she had been teaching for thirteen years. She began by forthrightly and roundly condemning the popular "catechetical" method in general use, of teaching by questions and answers which tested only the pupil's stock of factual information. That this was an error she had been made aware of by little girls like the one whose "Minute Men" were on all sides. She revised Emerson's old saw to read: "Not knowledge, but the capacity to acquire knowledge is power," and then went on to attack the schooling of youngsters for specialized crafts or careers which "would tend more strongly than any political or economic measures, to nurse class and caste feelings, by almost forcing the child to enter upon his father's trade or pursuit"—an undemocratic, un-American procedure. The elementary school should be "a training school such as will enable graduates to judge what course lies within their mental and physical reach, and, having once decided upon a career, to persevere in it understandingly and with discretion.

"The true utilitarian is a psychologist . . . he will confine his attention to those elements that educate the *man,* be he in the guise of a carpenter, a banker, a shoemaker, a hod carrier or a college professor. Above all things will he most assiduously acquaint himself with the workings of the child's mind. It is spread out before him like a map and the most prominent landmark there engraved is the child's repugnance to all abstractions. It is the living, the organic, the concrete, that in life which throbs and pulsates like his own quickening blood that attracts the child. In every study he must be shown growth, which is life." This she said with the fervent quivering passion with which Papa said, *Le-Ḥayim,* the Hebrew toast: "To Life!"—or, more literally, "To the Living!"—and then she proceeded to say how this good teaching was to be done. "If analytic we must be, let us analyze backward, beginning with what is complete. At present we begin at the beginning and enumerate for the child the varying elements which we with our wider experience know how to constitute into an harmonious whole. But is it just to expect of the child that he should combine, fit together, and from the elements construct an image of a whole that he has never seen or conceived of? Let us try to recall our own experience. . . ."

She tried to tell them what she thought an elementary school should teach: "In order to banish any tendency toward specialization, an elementary course should consist throughout of the three departments, Science, Mathematics and the Humanities—no matter what branch of science, what development of belles lettres. . . . I wittingly put science first, because observation precedes even language, language presupposes observation. . . . If the science taught be one of the group called natural, we can scarcely be said to be introducing a new element to the child's attention. He is quick to recognize his oneness with nature. Certainly that notion is soon dismissed as an illusion if you begin by telling him that he is studying botany or entomology or mineralogy as sciences that treat of certain abstractions. . . . No need to mention botany, chemistry, physics or physiology at all; no need in fact to teach any one of these systematically, at first. Take a flower one day, an insect the next, dwell upon such familiar phenomena as rain and dew, make it a rule never to overstep the horizon of the child's actual or possible experience. But mindful of your position as *trainer* of youthful minds, let your instruction in science be as unremitting as those in reading and counting. Gradually they may crystallize and assume a more systematic form; at the end of four or five years of school life you may even allow yourself the luxury of a textbook. Finally, when a multitude of facts has been not taught but most carefully observed as phenomena by the trainers, when your pupil is about to leave you, the crowning lesson, the abstractions, the inferences, the inductions, the general law may be methodically evolved."

She objected to the teaching even of arithmetic as a meaningless memorizing process, for "understanding must precede application. The truth is that in this, as in all other matters, we Americans are in a tremendous hurry." In criticizing the teaching of the humanities, she scathingly denounced the venerable *Common Reader,* "a book that abounds in poems—jingles conveying in whiney commonplace language, sentiments surely spurned by every healthy-minded child . . ." and decried "the misuse of the great literary text so that the student sees in Milton's 'Paradise Lost' merely an exercise devised for his torture, as Caesar is supposed to have written of the Gallic Wars for beginners in Latin." She attacked the chronological study of literature, so that one begins by a struggle with Chaucer, which discourages interest in contemporary literature; and similarly, the study of history which begins with the incomprehensible past instead of the familiar present. As for the teaching of grammar: "From the persistence with which we force it upon our pupils, it might be supposed that grammar is nectar and ambrosia to their parched hungry souls. In reality, however, they hate it with an almost vindictive, certainly a justifiable hatred." English should be taught, using the best literature, so that the pupil's "taste and judgment will have developed, his language will be clear, direct, accurate and correct, from mere force of habit, his vocabulary enhanced, his language sense in general be made keen and unfailing and his mode of thinking will have become logical from intercourse with the best, though perhaps the simplest of the best, the ages have produced. . . ."

She pointed out, however, that the large size of their classes was a "stumbling block to all reforms"; and, drawing on Talmudic lore she had got from Papa, "In what striking contrast with the ofttime shallow boasts of our nineteenth century that deems itself so far advanced in educational methods, is the custom that obtained in Palestine, as early as two centuries before the common era: namely, that any community that allowed a teacher to teach a class more numerous than twenty-five without granting him an assistant was to be branded as degraded." She counseled the need of a more intimate relation between teacher and student, whose whole personality should be trained in the process of education.

Looking then to the future, she undertook to justify the need for the reforms she advocated. "We are in fact drifting toward the solution of problems unique in the history of mankind, so far as the attitude of the masses of the people will have to assume toward them is concerned. These problems, only beginning to look formidable, but portending hard struggles, will not be solved by the sword, nor by dictum of a titled nobility, nor by the ingeniousness of the financial speculator; not even genius, nor the versatility of the journalist will stand in good stead. . . ." She proclaimed prophetically that "everywhere can be discerned prognostics of the fact that life in the twentieth century will not be easy to live, that it will call for high courage to face the truth, steadiness in action, steadfast opinions, and unflinching purposes.

The world will stand in need of a *host* of noble, perfect men, planned and executed according to the models that previous ages have shown only as isolated specimens of humanity, upon their pinnacles and in their foremost ranks. Such are our pupils to be. . . ."

Well aware that, like Cassandra, she had probably failed to convince her self-satisfied nineteenth-century audience, if she had not indeed shocked and offended them, she was not altogether sorry to leave Old Point Comfort and go home. However, the latter part of the summer compensated for that disappointment, when she went to Germantown outside Philadelphia, where Rachel, who was by then engaged to Joe Jastrow, was visiting his family. The three of them went to New York to attend the session of the American Association for the Advancement of Science, of which Henrietta had become a member, and she enjoyed not merely the stimulating meetings held at Columbia College and addressed by some of the most celebrated scientists of the day, but the stimulating quality of the scientists themselves—"a fine set of men, physically and intellectually."

So she wrote Harry Friedenwald, her long-time neighbor and friend, who had gone to Germany for his postgraduate studies in medicine and was corresponding with her, very much—although not as frequently, since mail took months to and from Europe—as had Morris Jastrow, who by now was back in Philadelphia, and a Professor of Semitics at the University of Pennsylvania. Harry Friedenwald's letters, which at first were addressed to the "Misses Henrietta, Rachel and Sadie Szold" but then confined themselves to Henrietta, covered a wide range of subjects rising from his intelligent observations of European life. Although he was about three years younger than Henrietta, his thinking was mature and sophisticated; he could discuss even such matters as the attitude of the sexes toward each other in Europe—a strained, formalized relation which, to his mind, resulted in a loss to them both, morally and intellectually. To this Henrietta was prompted to reply that "our free and easy intercourse may to a European seem to be fraught with dangers of all kinds, but our very scorn of all danger and forgetfulness thereof shows how healthy and uncontaminated we Americans still are. For this reason, too, I do not hesitate to condemn all those who desire to ape European manners by introducing the safeguards by which the 'females' are protected. They are thus indeed inviting the danger against which they fondly imagine they are protecting us." These, she knew, were pretty daring notions for a young woman in the year of Queen Victoria's Golden Jubilee.

For all that, and for all the apparent sophistication of her commentary on the dangerous relation of Sara Sullam and Ansaldo Ceba, Henrietta knew very well, while writing glibly of her "scorn of all danger," that, although very well informed and educated in most other fields, she was still fairly ignorant in this one, knew very little indeed, as a matter of fact—and that little with her intuitive mind and not her impassioned heart—about this "danger"; and that what protected American "Little Women" like the Marches and the Szolds, despite their freedom from those despised European safeguards, was the careful elimination of all sexual interests from their environment until such time as a suitable man chose to come and take one of them out of that encircling Victorian innocence.

Before Joe Jastrow came to take Rachel to Germantown for that visit to his family in the summer of '87 he wrote Henrietta that he was coming for his "sleeping beauty"—an apt expression. Henrietta, then past twenty-six, was still "sleeping" too, in that sense; for interesting as Morris Jastrow and Harry Friedenwald were, and others of the bright young men who were obviously attracted to her, none of them had really roused her or distracted her from the round of activities which took all her serious attention and abundant energy.

Henrietta had occasion about this time to observe at close range a girl who had been really aroused to love. Rebekah, the daughter of Rabbi Albert Bettelheim of San Francisco, who had been Papa's fellow student at Presburg, came to Baltimore in advance of her family and stayed with the Szolds until her father arrived to become rabbi of a Baltimore congregation. Rebekah, an attractive, energetic and intelligent girl, had fallen in love with Rabbi Alexander Kohut, whom she met in New York, a very handsome man with a blue-black beard, but a widower more than twice her age and the father of eight children, the eldest one near Rebekah's own age. As her father and friends were not in favor of the match, Rebekah was greatly distressed; and Henrietta, with whom she roomed, would hear her talking in her troubled sleep. But, to the admiration of Henrietta, Rebekah had persisted in her resolve despite all opposition, and happily married Alexander Kohut. Papa performed the ceremony; and Henrietta, who played Mendelssohn's "Wedding March" for them, would herself doubtless have welcomed this kind of impassioned attachment at that time. For if the "sleeping beauty" sleeps too long, the prince who comes to waken her may be too young.

In the following summer, Joe Jastrow, who was making good progress professionally, and publishing in the psychology journals, got an appointment to the faculty of the University of Wisconsin. So Rachel and Joe had an afternoon wedding at the Oheb Shalom Synagogue, with Papa officiating, of course, and went off to Madison. Sadie attended the Bryn Mawr preparatory school in Baltimore, but her frail health interfered with her studies and she spent a good deal of time trying some new treatment or recuperating from her chronic illness. Bertha was getting ready to go to Bryn Mawr College. That left in Lombard Street, besides Mamma and Papa, who was also away a good deal officiating and speaking, dedicating institutions and receiving honorary degrees in distant cities, only Henrietta and sprightly young Adele, who was finishing grammar school, still struggling with her spelling, and engrossed mainly in disciplining her dog, Don.

Adele had become greatly attached to Henrietta, looked to her for guidance even more than to Mamma, whom she could tease to sputtering distraction, and to whom she might say, "I have Henrietta's permission to do this." She could also be resentful of Henrietta as a child is of a disappointing parent. If Henrietta promised to go out with her and then let some important business interfere, Adele would be furious with her. Adele differed from her sisters in her strong streak of rebelliousness. Perhaps she had missed being the pet of Papa, who by the time she arrived could not devote himself to any one of the younger children and spent more of his spare time with Henrietta, his indispensable assistant. Adele would sometimes express her rebelliousness by skepticism in matters they both considered important. It was typical of Adele that she should tell Henrietta that, until the Johnstown Flood in Pennsylvania, she could not believe the Bible story of the Deluge. It was also typical of Papa that when Henrietta reported this to him, suggesting that he talk to Adele about her skepticism of the Bible, he said nothing directly to Adele about it. One day at the dinner table, however, he referred to the Johnstown catastrophe and remarked that when he first read the account in the papers about how thousands of people had been drowned, he could not believe it, until he was reminded of the Flood in the Bible. Adele looked up from her plate, rather startled, but said nothing. And it was like Papa that he should enjoy telling this story one day when he and Mamma and Henrietta went to dine at the Aaron Friedenwalds', where they learned that Harry would be returning from Germany with his medical degree early in the new year.

On the last day of 1889, Henrietta wrote Harry Friedenwald: "It was indeed good news to hear of your early return. . . . To-morrow we shall be able to say, '*This* year he comes back.' Your letters have testified to the full to your enjoyment of all your European experiences; still, I am looking forward with delight to the time when you can enter into details and relate your impressions. I am presuming that these three years will not have changed you, that you will be as willing as before to describe what effect sights and incidents make upon you, in short, that the old Sunday evenings will be restored. What right I have to expect any such delightful restoration I do not know. It seems to me everything has changed. Naturally, Rachel's going away has made a different family of us. I still miss her as deeply as at first. In fact more so. I am becoming conscious of the irrevocableness of the change. It is a fearful thing—this setting aside a certain period of one's life and saying in one's mind: 'This is done with, that is a sealed book; nothing to be added, none of its pleasures to be tasted over again. . . .' "

And as if to herald the end of that pleasant era of the "Little Women," the maids, Maggie and Lizzie, had left in the fall to open a boardinghouse; and Mamma, after sixteen years of perfect, smoothly run housekeeping, was hard put to it to find a good housemaid and train a "greenhorn" cook from among the new stream of immigrants then pouring into America.

1890s: THE SPINSTER

THE NINETIES were far from gay for Miss Henrietta of Baltimore. In addition to the burden of her daily labors, the alleviation of suffering became her constant preoccupation—first the suffering of her people, and then of her most beloved kin. Of the persecutions her people had suffered since Pharaoh—the archetype of all anti-Semites, recalled every Passover—she had been hearing and even writing since childhood; but those suffering generations of Jews were of distant times and places, far removed from herself. The righteous indignation they aroused, like her anger before the old ghetto gates at Presburg, was evanescent, and could no longer lead to action. Even the story Papa used to tell of the persecution he and his brother suffered at the hands of the gentile boys in their Hungarian village was like a childishly cruel fable out of a primitive bygone time; and the Corbin affair, right here and now in America, had seemed less sinister and dangerous than contemptible, like the stupid social discrimination sometimes directed by one caste of Christians against another. The generally indignant reaction to both Corbin and Hilton had served to demonstrate most reassuringly the inherent strength and reliability of American progressive democracy. And the Judophile writings of gentiles, like George Eliot's *Daniel Deronda,* evidenced not merely a growing tolerance but an appreciation of the Jewish spirit in the modern world.

It took personal contact with flesh-and-blood victims of virulent, contemporary European anti-Semitism to make it an immediate and dreadful reality for the proud Baltimore Jewess who had been living and working so amicably in and with her gentile environment. It was from Russia that this contact came.

The assassination of Czar Alexander II in 1881 by fanatic revolutionaries with whom a young Jewess was said to have been involved had served to unleash the beastly fury of anti-Semitism in the Russian government and, with its acquiescence and instigation, in the Russian people. The May Laws of 1882 further restricted the residence of Jews to crowded pales of settlement; they were denied the right to own property or hold mortgages, to practice the professions, to enter the universities beyond a very limited *numerus clausus.* They were subjected to every degrading indignity. Spurred on by this official persecution and the obvious indifference of the police, the benighted, downtrodden folk fell upon the defenseless Jews, offered to them as a scapegoat, in pogroms where men, women and children suffered horrible maltreatment—beatings, dismemberment, rape, and death—while their homes and synagogues were looted, desecrated, and burnt to the ground.

Like the Jews of Spain centuries before, thousands who could escape fled, destitute and under the most miserable conditions; and, finding no asylum in neighboring countries, they came, packed in the noisome steerage of ships which took weeks to cross the stormy Atlantic, to the "land of the free." Of these, most went to New York, but many landed in Baltimore; and Rabbi Szold, of course, went to their aid when they arrived and helped them find places to live and work.

In this he was assisted by Henrietta who went with him down to the harbor at Locust Point to meet the immigrants disembarking in the long sheds with their double rows of benches on which hundreds of the bedeviled, bewildered Jewish refugees came to rest. Their accounts of what had happened in the smoke-filled streets of their towns and villages, with feathers from their bedding flying through the air and blood flowing in the gutters, made anti-Semitism a terrible reality for Henrietta—a reality that called for action.

But after the immigrants had been helped to find homes and

work (for which she suggested the establishment of a labor bureau), Henrietta saw that there was still a great need to be met. They must be taught English as quickly as possible so that they would be equipped to become Americans, able to find the best possible kind of employment, and not to be exploited as inarticulate "greenhorns" were in the mills and the sweatshops, so that they had to live in such slums as were depicted by Jacob Riis in *How the Other Half Lives*. Henrietta set about starting a night school for adults, the first of its kind; and by November of '89 she had found support for her plan among members of the Hebrew Literary Society, and enlisted the active assistance of B. H. Hartogensis, a Baltimore lawyer, and others, in securing the requisite funds to open the class in a room on Gay Street.

Thirty men and women gathered on the first evening, but so many more came for the second session that an additional class had to be formed, and before long a third; and still more came, for two-hour classes, four nights a week. Henrietta's days were full of her regular teaching and writing, but she could not deny these Russian Jews what they eagerly sought, not merely because of their great present need after their great suffering but because their character evoked her love, something warmer even than that *Menschenliebe* she had learned from Papa; and this was strange, because she had been accustomed to hearing the East-European Jews of Russia and Poland looked down upon by the Western Jews of Germany, Austria and Hungary, as comparatively uncultivated, uncivilized folk. And it was true that they spoke the Yiddish jargon instead of the pure German to which she was accustomed; it was true that they hadn't the Western refinements of manner and speech, the decorum in which she had been reared; but, beneath their uncouthness, she found, they were intensely intelligent and idealistic. They were noisy and they gestured; but it was the vitality of their minds which drew her to them, the avidity with which they seized the learning she offered them; it was the irrepressible warmth and vigor of their spirit which appealed to the carefully repressed passion of hers, and endeared them to her. They were of all ages, from men and women in their fifties down to teen-age boys and girls who had to work in the shops. Husbands and wives came together; parents and children studied from the same book.

Henrietta called them "my Russians," and happily went without suppers and sleep to keep the school going and growing.

By the beginning of 1890 her budget for the next half year—rent, books, stationery, and gas—came to $141, toward which the students paid $18 in dues (those who could, paid a small fee) and raised $25 from a raffle—"much to my disgust," finicky Henrietta wrote Mr. Hartogensis. He managed to raise the additional $100 and to enlist the interest of the Baron de Hirsch Fund, which made it possible for the school to rent a whole house on Front Street. By the following season, however, two extra rooms had to be rented outside the house, and by 1892 hundreds were applying for admission and the school had to remove to a still larger house on East Baltimore Street. In addition to English, grammar and arithmetic were taught, and American history, and sewing for the women. By then they had seven rooms and six teachers besides Henrietta. She not only taught but acted as superintendent, handled budgetary matters, was concerned with such details as hanging curtains and lambrequins, and enlisted the interest of useful people like Dr. Aaron Friedenwald who became Chairman of the School Committee, and of Louis Levin, a young colleague of Mr. Hartogensis who was interested in social service, and who undertook to attend to the printing for the school, and to give a course in bookkeeping. As a consequence of this interest, Louis Levin got to know sister Bertha when she came home from Bryn Mawr, and then began courting her.

So Henrietta, who had not wanted to become branded as a Teacher, although she still enjoyed teaching and did it with less effort and preparation, now found herself teaching days and nights and weekends with so little time for leisure that red-haired, energetic Mr. Hartogensis failed in his efforts to get her to go off with him for some diversion—even so much as a tramp in the country. "I have little heart left to contemplate any pleasure of my own," she wrote him in reply to his invitation, a condition she found herself accepting without question. The Sunday evenings she had looked forward to with the return of Harry Friedenwald had indeed become a thing of the past. Cyrus Adler, Joe Jastrow and Rachel were gone; Bertha was away at Bryn Mawr except for summers; Sadie, undeterred by her ailment, was in Cambridge at the Harvard Annex for Women; and Harry, when he returned, was busy with his new practice. Besides, her three years' seniority over Harry Friedenwald was more apparent now that Henrietta was getting into her thirties, although she didn't look it without the pince-nez she now affected. She kept her wavy hair beautifully brushed—a hundred strokes every morning, her figure trim by daily calisthenics, and she always dressed daintily down to her pretty ankles. But mature men preferred the company of women younger than themselves. Had not Papa chosen a girl ten years younger than himself—indeed the youngest of four sisters? Anyway Harry Friedenwald was soon married to Sadie's young friend Birdie Stein; and Mr. Hartogensis, although extremely helpful with the school, could not divert Henrietta outside it. She introduced him to her dear friend and colleague in the school, Grace Bendann, whom he courted and married; and Henrietta exquisitely embroidered a bridal handkerchief for Grace's wedding. At that time the idea of doing anything merely for her own diversion seemed preposterous, when the demands of the "Russian School" were so pressing; and she found herself indulging again in the girlhood envy of the male, because she knew that if she were a man she could venture on certain plans for her "Russians" which she could not now undertake.

She not only loved them, she respected them; their aptitude for the improvement she afforded them was heartwarming, as was the vitality with which they put behind them the horrors they had survived, and directed all their energies into the struggle for a good life here in the new land. They asked for neither pity nor alms; only for the opportunity to work hard and make progress. "These people are independent," she warned Mr. Hartogensis, "and moreover they can be trusted to make their own way, they understand their own needs—and shortcomings . . . Will it convince you that these men have stamina when I tell you that Mr. B. timidly questioned whether the acceptance of . . . a gift would exact deference on their part to any of the patron's wishes or theories?" She loved and respected her "Russians" also because being Jewish was as important to them as it was to her, and because the suffering they had borne as Jews had not weakened but had strengthened and matured them as men and women. Not once was there any occasion for disciplinary action in the school, although the deprivation of contact with cultural influences and amenities had inevitably left its marks on their superficial manners. But that, she knew, would be corrected in time by their eagerness for improvement, if only the opportunities for improvement were available to them in this land of freedom.

As for the violent anti-Semitism from which they had fled, she began to see its peculiar rationale—how it strove to make over its intended victim into a contemptible form which would justify its hateful action; and she was no longer able to ignore the fact that it was not to be explained away merely as a manifestation of Russian barbarism. Harry Friedenwald, in the last year of his stay in Germany, had written his father of a growing overt anti-Semitic movement in that most enlightened of Western European nations, the country where European Jewry had made its greatest modern progress and contribution, and to which enlightened young Americans, Christian and Jewish, went as a matter of course for their advanced studies. Harry had written his father about an avowedly anti-Semitic convention held at Bochum in Westphalia where a Dr. Turk had also talked of "The Judaization of Austria," predicting that the government there was merely awaiting the will of the people to take action against the Jews; and Dr. Friedenwald had discussed that report with the Szolds. There was no ignoring the possibility that such movements boded no good for Jews in Germany and Austria-Hungary, and their only hope, Dr. Friedenwald thought, lay in the true democratization of those countries along American lines. Apparently culture alone was not enough to eliminate the dark medieval blight of anti-Semitism; it took democracy too. And the Szolds and the Friedenwalds agreed that many German Jews had been foolishly relying on German civilization for their security and had moved away from fundamental Judaism toward assimilation, unlike their afflicted Russian and Polish brothers, who had never been tempted to relinquish their Jewishness either under duress or the most tolerant conditions, so long as they had not got that democratic freedom which alone, as here in America, gave men the right to the maintenance of their spiritual distinction. All the same, it was difficult for men like Aaron Friedenwald and Benjamin Szold—and for Henrietta, too—to accept the fact of German anti-Semitism, accustomed as they were to thinking of German culture as an important part of their own culture. Germany was for them the land not only of Goethe but of Moses Mendelssohn, who in the eighteenth century had established the fact that Jews could remain loyal to Judaism while, as German nationals, contributing to German culture. He had translated the Bible into German, successfully demanded civil rights for the Jews, and was greatly admired by both Kant and Lessing. His *Jerusalem* convinced Kant that Judaism was a true world religion; and Lessing had used him as the model for his *Nathan the Wise*. Dr. Friedenwald and Rabbi Szold had come to America not in flight from anti-Semitism but as the bearers of their high cultivation to a cruder, new pioneer world where opportunities for the exercise of their talents and the need for them were greater than in the old. It was just a matter of time, they thought now, until a democratic Germany would dispel this eruption of vestigial anti-Semitism.

But the idea that anti-Semitism could not exist in a democracy became untenable when a wave of anti-Jewish literature and politics swept emancipated France in the early nineties, culminating in the Dreyfus affair and its accompaniment of dreadful overt hatred. It became undeniable then that anti-Semitism was lodged in the body of Christianity like a virulent germ which lay quiescent until some irritant lowered the threshold of resistance and gave it an occasion to erupt and flourish feverishly.

Henrietta, awakened by her beloved "Russians" to the painful reality and persistence of this scourge, had cried out in one of her letters to Harry Friedenwald: "Why do they hate us so?"—a cry expressing that vague sense of guilt which the anti-Semite manages, like the mad paranoid, to arouse in his baffled victim, whom he charges with fictitious provocations to conceal the compulsion in himself. But the question was as unanswerable as the question of Job, to whom his affliction was as unjustifiable and as incomprehensible. We know *how* deadly germs function in the human organism; we cannot say *why* they were put there by a provident Creator.

Eighteen ninety-three was a year of great trial in America, afflicted by severe economic depression and panic, so great that President Cleveland, Rabbi Szold's admired, high-principled, liberal conservative, had to send troops to break a railroad strike. And in

1893 Henrietta and her father had good reason to turn from her question about the affliction of the Jews to Job's more personal question. Early in that year sister Sadie, preparing for her marriage to Max Löbl, who was then on a business trip to Europe, went shopping for her trousseau and was stricken with pneumonia. In February, Sadie, who used to make light of rheumatism as "all pain but no danger," spent her twenty-sixth birthday in bed, ripping a wash-silk dress of Henrietta's which Mamma was making over for her. Adele had given her a Japanese purse in which was a five-dollar bill from Papa and Mamma and another from Henrietta. She got a profusion of tulips, roses, and fruit from Baltimore friends, and the Jastrows sent her a pretty bed jacket from Philadelphia. But by the end of April Sadie was gone; and Henrietta, reading Dr. Billingslee's combined letter of condolence and bill for over one hundred visits at two dollars—which he "cut in half for clergy of all denominations and sects"—could not but sense the inscrutable dilemma of all aspiring mankind in the doctor's regret for "the loss of one so pure, so bright, so unusually smart," and for his unsuccessful efforts to save her. . . .

Dauntless, indestructible Mamma, who could be upset by trifles but bore great afflictions stoically, took up her daily burdens and went on; but for Papa, this was, as for Job, but the beginning of a long trial. As if the Adversary, as after the destruction of Job's children, had said of Rabbi Szold, too, "But put forth thine hand now and touch his bone and his flesh, and he will curse thee to thy face," Papa, who had been troubled from time to time with a vaguely diagnosed ailment, was now afflicted with what was first thought to be an abdominal tumor and then proved to be an inflammation of the bladder, terribly painful and debilitating.

At that time, Oheb Shalom Synagogue was removed to a fine new building on Eutaw Place. Even its conservative members, prospering merchants and manufacturers, who were moving into mansions furnished in gilt and plush, had become Americanized to the point of thinking that English rather than German—besides sacred Hebrew—would be a more acceptable language to God, and that a younger rabbi might be more suitable to their new synagogue. So they retired ailing Rabbi Szold. Now when he took his place on the dais on the Sabbath it was to see another man serve where he had served for over three decades; and Mamma was rather resentful of what seemed to her the unseemly haste with which he had been deposed and supplanted.

Despite the ministrations of the great Dr. Osler of Johns Hopkins and of its foremost surgeon, Papa's ailment became chronic. He would be bedridden or confined to a wheel chair for weeks and months, requiring constant attention day and night by Mamma or Henrietta, for he got little sleep; but remissions between the severe attacks made it possible for him to recover enough strength to continue his writing on such subjects as "Jewish Scholarship," "Scriptural Poetry," "A Commentary on Daniel," which he could do now only with a soft pencil; and occasionally he could even go out and deliver a sermon or read a paper in public. Nevertheless he quickly became an ailing old man, his once thick black hair and beard thin, straggling and white, except around the mouth where a dark yellowish stain remained; his once warm flashing eyes pain-filled and sunken, his cheeks and temples gaunt. His appetite failed and food often became repugnant to him, so that he had to be tempted or persuaded to take enough nourishment to maintain the flame of life in his still unimpaired vital organs. And there were times when, in his agony, he withdrew with that flickering flame into a silence which seemed like apathy. It was as if he were mindful of his own dictum in his Commentary on Job that it was useless to ask why he, a virtuous, pious man, should be so afflicted, and that Job having, in unsurpassable poetry, expressed for all time the thought and feeling of a man so afflicted, there was surely no need for him to speak of his suffering.

In the periods of remission and partial recovery, when Papa could sit up in his study or be wheeled out into the garden, or during the summer in a cottage they rented at Berkeley Springs in West Virginia where the mountain air sometimes revived him, Papa became his old self for a while, benign and wise, loving and lovable, his witty talk seasoned with abstracts from Torah and Talmud, the dark eyes brightening in his ravaged face. Then Henrietta hopefully rejoiced, thinking that the doctors who had been wrong to begin with might still be wrong in their hopeless prognostication, and that, like Job, Papa, who was surely as piously faithful, would be spared. Thus for years she steeled herself daily against the inevitable end, praying each time she had to leave him that he would still be there when she returned.

She insisted on Bertha's remaining at college and having what she had missed; and she had Bertha send her copies of her examination questions which she would answer and then compare with Bertha's answers. And when Adele graduated from high school, Henrietta saw to it that she went on to the University of Wisconsin, where she stayed with Rachel and Joe. So the care of Papa devolved mainly on Mamma and herself, and it knit an even stronger bond than that of mother and daughter between the two valiant women. Sometimes it took each of them many hours more to get her daily work done because of the innumerable interruptions of desperate calls for help from the sick room. The anguish of those years Henrietta expressed, in passing, in a paper she had occasion to write while Papa was suffering greatly:

"We all unfortunately have experience of situations in life when our best-beloved are isolated from us. They suffer, and we stand by idly wringing our hands. They plead with us across a vast space, as it were, to come to their help, and we cannot reach them. They are as effectually separated from us as though they were confined in a prison cell or in the grave. They bear pain, doubt, guilt, alone, though surrounded by loving hearts. That is the awfulness of human life, the isolation of the human soul in supreme moments. When we are young, we rebel against it. We refuse to credit it. One morning we awake—the morning it is apt to be on which we discover the first gray hair—and we bow to the decree that life must be accepted on its own terms. Yet hard as life's terms are, they never dictate untruth, dishonor, unrighteousness."

Papa needed and sought Henrietta's help with his writing more than ever before; and for Henrietta there was no question of her right to freedom from the gentle tyranny of her father's love for her. Nothing could have drawn her away from his need of that help which only she could give him—not even the prospect of enjoying the life of a beloved wife which was presented to her as a possibility from time to time. There was, for example, Joseph Hertz, a high-spirited, promising young rabbi from Syracuse, who stopped in Baltimore to see Rabbi Szold, as many young rabbis did in those days; and Papa, who found him a most estimable young man, treated him like a son. Upon his departure from Lombard Street he began a steady correspondence with Henrietta which persisted after he had gone on to serve the Jewish community in far-off Johannesburg. He tried in his letters to interest her in his work and life there, but the mere thought of deserting Papa, of going so far from him in his extremity, was inconceivable to Henrietta, and she countered with the argument that the talents of a Joseph Hertz were wasted in the wilderness of darkest South Africa, and advised him to return to a substantial Jewish community like Baltimore or Philadelphia or New York, where he would be appreciated. But he remained there until his outspoken opposition to a benighted government during the Boer War and his demand for religious liberty made it necessary for him to leave South Africa for a while. He stopped to visit the Szolds in Baltimore en route to London, where he was on the road to becoming Chief Rabbi of England.

Henrietta's attachment to her ailing father made it necessary for her to give up her time-bound teaching activities at both the Misses Adams' School and the Russian School, which was by then well established and could be left in the hands of Mr. Hartogensis and the others. But her interests and activities were not confined by that filial attachment; indeed with the release from teaching, the volume and diversity of her writing increased and her activities became freer of the confines of Baltimore.

For this development she was to some extent indebted to her old friend Cyrus Adler, who had been abroad for three years on a mission to get European and Near Eastern governments to participate in the World's Fair in Chicago in 1893, a slightly belated celebration of the four hundredth anniversary of the discovery of America. Cyrus had been hobnobbing with the very important people—rulers, statesmen, magnates—of many lands from England to Turkey, and he was now in a position at home to open doors to new avenues of interest and activity for Henrietta. Enjoying the personal and influential progress he was making—the Chicago Fair mission was followed by his appointment as Librarian to the Smithsonian Institution in Washington—he did not share Henrietta's prophetic anxiety about the precarious state of the world in the century ahead.

Behind a shining pince-nez his bright eyes beamed with that nineteenth-century American optimism which transcended the immediate and obvious problems of this burgeoning pioneer society. No great upheavals were expected in this world, only that it would be getting better and better, that scientific learning, invention and development would make steady progress toward an end which was sure of attainment: if not perfection, at least great improvement in the state of the individual and of society. No one talked or worried much about capitalism, which was apparently the normal economic form of modern progressive society. There were, to be sure, some disgruntled socialists around who disagreed, but they were just talkers to men like Cyrus Adler, who thought of the nineties as a time when materially growing America was ripe for culture, for purely intellectual and esthetic development and enjoyment. Hence his preoccupation with such things as the Chicago Fair and the Smithsonian Institution, which incidentally brought him in contact with influential men of the administrations of Cleveland, McKinley and Theodore Roosevelt.

The Fair itself was a manifest symbol of this irrepressible American optimism. When President Cleveland opened it, banks were closing, commerce and industry were largely disorganized, mills, factories, furnaces, mines were shut down, unemployed workers went begging for work or food in the streets of the cities, augmented by bankrupt farmers abandoning the land which could not maintain them, and a half million immigrants flocking each year to this "golden land." Yet the white wedding-cake buildings of the Fair glittered with Edison's electric lights, its gay Midway was raucous with the music of his gramophones, and crowds gathered to gaze with hopeful wonder at the exhibition of Charles Duryea's horseless carriage. For a cultural plum there was the World Parliament of Religion, a gathering of representatives from all religions, Oriental and Occidental, in the new Art Institute, which opened with the song: "Praise God from whom all blessings flow . . ." and adopted as its theme: "Have we not all one Father? Hath not one God created us all?" At the end of this Parliament, Harlow Higginbotham, President of the Fair, was moved to write: ". . . our Parliament of Religion was the crowning glory of our Exposition and, in fact, of all time. It did more to unify the peoples of the earth and make them more kindly than any other event in all history." It had no observable effect, however, on the violence of anti-Semitism in Europe.

To this Parliament Cyrus Adler's friend, Henrietta Szold of Baltimore, was invited to deliver a paper. Her invitation came from Hannah Greenebaum Solomon, a member of the Women's Committee of the Parliament, which was, as a matter of fact, an expression of one of the dissenting forces actually underlying and disturbing the current American optimism: the feminist movement. There were women in Chicago who decided to use the World's Fair as an opportunity to demonstrate their potential equality with men: they organized their own contributions to the activities of the Fair, and one of them, Mrs. Solomon, was made Chairman of the Jewish Women's Committee. This committee was invited by the Jewish Men's Committee to co-operate with them in a program they were preparing for the Parliament of Religion, but when the women saw that the men had no places on their program for speeches by women—that women would be expected merely to participate socially, in such traditionally female functions as hostesses, decorators, etc.—they refused to co-operate with the men and organized their own program, to which Henrietta contributed her paper on "What Judaism Has Done for Women."

The feminist war between the sexes, of which this was an early and minor side skirmish, found Jewish men in a rather equivocal position. Scripture and Talmud paradoxically contain the most exalted opinions and pictures of womanhood together with the most primitively masculine derogation. In Proverbs alone, where wisdom and knowledge are repeatedly apostrophized as female, and which ends with that paean of praise to *eshet ḥayil,* the "woman of valor," there are repeated warnings to men of the dangerous seductiveness of women's charms. And in Deuteronomy countless ritual injunctions regarding the "unclean" periods of women reflect early man's fearful ignorance of the mysterious nature of the helpmate God had given him. Indeed, in her very first appearance in his history, Eve, the epitome of all womanhood, defies the will of the Almighty himself and brings mankind to eternal suffering. Even so enlightened and progressive a Jew as Rabbi Szold, loving and highly esteeming his wife and his daughters, and subscribing to the dictum in Midrash that "No generation can be redeemed except through the merit of the righteous women of that era," could nevertheless not, during his first decade at Oheb Shalom, consider dispensing with the traditional separation of women from men in the synagogue as the reformers were doing. On the other hand, there were orthodox Jews who would have questioned the propriety of Rabbi Szold's encouraging his daughter, as if she were a son, to study sacred Torah and Talmud, a pursuit for which they considered women unfit. Henrietta's old friend, Rebekah Kohut of New York, who had also been invited to speak to the Parliament of Religion, discovered after she had prepared her paper that her beloved husband, Rabbi Kohut, was unhappy about her going to Chicago, and, as he was seriously ill at the time, she humored him and did not go. The masculine idea that women had definitely limited feminine functions was not, of course, then confined to Jews, and the decision of the Jewish Men's Committee not to have women speak on their program was merely part of the prevailing masculine attitude toward women. Many a Christian whose wife sat beside him in church didn't want her to vote, an attitude which women were then beginning to fight.

Henrietta used to cite as an early instance of Hebraic emancipation of women the decision of Moses regarding the daughters of Zelophehad, who had left no sons: that they should not only share their father's inheritance but should be free to marry whomever they chose—within their tribe, however. But, being conservative like her father, Henrietta would not think of joining the feminist war against masculine authority; she believed that women could demonstrate their capacities and make progress without resort to overt and violent opposition to that authority. Nora, in Ibsen's *A Doll's House*, slamming the door on her husband, was not Henrietta's heroine. She saw the emancipation of women not as separation and flight from the domination of man but as part of the total progress of humankind within which women, as human beings, would realize their womanly potentialities.

Two years before in a lecture to immigrant women at the Hebrew Literary Society of Baltimore, on "Tales of Good Women," she began with a disavowal of any intention of being a female rabbi—but, recalling her visit with Papa to the Alt-Neu Shul in Prague, she proposed to relay to them, like the woman standing in the window of the old synagogue gallery, what she had learned. "I have all my life been hearing sermons that have a great influence on me, because they have been spoken by someone who is dear to me. . . . I believe, too, that the Bible gives me the right to do this sort of saying over again. . . ." and she cited Miriam, sister of Moses, who after the Red Sea crossing, led the women in a song of thanksgiving to the Lord, after Moses had led the men. She then urged Jewish women in America to engage in social service and education, citing as examples such celebrated Jewesses, who made great contributions to American cultural development, as Rebecca Gratz of Philadelphia, Peninah Moïse of Charleston and Emma Lazarus of New York. "Now when I urge you," she said, "to become like American women, I do not say do the foolish things some of them wish to do. I do not say become like men. I do not tell you to vote any more than I tell you to wear trousers and coats. But I do tell you to help your sons, your brothers, your husbands, to lead a noble, true life." And in Chicago she met Jane Addams of Hull House, a woman who, like herself, did not need the vote to function effectively for the good of her kind.

As an outcome of the Committee of Jewish Women at the Chicago Fair, the National Council of Jewish Women was founded under the leadership of Hannah Solomon, dedicated to social service, and affiliated with the National Council of Women which had been organized by Elizabeth Cady Stanton, a pioneer in women's suffrage. Henrietta's friend Rebekah Kohut, after the death of her husband, organized the New York section of the National Council of Jewish Women, and as the Council was engaged in doing, among other things, just the sort of educational work for immigrants that Henrietta had initiated with her "Russians" in Baltimore, it was natural that she should be asked to join and become its national secretary. But she declined that invitation —although she spoke to its Baltimore section on "A Century of Jewish Thought" and to other sections on similar topics—because to her conservative mind its attitude seemed radical; its leadership was generally of the reform persuasion in religion; its affiliation with the feminist movement and its determination to work as an autonomous women's organization did not appeal to her. Jewish tradition, announced at the very beginning in Genesis, made woman the helpmate of man, for all that she might be a trouble and even a danger to him. And all through the Old Testament there were instances in which women had acted decisively to get misguided men to take the proper course in their history, even if women had to stoop to deception to achieve the worthy destiny. Rebekah deceiving blind Isaac in order to make gentle Jacob and not wild Esau the father of his people, and Rachel deceiving her father Laban and hiding his gods in order to save Jacob from his wrath, were both making history deliberately; and even Tamar, blindly driven by her womanly desire to bear a child, in deceiving Judah, her father-in-law, into giving her a son, also served history greatly, for out of this ultimately came Boaz, whose seduction by Ruth with the help of Naomi brought to pass in time the birth of David, and Solomon in all his glory. . . . The ancient Hebrews, romantic yet unsentimental, saw woman whole: had she not eaten first of the tree of the knowledge of good *and* evil?—and then "gave Adam that wretched piece of advice to eat of the apple," as Henrietta put it when she spoke to the women in Baltimore. Henrietta had learned from Papa how important the service of women like Mamma and herself could be to the creative work of man, physically and spiritually. And she had herself demonstrated in the "Russian School" the capacity of a woman to get men, drawn to her by her womanliness, to work with her for a worthy cause. Her ideal woman was not the manlike Amazon, but *eshet ḥayil*, the "woman of valor."

At this time her good and influential friend Cyrus Adler opened a door to another activity in which she demonstrated her ability to function as well as any man in a capacity not often available then to women; and she was certainly indebted to her father for the erudition which made it possible for her to perform this function. In Philadelphia Cyrus had founded the Jewish Publication Society of America with the primary purpose of making great Jewish literature available in English, and Henrietta was appointed its editorial secretary—a post for which her years of collaboration with Papa had perfectly prepared her. She expressed her feeling for this work in her talk on "A Century of Jewish Thought":

"There is a vast literary storehouse filled with treasures; the key, the Hebrew language, is in our guardianship. Have we a right to throw the key into the ocean of oblivion, and deprive the world of the enjoyment of those treasures? More than that, when we have ceased to be the efficient guardians of our treasures, of what use are we in the world? I fear that in the case of such flagrant dereliction of duty the twentieth century will have in store for us not a Ghetto but a grave. . . ."

She was also concerned with the revival of "intellectual Judaism" as an important adjunct to religious Judaism. This concern she had expressed in a paper on Yehudah Halevi, "A God-kissed Poet": ". . . We are too apt to despise the intellectual Judaism. There are many among us who . . . believe that the fear of the Lord is not only the *beginning*, but also the *end* of all wisdom, and hence criminally refuse to be students of our literature and our law. Again there are those, in these days overshadowed by the threatening cloud from Russia, who believe that our salvation is to be sought on the soil of Palestine, but who refuse, in their national program, to acknowledge any of the religious responsibilities that possession of the land must carry with it. And who does not admit that racial Judaism, even when idealized by national fervor, is a revolting anomaly in the nineteenth century? And finally, the fear must possess even the staunchest, most pious heart that, unless fed from intellectual springs of unsounded depths, our sublimest spiritual truths, seeking expression in ceremonial observances, may in our safekeeping degenerate into sentimental or mystical speculations, and our symbols, instead of remaining vehicles, become ends in themselves."

For the Jewish Publication Society she revised the English translation of Graetz's five-volume *History of the Jews*, adding a sixth volume of indexes, historical tables and annotations, which was hailed as an invaluable aid to the use of that monumental work by scholars. She wrote fifteen articles for the Jewish Encyclopedia which included part of her biography of Sara Copia Sullam, and studies of other Jewesses: the German intellectual Henrietta Herz, the early nineteenth-century English writer Grace Aguilar, the American poetess Emma Lazarus, who, moved by the persecution of Jews in Russia had written eloquently on Jewish subjects. She edited for American publication Israel Zangwill's *Children of the Ghetto* and *Dreamers of the Ghetto,* and the early novels of Sholem Asch. She undertook under Cyrus Adler's direction the compilation and editing of the annual American Jewish Year Book, a most painstaking job of checking and rechecking statistics, dates and thousands of other details, a work which had to be done in the hot and muggy summer months of Philadelphia and Baltimore between which she commuted. Much of this work was menial, but she had learned from Mamma, the good *Hausfrau,* how important menial services were in the creation and maintenance of anything *ordentlich* and admirable. The *eshet ḥayil,* as Proverbs describes her, saw to small matters as well as major ones. Henrietta read manuscripts, read proof, saw books through the press, did translations from German, French and Hebrew, read books for review in several languages, balking only at the Scandinavian, the meaning of which she could only guess at, and at books for the criticism of which authoritative scholarship was required, since, for all her erudition, she did not consider herself a "scholar." She had learned from her father how profound and thorough a knowledge that term implied.

She was by now a fine writer—had come far from that overexuberant tyro whom Dr. Isaacs of *The Messenger* had wisely criticized and encouraged. Her prose was lucid and vivid, vigorous or lyric as the subject required; and it was informed by a well-stocked and agile mind. She had the artist's imagination and sense of composition, and had even written some verse, published anonymously. Since childhood she had loved language and she had the highest regard for the function of the "writer." In her address to the Baltimore section of the Council of Jewish Women, she said: "Man's every act has a religious bearing; therefore true literature, the unfalsified record of man's acts and thoughts, is religious." She recognized that "unclean language fosters confusion of thought." She asserted that "the sublimest of thoughts has no effective reality until it appears in the garb of suitable language." She knew that expression is part of creation: God *said,* "Let there be light" before there was light. But on one occasion when her great admirer, Mr. Hartogensis, urged her to write something for *The Jewish Exponent* she replied: "My sterility will go thundering down the corridors of time. . . . There is nothing in me that cries out for utterance. As I grow older (and wiser?) I find that multitudes have said what I can say much better than I can. And what lies deep down at the bottom of my soul, and what as yet I have not heard from others, I myself am unable to frame with words. So, until the spirit does move me I shall keep silence, and at least be true to myself." And, rather than become a "writer," she chose to be the helpmate of Jewish scholars and writers like her father, to work arduously for the Jewish Publication Society in order to bring to American Jewry that spiritual heritage out of its past and present literature which she felt it needed as fortification against the anti-Semitism which was raging in Europe and might possibly even come across the ocean.

In 1895 Herman Ahlwart, a notorious member of the anti-Semitic Christian Socialist Party, came from Germany to launch an anti-Semitic party in America. He held a mass meeting in New York and asked for police protection for it. The Commissioner of Police, young Theodore Roosevelt, sent a hand-picked squad of New York's "Finest," stalwart policemen, all Jews, who guarded Herr Ahlwart and set the town laughing at his effort. Yet, but for the grace of a progressive and vigorous Roosevelt, could it not happen here? Could not anti-Semitism flourish?—despite the fact that the two great symbols of American freedom were to bear inscriptions of Jewish origin. In Philadelphia Henrietta had stood before the old Liberty Bell and read with pride the glorious words of Leviticus: "Proclaim liberty throughout the land to all the inhabitants thereof. . . ." And at the base of the new Statue of Liberty, which had been erected in the great harbor of New York, they were going to put a bronze plaque bearing the moving words of Emma Lazarus:

> *Give me your tired, your poor,*
> *Your huddled masses yearning to breathe free,*
> *The wretched refuse of your teeming shore,*
> *Send those, the homeless tempest-tost to me.*
> *I lift my lamp beside the golden door.*

Surely there was no people on earth who could speak with sincerer eloquence of liberty than the Jews, who since their exodus from slavery in Egypt had suffered incessantly for the freedom to be Jews.

If life in the nineties was not gay for Miss Henrietta it had its profoundly satisfying developments and even its delights. In Philadelphia she saw Edwin Booth, Modjeska and Otis Skinner in *Macbeth*; she heard Paderewski play . . . and her work and interests there took her into a wider world, freer and more mature, though with somewhat less of the optimism of her girlhood when she had thought that democratic education would make everything right.

In a talk to the Philadelphia Section of the National Council of Jewish Women early in '95 she took as her subject the "Evening Classes," private as well as public, which had spread like a rash in the cities of the land since her inception of the idea in the "Russian School" in Baltimore. Crackling with ironic epigram her talk turned an unsentimental light on some of the widely advertised and lauded institutions her own idea had spawned, and on the go-getting spirit which was using education merely as grist for its materialistic mill: "It is true that the self-made man worships his creator; it is no less so that the self-taught man makes a fetish of his teacher. . . ." She turned a disillusioned eye upon what she herself had once been: the volunteer teacher. "Nowadays, when social conditions attract earnest students and inspire popular exposition, everybody not a bundle of egotism is made keenly alive to his duty to society, and volunteer teaching is a favorite way of discharging the duty. Oddly enough, people . . . do not . . . understand this to be the age . . . when at last it is acknowledged that even a pedagogue needs efficient and special training. Too many still believe that teaching can be done by anybody not fit for anything else. . . ."

She turned her unflattering light then upon some of the Jewish product of this well-intentioned but uninformed mass melting-pot cultivation: "Scratch it until its very blood flows and . . . the Russian Jew will not appear. Every sign of outlandishness has vanished: dress, language and manners are native, gum-chewing itself stamps the American product with the seal of genuineness. Yet there is something lacking—a touch of idealism that transfigured the very sordidness of the fathers and endeared them to us. . . ."

The mid-nineties were years of disillusion for Henrietta, depressed as she naturally was by Papa's painful and hopeless affliction and the sense of her own failure to find fulfillment as a woman. This she expressed, however indirectly, in the reply she sent to a questionnaire from *The Reform Advocate* on "Woman in the Synagogue":

"I believe that woman can best serve the interests of the synagogue by devoting herself to her home; by filling any administrative position for which her executive ability is admittedly greater than that of any available man—'Where there are no men, be thou a man' is addressed to both sexes—and by occupying the pulpit only when her knowledge of the law, history, and literature of Judaism is masterful, and her natural gift so extraordinary as to forbid hesitation, though even then it were the part of wisdom not to make a profession of public preaching and teaching, the old Jewish rule of not holding women responsible for religious duties performed at definite times having a deep-seated rational basis and wide applicability. I further believe that religion being sexless, no necessity exists for Jewish women's organizations, whose interference in religious affairs I should therefore deprecate. . . ."

But she was developing a vital and hopeful interest which, until then, had been more ideological and traditional than actual and imminent. As in the case of anti-Semitism, she was indebted to her "Russians" for her realization of Zionism, and her ultimate involvement with it.

Since childhood, every spring, in the Christian Eastertide, the Jewish Passover had recalled the epic story of Israel's trek from Egypt to the Promised Land, and every *seder* ended with the words said in unison by all at the table: "Next year in Jerusalem!"—although, of course, you knew very well you would be in Baltimore next year. Every winter, in the Christmastide, she had celebrated *Ḥanukkah,* the heroic resistance of the Maccabees to Greek tyranny; and every *Tisha b'Av* she had heard in the synagogue the reading of Lamentations for the fall of the Temple in Jerusalem. How often had her heart quivered to the words:

By the rivers of Babylon, there we sat down, yea, we wept,
when we remembered Zion.

We hanged our harps upon the willows. . . .

If I forget thee, O Jerusalem,
let my right hand forget her cunning. . . .

But the pang at her heart was like the pain one feels in a theater or on reading a tragic book, the suffering one shares almost pleasurably with a distant sufferer.

Among her "Russians," however, were young men and women for whom this song had an immanent reality that was contagiously exciting and moving when they spoke to her of it, as the fervently hopeful and faithful devotion of humanity to an ideal aspiration always is no matter how unpromising its prospect. These men and women called themselves *Ḥovevei Zion*—"Lovers of Zion"; and they were dedicated to the re-establishment of Israel in its ancient land. If they could not themselves all go, they could gather enough, saving and collecting coins from their meager earnings, to send and help support a few who could go and settle there. They kindled in the heart of Henrietta the spark of their passion for the revival of Israel. They revealed to her the passion of the Jewish people which is the sign of their greatness, though that passion was well-nigh hopeless then, like the unrequited passion of a lover who can get no response from the beloved.

Cyrus Adler, in the course of his mission in the Near East for the Chicago Fair, had visited Palestine and seen colonies of Jews maintained there by collective philanthropy, *ḥalukah,* from Europe and America and from organizations like the French *Alliance Israélite,* or by such wealthy individuals as Sir Moses Montefiore of England, who went seven times to Palestine and took the first steps to settle Jews there, and Baron Edmond de Rothschild of France, who supported the wine-growing colony of Rishon le Zion. Cyrus Adler, whose eyes were fixed on the glittering new world, was not impressed by what he saw in the romantically ruinous ancient Holy Land, once flowing with milk and honey, but now the neglected territory of backward, corrupt Turkey—a worn-out, treeless, stony, somnolent country inhabited mainly by malodorous Bedouins and fellaheen, camels, goats and donkeys. The Jews, many of whom had come there in the early eighties, although forbidden by Turkish law to own any land, managed by dint of bribery and austerity to maintain a far from satisfactory existence, even in the most flourishing of their colonies at Rishon le Zion. There they were subject to the autocratic control of their donor—a condition which, as Henrietta had already learned from her "Russians," was intolerable to such freedom-loving folk. Even their God had found the ancient Israelites a stiff-necked people not overly grateful for his gifts, an independent people whose Old Testament had powerfully influenced freedom-loving American leadership from the Puritans to Abraham Lincoln.

In the Western world, in civilized Europe and in free America, most Jews like Henrietta's father had practically given up thinking of the national return to the Holy Land as a possible reality. Like the coming of the Messiah, to which that return was linked by tradition, it had been relegated to the fabulous future. The generally accepted idea of the mission of Israel was to serve in the Diaspora as a civilizing peaceful leaven among the warring nations until the time when, as Micah said, "They shall beat their swords into ploughshares. . . ." If ever the Jews revived their land, such men, whose great spokesman was Ahad Ha-Am, the Russian-Jewish philosopher of Zionism, believed it would not be as a political state but as a spiritual Jewish center and light to the nations—as it was prophesied by Isaiah: "Out of Zion shall go forth the law, and the word of the Lord from Jerusalem."

In the seventies, during the Turko-Serbian War, Rabbi Szold had written an article, characteristic of the attitude of such Jews, on "The Return to Palestine," in which he criticized Christian commentators who "assigned a particular role for the Jew to play in that drama: It is for the Jews to lend—with their finances, of course—the most efficient support to the antagonistic powers of the Crescent. The realization of their long-nourished hopes and wishes to restore their ancient kingdom—so many Christian writers argue—depends upon this final solution to the Oriental Question. Should the Turks be defeated and the Ottoman Empire be brought under the Christian sway—then the road will be paved for the Israelites safely to return to Palestine, their forefathers' country." And Rabbi Szold had then raised the questions: "But do the Jews in general really entertain such a desire? Are they indeed longing for a restoration of their ancient home?" and answered them, "in order to enlighten upon these topics—not the adherents of our faith: they know that there is nothing more ridiculous than to ascribe to them the entertaining of such vague and dreamy notions—but the Christian public. To them we want to say once for all that our home is the whole earth, every land of our birth or our adoption." He had proceeded then to explain how and why this change had come about, and, proud Jew that he was, incidentally took the opportunity to enlighten the Christian world forthrightly on some of its shortcomings. "When in the former centuries, ere freedom and enlightenment were dawning upon mankind, the Jew lamented for having been exiled, and prayed for the restoration of his old national glory, then it was a matter of course. He could not consider the soil on which he had to endure all the imaginable sufferings as his home. But thank God since the dawn of the present century our lot as a particular religious body among the nations of the earth changed. Mankind has been aroused to the consciousness that religion is an individual matter, and that it is left to everyone to decide for himself what shape to give to his religious feelings. With regard to religious matters, we, at the present time, follow as we did at all times, the dictates of our conscience; but in everything else which interests men in general, we are men among men, citizens among citizens. We have no particular interests, social, political or mercantile. We look upon every question and upon every problem that is offered outside the sphere of religion—social, political, scientific, industrial and commercial—not as Israelites, not from the standpoint of our particular religious consideration, but as men and citizens, and according to the ideas of the respective country we belong to. In all those concerns, we are Germans in Germany, Frenchmen in France, Englishmen in England, Americans in America, Russians in Russia, and Turks in Turkey.

"Being thus naturalized in whatever country we live, where the graves of our sires are, and the cradles of our children stand, there is not the least desire on our part to leave our dearly cherished native homes and return to a land that was the home of our forefathers eighteen centuries ago. The great fault with many of our Christian brethren is that they take us for Orientals because we were such in the earliest antiquity. But what justifies such an opinion? Our habits are occidental in every respect. Our religion bears more the stamp and color of the civilized Occident than many creeds in Christianity. . . . We fulfill in its widest sense the command of our Scriptures: 'Love thy neighbor as thyself!' and carry out conscientiously the interpretation given to it by one of our sages who lived long before the common era: 'Do not unto others what you do not wish that others should do unto you!' Christianity, however, makes itself guilty of violating this behest; it does unto others what it hardly wishes should be done unto it. . . . The paramount demand of the present civilization of the Occident, not to interfere with the religious convictions of others, is by none so fully respected as by the Jew. There is not a vestige of the tyrannical spirit of the Orient in our religion. Our religion is in every respect one of progress, tolerance and humanity. This impresses the modern Israelite with the belief that the design of Providence in scattering us all over the globe had been the propagation of religious freedom among the whole human race. We therefore feel and find ourselves at home everywhere."

This was believed by many Jews in the seventies; but in the eighties, alas, it became clear that, for all the dawn of freedom and enlightenment, Jews could not be Russians in Russia, might not be Germans in Germany, and, to the likes of Messrs. Corbin and Hilton, they were not even Americans in America. And although Turkey had been defeated by the Christian powers, the Holy Land was still not accessible to the Jews. It was still under Turkish rule and no Jew could own land there.

But in the mid-nineties something happened in Europe which turned a Messianic dream into a dynamic force—Zionism. Theodor Herzl, successful Viennese playwright and journalist, while correspondent in Paris for the *Neue Freie Presse* of Vienna, witnessed the public condemnation of Alfred Dreyfus and the wave of overt vitriolic anti-Semitism in France which accompanied that scandalous affair. Herzl, an assimilated Jew, with very little knowledge of Judaism or feeling for it, was so outraged by the shameful injustice of the treatment of Dreyfus and became so keenly aware of the unjustifiable persecution of Jews everywhere in Europe that he brooded upon the matter until he was inspired to write *Der Judenstaat* presenting his solution of the Jewish problem: the establishment of an autonomous Jewish state. So little was he then a Jew in spirit, or in contact with the Jewish spirit, that it did not greatly matter to Herzl, in the beginning, where this state was to be. When he could not persuade the Sultan of Turkey to let the Jews revive their national home in Palestine, he thought they could find salvation in any haven from Christian persecution, anywhere, and that it was up to the Christian world, which could not tolerate them, to supply the Jews their place in the sun. Herzl became a true Zionist only after he learned two things: first, that although anti-Semitic Christians wanted to get rid of the Jews, they were not eager to supply them with a suitable place to settle; and then, that even when such a place was available to them, most of the Jews who sought that haven were at heart, like Henrietta's "Russians," *Ḥovevei Zion*—lovers of Zion who would willingly leave their adopted gentile countries only if they could go to the land of Israel, which had been promised them, and to which they were tied by centuries of history and hope. When Argentina in 1889 actually offered Jews land for colonization, only a thousand went there. It was more than a mere haven the Jews wanted.

Aside from the coincidence that they were born in the same year and were both of Hungarian extraction, there was apparently nothing to link the careers or characters of Theodor Herzl and Henrietta Szold. He had an uncle who, like her father, had been involved in the revolutionary activity of 1849; and his parents, like hers, were lovers of German culture. But Judaism, which had been since her childhood part of the fabric and strength of Henrietta's spirit, was for Herzl like a forgotten cast-off cloak he was hastily learning to wear in a time of storm; not as protection, to be sure, but as his identification with the persecuted people whose leadership he was powerfully moved to assume. Henrietta would have been a staunch Jewess even had Jews never suffered persecution; it was anti-Semitism which brought Herzl to Judaism, and he came in time to believe that the return to Jewishness must precede the return to the Jewish land, whereas Henrietta never had to make that first return. But they were alike in one respect: both had fervently impassioned spirits—hers hidden under the prim, genteel guise of the Baltimore schoolteacher, and his under the elegant guise of the sophisticated Viennese writer. Both were capable of strong feelings, decently controlled and expressed with dignity. Like Henrietta, Herzl in his teens had been deeply moved by the loss of a beloved sister. By another curious coincidence, in 1881, when Henrietta was in Vienna with Papa, Theodor Herzl was also there, a student, who got his first faintly bitter taste of anti-Semitism when the student society to which he belonged voted to disbar Jews.

Herzl never heard of Henrietta Szold; but she got a clear picture of him—the handsome black-maned and black-bearded man whose motto was: "If you will it—it is no fable," the man who did not fear to ask what he wanted of kings and princes, and who moved men whenever he spoke. When some delegates to the first World Zionist Congress which Herzl had called in Basle in the summer of '97 returned to Baltimore, Henrietta went with Papa—who was by then converted to active realistic Zionism—to hear their report and was enthralled by it; and the next year, when Cyrus Adler returned from a trip to London for the Smithsonian Institution, he told of hearing Herzl speak there in an effort to get the support of the British government and English Jewry for his project. He got from the government the offer of territory for Jewish settlement in Uganda, East Africa, but he could not win the support of the English *Ḥovevei Zion,* whose hopes were unalterably fixed on the ancient land of Israel. Yet there was no gainsaying the man's impressive and magnetic spirit and personality.

By then, Henrietta, who had been going to hear great Zionists like Masliansky, and reading the eloquent writings of Aḥad Ha-Am, was herself a confirmed Zionist; but she would not write about it when Mr. Hartogensis asked for an article in *The Jewish Exponent:* "Precisely because Zionism . . . [is] near and dear to me; precisely because the weal and woe of Judaism is bound up with it, I do refuse to foist my immature views, my intuitions, my strong, biased feelings, upon an innocent trusting public. . . ."

There was a large and growing literature on Zionism which she avidly read, and one of the finest statements about it—expressing her own attitude toward Judaism—had been written by George Eliot, a gentile, as far back as 1879 in *The Modern Hep! Hep! Hep!* Henrietta copied it out for her scrapbook:

"If we are to consider the future of the Jews at all, it seems reasonable to take as a preliminary question: Are they destined to complete fusion with the peoples among whom they are dispersed, losing every remnant of a distinctive consciousness as Jews; or, are there . . . in the world-wide Jewish communities . . . and . . . in the political relations of the world, the conditions present or approaching for the restoration of a Jewish state, planted on the old ground as a center of national feeling, a source of dignifying protection, a special channel for special energies, which may contribute some added form of national genius and an added voice in the councils of the world?

". . . Why are we so eager for the dignity of certain populations, of whom perhaps we have never seen a single specimen, and of whose history, legend, or literature we have been contentedly ignorant for ages, while we sneer at the notion of a renovated national dignity for the Jews, whose ways of thinking and whose very verbal forms are on our lips in every prayer which we end with an amen? Some of us consider this question dismissed when they have said that the wealthiest Jews have no desire to forsake their European palaces and go to live in Jerusalem. But in a return from exile, in the restoration of a people, the question is not whether certain rich men will choose to remain behind, but whether there will be found worthy men who will choose to lead the return. The hinge of possibility is simply the existence of an adequate community of feeling as well as widespread need in the Jewish race, and the hope that among its finest specimens there may arise some men of instruction and ardent public spirit, some new Ezras, some modern Maccabees, who will know . . . how to triumph by heroic example over the indifference of their fellows and the scorn of their foes, and will steadfastly set their faces toward making their people once more one among the nations.

". . . A modern book on Liberty has maintained that from the freedom of individual men to persist in idiosyncrasies the world may be enriched. Why should we not apply this argument to the idiosyncrasy of a nation? . . . Every Jew should be conscious that he is one of a multitude possessing common objects of piety in the immortal achievements and immortal sorrows of ancestors, who have transmitted to them a physical and mental type strong enough, eminent enough in faculties, pregnant enough with peculiar promise, to constitute a new beneficent individuality among the nations, and, by confuting the tradition of scorn, nobly avenge the wrongs done to their Fathers. . . ."

The reports Henrietta read which came in '99 from the Third Zionist Congress at Basle told of world-wide action and propaganda rousing Jews in the countries of Europe, in North and South America, and as far as South Africa and New Zealand to support of the movement, and informing non-Jews of its aims and soliciting their sympathy. Influential leadership was developing. Herzl was strongly reinforced by the brilliant and popular writer Dr. Max Nordau, who was also an eloquent speaker, and by many others in Europe; in America men like Rabbi Stephen Wise and Professor Richard Gottheil of Columbia were equally persuasive. But there was also a strong anti-Zionist movement—the expression of those nervous Jews who saw in the national revival of Israel a threat to the hard-won and precarious status achieved by Jews in the more liberal countries—especially in the United States—and who saw inevitable failure and annihilation for those Jews who would embark on that visionary project.

It was this opposition which overcame that reluctance to write about Zionism which Henrietta had expressed to Mr. Hartogensis, and in November 1901 she published an article in *The Maccabean* —"The Internal Jewish Question: National Dissolution or Continued Existence"—which not only answered the anti-Zionists but envisioned the future Israel as more than merely Herzl's haven for homeless Jews, or Ahad Ha-Am's haven for metaphysical Judaism. To the anti-Zionists she said: "They express doubt in the ability of Jews to govern themselves, which is tantamount to mistrust at once in the spiritual strength of the Jew and his practical skill. They confess fear of a movement that purposes to concentrate Jews in one locality and constitute them a body independent of other peoples in the making of its laws and the guarding of its welfare. For a state Jewish in composition and complexion, they foresee anarchy and corruption within, war and annihilation from without. They hold that Jewry would gather itself together from all corners of the globe, for a Nero of the Jew-haters the better to fell the whole nation at a single blow, and they prophesy that floundering Jewry will prove its own Nero.

"Of such paradoxes is Jewish history made up: libraries of books have been written to solve the mystery of a nation stripped of land and language, existing for centuries; and now it is feared that the same nation cannot live, or cannot live worthily, if it should come into possession of its land and its language.

"Their distrust is a serious indictment, more sweeping than they seem to know. It is distrust, not only of the efficacy of the Zionist movement, of the comity of the nations, of the powers and the character of the Jew, but, bluntly, of Judaism itself. The inference from their inconsistent opinions of Zionism is that Judaism is what its enemies for two thousand years have been asserting it to be, an effete system, a dead-alive issue, an agglomerate of legal quibbles and antiquarian curiosities, without generative power or progressive vital impulse; at best, an utopian vision whose realization would be an anachronism."

She did not try to argue with such anxieties. She stated flatly that "Zionism rests its case, not upon what some Jews have or have not done, but upon what all Jews may do by reason of the progressiveness, the native forces, the potentialities of Judaism"; and then revealed her vision of the function of Zionism as the savior of Judaism.

"If Zionism had but one Jewish question to solve, the external one—the question created by anti-Semitism and industrial and economic disturbances, then the solution it proposes, the re-establishment of the Jewish life for the Jew, might well awaken misgivings. An impulse shaped by such accidental considerations might bring together irreconcilable elements not to be fused into a national unit.

"Besides the external Jewish question, there is an internal one, the Jewish question created by the needs of the Jew as such, the question of national dissolution or of continued existence, together with the terms on which continued existence will be a blessing to the race and to mankind."

She attributed the Jewish survival in the Diaspora for two thousand years to the Talmudic system and its study by Jews all over the world. "Today, however, he who runs may read that the

Talmudic inspiration has lost itself like a river in a sandy waste. The bond of fifty generations has been ruptured, no one knows how, and twentieth-century Israel is left without a national anchor." It was Zionism, she contended, which was reviving not only national feeling but the Hebrew language and literature; and with prophetic fervor she predicted that in the revived Israel "The potentialities of Judaism will be made realities by its skilled and faithful adherents. To it they will devote themselves, illustrating its system and applying its theories in the varying circumstances of life. Its spirit will pervade their work and their play, their hours of devotion and their hours of struggling for material existence. They will consecrate to it their spiritual endeavors and their manual toil, their intellectual, physical, and moral strength, their heart, soul and might. Jewish vitality—the vital abilities of the Jew and the vital force of Judaism—will be poured like a stream into the sciences, the industries, the arts, the literature, the political activity, the daily humble walks of the Jew. His going up and his going down in the land will be Jewish. If Zionism is, indeed, a spiritual force, then it has the power to make its adherents not only shout until they are red in the face, but also live out Jewish ideals in religion, in philosophy, in government, in business, in every work of hand and brain. The world has not progressed beyond the need of Jewish instruction, but the Jew can be a witness and a missionary only if he is permitted to interpret the lessons of Judaism as his peculiar nature and his peculiar discipline enable him to interpret them. And so will arise the fabric of Jewish civilization, granting shelter and opportunity to the Jew, and instruction and inspiration to the world.

"The Jew who fears to make trial of this complete Jewish life lays himself open to the suspicion of insincerity in his professions regarding the spirituality of Talmudic Judaism. Talmudism is nothing but all this many-sided Jewish life concentrated—put into portable shape for the Jew during his *Wanderjahre*. It is all there, though all under the one name, religion. When the Jew makes for himself a home in which he can live out the whole Jewish life honestly, every conception of Jewish living side by side with every other conception of it, each made clearer by attrition with every other, then religion will still be all-embracing, but not all-exclusive. The whole of life will subserve the religion of the Jew, and his religion will penetrate every one of his activities. He will at last be at one with himself, his life will be a unit, and as a unified force it will operate in the modern world.

" 'Difficulties!' says George Eliot's Ezra. 'I know there are difficulties. But let the spirit of sublime achievement move in the great among our people, and the work will begin.' "

Much as Henrietta was inspired to do so, there was little of a practical nature she could then contribute to Zionism, with all her time taken up in shuttling back and forth between her labors in Philadelphia for the Publication Society and helping sick Papa in Baltimore. He was the fast failing tie which held the remaining Szolds there. They had already given up the beloved house on Lombard Street and moved to a smaller one on Callow Avenue, which was also nearer the new synagogue.

Indeed, the whole of their stable nineteenth-century world seemed to be disintegrating. In February of '98 the battleship *Maine* blew up and sank in Havana Harbor and President McKinley sent Admiral Dewey with the fleet to beat the Spaniards. Pimlico race track in Baltimore was turned into a military camp. Bands blared "There'll Be a Hot Time in the Old Town Tonight," "Goodby, Dolly Gray," and "Break the News to Mother," as typhoid and dysentery took a heavier toll of American lives than Spanish bullets. Teddy Roosevelt charged up San Juan Hill on his way to the Presidency—after McKinley was killed. Women rode around on bicycles—wearing shirtwaists with stiff collars, neckties, and men's hats. Queen Victoria, too, was dying.

Israel Zangwill, whose works Henrietta was editing for the Jewish Publication Society, came to America to lecture and to attend the production of his *Children of the Ghetto* as a play. His portrayal of the less palatable aspects of contemporary Jewish life was disturbing those nervous Jews who were less interested in truthful art than in what the gentiles might think and say about them. It did not comfort such Jews that Dreyfus had been proved innocent; they didn't relish being martyrs. Henrietta tried to persuade them in an article in *The Jewish Comment* that "Jews can afford to meet the effect [Zangwill's play] will produce with equanimity, even though our foibles are published to serve the cause of truth. Not our foibles bring us to grief in the court of nations. . . . Can a picture be painted with all light and no shadows?"

On the first day of the new century Henrietta, recently turned thirty-nine, set down her thoughts for some youthful Jewish readers; and because the current behavior of mankind seemed to her uninspiring, and because the midnight celebration "when the wild ringing of the church bells begins, the tooting of horns, the savage yelling, and the firing of crackers, and all the noise that ushers in a new year every first of January" seemed to her un-Jewish and pagan rather than Christian, she turned for inspiration to the New Year of the Trees, *Tu bi-Shivat*, the ancient celebration of the time when the sap rose in the trees of the land of Israel, which would be observed by Jews that month. She wrote: "Has not a good God set men down in the midst of a vast and beautiful temple, ornamented with trees and flowers, with curious shells and varicolored rocks, resounding with the carol of birds and busy hum of insects, gleaming with color, and offering surprise after surprise to open eyes and ears and alert minds? To pass by such beauties and wonders is to abuse God-given opportunities. What we see all around us is to stimulate our curiosity, lead us to examine the manifold and wondrous works of God, and make them yield up to us the lesson of His wisdom. It is our duty to search out the law of every being, every plant, every pebble, every grain of sand, and learn what the tiniest mote can teach. . . . Silently, day by day, second by second, the sap rises unseen through millions of the tiniest of tubes and cells, up and up, and still higher, until it carries the nourishment absorbed from mother earth to every last twig. Suddenly one day the sunshine touches the swollen branches, the tree bursts into leaf and blossom, and stands there the picture of vigor and grace combined. Life is made up not only of the objects seen by our eyes, perceived by our ears, grasped with our fingers. The most powerful forces are those that work unseen with patience, with perseverance, and in silence. We know them only by their effects. The man or child who insists that only 'seeing is believing' loses half the meaning and truth of life, and all its wondrous beauty. Let him apply his mind and study how the sap rises, brings life to the driest stick, clothing it with verdure and color, and he will at the same time learn that beside the life of material things, the life spent in eating, and drinking, and pleasuring, there is a hidden life, which we call the life spiritual, a godly life, full of the beauty of holiness, a life of love, of charity, of hope, of faith in God, of noble self-sacrifice. He will understand that though he be deprived of the good things some others enjoy, he can acquire possession of that of which neither man nor cruel fate can rob him. Above all, he will learn from nature about nature's God, the great and good God, who makes the sap to rise, who lays down an unchanging law for all His creatures, and has crowned man with understanding so that he may know, and love, and hope, and pity, and believe in the power and beauty of the unseen." Thus she reinforced in others as well as in herself that love, and hope, and pity so sorely needed in this life, which just then seemed to hold less light than shadow.

In November of '99 Rabbi Szold's seventieth birthday had been celebrated at the handsome new Oheb Shalom Synagogue, a book of tributes to him was published, and the press of many cities praised him and his accomplishments. The whole city of Baltimore, Christians and Jews, prayed for his recovery; but Papa was a hopeless invalid by the end of the year and the century. He lived long enough into the new one to see Bertha happily married to Louis Levin in 1901 when Henrietta remarked to Louis that "married sisters at least enable [the single woman] to rejoice in the possession of a brother, even when nature has been grudging in this direction." Papa, however, did not live long enough to have the pleasure of seeing his first grandchild.

When he died on the last day of July of 1902 in the summer cottage at Berkeley Springs, Mamma and Henrietta were there. He had talked a while that morning with Henrietta about some ideas he had in mind, quoting from memory passages of Torah and Talmud; but for all her long vigilance, for all her self-preparation and fortification for that event, she was not with him at the end. She had left his room for a few hours, and when she returned he was gone. Near at hand lay the books he had been using: a small Letteris Bible, Yehudah Halevi's *Kuzari,* Horace's *Ars Poetica, The Art of Poetry of Horace* by Reverend Daniel Bagot, a Hebrew lexicon, and the papers on which he had been working, unfinished.

Fifteen years before, writing of Sara Sullam under similar circumstance, Henrietta had said: "Great sorrows are usually borne silently and more resignedly than petty trials; and the heart may become dulled to bear heavy inflictions while trifling woes are perpetual grievances of which the wounds open afresh as soon as they seem healed." Looking for the last time upon that gaunt ghostly face, she felt that this was the greatest sorrow she would ever have; but the dullness in her heart, which felt as if its quivering, too, had been stilled forever, was not of resignation so much as if all ideal aspiration in life had died with him. As she had written of Sara Sullam: "She appreciated how deep was her obligation to her father . . . for she never ceased to regret him, and her choicest thoughts were ever dedicated to his memory," so it would be for herself. But she would have to find some purpose for going on without him whom she had served so long; and this became the burden of her thoughts in the year of mourning, during which she went daily to the synagogue to say the *kaddish*, the Hebrew prayer for the dead, which is customarily said only by a son.

Condolences came from all over the country and from across the sea, and Henrietta acknowledged these and set about putting her father's works in order and settling his estate.

In December of the year he died, the National Council of Jewish Women held its convention in Baltimore and met at the Oheb Shalom Synagogue where a heap of red roses was placed on the seat Rabbi Szold used to occupy. Henrietta addressed the convention on "Aspects of Judaism in the Cities of the United States" —a social scientist's survey, based on information gleaned in her work on the American Jewish Year Books, of the current activities in urban Jewish communities—charitable, educational, religious, and Zionist, all complicated by the divisions and differences between the long-established and recently immigrated members of those growing communities. But she laced her technical report with eloquent prophetic passages in the spirit of her father, using biblical examples, pleading for Jewish spiritual integrity, for the preservation of "Judaism, and the holy living inspired by it," of "the Sabbath, the historical seventh day of rest bidden in the law that the founder of Christianity did not come to destroy," and of

Zionism which "demands more than machinery . . . it demands hearts and souls."

Jane Addams, who came from Chicago to address the meeting, spoke on "The New Social Spirit"; and Henrietta had occasion to consider the possibility of joining such distinguished spinsters as famous Miss Addams of Hull House and handsome Lillian Wald of the Henry Street Settlement in New York, in the fast growing field of social service which increasing immigration made necessary, a career for which she was eminently well equipped. For Miss Henrietta, too, was by now undeniably a spinster: she was forty-one, and no prince had appeared to rouse her for his helpmate, although she still paid meticulous attention to her trim appearance, from her well-brushed hair to those dainty ankles of which she was still rather vain. Had not Solomon himself begun his paean to womanly beauty with "How beautiful are thy sandaled feet . . ."?

Miss Henrietta was not by nature a spinster, and she resigned herself to that fate only reluctantly. She had eloquently expressed her vision of the role of wife and mother: "Jewish custom bids the Jewish mother, after her preparations for the Sabbath have been completed on Friday evening, kindle the Sabbath lamp. That is symbolic of the Jewish woman's influence on her home, and through it upon larger circles. She is the inspirer of a pure, chaste family life whose hallowing influences are incalculable; she is the center of all spiritual endeavors, the confidante and fosterer of every undertaking. To her the Talmudic sentence applies: 'It is woman alone through whom God's blessings are vouchsafed to a house.' "

Now she was nearing that turn in a woman's life beyond which she could not hope to perform this blessed function. And at that time women who had missed, for whatever reason, nature's road to that function were apt to turn, as spinsters, to the field of social service. But Henrietta did not take this path.

In the year before her father died Miss Henrietta had been invited to address the graduating class of Western High School—which had by then dropped the word "Female" from its name. Twenty-four years had passed since she addressed her own class on the stage of Ford's Grand Opera House, and she took this occasion to recall how she and her classmates had permitted themselves only to dream of going on to Vassar and preparing themselves for anything other than domestic destinies. Now college scholarships were being offered the graduates, and women were being trained to work alongside men in industry and the professions. Her plea now was for a higher education of women which would not be limited to the intellect—that not merely the mind, but the hand and the heart, should be trained so that women would retain that deftness and spirituality which men had long recognized and cherished as feminine traits invaluable to the home and family. "It is well enough to remind women," she admitted, "in season and out of season, that their place is in the home. That is an undeniable truth, their place is in the home; but it is an equally undeniable truth that a large proportion of women cannot exercise any choice in the matter. Industrial conditions in the past have forced women out of the privacy of their homes, and continue to force them out into the turmoil of the world. They must supplement the family income. . . ." And she warned them: "The enemies of woman's higher education and of her entering into the life of the larger world have not yet disappeared. They have a great fear that woman may lose her womanliness. They believe that self-confidence that comes with knowledge and skill must perforce be boldness. There is a simple argument that ought to silence them. Is it or is it not time that under the present industrial system woman must earn her livelihood? And if woman is thrown upon her own resources by the existing constitution of things, then it is her bounden duty to equip herself as well as her means and advantages will allow regardless of masculine fears. . . . As you go on in life you will discover a peculiar condition of affairs. Though your art, your science, your craft makes you more self-reliant, experience in one art, in the art of living, opens your eyes to an ever increasing number of difficulties and problems. The details may become simpler, but the whole grows infinitely more complex. It is for this greatest and highest of all arts, the art of living, that men and women need the preparation given by a cultivated heart. . . ." And in conclusion she quoted them the aphorism of Hillel, teacher in Israel in the time of Jesus;

If I am not for myself—who will be for me?
And if I am only for myself—what am I?
And if not now, when?

She took this counsel for herself; and it was while setting in order her father's accumulated papers—all the pathetically perishable expressions of the passion of his spirit such a man leaves behind him—that she came to her decision regarding the future. She would continue working for the Jewish Publication Society, which afforded her a modest livelihood and the opportunity to serve scholars and writers and the spirit of American Jewry; and she would further serve humanity by applying herself to the editing of the works—many of them still unpublished and some incomplete—of her father, who had been concerned for humanity. Never had he given her any instructions or indications of his wishes in this regard; but it was unbearable to her that so much precious learning and creative thought should be buried with him. She would dedicate herself to saving his works for posterity, and in time she might say, as had Sara Sullam in dedicating her work to her father: "O thou, author of my days, . . . then thy name and mine will descend together to future generations."

For this task she felt she needed further formal training in that scholarship in which her father was steeped, and to this end she would have to leave Baltimore. Mamma no longer had any happy attachment there, except for Bertha, with whom they were temporarily staying, and who was preoccupied with her own growing family. Her son, who was born a few months after the death of Papa, was named Benjamin after him. Even their dear friend Dr. Aaron Friedenwald died in that year. As for Adele, who, far less influenced by her father than were her sisters, was developing into a very modern young woman interested in the contemporary ferment in socio-political ideas, she was an avowed feminist and socialist, and was quite eager to make the move from quiescent provincial Baltimore to metropolitan New York, where everything exciting was going on.

The Jewish Theological Seminary, recently developed in New York as the training school for the growing conservative rabbinate, was being reorganized and strengthened as an important center of modern Jewish learning. Cyrus Adler, who was on the board, had brought the distinguished scholar Dr. Solomon Schechter from Cambridge University in 1902 to head the new Seminary. Dr. Schechter, who was renowned for his studies of the Genizah, remnants of ancient manuscripts and scrolls hidden for centuries in the *Genizah,* or storeroom of the Cairo Synagogue, was in turn recruiting here and abroad, for his faculty, several brilliant younger scholars, trained in both the classical Jewish Seminary, the *yeshiva,* and in modern universities—such men as Alexander Marx, the historian, Israel Friedlaender in Semitic languages, and others, each one an authority in his field of Hebraic learning.

The Seminary was, of course, intended for male students only; but Henrietta's friend Cyrus Adler could vouch for her good intentions, and the reputation of her father was well known to Dr. Schechter, who had, in fact, visited Rabbi Szold in 1902 and met Miss Henrietta then. Early in 1903, after she had given her assurance that it was not her intention to become a rabbi—something even the most liberal conservative, even Papa himself, could not have countenanced—Cyrus Adler wrote her that she would be admitted to the Seminary in the fall as a special student—in fact, as the only woman.

In the summer of 1903, after a massive white marble monument, simply inscribed, was set on Papa's grave in the presence of a large delegation from Oheb Shalom Synagogue, Henrietta went to New York to seek a new home. She found a flat on the third floor of an apartment house diagonally across the street from the Seminary, a sedate, substantial new building of brick trimmed with the carved stone, garlanded pillars and pediments of the period. It was on West 123rd Street in a decent, comparatively quiet area of the bustling city, Morningside Heights, an area dedicated to scholarship, with Columbia University's new campus a few blocks away. The apartment house was one of three with brownstone entrances. There was a row of polished brass letter boxes and push buttons in the entry, which was decorated in the neo-classic manner, with the heads of Greek gods and heroes, in low relief, set in round medallions, and a tessellated floor of black and white marble. When you came out of the entry you could take one of two walks—and this was important to both Mamma and

Henrietta: west from Broadway to Riverside Drive with its verdant parkway dominated by the classic dome of Grant's Tomb, overlooking the lordly Hudson; or east, down the long steep hill to Amsterdam Avenue and beyond to Morningside Park, a "bosky dell," a small reminder of their beloved Baltimore woodland parks, with shaded pathways meandering among outcroppings of the pre-Cambrian granite underlying the great city.

Almost directly across the street from the entry to their apartment was the Seminary's dignified wrought-iron and glass entrance with stone steps. This location suited Henrietta perfectly, not only because of its proximity to the Seminary but because, sprinkled in the neighborhood within easy walking distance, lived a community of its scholars and their wives, just the kind of congenial, cultivated, German-speaking company Mamma would enjoy, as well as herself; and within the Seminary was its synagogue—the center of their social as well as spiritual life. It was a chapel-like room with an antique ark which Dr. Schechter had brought from Cairo. On either side would sit his young professors in frock coats with striped trousers and top hats, giving the services he conducted an air of conservative dignity, which was enhanced by the presence of such visiting dignitaries as Jacob Schiff, Cyrus Sulzberger, and Louis Marshall, well-to-do members of the Seminary's board. In accordance with conservative custom, the women sat to one side, apart from the men, although there was no partition between them.

For Adele, too, the flat on 123rd Street was conveniently located for those more secular interests downtown, with which she was preoccupied and to which the nearby Broadway horse-cars could take her. After her return from Wisconsin she had taken a job with Funk and Wagnalls, who were publishing the Jewish Encyclopedia, and had gone to New York before Henrietta and Mamma.

By the fall of 1903 the three women, with Anna, their maid, were comfortably established in the flat furnished with friendly old Victorian pieces from Baltimore—the round dining-room table, Papa's Morris chair, the wine-colored Chippendale sofa, a warm red rug, bric-a-brac and pictures. Mamma's bright flowering plants were set in the wide bow window of the front room, where Henrietta's desk was also installed—under the benign vision of Papa in his prime, gazing down from the large portrait nearby.

Henrietta, between trips to Philadelphia for the Jewish Publication Society, began attending classes across the street, classes conducted by a man who was already considered one of the most brilliant members of Dr. Schechter's fine faculty.

PART TWO

The Turn

She was exposing herself to temptations which it is best to avoid where it can consistently be done. One who invites such trials of character is either foolhardy, overconfident or too simple and childlike in faith in mankind to see the danger. In any case but the last, such a course is sure to avenge itself upon the individual; the moral powers, no more than the physical and mental, can bear overstraining. And, in the last case, a bitter disappointment but too often meets the confiding nature.

—HENRIETTA SZOLD 1879 *

Painful effort is preferable to unconsciousness.

—HENRIETTA SZOLD 1895 †

Can a picture be painted with all lights and no shadows?

—HENRIETTA SZOLD 1899 ‡

Does [being] extraordinary mean to rise above human feeling? It means to be intensely human, it means to raise ordinary feelings to an extraordinary plane.

—HENRIETTA SZOLD 1908 §

* Biography of Sara Copia Sullam
† Address to National Council of Jewish Women
‡ In an article on Zangwill in *Jewish Comment*
§ In her journal

1900s: TRIAL AND TRANSFIGURATION

SHE HAD MET him earlier that year, 1903, on Lincoln's birthday, when she had come to New York apartment hunting, and had gone to a reception at the Clara de Hirsch Home. Her old friend Rabbi Marcus Jastrow of Philadelphia, who knew him, had prepared her for the scholar; but she saw at once only the man—the idealist, the single-minded searcher for truth. His eyes were keen, violet blue.

The next day she saw him again at a meeting of the American Jewish Historical Society. She had to leave before the meeting was over, and caught sight of him sitting on the end seat of one of the back rows. As she passed, instead of merely nodding to him, she held out her hand to this man she had seen only once before. The impulsive act alarmed and abashed her; for weeks the memory of it returned to haunt and embarrass her. Yet when Adele referred to him humorously, mimicking what she thought was his conceited manner, Henrietta was not amused and, to Adele's surprise, said quietly, "I think you are mistaken."

Toward the end of September, when they moved into the new apartment, he had not yet returned from Europe, where he spent the summer vacation; but he arrived within a week, because Rachel and she saw and spoke to him at the Seminary Synagogue services the second Saturday they were living there. Being still unfamiliar with the city, they asked him the way down to Cooper Union, where the delegates to the Sixth Zionist Congress at Basle were to give their report that evening. He offered to call for them and take them there; but, suddenly mindful of the strange attraction he had exerted upon her at their last meeting, Henrietta quite brusquely declined his offer; and when Rachel afterward reproached her for her brusqueness, she could offer no defense. She did not tell Rachel how the memory of her impulsiveness at the Historical Society meeting had troubled her, nor how curiously thrilled she had been when Rachel spoke to him and he replied.

Then and there the question rose up in her mind. Never before had she loved any man; was she to begin then? So late in life? And with a man years younger than herself?

At the meeting in Cooper Union, the American delegates to the Zionist Congress described how Herzl had laid before the Congress the offer he had received from the British government of a refuge for the Jews in Uganda, East Africa, and the resulting debate which had rent the Congress in two. The long persecuted Russian Jews for whom the refuge was mainly intended, being *Ḥovevei Zion*—dedicated to the return to the land of Israel—were its most stubborn opponents. Henrietta heartily approved of their stand, despite the fact that on Easter Sunday of that year had occurred in Kishinev the most terrible of a series of pogroms instigated by the Russian government, in which fifty Jews were killed, six hundred horribly wounded, and fifteen hundred homes and shops looted or destroyed. Herzl had barely saved the Congress by getting an agreement to suspend decision until a Survey Commission could go to Africa and report on the project, considered merely as a temporary "night shelter," as Max Nordau aptly phrased it.

Henrietta's attention to this discouraging report was disturbed by her remorse over the invitation she had spurned; but *he* was not to be seen in the crowded auditorium.

She did not enter his Talmud class; she took only a few history sessions with him while he was conducting the class of Dr. Marx, who was still abroad; and throughout that term she went just once a week to his class in Aramaic grammar. He was frequently ill at that time, sometimes absent or late; and the few times she saw him she had to force herself to be critical of him, especially when she learned that he actually objected to her attending his class. Curiously, she who had such definite convictions on higher education for women, did not resent so much his opposing their scholarly education as his doing so when she felt he must know she was taking this way of continuing her father's work.

Yet it was he who made the first approach which tied her to him. In October, on the last day of the Holy Days, Dr. Marcus Jastrow of Philadelphia died; and he was asked for a eulogy. He wrote it in German, and stopped her in the Seminary hall to ask if she would translate it. She demurred—not very graciously, conscious that she was behaving contrary to her habit and nature. It was especially peculiar as Rabbi Jastrow, Rachel's father-in-law, had so long been the good friend of her father and herself, and she had assisted him in the new translation of the Old Testament of which he had been in charge for the Publication Society. She was, in fact, herself preparing a paper on Dr. Jastrow for the Jewish Year Book. But when he pleaded a little with her she consented. She did the translation and handed it to him, again in the hall of the Seminary, pointing out, incidentally, a change she had made in the text which she thought necessary. She barely talked to him again all that winter; met him only once at some gathering, and then almost quarreled with him in the discussion of some quite unimportant matter.

The first gracious words between them were exchanged in April 1904 at the end of the Passover *seder* at Dr. Schechter's. It was a wild stormy night, and when Dr. Marx and Dr. Friedlaender, who were also there, offered to take them home—Mamma, Adele, and herself—*he* apologized for not accompanying them, explaining that he was not sufficiently recovered from a recent illness to expose himself unduly; and she had promptly scoffed at the very idea of his having thought of doing it.

His colleagues, Alexander Marx, the historian, and Israel Friedlaender, Professor of Biblical Literature and Exegesis, both foreign born like himself, had been coming to her apartment Saturday evenings for an informal lesson in English. After one of those evenings Dr. Friedlaender rallied her about an anonymous article he had read on the personalities of the Seminary faculty. His main reason for ascribing the paper to her was that it had done scant justice to their most distinguished colleague—for he was so considered by Friedlaender and Marx and even by Dr. Schechter—intimating that her antagonism to *him* had been noticed. When she insisted she had not written the piece and had no objection to the man, they asked why she had not invited him, too, to her English evenings. To this she rejoined that she had not thought so brilliant a man, who had been in the country for several years, would need her instruction—which was the truth—but she did not say how relieved she was that she need not invite him.

Later that spring she had a severe attack of earache which kept her from going to the synagogue one Saturday morning. In the afternoon Dr. Marx and Dr. Friedlaender came to inquire about her health, and asked whether the English class would meet that evening. He was with them; and that was the beginning of her struggle. She told them to return for supper and the English lesson and, naturally, had to include him in the invitation, although the words she addressed to him directly almost stuck in her throat. From that time on he came regularly Saturday evenings, and the torment of her bittersweet happiness in his presence became a constantly recurrent accompaniment of her days.

At the Seminary commencement in June she saw only him on the platform—the bright violet eyes under the broad brow with its unruly brown hair, and the sensitive lips framed in the ruddy brown Vandyke beard. His face seemed to signify to her everything in life that was ideal and desirable.

It was the first graduation exercises of the Seminary under the auspices of Dr. Schechter, who gave the fledgling rabbis a rousing invitation to fight for Judaism, incidentally offering them wise and witty advice regarding their personal conduct. "But chief among those you will have to fight will be your own selves. Rabbi Bachya ben Pakudah gave us the wise counsel: 'If you want to praise, praise God; if you want to blame, blame yourself . . .' "—advice which Henrietta, too, might have heeded. Dr. Schechter was an impressive and delightful man, with reddish shaggy hair and beard, and blue eyes twinkling under bushy eyebrows and over the half reading glasses he wore well down on his nose. Toward the end of his address he referred to the Torah as "Mother Torah" and to the graduates as her children—a designation in gender which was new to Henrietta. But she could hardly heed what Dr. Schechter was saying, fascinated as she was by *his* face nearby.

After the exercises he came over to her apartment with a number of other people. It was a hot summer day and Mamma served them lemonade. A discussion arose regarding the higher education of women, and it was evident to her from what he said that he must not have wanted her in his class, that he felt she was out of place there. Still, this, curiously, did not affect her feeling for him.

In July came the depressing news of Theodor Herzl's untimely death at forty-four. Zionism at this point seemed to have come to a standstill in the midst of endless and fruitless debate about whether to consider the possible reality of a settlement in Uganda or to hold firm to the hope of a return to Zion, which still seemed unrealizable for all of Herzl's efforts.

Here, too, as in the case of education for women, the lack of *his* involvement in a matter which concerned her so deeply did not seem to affect her feeling for him. His interest in Zionism as a historical development appeared to her scholarly rather than personal, although theoretically he saw Conservative Judaism as inherently pro-Zionist.

Later that summer his brother came from South Africa and they went off on a trip. While he was gone she wrote a piece on Herzl, "The Practical Idealist," for the Zionist *Maccabean,* saying, "That he with his non-Jewish education and environment should have conceived the idea of political Zionism was a flash of inspiration, a manifestation of race atavism perhaps. That he grew Jewish . . . learned day by day to read life and its problems in Hebrew fashion—therein lies his genius and our comfort. . . . His ideal grew, he grew with it, and as they grew together the means of realizing the ideal took on larger dimensions, deeper fervor, spiritual force. . . . Upon us, now that the leader is no more, it is doubly incumbent to labor for the hoped-for consummation."

On his return she was in the thick of work on the Year Book for the Jewish Publication Society, tedious work all the hot summer days. He came to the flat and asked her to write a letter for him, his English being still rather poor, to the Commissioner of

Immigration regarding some relative of his being detained at Ellis Island. His coming to her even for this slight service gave her inordinate happiness.

In early October—it was a golden day, a Monday, the day the Seminary reopened for its regular session—she was invited to the Schechters' for lunch to meet a distinguished visiting scholar. *He* was there, and he joined Dr. Friedlaender and her on their walk back from 115th Street where the Schechters lived to the Seminary on 123rd. On the way Dr. Friedlaender asked her whether she was also going to the formal Seminary dinner for the visitor, to which she replied that, although an enrolled student, as the only woman she had decided not to attend official Seminary dinners. Dr. Friedlaender professed not to see why she should discriminate against herself, but *he* shot out: "Ridiculous!" with a little chuckle of his she found delightfully eloquent. It thrilled her to feel that in his approval of her self-discrimination he was recognizing her womanhood, in curious contrast to her feeling about such discrimination a decade earlier when she spoke for women at the Chicago Fair.

As they walked on, he turned to her and said that he had expected to see her that morning in his Talmud class. She reminded him of the opinions he had expressed at her home on Commencement Day about scholarship for women, who apparently were unfit to study "Mother Torah," and she asked him if that should not have kept her from enrolling in his class. He said nothing to that. But the next morning at breakfast she had a note from him. Her hands trembled so she could hardly open it. He said he wanted her to come to his class; he wished he had more "disciples" like her. The words were polite, conventional. Even in her excitement she knew that. It was the mere fact that he had written and would let her come that transported her.

At the end of her first attendance at his class he called her aside and asked if she would call to his attention any errors in English he made in his lectures; and this she proceeded to do most conscientiously and thoroughly, stopping daily at the end of class to explain each error. She was careful to remain not a moment beyond the time this took, realizing very well the danger to which she was exposing herself, but knowing before very long that she was already its victim, and that any happiness which came from this could not be tranquil.

In November her sister Bertha came from Baltimore for a visit, while Mamma stayed there and cared for Louis Levin and little Benjamin. Bertha looked lovely, a blooming, enviable young mother; and they had much to talk about. Bertha's news of the death of Miss Charlotte Adams in Baltimore recalled those calm though busy days of her teaching there, and her writing so wisely at nineteen of Sara Sullam whom she had criticized for "exposing herself to temptations which it is best to avoid . . ." But Henrietta said nothing about that to Bertha.

Soon she had learned to distinguish his footfall in the corridor as she sat with her back to the classroom door—she was always early, he was often late—and listened to the shuffling of the feet of incoming students. Never was she mistaken; and she would watch him enter with the big folios under his arm and the small black silken skullcap on the back of his fine head that was like a Van Dyck portrait. Thanks to her father's teaching, she was sometimes one of the few in the class to grasp his Talmudic exposition. The mazes of the subject, made somewhat more involved by his awkward English, opened before her without effort on her part; the brilliance of his interpretations deepened in turn her understanding and appreciation of her father's scholarship. Whatever he said, he seemed to be saying directly to and for her. When a knotty point came up for discussion, he always looked in her direction; when her fascinated gaze rested upon him, he half turned away, averted his eyes, but soon sought hers again. . . .

In January 1905 they came to the section of Talmud entitled *Kiddushin,* on marriage, which in part dealt with certain delicate matters regarding the relations between the sexes, divorce, etc.; and when she heard that to spare her feelings, he intended to eliminate those passages from class discussion, she wrote him:

"An innocent word dropped inadvertently in my presence warned me of the approach of an awkward passage in *Kiddushin,* to be omitted, it seems, on account of me. I am not writing because I do not trust your tact and judgment implicitly. I want more to assure you that if you exercise your right to exclude me from the class when my presence is trying, I shall take it as an indication that ordinarily I am *persona grata*. You need not refer to this, unless it is to tell me to absent myself from your class."

He said nothing about it, so she attended the class; and he adhered to his intention not to discuss those passages which he thought would be offensive to feminine ears, although his general approach to his subject was anything but formal. His critical study of the Talmud was original as well as erudite. With encyclopedic knowledge of his subject he examined its social, economic, and political background, and revealed how Judaism had remained alive by reinterpreting its traditional ideas and practices throughout its history. His conservatism, like her father's, was the synthesis of a traditional and modern education, resulting, in *his* case, in an almost radically progressive spirit functioning within the confines of tradition.

In February he brought her a lecture written in German, which had been partly and poorly translated by someone else, and asked whether she would translate it for him. It was to be delivered soon. She translated and edited it, and got it done in time by sacrificing some sleep; and was delighted to do it. She also advised him about the delivery of the lecture in English, where to place emphasis, and so on; and, although she knew every word by heart she went to hear him deliver it at a synagogue. There she met the sister-in-law with whom he was living, who thanked her profusely for the help she had given him, until she felt like saying: You little know how happy I am to make any sacrifice to have him near me! By then she was beginning to question the wisdom of her move to New York, but she could not honestly answer that she was sorry she had made it.

Soon after that he asked her to read proof of one of his studies for publication. And so eagerly and happily did she engage in this work for him that it was not long before he was dictating directly to her the basic substance of what were to become his major works.

To be sure, out of that devotion to scholarship which her father had instilled in her, she had been performing similar if lesser services for other Seminary faculty members—and even for an occasional student. Just as she had been moved by the urgent need of her "Russians" in Baltimore, she could not deny her assistance to fine minds which might fail to gain recognition or, indeed, to reveal their force and ability because they happened to lack an adequate command of English. But it must have been plain to him, she thought then, that her service to him was of quite another sort; it was for her like the service she had given Papa—without question or stint—out of love.

By the *Purim* holiday in March of that year she had learned the full extent of her involvement. For a *Purim* gift he sent her a book of Hebrew legends with a poem he had written on the flyleaf; and hours after it arrived she found herself sitting in darkness, her hand on his writing, her whole being a-quiver; and when she met him that evening at Dr. Schechter's she was too shamefaced to speak to him, nor could she swallow a bite of what Mathilde Schechter served, until a remark from Dr. Schechter about her lack of appetite recalled her to her senses. Then she heard *his* reply to Dr. Marx, who was jokingly deploring his own inability to flirt: *he* said he could flirt with any woman he chose; but his way of saying it made him seem not so much conceited as forthright, and manly. Then when she mentioned that she was going downtown to a synagogue on the East Side to hear the *Purim Megillah*—the story of the Jewess Esther who, to save her people, married and beguiled the King Ahasuerus, and defeated his anti-Semitic minister Haman—he asked to go with her; and when they were late getting started she warned him it would be on his conscience if for the first time in her life she did not hear the *Megillah* read. It was an orthodox synagogue, so she had to sit upstairs in the women's gallery; and when she was seated, and found that she could not see him in the congregation below, she moved over to the other side of the gallery where she could see his head, and for the first time in her life she did not listen to the reading of the *Megillah;* she read only that beloved face. Afterward, they went to a dingy little upstairs restaurant and ate *Purim* poppy-seed cakes.

In the last line of his inscription in the book he had given her he expressed the hope that their friendship would never be broken. But, alas, the bookbinder with whom she left the book to be leather-bound lost the inscription page, and she was sadly depressed by that loss which seemed somehow prophetic; and then was plagued by the fact that this passion was making her superstitious.

Then one Saturday morning after synagogue services he asked

her to stop a moment—he had a favor to ask of her. It was quite unlike him to put it that way. Would she take down a lecture he was going to deliver on one of the coming holidays? So she sat up night after night reworking the notes she had taken into a piece as fluent in English as the one he had given in German, jubilant over the very feeling that she was wearing herself out for him, and happy in the ease with which she could now approach him with questions about his collection and interpretations of Jewish legends, which was one of his most important projects. He was working on the first of several volumes; and so happy was she to be helping him in this work that she hardly considered the suggestion of Dr. Schechter that she undertake the writing of a prayer book in English for women. To do that she would have to give up working for *him*. It was not women she now wanted to serve, as she had thought when she and Papa stood in the Alt-Neu Synagogue in Prague. She had been diverted even from the service to her father which had brought her to the Seminary. She had not yet started that work.

Even the notable fact that—unlike courteous, grateful Papa—he never explicitly thanked her for anything she did for him became a source of pleasure to her, because it made her feel so close to him that such formal acknowledgments were no longer needed between them.

And then it came about that every Saturday after synagogue services that spring they went for walks which became for her the joyous culmination of each week. Usually they went west to Riverside Drive and then turned north or south along one of the railed walks high above the majestic river where ships stood at anchor and long strings of barges were hauled by puffing towboats. There were benches to rest on, where mothers and nurses sat airing their charges, and sailors in pairs, from gray battleships below, sat avidly eying the passing girls. Elderly folk would be sunning themselves and staring across the river at the distant Palisades of the farther shore, which changed as the seasons passed from the bare wintry gray rock to the thick green curtain of summer, to the colorful tapestry of autumn.

That Passover eve she conducted the *seder* at the Clara de Hirsch Home downtown; and when everyone complimented her on the grace and erudition with which she interpreted the legendary symbolism of the freedom festival, she was happy in the realization of what she was learning from him, and that the idealism she had lost with the death of her father was returning to irradiate her life. She had to spend that night at the Home; but the next morning she rose early and walked all the way uptown to the Seminary Synagogue because of a burning desire to see him, although she knew she would have to wrench her eyes from that fine and noble face to her prayer book. And it seemed to her that no woman was more royally rewarded for an effort than she was that beautiful Passover morning when, footsore, she entered the synagogue and he raised his eyes from his prayer book. They lighted up; he stirred in his seat, and called the attention of Dr. Schechter beside him to her presence.

Often now she found herself sitting over his words, as she had over the poem in the book he had given her—capable of no thought or work, only of inexpressible feeling. And often she had to give up even more sleep to make up at work the time lost in this distraction. And how blind were her friends and her family—even wise Mamma and sharp-eyed Adele right there in the flat; how impossible it was for her to convey to them by word or manner this discovery of herself—the simple fact that she was a woman, with a keenly emotional nature, a profoundly feminine woman, not just an abstracted intellectual!

Yet she did not feel then impelled to confide her problem to either her sister or her mother. Adele, for all that she lived right there and was working with her on some translation from the French for the Publication Society, actually inhabited quite a different world from Henrietta—the world of sophisticated literary radicals, feminist and socialist, and she was being courted by Thomas Seltzer, an editor of the left-wing *Masses,* and a publisher of foreign literature. Adele, Henrietta knew, would be unsympathetic anyway. She had never liked him; and once when she was working as a probation officer, Adele had deliberately embarrassed him with her frank talk about prostitution and white slavery, which a current vice investigation had revealed was no longer uncommon even among immigrant Jews.

As for Mamma, Henrietta was loath to disturb her then with a new problem. For a while after the move to New York, Mamma had found it difficult to adjust herself to the change. It was like leaving one's own family to become part of another; for the communities of cultivated Jews in cities like Baltimore, Philadelphia, New York and Chicago were like close-knit families. The wife and daughters of Rabbi Benjamin Szold were heartily welcomed into the Seminary family headed by Solomon Schechter and his wife, Mathilde, an amiable woman who kept her mercurial husband in hand and befriended the brides his faculty brought into the community. But Mamma, who as the wife of Rabbi Szold had herself presided over such a community, now found herself relegated to tending her small ménage with the help of Anna, while Henrietta and Adele were busy with their labors. Mamma would make frequent trips to Baltimore to visit Bertha, where it was pleasant to be called *Grossmutter* by bright little Benjamin; but she was depressed there by reminders of the past, the lost joys and unforgettable sorrows. Mamma herself had changed very little. When she went out, she still wore the jet-trimmed bonnets, the boned basques and voluminous skirts under which she would delve for the coins she kept in a petticoat pocket. Her hair was still brown, her complexion fair and florid and her eyes bright blue. She was only just beginning to enjoy social life in New York with Henrietta's friends, to feel more at home with them in the Seminary Synagogue and to enjoy helping Henrietta entertain them on her Friday evenings at home. They were mostly younger than Mamma, but young men still liked her, as they had on Lombard Street, and enjoyed her vivacious hospitality.

Since Henrietta had no wish to disturb Mamma with her troublesome confidences, and saw nothing to be gained therefrom at this juncture, she had no way of knowing what her mother thought of her situation. It was plain that *he* liked Mamma very much, and that she enjoyed feeding and treating him like a welcome guest, however frequent. But just as in the old days in the house on Lombard Street, each one of the Szolds had some personal belongings the privacy of which was to be respected, so until Henrietta saw fit to confide her problem, even Mamma would not intrude. Even as a young girl, Henrietta sitting beside Papa and discoursing learnedly with him had not been Mamma's dependent daughter so much as her colleague; and to this day, when she was away and wrote Henrietta, she signed herself Sophie, more like an elder sister than a mother.

As Henrietta did not discuss her disturbed state with anyone, not even Mamma, she began lecturing herself—that such emotions were absurd in a woman her age, particularly for a man thirteen years her junior. She would examine herself in the mirror, and she saw a face sweetly rounded and framed in softly waving, slightly graying hair. She would have looked years younger, as much as a decade less than her forty-four years, were it not for the prim pince-nez through which her warm dark eyes looked with intent intelligence. Everything about her expressed her femininity —her tastefully clad figure, the psyche knot on the back of her smoothly brushed hair, the well-kept, sensitive hands and still shapely ankles. But she could not deceive herself, and she would end her self-examination saying that never again should this foolish, hopeless feeling master her—only to succumb again the next time she saw him. And what was worse—it was making her jealous. She began studying the faces of young girls, envying them the fresh color, the light laughter, the lineaments unmarked by experience, the buoyant step, the insouciance of manner. She foolishly prayed for at least the semblance of youth, but when she saw his eyes resting upon a lovely young girl in the street, at the synagogue, she despaired.

She became jealous even of her sister Adele. Once when he came to the flat, he asked Adele to walk with him, and she refused; then he turned to Henrietta saying: "I do not ask you because you are so busy." His disarming frankness made him appear to be perfectly innocent of the anguish he was causing her. When he and Adele discussed nationalities and Adele expressed a scorn of Germans, he looked hurt, for he liked to think of himself as practically a German although he hadn't been born one, but had come from Lithuania. He had, however, been educated in Germany, at Strasbourg and Berlin and at Heidelberg, where he took his degree. Like her father, he had been steeped in German culture and he wrote in German. Despite Adele's antagonism, he treated her with a piquancy that made Henrietta feel a difference in his vision of them—Adele was the young woman, she the old one. And when he bade them both farewell before he went abroad that summer to visit his father in Amsterdam, saying he would write if they permitted it, Henrietta had, quite unreasonably, the feeling that she was included only that he might write the more naturally to Adele.

The night after he left, she gave way to despair. For days and nights she wept and tried to renounce him, seeing the folly of it; and went on weeping and getting grayer and thinner and older-looking; and Adele, who once found her weeping, discovered her plight. Fortunately she did not have to face Mamma, who was away in Baltimore. Bertha was having her second child, a girl, whom they named Harriet.

Despite her distraction Henrietta worked prodigiously, editing and writing. She prepared a paper on "Jewish Nationalism" and went to Atlantic City in July to read it before the Jewish Chautauqua Assembly, a vast cheerful audience gathered beside the cool, sunny sea, an audience totally unaware of the feat she had performed in organizing this eloquent and convincing statement, despite the turmoil in her unruly heart.

It was less than three weeks before the Seventh Zionist Congress was to take place in Basle where, lacking the magnetic leadership of Herzl, the Zionist forces for the first time would be divided into two camps—camps, not parties, she emphasized. Parties there had been from the first, and they attested the vitality of the movement. But Uganda, or territorialism as it was called, had been injected artificially into the movement, through fear and anxiety—for the Jew was being slaughtered in Russia, degraded in Roumania, scoffed at everywhere in Europe, spurned with ill-disguised scorn even in some of the countries of refuge. Seeing all this, the magnificent leader flinched at his post and a moment's quailing cost him his life.

Henrietta was learning the courage to say that even the revered and beloved dead might have erred: "Herzl had but returned from Russia, where, with his own eyes, he had beheld the suffering and the hope of the Jew, but not even he had yet risen to a conception of the Jewish force that impels the Kishinev martyr to choose more suffering and still longer deferred hope in preference to a debased ideal. With compassion for his brother Jew outranking his newborn knowledge of the Jewish spirit, no wonder that he yielded to the temptation of the apparently brilliant offer of Great Britain." The great if erring leader gone, and Uganda having been found unsatisfactory and refused by the investigating commission, Henrietta now turned her attention to the danger of the residual split in the forces of Zionism, between those territorialists who would still consider any adequate asylum and the die-hard *Ḥovevei Zion* to whom Zionism meant only the hope of return to Zion. With these last she aligned herself, and she defined what Zionism signified to such a Jew:

"It is not a political expedient, not a philanthropic panacea, not a temporizing advance guard of socialism, though it is somewhat of all of these. It is of the essence of his Judaism. Whatever happens, he can never again be merely a Jew without the Zionist qualification. . . . Not so much because the existence of the Jew is threatened by the excesses of barbarity, as that the existence of Judaism is threatened by the excess of alien civilizations. . . ."

Boldly she declared: "My appeal is to him who believes that the highest interest of humanity will be served by the preservation of the Jews as the exponent of Judaism." She then examined the unique relationship of Jews to Judaism regardless of their religious affiliation: "There is the historic fact that so long as a man calls himself a Jew he is a Jew—and when he ceases to call himself a Jew, the anti-Semite does it for him. The world sees to it that we shall not forswear the heritage of our birth . . . by thus classifying the nonreligious with the religious Jew, the world tacitly admits what Dr. Nordau and Aḥad Ha-Am have pointed out, that a nation need not justify its being by a mission. It is—that is enough. As in many other respects, so in this, too, the Jew is unique: he alone has been always called upon, and has called upon himself, to justify his existence." This condition, this unique solidarity, she submitted, was the justification of Zionism and Jewish nationalism, and she frankly described the contemporary condition under which uprooted Jews hopelessly strove to maintain a healthy Judaism even in the havens which welcomed them. "The Jew is being morally crushed in the lands of persecution when he is not actually deprived of life, and everywhere, in the lands of sunshine as in the lands of shadow, he is driven to juggle with the verities of the faith consciously or sub-consciously within him. It is my firm belief that we can be saved from a phantom existence, and our Judaism from being crippled, to the detriment of human progress for generations and ages, only if we say frankly we are a nation . . . if we take practical steps to establish ourselves as a normal nation . . . when we shall be looked upon by the nations, not as an archaeological marvel, not as a trick of history, not as a horde trading upon its glorious national past, but as a fellow nation, begging neither indulgence, nor pity, nor patronage, but standing shoulder to shoulder with them, doing our share of the world's work healthily, and compelling recognition for work well done.

"Zionism is the practical shape Jewish nationalism takes at present . . . nationalism as a principle will, I believe, remain as the only solution of our Jewish problem, which primarily is how to bring freedom to the Jew enslaved in spirit, and secondarily how to bring freedom to the Jew enslaved in body."

From the exhilaration of her evident power to move the minds and hearts of the many who listened intently to her small but earnest voice and applauded her heartily, she returned to the oppressive air of the sweltering city and hurried home, her heart still buoyed up with hope. But in the heap of mail awaiting her there was nothing from him. She tried to settle down to the dry-as-dust routine work on the Year Book, but she was in too much of a turmoil even for that. All interest and satisfaction in her accomplishments were gone.

It was intolerable that she should have come to this pass—she, a woman in her forty-fifth year, editor of an important publication society, herself an influential writer and speaker well known to a wide audience, respected and beloved among her scholarly and talented friends, some of them of world renown.

The flood of love which had swept over her like an irresistible torrent in the weeks before his departure became unbearable now as, day after day, she hoped for a letter from him and none came. And finally, on a hot July day, when she had been greatly moved by a melancholy love poem she had read, she tried to end the commotion within her by sitting down at her desk and writing out her renunciation in a letter addressed to him as if in answer to his proposal.

Mamma was still in Baltimore, and Adele was out, so she would be undisturbed in the writing of this letter, to which she might well apply that dictum she had so prophetically given her pupils at the Misses Adams' School: "A fictitious letter should have exactly the tone and color of a genuine one. . . . A letter—remember this—is always a *talk*—what you would say to your correspondent if you were with him; and as he is abroad, you talk on paper instead of with your lips." She reached for a sheet of her folded note paper, and taking her pen began writing steadily in her small but clearly legible script running across the page in even lines, evenly spaced. . . .

Dearest Friend:

I have been sitting with your precious letter in my hand all day long . . . Though there was no letter from him on the desk before her, she wrote with determination what seemed to her like her own death warrant. *I feel I am going to be un-Jewish, unwomanly. Perhaps before I reach the point of returning the treasure of love your letter gives me, my unreserve will have forfeited it* . . . But she could not do otherwise, could no longer be prudent. . . . *must once, before I renounce, pour out my heart to you* . . . Not that she thought it would be news to him. *In these hard months of my solitary struggle, I must have betrayed myself to your clear vision* . . . As if standing before her she could see those piercing blue eyes in the brown-bearded face . . . *over and over again by my very efforts to exercise self-control. You must have divined it, that I was tranquil only when I was near you, only when you permitted me to do something for you* . . . Slight services, she called her long unremitting labors for him. . . . *that at all other times I was restless, disturbed, unable to do the tasks I set myself, and which never before had found me distracted. Why then should I refrain from telling you in explicit words that my whole happiness lies with you—that you are the first to give my soul its woman's heritage, a soul that up to the time it was awakened by you—Oh! so many happy months ago—had known only filial passion.* . . . Papa's darker, gentler eyes in the black-bearded face gazed benignly down at her from the portrait on the wall, as they had in those dear, dead days when she was his pet, his "Henriettchen." *You guess all the rest, all I have suffered to pretend indifference to you, all I would suffer to win you and hold you forever. You remember my definition of woman's love—the opportunity for self-effacement. And your favorite Zarathustra says: "Das Glück des Mannes heisst, Ich will; das Glück des Weibes heisst, Er will."*

Through the wide window with its row of bright flowering plants, she could see the sunlit Seminary with its dignified entry of wrought-iron and glass and the stone steps he had trod almost daily. The tidy coziness of her Victorian room, the ordered profusion of papers on her desk—some of them his—belied the tumultuous commotion in the heart dictating the words she wrote.

Yet there remains a good deal to be said; and it is hard, bitter to say it, but it is better I send it across the waste of waters. Then when you come back, I shall be fortified to look you in the eyes without flinching. And then, as if stung by those keen eyes, her words spurted out:

Somebody has sinned, or I should not have been exposed to the temptation of loving you—loving?—of adoring you—and you would have been spared the disharmony of being loved by me. Either I sinned against myself, or others sinned against me. But, like Job from the counsel of his friends, she got no comfort from such explanations. There was no comfort now for her even in Papa's benign and loving eyes. Could even the purest filial love be sinful? *But whoever sinned, one sin is not expiated by another. And I should be committing a grave sin against you, your young manhood, your high scholarship and ideals and gifts and prospects, were I to hang myself as a millstone about your neck. When you went away I wept and wept and prayed that this one time yet you might come back to me heart-free, so that I might have a space to grow accustomed to the idea that you would belong to some other woman. And then I grew bolder—I prayed for what has happened—I prayed that you would learn to love me. Happened, do I say? How we delight in deceiving ourselves! It has happened only because you guessed at the tumult in my soul and because you are chivalrous. For how can one like you spontaneously love one like me?* And now, having let logic and fantasy have their way, she proceeded to speak the simple truth:

But whatever wild idea came into my disordered head and heart, I never lost sight of this one—that in the end I should have to practice renunciation, a more absolute self-effacement than even my definition of woman's love calls for. I dare exercise no claim upon you. You belong to a happy, sprightly young creature, one that has not known the heat and burden of life, who will not so much give you intellectual sympathy—you do not need it, your penetrating, sane, unclouded mind suffices unto itself—as she will give you warmth and color to glorify your life. With me you would walk in the gray shadow of sorrow. Now she could not stem the flow of self-pity. Like Job, she fairly reveled in the expression of her tragic anguish.

Only one thing I ask of you, my dear friend. Do not think it easy for me to give you up. If you would see what I see before me now, my own future dark as night, cold as death. I can never go back to the ignorance of my passionless days. You have made me to eat of the fruit of the tree of knowledge, and my eyes have been opened—only to behold my own misery, only to pity my past self which was so stupid, to pity my future self which is doomed to unhappiness. And yet I kiss your hand for the fruit it gave me to taste of, for I still may love you, worship you, only I may not purchase my happiness with yours. And so I hug my misery; it is at least a pale similitude of the happiness I know exists for another.

I give you back then what you offer me, I shall bear my lot bravely. You will see how I shall control myself though my heart break. And if my strength gives out, I shall go away from where you are, and shall thank you evermore for the moment's glimpse of genuine living which you in the richness of your ample nature granted me—I shall thank you for the happy "might have been," God bless you and that other one!

In the lower left-hand corner of the page she wrote *July, 1905*, and there stopped writing. She sat, pen poised in hand, feeling suddenly becalmed, as if all the tumultuous commotion in her heart had been drained away in the writing. It had succeeded: her resort to this desperate measure. She saw clearly now how he had taken the place in her heart of Papa, whose loving spirit had perhaps erred in holding to hers too long, so that she had been roused to this love too late. For all her insight, the strength of her passion was undiminished. But it had done her good to pretend that chivalry had led *him* to offer himself to her when he realized her plight. By this pretense, while wittingly indulging herself in this fantasy, she had made herself realize that he could not feel any love for a woman thirteen years older than himself—he was too normal for such an aberration—and that even if he had chivalrously offered himself she could not possibly have taken him on those terms.

Her eyes fell upon the poem that had sparked her pent-up passion to this impulsive act. She took another sheet of paper and copied it out:

The Solitary

Upon the mossed rock by the spring
She sits, forgetful of her pail,
Lost in remote remembering
Of that which may no more avail.

Her thin, pale hair is dimly dressed
Above a brow lined deep with care,
The color of a leaf long pressed,
A faded leaf that once was fair.

You may not know her from the stone
So still she sits who does not stir,
Thinking of this one thing alone—
The love that never came to her.

The melancholy verses which had stung her to express her own unbearable anguish now seemed to strengthen the rebuke she had administered to herself in writing the letter. But, like the poet, she was moved to preserve the expression of her pain, the fantastic creation which had come of it. Calmly now she put the pages together, the letter and the poem, folded them once and dropped them into the drawer where she stored certain keepsakes. Still, as she shut the drawer, she could not help hoping for a letter from him.

And when the postman rang and she ran downstairs for the mail she found in the box—joy of joys!—what she had hoped; and not even a postcard for Adele—he had written only to her! And a second letter came for her before one came for Adele; and she had a third one that summer, this last a long one in German, telling her all he was doing and seeing.

And then in the fall he returned. On the morning of his arrival, a Monday morning it was, sitting in the Broadway horse-car on her way to an errand downtown, she saw in the newspaper of the man next to her that *his* steamer had had an accident. Not a serious one. But the pang that went through her told her that—Oh! her renunciation was wearing off.

When she came home from her errand he was there! And the struggle began again. He had brought her a handsome inkwell and some Dutch china. She wished he hadn't. She didn't want even conventional gifts to make a bond between them. And on the first Saturday, after services at the synagogue, she moved away to the other side of the foyer from where he was, but he came after her and asked whether he might walk with her; and when they started out she could not help saying, "Ah, this is good—to resume the old ways." To which he replied, as if puzzled, "But why shouldn't we resume them?" Still, she told herself, this could only be temporary; in two years she would have got all she could at the Seminary and she would return to Baltimore and live a quiet industrious life, like those Quaker women on Lombard Street she used to envy. Had they been as peaceful as they looked?

That fall she went so far as to suggest that she write out for him her notes on a new series of lectures he was giving that year. She made of them a handwritten bound volume of over four hundred pages; and this brought them together a great deal because he had to go over each lecture with her in detail. But she behaved well. She always kept in mind her age, her graying hair, her faintly lined face, even when that irrepressible feeling of youthful happiness took possession of her in his presence. Nothing but his work seemed important that fall; nothing else concerned or could distract her.

In September Cyrus Adler married her Baltimore friend Racie

Friedenwald, who had moved to Philadelphia. In October Israel Friedlaender brought home his bride from England—Lilian Bentwich, a radiantly beautiful girl of a distinguished family. She had already written Henrietta thanking her for the help she had given Dr. Friedlaender with his English; and she told Henrietta, when they came to call, that her husband had said he was taking her to meet the woman who had more to contribute to American Jewish life than anyone else. Henrietta envied neither Racie Adler nor Lilian Friedlaender. No woman was enviable to her now that he had returned to her.

One afternoon in October a hundred thousand Jews from the East Side, Brooklyn and the Bronx marched up lower Broadway and Fifth Avenue in protest against the Russian pogroms which had continued since Kishinev. They were headed by Judah Magnes, a handsome twenty-eight-year-old rabbi from Brooklyn, a rising Zionist leader who had attended the Congress at Basle, and was leading a drive for money to send arms with which the Russian Jews might defend themselves. But, moving as was that demonstration of her beloved "Russians," it could not deflect her from the tide of emotion in which she was again engulfed.

It did not matter now that, as she had written so long ago of Sara Sullam and the Genoese monk, "In their relations, she was the giver and he the receiver, nay the demander." He came regularly on Tuesdays for supper, and for other meals which Mamma delighted to make for him. And on Sunday mornings he would send Henrietta a message saying he wanted to take a long walk with her in the afternoon. Yet she usually kept herself well in hand. To be sure, there were times when jealousy got past her guard, as when he asked Adele to translate a piece for him in the fall, when Henrietta was already overburdened with his work and her own; and he presented Adele with the published article with his inscription. And again in November, when Adele read a paper on Emma Lazarus at a memorial meeting for the poetess in Temple Beth El, and he went to hear it and praised it extravagantly as he had never praised any of the work she had done for him. He sat by Adele in the streetcar coming home, leaving her to sit alone in the opposite seat, smarting with envy, until a seat beside him was vacated and he sent her an irresistibly inviting look.

There were times when passion quite overcame her. One wintry evening, when the daylong snow, rain, and sleet suddenly stopped and a high whistling wind arose, the pain at her heart drove her out into the darkness and she hastened down the long hill to Morningside Park and there raced around the solitary paths with the wild wind. That calmed her, and she returned to her desk feeling that she would never again give way to her anguish. But she was mistaken. There were sleepless nights spent praying and wrestling with herself; and days of utter, blank, dull despair.

One Sunday toward the end of December, she had an appointment to go walking with him in the afternoon; and she went despite the appearance of her old friend of the "Russian School" days, red-haired Benjamin Hartogensis, who had come from Baltimore, and asked to see her that day. His wife, Grace, had died five years before, leaving him with a young daughter; and it was plain to Henrietta what his hopeful errand was. But she cut short his visit because by then nothing could stand in the way of her going out with *him* if he wished it.

It was a bitter cold day and they walked on Riverside. The wind from the icy river cut her face cruelly although she wore a veil. He had brought with him the first pages of a new lecture, and he read them to her as they walked. Then they discussed the new ideas he had presented, and finally, as a matter of course, he handed the manuscript to her for translation and editing. There was no longer any question as to whether she was to do it—it was her privilege, her duty, her joy, even if, since he had delayed its preparation, it meant working night and day to get it done in time. And that walk was to yield her yet another joy. For the wind, becoming fiercer, tore part of the veil from her hat; and when she tried to pin it back the wind tugged it from her hands. Then he bade her sit down on a bench while he tied it on firmly. And when she came home, she removed the veil without opening the knot he had made, and kept it in her dresser drawer where she could touch it from time to time, for she never wore it again.

Early that spring, as if to counteract the disordered state of her life, Henrietta set her mind to the writing of a paper for *The Maccabean* on "How the Torah Grows." In simple, lucid, almost childlike style, she revealed the essential Hebraic genius of Moses, his emphasis on lawful order. " 'The Law which Moses commanded us is the inheritance of the Congregation of Jacob.' This sentence is to be found in the Fifth Book of Moses. . . . Once more, before he left them . . . he wanted to impress upon them the need for observing the laws he had given them as the servant of God. . . . The Hebrew word for Law used in the sentence is Torah. It became, and to this day is, the most important word in the dictionary of the Jew . . . because the Jew believes that the whole of his life must be carefully thought out . . . that the whole of a human life must be regulated by law. An animal does what the feeling of the moment wants it to do . . . But a real man who feels and thinks properly . . . bears in mind his experiences of yesterday and many yesterdays, even his ancestors' yesterdays, and he takes the meaning from all the yesterdays he knows, and packs it away in a short law, which he can easily learn by heart and use on all the tomorrows when he and his children need it. Such a man says to himself that the foolish deeds he does today have to be paid for tomorrow. This means there is a proper way of living and an improper way of living, and the proper way of living is arranged according to laws given by God and used by generations upon generations of thinking men . . ." And she then showed how, because of the changing conditions of life through the centuries, these basic laws had been interpreted and elaborated by the Talmudists so that the Torah had grown to its present vast proportions.

For much of this vision of Torah and Talmud she was indebted to *him*. Yet, in all that collection of lawful wisdom, Henrietta had, ironically enough, found no guidance for her present perplexity. The great Maimonides' *Guide to the Perplexed* could not help her. She had been only too sadly prophetic in 1901 when she wrote that "Today, however, he who runs may read that the Talmudic inspiration has lost itself like a river in a sandy waste."

The spring of 1906 was a time of constant tension for her. When he was not near she was restless; when he was with her she grew calm; but all the time she walked the earth with a feeling of painful heaviness in her heart. At Passover, under an accumulation of labors from the Publication Society, the burden became insupportable; she suddenly collapsed. She abandoned the Seminary courses, feeling she had no business there with that pent-up passion in her, and went down to Baltimore to visit her sister Bertha. In over two years she had spent in New York, she had done nothing about what she had come there to do—editing her father's works; *his* works had taken all her spare time. Guilt plagued her, a guilt heightened by her awareness that his scholarly brilliance manifestly outshone even her father's. Yet even in flight she could not banish him from her mind; but she kept her age steadily before her eyes, insisting to herself that only a miracle could give her what she really wanted—to keep him beside her for life.

The visit with Bertha and Louis Levin and the children, Benjamin and Harriet, the old feeling of family coherence, was stabilizing and refreshing. She returned to the flat in New York fortified in spirit, and resumed the routine of her life for the summer. The Year Book was the usual oppressive nightmare, but it served to arouse his concern for her: he took her away from her desk for walks with him; and she kept herself well under control, although her having given up the Seminary courses seemed to have the unexpected effect of bringing them closer together, of freeing them for a closer relationship.

On Riverside Drive they would sit in silence on a bench overlooking the broad sunny river, so calmly majestic despite its powerful restless flow to the sea—silent sessions that made her feel they understood each other perfectly now, and that, if she could keep just his friendly companionship, she would be happier than she had ever thought it possible to be.

In August came *Tisha b'Av*, commemorating the destruction of the Temple in Jerusalem, and on the eve of the fast day they went together to a downtown synagogue, but both of them came away dissatisfied with the perfunctory, pedestrian singsong reading of Lamentations in the crowded orthodox synagogue. In the Elevated train coming home a disturbing thing happened. She wore a dress with short sleeves, and as the evening was very warm, had not put on her long gloves. By chance, as the car swayed, her bare arm touched his hand, which he withdrew so hastily that it seemed like a physical repulsion, and she guarded against its recurrence.

Together they composed a letter to the *Nation* about cruelty to animals and the Jewish law, and she was happy to have persuaded him to write something which would reach a wider audience.

In June he went for his vacation to Tannersville in the Catskill Mountains, where a meeting was being held of the American Federation of Zionists. The evening before he left for Tannersville she had the temerity to tell him that she would miss him; and he urged her to continue taking walks without him.

She was much alone that summer. Rachel and Joe Jastrow had come east from Wisconsin and rented a large cottage at Mount Desert in Maine, and Mamma went up there for six weeks and Adele for four. The weather in town was what New Yorkers called "fierce." There were days and weeks when Henrietta had to force herself to go on working because the humid heat made even thinking an effort. Most of her friends were away: the Friedlaenders in England, the Schechters and the Marxes in Tannersville.

From Tannersville came reports of the Zionist meetings enlivened by Solomon Schechter's exposition of what he called "Catholic Judaism," which would hold all shades of Jewry together, and his vigorous espousal of Zionism as its instrument. There was also the eloquence of the recently elected rabbi of New York's most affluent synagogue, Temple Emanu-El, handsome young Judah Magnes, an ardent Zionist, of whom it was said that he believed the world might have got along without God but not without the Jews. Judah Magnes had become one of the bright young men who flocked to Henrietta's friendly Friday evenings as to a sanctum.

Reports also came from Tannersville of tennis and horseback riding and hikes over wooded mountain trails, which made it no easier for her to work at her desk, looked down upon by the dark benign eyes of Papa from one wall and the dark commanding eyes of Herzl from another. And snapshots came from Tannersville in which *he* appeared, easily distinguishable from his Seminary colleagues, even superficially. Among their bushy beards, their stiff-upstanding collars and thick cravats, his curly hair and beard trimmed short, his soft-collared shirt and necktie negligently knotted gave him a jaunty air, more youthful even than his years. That he felt himself freer than they from restraining responsibilities, less dedicated to causes outside his own scholarly interests and pursuits, was apparent. He was egocentric, but that she took to be the necessary concomitant of genius; to achieve its potential productiveness, it had to be self-centered.

His stay in Tannersville was for her one long drawn-out waiting for a letter, a letter, a letter. He wrote once a week, saying in one of them that he was glad for her sake to hear people speak approvingly of the *Nation* letter—for its effectiveness was due to the form she had given it; which was not true, she thought, but it made her happy.

He returned on Labor Day to be best man at the wedding of Dr. Davidson, an old friend of his, and an authority on medieval Hebrew poetry, whom Dr. Schechter had brought to the Seminary faculty the year before, on *his* recommendation. Henrietta was unhappy at the wedding because she would be leaving the next day for Maine; and he seemed very weary despite his vacation.

She hated the idea then of that trip to Maine, much as she needed it, for she had resolved there was to be no correspondence with him unless he expressly wished it. This was her opportunity for a test of her self-discipline. Since it was she who was going away, it would depend upon her to start any correspondence. A brave resolution, but how she suffered for it! She did not write; but she trudged to the village post office, hoping for a word from him. There was none. The country was ineffably beautiful, but everywhere she looked she saw him and only him. On walks with the others—Mamma, her sisters and Joe—she could hardly follow their conversation for unending thoughts of him. For the whole of her last week the others went off to New York and she remained alone, taking long solitary walks under clear blue skies, through the lush green landscape down to the deep blue sea, longing constantly for his companionship, to enjoy with him this comely countryside, to speak out for him all the thronging thoughts disturbing her unwanted, solitary leisure. Still no letter came from him, and still she maintained her stoic silence. Finally, when she sent his little nephew a collection of botanical specimens, along with the boy's acknowledgment came a single line from him of greeting for *Rosh Hashanah*—the Jewish New Year—which drew from her a long letter she could not then withhold.

She was desolate on the ride down from Boston; but when she reached home her pulses leaped when Mamma greeted her with the report that he had telephoned twice that day to ask if she had returned. But, as for that long letter she had written him, he must hardly have read it, because when next she saw him he asked questions about Maine and her stay there which had all been answered. No matter; for a few weeks she gave herself up to the magical joy of his companionship without any self-restraint—she had deprived herself of so much.

In October, Adele was married to Thomas Seltzer at Bertha's home in Baltimore; and Henrietta and Mamma returned to their flat without her; but Adele and Thomas took an apartment within walking distance of them.

All that winter Henrietta worked with *him* on his lectures and his various writings, including some new studies of the *Genizah* manuscripts discovered in Cairo by Dr. Schechter. But he helped her too. When she had to write an article for the *Hebrew Standard* he suggested she take as her subject the literature which had long ago been written especially for Jewish women. He got the books together for her and discussed with her the materials she gathered.

Under the title "What Our Grandmothers Read" she reviewed those books which for three and a half centuries had been provided for Jewesses of Germany and Eastern Europe who, being ignorant of Hebrew, "were barred from the great and beautiful literature of the Jew, the centuried stream flowing from the Bible as its fountainhead and fed by tributaries from the Talmud, the Midrash, the Kabbalah, and divers philosophies." What could they know of God and man, of the creation of the world and its government, of life and death, of conduct and character? For them was this special literature created in the language called *Weiber-Teutsch* —"woman's translation"—in that Judeo-German with its admixture of Hebrew and words from the modern country in which it is being spoken and read, that jargon which is now known as Yiddish, a pliable, plastic language, serviceable and salty. Henrietta's study of this naïve literature was gently humorous, ironic yet sympathetic. "It is conceivable," she wrote, "that even a modern woman, with all of literature open before her, with the freedom of club life her own, and untrammeled by the strict customs and intrusive duties of a religious household might fall under the spell of this literature." But her final observation was that "in the whole range of it there is not a suggestion that a Jewish woman could have a sphere other than that of wife and mother. Her invariable fortune was to found a house, a home, wherein she should reign as patriarchess, the living bearer of a tradition making for purity and holiness of life. . . ."

When she was writing the article, he asked her to let him see it before it went to the printer; and she awaited his reaction with particular interest because she had expressed in it her own ideal of Jewish womanhood. He praised it only moderately, but said he hoped it would encourage her to do more independent writing. This time even the moderation of his praise did not matter; his interest in her future was enough to make her happy.

Never had she any pleasanter hours than those he spent with her on Tuesdays that winter, between his afternoon lecture and dinner-time, helping her polish her translation of one of his works. Then, if there was a bit of spare time, he might read her a humorous Yiddish tale with that delightful little chuckle of his. Oh, he made her happy as well as unhappy that winter; and the happiness she got far outweighed the unhappiness. She felt certain now it meant something to him that she was devoting all her strength and ability in his service; and his acceptance of these labors, though without his ever actually thanking her, made her feel they were a bond between them, much as she had felt when working with her father. Now he took everything she gave him—not only the editorial work—almost as a matter of course, like the typing she arranged to have done for him, and the fine cigars she brought him from Baltimore.

That winter they never missed a Saturday morning walk after synagogue, but even then she was on her guard against any temptation to feminine coquetry. She was always fearful of walking on ice and, remembering that incident of *Tisha b'Av* in the Elevated train, she would withdraw her arm after he took it to steady her on slippery patches. But once, when they were walking down Broadway, returning from Sunday dinner at the Davidsons'—and it was noticeable by now that people were inviting them together—she repeatedly slipped on the icy pavement. He finally took firm hold of her arm and held it, even when the street was free of ice, all the way home. That was a happy day, which he ended with her, staying all the evening far beyond his usual time.

It was on one of their Saturday morning walks toward the end of March that the first frightening alarm was sounded for her. There had been snow and ice for days, but that morning a wonderful thaw set in, transforming the streets into streams, sparkling under the magical sunny sky. It was so wet that they could not go through Morningside Park, where the paths were turned to brooks, so they went north on St. Nicholas Avenue and walked along the length of the park in the quiet street of ivied brick buildings behind Columbia University. For several weeks he had been telling her, with that difficulty he always had when speaking of something affecting him deeply, of the precarious health of his father in Amsterdam; and on this March morning, when they had reached the northern limit of their walk and were turning back, he suddenly said he had got leave from the Seminary and was going to sail for Holland at the end of April. He would be gone for at least five months.

For her there was no more sunshine in the air; all the world was icy again. Her lips were locked; her head hammered; her eyes failed her. Was it possible to exist five months without him? All she could utter was: "Do you mean that you are leaving in less than five weeks?" He said yes; and no more was said between them on the way home although she felt his inquiring eyes upon her.

The next day she went to Philadelphia for the Publication Society and worked in a state of dark depression. She returned on Monday still unable to shake it off. Tuesday he dined with them as usual and she could speak a word or two with only the greatest difficulty, although he was very gentle with her. Wednesday when her gloom seemed to be lifting a little she set out for a solitary walk, and found him and Mamma standing and talking in front of the house. He had come to fetch her for a walk, and as soon as her mother had gone upstairs he asked her why she was depressed. She began with a recital of minor business and working worries and then ventured to add: "There is something else I dare not tell you," but he did not urge her to do so.

Somehow she endured those weeks before his sailing. She got the copies made of his new lectures and he had a set bound and sent to Judge Sulzberger in Philadelphia. He also asked her to prepare two more sets—for his good friend and colleague Dr. Marx and his uncle in South Africa, all of which she managed to get done before he left, although she was then working nineteen hours a day on a special Census Year Book.

Because his sailing was on a Saturday, and driving on the Sabbath was forbidden, he would have to walk down to the dock—a distance of several miles. She asked if she might walk down with him, and he seemed pleased, although he said no one else would be foolish enough to want to do that, which somehow pleased her, too. On Friday he came to say goodbye to Mamma, and because the typists she had employed for her work were going full blast they had to go into the dining room to talk. And there, for some reason, he mentioned that his ailing father was desirous of seeing him married. At that moment she had herself so well under control that she felt no tremor, inward or outward; and she said to herself: He will come back engaged to please his father; and I will be sad, but not in despair—for that is to be expected. On the way out, he said goodbye to Anna, the maid, and bade her take care of Miss Henrietta and make her stop work to take regular walks.

On the way to the dock Dr. Marx joined and accompanied them, which was fortunate, she thought; but for his restraining presence, she might have been moved to some desperate speech or action as they went down Fifth Avenue. It was a spring morning by Corot. Masses of rain clouds still hung in the sunny blue sky, and his solicitousness for the new hat she was wearing made her as happy as the beauty of the misty green trees rising from the clean, broad, rain-washed length of the avenue, along which the black hansom cabs rolled, their drivers in shiny wet oilskins. And when she turned her eyes to his face, that was a still more exquisite pleasure.

They stopped at noon to rest on the steps of the Astor Library where they were joined by a few friends, among them Rabbi Magnes. They were all to go to lunch nearby; but as Adele and Thomas, who were also expected, had not yet arrived, she urged him to go off with the others while she waited for the Seltzers. He refused with a masterful air and only Adele's arrival just then prevented her from losing all self-control. Adele, noticing her upset state, admonished her quietly to behave herself. At lunch she sat next to him and, of course, could eat nothing.

After seeing his stateroom, while they all stood on the deck awaiting the time for departure, she happened to be standing alone.

He, talking gaily with Adele and Thomas, Dr. Magnes and others, glanced in her direction, and seeing her utter dejection went over to her and remained beside her the rest of the time. When the time came to leave, she could no longer withhold the tears despite Adele's warning. And all the way home that afternoon with Dr. Marx she could speak only of him; and all that summer was one long thinking of him.

His letters came regularly and frequently and he seemed to need hers. He was in distress; people in distress had always come to her, and she was content that he needed her. Then came the cabled news of his father's death. In the first week of mourning, during which he was not permitted to write, she wrote him daily, comforting him with all the tenderness in her heart; and after that week came a letter asking her to write him as often as she possibly could. His grief broke down his reserve as well as hers. His letters were brokenhearted. He had been through an ordeal which she, too, had once suffered; and when she wrote him how well she knew his feelings because she vividly remembered her own, he answered tenderly, regretting that he was recalling her grief. The loss of their fathers, too, was a bond that brought them closer together. But she did not let this lead her to hope for a change in his feeling for her. When he recovers from this sadness, she told herself, when he has braced himself and returned to see your face again, you will look old to him.

In one of his letters he lamented that he had not been a joy to his father in his declining days: his father had wanted him to be an old-fashioned sage, not a modern scholar; his father had wanted to see him married; and he feared that his father had discovered his lack of orthodox piety during his last painful month. For his own part, he wrote, he did not regret having become a modern Western scholar; and as for marriage he put it to her quite plainly: she knew very well, he said, "how happy I am in my bachelorhood." And this she took to be a declaration to her. So be it, she thought. If he was happy as a bachelor, she, too, was satisfied—far more than satisfied; she would be happy to go on forever, doing what she had been doing for him and having his friendly companionship.

She was well aware that this was an un-Jewish relationship—that her father, like his, would not have approved of a man who considered bachelorhood a satisfactory state and accepted the services of a woman without making her his mate. For Jews did not consider celibacy a virtue in a man; it exposed him to evil temptation; marriage and children were enjoined as his moral duty, to himself as well as to his society. And *eshet ḥayil,* the woman of valor, whose praises Jews have sung for centuries, was a wife, not just a devoted companion. But that realization did not help; she seized upon his declaration as a hopeful signal to her. If she could have but this she would be content.

She tried, however, to divert her mind to a renewed interest in Zionism which was reviving that year. Rabbi Judah Magnes, who had become her admiring friend, went to Palestine that summer and brought back reports of new settlements and schools, of the discovery of wild wheat by a young agronomist there named Aaron Aaronsohn who had started an Agricultural Experiment Station; and Magnes brought back his own dream of founding a Hebrew university on Mount Scopus in Jerusalem. He told of how a man, standing on a box among the hot sand dunes outside ancient Jaffa, where Jonah set out to sea, had planned the creation there of a new Jewish city—Tel Aviv. Chaim Weizmann, a brilliant young chemist from England, also went there that year for the first time and saw great possibilities of developments in his field: there was a priceless accumulation of salts to be mined out of the Dead Sea. . . . There was also, at that time, a good deal of anti-Zionist expression, especially among the wealthy, like Jacob Schiff, who feared that nationalistic Zionism would imperil the status of Jews as Americans.

Henrietta joined a group of women in Harlem who called themselves "Daughters of Zion," and she sent her secretary to the Zionist meeting in Tannersville that summer, since her labors on the Year Book prevented her going herself. But all this did not keep her from writing *him* regularly in an effort to tide him over the death of his father.

Sometimes in their correspondence their similar thoughts would cross. As the Holy Days approached, she admonished him to merge his personal grief, in good Jewish fashion, in the general sorrow of his people expressed in the prayers of the season; and at the same time he wrote her of his feelings while he read the *Seliḥot,* the Penitential Prayer, at the *Yom Kippur* service. In his letters, for the first time, although he still addressed her as "Dear Miss Szold," he seemed impelled to reveal to her his innermost feelings, even when they had seemed inappropriate: "I had not shed a tear during all the time of my suffering and while reciting the *kaddish* at the grave of my father I was nearly unconscious and regained my self-possession only after being shocked by a grammatical fault in the vocalization of the Aramaic in the *kaddish*! The mind of man works sometimes very strangely. The grammatical error caused me a real unpleasant feeling while my great misfortune had made me for a time unconscious of any feeling. . . . I feel more and more how deep I root in old-Jewish feeling notwithstanding my modern intellect. One who hears me recite *Seliḥot* will not understand if told I am an admirer of Nietzsche. And indeed many a time I do not understand myself. But you do not need to worry about me getting excited too much. I have regained my old tranquility though at the expense of great physical suffering. . . ." In his still imperfect English, he made clear that he took a detached view of her Zionism, and even of anti-Zionism: "If Mr. Schiff is convinced that the Zionist movement is harmful to the Jews and to Judaism then it is his duty to combat against it even if the anti-Semites should make use of his weapons. Mr. Schiff may as well reply to you and your co-Zionists that you with your denouncing the nationality of the country in which you lived that you give the sharpest weapons to the anti-Semites. . . ." But this in no way affected her feeling for him; and he expressed an intimacy of interest in her personal affairs which gave promise of further development: "I rejoice that your Benjamin is present in New York and only regret that I am not there. I have a number of questions to put before you but as I am to be in New York before your answer could reach Europe I will keep them for an oral conversation."

She was distracted, however, from further concern about him by a calamity at home—an accident to little Benjamin, Bertha's son, who had come to stay a while with Grandmother and Aunt Henrietta, who adored the child, her father's namesake. She had watched his development with enchantment, and now he was a precocious and sensitive boy in his fifth year whose bright spirit and aptitude for learning delighted her. He developed a cold; and to relieve it Mamma set a steam inhaler beside his bed. In a moment when he was unattended the curious child reached out and upset the hot liquid inhalant, which severely scalded his arm and chest.

Henrietta got little Benjamin to St. Luke's Hospital and spent anxious nights there with him. Rachel, who had come east on a visit, also helped. On *Yom Kippur* Mamma prayed God for his recovery and return to them. The child slowly recovered; and the resultant scars were fortunately confined to an area concealed by clothing. His father came to fetch him home to Baltimore and Mamma went with them to care for Benjamin during his convalescence, and to help Bertha who had had a third child, Sarah, in May. Henrietta was left alone, free to return to her own painful preoccupation.

The morning he returned—just after the Holy Days—as soon as he got home he telephoned and asked if he might come in the afternoon; and he brought her, not a conventional gift this time, but his mother's *Teḥinnah,* her personal prayer book, which he had found among his father's effects in Amsterdam. It was one of those books she had described in the article he had got her to write in the spring; and it seemed to her a sign, saying everything she wished him to say. She got him to talk freely about his father. It was a great relief to him.

When he resumed his Tuesday lectures he would discuss them with her. That fall and early winter he spent practically entire Tuesdays with her; he came for midday dinner, after which they worked on his book of legends and some letters until time for his lecture at four o'clock, and on leaving he would say: "I shall ring the bell at five; will you take a walk?" She never refused; and when they returned he would stay for supper and after that would discuss the progress of his works—the printer was delaying one volume, so she urged him to finish off his studies of the *Genizah.* He agreed; and in December he came two or three times a week and dictated to her. It made her happy just to look up from her pad after his retreating figure as he paced up and down the room, or watch him thoughtfully puffing his cigar as he paused to one side of her, thinking out some new point. He would start dictating again, part English, part German, part Hebrew. Then she would read back what he had said, and the sentence might be awry. It had to be reshaped; but how? He would stand beside her scanning what she had written, and she would study that beloved face though she knew it so well. And once, as she started writing again, he reached down and put a detaining hand, the slender, sensitive hand of the thoughtful man, over hers holding the pen and kept it pinned down for many minutes, it seemed, as she sat with bated breath. To have withdrawn her hand, she thought, would have made him aware of what he was doing. She fairly shivered, but remembering that evening of *Tisha b'Av* in the Elevated train, she thanked God there was no longer any physical repulsion between them.

On Saturdays, after services, he no longer asked in words, "Shall we walk?" He merely put the question with his eyes, and she would answer with a nod. Often he was not near her when question and answer passed between them, as people came crowding into the hall from the synagogue. Sometimes one of their friends would join them out in the street, but he would shake off the talking intruder and with an unmistakable air of relief begin his conversation with her and take her off with him. And on their return, as he held out his hand for goodbye, a quick, indescribable look came into his eyes. Equally indescribable was the light in them when he came in on Tuesdays, and many other times, for that winter he invited himself frequently to the noontime meal, always making a most endearing, apologetic excuse to Mamma, much as Papa used to do when he wanted something. Then he would stop on the rug at the door to the front room, hesitating until he caught Henrietta's glance, while that soft, half-pleading light came into his eyes—a love light, it seemed to her.

By then they had accumulated a common fund of allusions to stories, incidents, opinions, prejudices—it needed but a word or a look to bring these up between them. Sitting at table opposite her he seemed to direct all his conversation to her no matter whom he addressed; and then, when he glanced at her, there it would be, that light. Sitting together over a piece of work, when she caught his meaning before he completed a sentence, there was that light in the look he gave her. And that look, whatever it meant, weakened her resolution. She told herself: That look, even if it be love, does not mean happiness for you. But her resistance diminished from day to day; until one day in December, for no particular reason, she realized what inroads he had made on her fortification, that wall she had raised by constant reminders of her age and his, and she resolved to drive him out again. She reasoned with herself: the death of his father had laid bare the dependence of his nature, and he found her understanding and sympathy soothing; that was all.

In mid-December, the Saturday evening of the *Ḥanukkah* week, he came at sundown and, after lighting the little candles commemorating the heroic resistance of the Maccabees to the Greeks, they worked on his studies of the *Genizah* until supper. Then she changed her dress while he waited, and they went over to the Seminary for the celebration of Dr. Schechter's sixtieth birthday. On the way he discussed with her what he would say when called upon; and all evening she sat where she could watch his face as he talked. She left before him, but he followed at once and caught up with her as she crossed the street, eager to hear her judgment of what he had said, and was pleased to hear that it had pleased her. He depended upon her; but she had allowed herself to get soft, too. She must stop thinking of him. So she wrote out on small slips of paper Hebrew poems, psalms and prayers, which she carried with her wherever she went, and the minute he came into her mind, while walking, or on the streetcar, she got out one of the slips and began to study it, to learn the poem by heart; and if, while bathing or dressing or even at synagogue, she thought of him despite her determination, she would recite one of the prayers she had learned, like an incantation against her passion.

But one day that winter it seemed to her unmistakable: the miracle had come to pass. She almost cried out aloud: He does not care how old I am! He loves me, he needs me; he loves me—not for a smile, or my looks, or for a trick of speech or thought, but for myself, and in spite of my years. She could not mistake it any longer. She believed that his every word and look made it evident. He might never marry her; but no matter; it was as he had written: he was content in his bachelorhood, but he wanted her companionship. And as for herself—what more did she want? Was she thinking of ease for herself, of surcease from arduous work, of the dignity of being a professor's wife? She thought only of being with him, of bringing something to him, of functioning for him as the helpmate she had always seen as the appointed role of Jewish women. Nothing specific had happened to bring this conviction of his love for her; but certain conviction there finally was in her long tormented mind.

And now, she relinquished all self-repression and abandoned herself to happiness. She was a queen; she trod on air; she sang within herself! If before then she could not sleep for hopeless longing, now she could not sleep for sheer joy. And when she fell asleep she would waken with a start to the realization of still greater joy. Each day confirmed this conviction of his love for her. She had used to dread the days between Tuesday and Saturday when she might not see him; now he found reasons for coming on Wednesday, when he worked all day at home; and he came Fridays for dinner and wrote his weekend letters there; and Saturday nights; and Sunday afternoon and evening. He went nowhere else, even to his good friend Dr. Marx. And if he did not expect to be at synagogue Saturday he always forewarned her so she knew they could not go walking afterward. And if the weather looked threatening after the service he parted from her reluctantly, but if there was any chance of its clearing he would say, "Let us try."

As the season wore on toward the spring of 1908 and the weather improved, their walks increased and one aspect of them became more and more frequent: long pleasant silences which neither one wished to break. How much more there was to talk about she did not say—how much she had laid up to tell him in some happy future when every conventional restraint between them would be broken down. And to her wonder this self-contained man talked more and more of himself, poured himself out to her. Sometimes only *he* talked. Then at the point of return they would sit on a bench on the Drive silent for half-hours at a time. He would smoke a cigar and they would look out over the beautiful river—but she looked beyond it to an even more beautiful shore, a harbor. Occasionally, almost reluctantly, one of them would break the silence to call the attention of the other to a stately ship at anchor, or a flashing speedboat leaving a curved wake like a skater on the smooth water; to a flock of white gulls screaming over some food in the stream, or to a solitary bird chirping in a nearby bush.

In May he began writing his Introduction to the *Genizah* studies. He assured her that it would not be more than ten or twelve pages; and she teased him about other such predictions he had made. Under his fertile touch the Introduction grew and grew, and she translated almost as fast as he wrote, getting up early, sitting up late, taking a day off from her other work to keep up with him. When it had lengthened to about twenty pages he protested she should not go on with it but should find a translator for him. Then she was bold enough to say that would make her unhappy; and the next time he made the suggestion again she had the audacity to tell him that so long as she had even a subordinate part in his work she felt she could keep his friendship, which she very much needed. He protested no more after that. It became natural for him to tell her each evening as they walked westward toward the river what he had written that day, explaining it to her in advance to make it easier for her to edit and translate; or, seeking a bench by a lamp, he would read her his manuscript in the balmy perfume-laden air of the summer night, while the shadows of fluttering moths fell upon the pages. The extinguishing of the lights of Palisades Park across the river would be their signal for going home—with a sigh.

On a Saturday night toward the end of June, at a memorial service in the Seminary Synagogue, she suddenly felt her head turning to see him enter, but he went to the opposite side of the hall from her. The service was long, and as she went out she was stopped and consulted by a committee about the memorial fund of which she had been made treasurer; and then someone asked her about making a speech, which she refused, as she so often did now, because she knew he disliked women making speeches in public; so far had she changed for his sake, so willing a subject had she become to *his* gentle tyranny. Out of the corner of her eye she saw him go out the door and then turn back to re-enter the hall and stand where he could catch her eye, and then one of those wonderful looks passed from him to her and under its spell she nodded, knowing it meant Riverside. And to Riverside they went, and while they sat, watching the yellow moon swimming through heavy heat mist and spraying the night between river and sky with its cool golden light, they spoke scarcely a word. He smoked two cigars, for which, for once, she did not censure him, feeling without will of her own, without self-possession, feeling that with that look he had wholly appropriated her. Nor was she concerned for the time, which was half past one when they rose to go home. Even the lights of Palisades Park were long out. And when he teased her a little later about the lateness of the hour, that too warmed her heart.

It was a very hot summer, trying the tempers of others while she was so happy. She worked steadily all through June and July up to the time he sailed for Europe, and managed to finish the Introduction to his *Genizah* book, notes and all, by refusing all invitations to the country, by going on no excursions, by keeping every minute for him. And she was happy; forgotten were her age and her fears. And it seemed to her that he, too, was reluctant to return to Amsterdam where, in settling his father's estate, he would relive the sadness of the year before; and sometimes she ventured to entertain the thought that it was because of his pleasure in being with her that he welcomed the work which was keeping him there, although his brother was urging him to go abroad as soon as possible. Yet once—it was on one of those occasions when she told herself: today, in so many weeks—four, three, two—he will be on the ocean—she wondered whether he was not telling himself: today, in so many weeks he would be shaking off all his quandary about her.

But up to the time he left he came daily. The last Sunday but one that they worked together they spent all day at the Seminary, and it was so hot a day and she was so unwell that at times she felt she would faint, yet she could keep herself going because it was for him. And on the last Sunday he was sick, too, but they worked away together at the notes. From the day she had first entered his class almost five years before, she could not bear it when he was not well, and she always knew it at a glance; his eyes were eloquent to her. On Tuesday he was better, and they went for a walk. Wednesday afternoon about five he came to say goodbye to Mamma and herself. He had a manuscript with him he was taking to the post office to register, so she said she would go there with him. She fought back her tears all the way to the post office where they met their friend, Max Radin, and after he had registered his manuscript he handed her the receipt and said in the presence of Radin, in the most matter-of-factly masterful manner, "You take care of that," implying that she was the custodian of everything else of his. After Radin left them, she walked a few steps from the post office with him and there bade him a speechless farewell, for her lips were trembling; and he, too, said nothing.

So she went home to weep all that night. The next morning, Thursday, she was tearfully at work when the telephone rang. Her heart stood still, for it was his voice telling her he wanted one more word with her just before sailing, and she barely managed to say "God bless you!" feeling that she was surely betrothed to him, forever. And at once she sat down to write him the first of a series of letters out of the fullness of her grateful heart—of the beautiful summer she had had, how all its beauty was due to him, how she would miss working with him . . . revealing herself to him thereafter in letter after letter as she had never revealed herself to anyone.

So absorbed was she then that an incident, the like of which in other times would have troubled and moved her to some form of expression as had the Corbin affair, now barely involved her: New York's Police Commissioner Bingham published an article in the *North American Review* on "Foreign Criminals" in which he asserted that half the criminals in New York were Jews. Judah Magnes rose to the defense of his people and with irrefutable statistics disproved the allegation and forced the Police Commissioner to retract his statement. Reassuring as was that retraction, the incident was a disturbing answer to the question of the seriousness of anti-Semitism in America raised by the contrasting action of Commissioner Roosevelt in the case of Herr Ahlwart. Rabbi Magnes made this incident the occasion for proposing the organization of a *Kehillah*—a Jewish community council which would concern itself with the welfare of the great Jewish community in New York, and would be prepared to deal with so unjustified an attack. It was the sort of cause Henrietta would normally have been among the first to espouse, especially alongside a good friend; but she was then too distracted, too preoccupied with her still unresolved personal problem.

She suffered greatly in the first weeks of his absence. He sent no card back with the pilot as she had expected; and his first letter from the ship, written just before landing, was hasty and brief;

then came picture postcards. And she, who had been writing long letters every other day, began to lose her assurance of his love, to revert to her determination to repress all her hopes. For two and a half weeks, painfully, she refrained from writing him. Then came his first real letter dated August 21 from a place called Heningsdorf, in which he thanked her for one of hers which had come the morning of *Tisha b'Av* and had cheered him so that fasting that day had been painless. She resumed writing him those letters in which she bared her soul to him—telling of her joy in his friendship and her need of it, of her happiness in sharing his labors and even his sorrows, of her pride and concern for his career. She reported what the Jewish press had said of his comment on a manuscript found in Copenhagen, telling him too of how she spent her days without him, how unsatisfactory were her solitary walks and works. Some of her letters he answered; and from Berlin he sent her a book on Jewish literature inscribed in his boldest hand: *Freundlichen Grüss aus Berlin* with the date August 28, 1908, and above this, in smaller, cramped handwriting, as though crowded in as an afterthought: *Meiner lieben Freundin, Frl. Henrietta Szold.* She kissed the inscription, observing that for the first time he had used *lieben*—beloved—instead of as heretofore the formal *hochgeschätzte*—highly esteemed; and imagining happily how it had been in his mind to write her an endearing word—how he had shrunk from doing so—and then finally had been impelled to add it. To be sure, in German one might use the word *lieben* casually as one wrote "Dear" in English; but in either case it *could* mean much more.

After that she got three letters from him which puzzled and troubled her. The first, dated September 4, a week after that blessed inscription, began by saying he was at last in Amsterdam, that he had lingered on the way there because of its painful reminders of his loss last year, that it might have been better had he not gone abroad. Then he apologized for the pain he caused her in return for her good letters, that he felt he must speak to someone who understood him, and, of course, *she* must be the "victim."

The second letter dated September 15 began by chiding her for the self-repression she had exercised—he did not want to be the victim of her virtues. He referred to himself as "the same old egotist" whose egotism caused her pain. But self-control failed him;

and she and Dr. Marx were the only ones he could talk to—and again he called her his "victim." He had tried to conceal this weakness of his from her but now in crisis he had broken down—she wondered about this "crisis," it must be some aftermath of his father's death—but he begged her not to worry, for he was quite sure that the crisis had passed and he was gradually regaining control of himself. He said he would return on the SS *Minneapolis* and sent greetings for *Rosh Hashanah,* the Jewish New Year, which would come on September 26.

His last letter, dated September 24, thanked her at length for her report on the *Jewish Chronicle*'s misrepresentation of his opinion on the new-found manuscript; to this he devoted two pages. In the third page he resumed the subject of his abuse of her friendship—again using the term "victim"—and again equating her friendship with that of Dr. Marx, but referring to the "cowardice" of his not having spoken out to her as he had to Dr. Marx who had asked for an explanation, assuring her again that his crisis was past and he was becoming himself again. . . . She was disturbed; she could not understand what he wrote; but all her uneasy feeling dissolved in delight when she reached the last sentence on the fourth page: "I know that this poor letter of mine is a very shabby recompensation"—even his inaccurate English delighted her—"for your three letters, but you may be assured that the wishes for a happy holiday accompanying it come from the depths of the heart of yours"—signed in his quite illegible scrawl. An irrepressible song rose up again in her heart that day, and it continued to sing until two days before he returned.

All the preceding year people had been telling her how well she looked, how animated; and she had explained it was due to her having given up the Year Book drudgery, though she knew very well it was because of her happiness with him; and in the last fortnight before he returned she met no one who did not look her in the face astonished at the transformation they saw there. Although when she reread parts of his letters, as she frequently did, she was troubled by those unusual, unclear phrases, by underscored words—by his three references to her as his "victim"—but when she came to that last paragraph—there was no mistaking *that,* she reassured herself.

That letter had been dated two weeks before his sailing time and she hoped for another; but looking into the letter box again and again brought no more, and by Saturday she was nervous about this. However, she sent her fears flying with the thought that after that last paragraph anything but a declaration of love would be an anticlimax; and since he did not wish to write that, he wrote not at all.

On Sunday, the last day of the Holy Days, after synagogue she went to the Schechter's with the Davidsons and was exuberantly joyous; and afterward, when she walked home alone, she decided to go by the lower promenade on Riverside—his favorite—and think of him at every familiar turn. But there came a change in her mood: suddenly, inexplicably, she felt depressed, nervous and anxious; all her blitheness was gone. Her dejection continued through the night, and when the next morning at breakfast she went through an unusually heavy mail and still found nothing from him, she was desolate. And to make matters worse, there was a letter from Judah Magnes, an exuberantly happy letter, boyish, enthusiastic, telling the secret of his marriage to Beatrice Lowenstein—and asking her to rejoice with them: "I wonder if you are as happy about it as we think you are. We are in the last of the heavens of bliss . . ." Her heart failed her then. She went into her room and wept, rebellious at her fate to be called upon to witness and find joy in the joy of others while her joy was withheld. On an errand at the Seminary she met Dr. Marx, who asked if she was going down to the dock that evening to meet the *Minneapolis*. She could manage only to say no, and left him looking puzzled.

When Tuesday morning finally came she felt cold but strangely composed. She kept herself from going to the window to watch for him. She nailed herself to her desk, working with her secretary.

At half past twelve came the familiar ring, held just so long; and then he was in the hall, excited, flushed, eager. He came toward her desk, their old stand. A few words passed between them, the aimless words spoken in public after long separation, because there is so much to be said. Then he said: "Can we go into the other room? I have something to tell you."

For a moment her heart knocked like a hammer, the blood rushed dizzyingly to her temples, she could scarcely see: her time of happiness had come at last, her heart cried out, singing, shouting, jubilant; and, in the next instant, was cold with dread, like marble. She had led him into her room and had hardly closed the door before he blurted out: "You will be surprised to hear that I am engaged."

"Engaged," she said simultaneously. Fortunately his back was still to her as he went to the bureau and leaned against it, which gave her an instant to collect herself, breathing a prayer for strength, not to break down, to keep calm.

"No," she said, "I am not surprised. I always had an idea that someday you would come back from Europe—engaged." She spoke in an even tone, suppressing the thought: But that you would do that *this* time, an angel from heaven could not have made me believe.

"A premonition—eh?" he went on. "You know, I always do the unexpected."

The room whirled about her, but she did not fall; and she felt grateful to God who had given her so much physical strength; it made up for her spiritual weakness.

"You know," he continued, "I wrote you of the crisis I underwent when I reached Amsterdam?"

What had been unclear was now to be crystal clear.

"I had seen the girl in Berlin," he said.

"What is her name?" she asked, as if merely curious, and he told her.

"I went to the synagogue and met a friend there, and I happened to look up to the women's gallery—I assure you it was not a frivolous thought that made me do so—and saw a girl, and I said to my friend, 'Rather a pretty girl,' and he said he knew her, and that she was a fine girl, too. After the service he introduced me to her. By the merest chance I met her again that afternoon. . . . Then came the crisis at Amsterdam."

And then came the first of his last three letters to her! With lightning rapidity she calculated that that Saturday—her doomsday—was the day after he sent her the book from Berlin with its inscription which had raised her to the seventh heaven; and that he wrote her the first of those three letters referring to his "crisis" and to her as his "victim" directly after the girl, whom he had seen just three times, said she would go to America with him!

He proceeded to tell her how he had written the girl's father, who objected to the engagement because he knew nothing about *him,* and would not give his consent until he had written for information to someone he knew in New York. He said he had answered her father that there was but one man who could tell him all about himself—namely himself. But she could not smile at the conceit which had somehow endeared him to her until then. Anyway he had won out against the father with the help of the girl. Nevertheless he spoke well of the family—he had inquired and found it all that was desirable—a Frankfort family: "You know," he said, "I have never cared for South German Jews; they are very pious. So is my fiancée, and she has the most beautiful eyes and mouth. She has a great deal of wit, a good German education, and is very domestic, I am told. . . ."

She interrupted him to say, with great difficulty, "I hope you will be very, very happy," feeling that once she had said that she could contain her anguish. Then she asked to see the girl's picture, which he took out and showed her, saying, "She is exactly as tall as I am."

By this time she thought she was safely under control. But then, as if released by her calmness, he turned to her with a lively gesture and said, "And do you know of whom I spoke most to my fiancée? Of you and your mother!"

The pain was unendurable, yet she kept telling herself she must do nothing to mar his happiness, and marveled that his elation remained undamped—that he could not see and feel what she was suffering!

She asked if he had announced his engagement.

"We did not do so in Europe," he said. "But I've told the people at the Seminary."

So she was to have no respite—no time in which to accustom herself to the thought of giving him up forever. He had, it seemed, fortified himself by first telling their circle. Or was it all unpremeditated, was all his behavior the natural result of this love that had suddenly possessed him? She prayed God to let her keep her ideal of him at least. As they turned to leave the room he said, "I asked my fiancée to write you, but she said that would not be proper. Is that so? Isn't that proper?"

"That is a matter of feeling," she replied and was thinking how, if he ever asked her to do anything, she would not have stopped to question its propriety, when he said, "Will *you* write to *her*?"

She felt faint. He was asking her to do something. It was outrageous; but in five years had she ever denied him anything? Perhaps writing that letter would be the final act of renunciation she needed to free herself. She said yes. Then he went down the hall, halting only to say he would return to take her for a walk in the afternoon. Almost mechanically she said she would not be home until six, numbly wondering if she could possibly have been so completely mistaken about his feeling for her; for here he was, on the day after his return, engaged though he was, expecting her to go for a walk with him as if it had all been just a cool friendly association they had had. And she stood there trying to accept that discovery, telling herself: Very well, it shall be as he conceives it—I was mistaken; he has done me no wrong. As he passed the kitchen door, he called gaily to Anna in German: "Well, next Tuesday prepare for me too, I'll be here as usual." She stood there numbly thinking: So be it. Nothing has really changed. When he was at the outer door, she said, "When you come at six bring me her address and I shall write."

"Oh," he said, "I'll give you that now," and returned with her to her desk and wrote out the address.

As he turned to leave again, she asked, "Shall I write in German or English?"

He said, "German, of course."

"You must look at the letter before I send it," she said.

They were again in the hall by the hatrack when something in her fast failing voice stopped him. He said, "You *are* happy about this, aren't you?"

And for the first time she faltered, "Ye-es," felt her brain reeling again, and saw that he was gone.

Fortunately Mamma was not there. Only Anna in the kitchen, and her secretary. She went to her room and sat down to collect herself—outwardly cold as ice, inwardly consumed by a sudden hot flame of rebellion. She groaned but did not weep. Was *she* not of good family? Was *she* not domestic? Ah! but she was not twenty-two; she had not those beautiful eyes, that luscious mouth. She was only a woman who knew how to serve her beloved boundlessly. And because love is blinding, and she had loved him, she had not seen that he *never* had loved her. Now those last three letters proved it, and his willingness to pick up with her where they had left off: going to walk with her; coming to dinner Tuesday. . . . He had never considered her as anything more than a sexless intelligence and she had misinterpreted everything. But now she would write to the girl, and with that letter put the past behind her and be the mere friend to him he had thought her. In the few minutes before dinner she dashed off the letter, and then sat down and made a pretense of eating. To Anna, who remarked that she was not eating, she said, "You know I am always too nervous to eat when I am to speak in public"—for that afternoon she was to address the Council of Jewish Women.

After dinner she dressed and went to the meeting. Several people asked why she was so pale. Had they touched her they would have found her cold as a corpse; but within her a great fire raged. Sitting on the platform awaiting her turn to speak, she was hardly conscious of what was going on around her. Yet when the time came she stood up and spoke for half an hour and was roundly applauded. After it was over she had to make small talk with about two hundred women who clustered about her, expecting her to remember them. It was torture. At last she got away, her teeth chattering, and hurried home lest she miss that six o'clock appointment with him, still dominated by his wish, still not realizing that she was nothing to him and he could be nothing to her.

At six he had not come. She waited, and when she could wait no longer, telephoned. His sister-in-law answered and said he was not yet home, a number of people were waiting there for him—and what did she think of the news? It was fine, said Henrietta. "And how much she will love you—that girl, who knows all about you," said his sister-in-law. To this she could give no response. And then came the Parthian shot: "I've known it some time; but I couldn't tell you, could I?" "No, of course not," said Henrietta and hung up, and collapsed, chills chasing over her and her senses gone until recalled by the telephone bell. It was he, saying he could not come. She said she wanted to show him the letter. He said, "Oh, just send it off, your German is all right, there will be nothing to alter." But driven by some dark compulsion unclear to her then, she insisted that he must see it. Very well, he would come to take her for a walk the next day. She then dragged herself to bed, and Anna nursed her through a horrible night.

She had an appointment the next day with Dr. Schechter at the Seminary. He looked at her and said, "You do not seem well."

"I have not slept much," she answered.

"Neither have I," he said. "The opening day at the Seminary is always distracting; and the engagement of Dr. –"

"You must be happy," she cut him off, "now that all your professors are married off." She realized then that her calamity was being talked about; that it must be the primary topic of conversation in the Seminary community.

Later Adele dropped in; and to Adele, who had always been against him, she had to say, "The catastrophe has come."

"He is engaged to be married?" Adele said at once, and insisted that she break completely and immediately with him; have nothing more to do with or for him. But she could not yet agree to that.

He came late in the afternoon, and she gave him the letter she had written. He read it, and thanked her; neither one made any pretense of discussing its form or content. He handed her a small white case he had brought, his gift from abroad, a beautiful buckle made in Denmark. It stung her that he should now, for the first time, have given her a personal ornament. "I bought it in Copenhagen," he said; and she thought: That was before he met the girl, when she herself was still possibly something more than a mere friend to him.

She refused the gift. He seemed astonished and threatened to be very angry with her; and she tried to resign herself to his wish, telling herself they would be friends, that they had never been anything else but friends.

They set out for their walk, but by the time they got to the corner, strength failed her; her lips were dry, her throat choked so she could hardly say, "I think I had better not go on." "What is the matter with you?" he asked, so plainly puzzled that she felt certain of his innocence. He urged her to walk; it would do her good; he would do all the talking. He admonished her not to work so hard. . . . He led her down their favorite path and as they went on—he talking about his work as he used to, discussing various points, asking her advice—she grew more composed, was almost happy again, until overwhelmed by the thought that she was permitting herself to go on loving a man who was practically married. And what would happen if she went on with him on his own terms, working for him, letting him come like this and take her for walks? She would be wicked, dishonest. Or would her feeling for him change to calm friendliness? Yes, she resolved then, it could; it must.

When they returned to her house, she spoke of his gift again, said that he must not think she disliked the buckle, it was beautiful, but she had never cared to have anyone but her family give her personal gifts; however, if he insisted, she would take it. He nodded silently, as if the matter no longer concerned him; and, as he did not leave, she felt obliged to invite him for supper, which he accepted just exactly as he used to.

While they were eating, Adele came in. She coolly congratulated him. He mentioned that his "future wife" bore the same name as hers; he admired her new hat; he gave her a small Dutch plaque he had brought her. He stayed all evening talking of history and other impersonal matters.

Just as he was leaving, Anna came home; and when he had gone Henrietta told Anna that he had got engaged while he was abroad; and Anna replied that she had heard it from Dr. Marx's maid, and added, naïvely, that she had almost fainted at the news.

Seeing him again that first Sabbath in synagogue was a great trial. She could hardly breathe. A friend sitting beside her offered to take her outside. Dr. Schechter, on the platform, shook his head at her in despair, and then averted it, as if unable to bear the sight of her distress. At the end she kept close to the Davidsons, with whom she was going to dine, hoping to leave without having to speak to him. To her consternation she found that he was to dine with them too. The dinner was sheer agony. And when that was over he said, "I will go with you,'" as if nothing had changed for him, and walked home with her. If she still had any sins to account for, she thought, they were surely expiated on that walk.

Tuesday he came for dinner, just as he used to, and she sat speechless at the head of the table. When it came time for him to go to his afternoon lecture, he said, as usual, that he would ring for her at five. He did, and she went for the walk with him, again agonizingly divided between a temporary sense of peace and a sense of the wickedness of what she was doing. This time he did not return for supper, and she bade him goodbye, as she was going to Baltimore on Friday. When he said that he would stop and see her the next day, after a faculty meeting at the Seminary, she told him she would not be at home, she had an engagement, instead of breaking that engagement in order to see him again as she would have done before.

This was the beginning of her practice of self-denial with him, whenever she could do so by an act of will. No longer did she stand by the window to watch him going home from the Seminary at the times she knew well, waiting to see if his eyes would glance upward. No longer did she reread his letters to her, as she had almost daily, carrying them with her on all her trips; although this self-denial hardly mattered, for she knew by heart everything he had ever written her. She put all his letters away in the drawer with that letter of renunciation she had written three years before; and with them she put the veil which she could no longer bear to touch. Unhappily, however, thoughts and tears are not to be denied with all the will in the world, and her irrepressible longing for him made her feel like an adulteress.

In Baltimore, at Bertha's, self-pity and bitterness overwhelmed her. She was ill; even her seemingly invulnerable physique could not stand the strain. She had resolved to speak to Mamma about it when she got to Baltimore, but she could not. For all Mamma's love for her, she feared she would not meet with sympathy, for in all those five years Mamma had not betrayed by the twitch of an eyelid that she observed what was happening to her eldest daughter. Mamma would probably say it was ridiculous, this passion of hers, unbecoming her age. In one simple sentence Henrietta had written Mamma the news of his engagement; had urged Mamma to write congratulating him; and had even suggested that she write the girl too, as Henrietta herself had. So it must have seemed to Mamma that she was taking it properly. This, too, made it difficult now to tell Mamma of her present state.

Only once during the Baltimore visit did she see an opening for such a talk, when their friend Dr. Benderly called and, having heard of the engagement, asked whether the girl was an old flame, to which Henrietta replied: "No, he saw the girl accidentally in the gallery of a synagogue and was practically engaged to her after their third meeting two days later." Mamma gasped, and exclaimed something indignant. But Henrietta could not bring herself to take that opportunity, knowing then that if she spoke to Mamma the result would be sympathy for herself and opprobrium for him; and this she could bear no more than ridicule and lack of sympathy for herself.

That trying visit came to an end; and she and Mamma returned to New York together, stopping at Philadelphia on the way—an added torture, for, there too, she heard his engagement being discussed. Philadelphia and Baltimore were like cousins in the close-knit though far-flung American-Jewish family. Chicago and San Francisco, too, in time would hear and discuss the news.

They got home Thursday evening, November 5. On Saturday Henrietta's good friend Alice Seligsberg went with her to the synagogue; that gave her a good reason for going off without him after the service. But in the afternoon he came to pay his respects to Mamma, whom he had always loved—a love that had reminded her of Papa's love for Mamma's mother, of which she had often heard as a child—a love on which, she realized now, she had hung some of her hope; for Papa used to say he loved Mamma's mother first and then loved Mamma, because he had seen her mother in her.

His manner toward them both was exactly as it had always been. He complained of her having gone off without him after synagogue, and proposed a walk then. She went with him, feeling again that she was on dangerously thin ice. Something had to be done, but what? She could not do what Adele counseled.

The following Monday she went to the Seminary library to look up references she needed; he joined her there and they arranged that they were to meet there again in the afternoon to go over some proofs of his. She returned to the Seminary library, but as she worked there with him in the book-lined room, tears would start falling from her eyes. Adele came, perhaps sent by Mamma who must have seen her perturbation, and tried to get her to go off with her. He came home with her for supper, and they worked afterward until ten, when he asked her to walk with him. She did with the usual consequence—a precarious peace compounded of heavenly pleasure and hellish torment. On Tuesday he came for dinner and again they worked together until time for his lecture. And then, in the evening mail, came his fiancée's reply. She read it, and passed it to Mamma, who, having read it, said, "But I do not understand!" to which Henrietta could only reply, "There are many things I don't understand either."

That evening, after reading that letter, she felt she had reached the nadir of misery, and must have either sympathy or the knowledge that she deserved no sympathy—the one would soothe her, the other would perhaps bring her to her senses. The only one to whom she had confided in those three dreadful weeks was Adele, who had, until then, tolerated him only for her sake, and Adele was too fixedly antagonistic to him now to be helpful to her. She decided then to talk to Mamma who had loved him. She did so that night when they were in their beds in the room they shared, and the lights were out.

She began with a reference to his financée's letter, and she had not gone far in her confession of those nine months of tumultuous happiness before he left, when Mamma interrupted her to say what a shock and a grief the news was when she got it in Baltimore; and then recalled how all day during prayers last *Yom Kippur* she had thanked God for the belated happiness she was then certain was coming to Henrietta, and how she had planned to live with Rachel and Joe in Wisconsin for a year after Henrietta's marriage.

For a moment as Mamma talked, the whole burden of humiliation and despair seemed to have been lifted from her heart. If unworldly Mamma exonerated her of folly and unwomanliness, if she, too, had thought his devotion was that of a lover, then Henrietta could not be the despicable, self-deluded creature she had been thinking herself. But that consolation did not last long, when she remembered that it was her own mother who was consoling her, as any mother would inevitably console her child. She was not yet justified; she had not yet been helped to the understanding she needed and sought of the unhappy fate that had befallen her.

Mamma criticized him unmercifully, so that she had to beseech her not to treat him cavalierly when he came. There was some reasonable explanation, she insisted, for what he had done to her. He was incapable of cruelty; passion had enthralled him in Berlin, had overpowered him, so that he had forgotten his feeling for her. This new love was so different from the old, if love that had ever been, that he could not consider the one in the presence of the other. So she argued; but Mamma—and also Adele—cited each act of his since his return, interpreting each one as a coldly calculated part of a plan to make her believe there had been nothing between them before but a simple friendship. And she insisted that there was still the possibility of his innocence, that what seemed to them calculated might be perfectly natural.

On Thursday evening he came to finish the proofreading of the Introduction. And after that was done she showed him his fiancée's letter. It contained two specific instructions: Henrietta was to ask him for one of the pictures they had taken together; and she was to see that her darling did not work too hard. As he read the letter she recalled how, in those summer days before he went abroad when she was working on the Introduction for him, she had tried to get up enough boldness to ask, as a reward, for a picture of him to have with her while he was away. But she had refrained, even when one evening at his home his sister-in-law showed her a number of portraits of him. Now she was instructed by a stranger to ask for his engagement picture, and to see that he, whom she had saved all manner of labor for years, did not work too hard.

The irony of it pricked her to a feeling of malice for the first time. She watched him read the letter, but his face seemed masklike; she could not tell if it pleased or displeased him. When he had come to the end she referred him to a passage in which the girl said that until Henrietta's letter came she had been fearful of the learned woman her darling had told her about. "So all you could tell your fiancée about me was that I am a learned woman? You know that is not true. You do not consider me learned; and you know I do not consider myself learned." "That depends on the point of view," he said, dodging her baiting, and asked her to go for a walk. With a tremendous effort she managed to say, "I cannot—I have struggled—I cannot control myself. . . ." He stared at her with wide-eyed surprise, his eyes quite void of understanding. And again like a hallelujah came the conviction: He is innocent! He is innocent! And for a moment, again, she thought that all was not irretrievably lost—they might yet achieve the friendship he sought with her. He left then; a moment later, when the spell of his presence was broken, she knew that a break was absolutely necessary to save herself.

The struggle to free herself began. On Saturday after synagogue she walked with Mamma toward Morningside Park. He and his niece overtook them. She paired off with the girl and left him to Mamma, but after a few blocks the mere sound of his voice became too much for her and she turned homeward.

Monday noon he telephoned about some manuscripts she had and then came for them. One was a still uncorrected copy; and when she pointed that out to him, he said in his usual manner, "Oh, you needn't bother about that." To which she replied, "I do not intend to," trying to tell him he need no longer expect her to work regularly for him. Then he said, "By the way, I won't come on Tuesdays any more. I have made a change in my afternoon lectures. They come later, and I can go home for dinner." And it seemed to her that he understood her at last; but she wondered why he did not talk the matter out with her instead of resorting to so patent a dodge; for she saw him that afternoon going to his lecture at the usual time.

On that evening, determined to talk it out at least with herself, she sat down at her desk and wrote at the top of one of her sheets of folded note paper the date Tuesday, November 17, 1908. And then in her small neat script she wrote: "Today it is four weeks since my only real happiness was killed. . . . Today for the first time I have been calm. . . . Today the thought comes to my mind that if I put all my memories down . . . so as to have them before me as an object, so to say, outside of myself . . . perhaps it will help me. . . ." She recalled how for eight years she had tried to prepare herself for the death of her father, yet when the catastrophe came she was neither prepared nor strong. So now, too, after four years, during which she had told herself many times what might happen, when the blow came, as inevitably as the other, again she was neither prepared nor strong. But while, when she lost her father, she had needed no justification for that act of God, now unless she could see herself and him, each of them, justified, she did not know how to go on living worthily. She must do something to wipe out what she now recognized as folly in the past and prevent it from becoming wickedness in the future.

She proceeded then to do a remarkable thing: She summoned up from her memory and wrote out on page after page her recollection of this relationship from its beginning when she met him at the Clara de Hirsch Home on Lincoln's birthday in 1903, recording the details of its progress and growth as evidenced in their activities and speech, in his behavior and hers, and in her feelings. And as she recalled and recorded these things, sometimes in the order of their occurrence and sometimes when they recurred to her by association, she would examine them, not for the purpose of judgment but for understanding, hoping that, in the process of expressing and comprehending it, perhaps she could rid herself of this painful affliction.

It was as if a surgeon, having discovered a malignant growth on his own body, set out to study its development, beginning with a case history, and then to examine its structure as he proceeded painfully to excise it, not all at once but bit by bit.

That first evening she covered the four sides of ten folded sheets, which brought her to the summer of 1907 when he went off for his vacation in Tannersville to attend the Zionist meeting, and there she stopped, when the anguish it caused her became unbearable.

At the end of that week, Bertha's husband, Louis Levin, came from Baltimore, and she confided in Louis and got from him a full measure of sympathy. Louis was sensible and understanding, and had been her good friend since the days of the Russian School. He spoke earnestly to her, and said all the things Adele had said about having nothing further to do with him; but it helped her only for a little while. Each new person she talked to restored her self-respect only temporarily; and it was her self-respect which suffered most. For it appeared to her that all tongues were wagging about them, near and far, in New York and Philadelphia and Baltimore, not ill-naturedly to be sure, but she was being talked about—Henrietta Szold, the daughter of her father, who would turn in his grave if he knew how his child had been spurned—and was now an object of pity.

Sister Bertha, having got the news from her husband, wrote: ". . . I feel really as if your trouble were mine. That *you* should have it! I wish I could tell you in some really clear way what you are in my eyes. Outwardly lovely, sweet, oh so much sweeter, I think, than anyone outside your family knows, gentle, generous, everything noble, lovely, lovable and womanly! I never in my own thoughts make half the fuss about your mental attainments the outsiders make. It is *all* of you! No one knows better than your sisters how you can pour out treasures and treasures of yourself into the laps of those you love, as you did us. . . . You are so much worthier than I, and I love you so! Your grief would not be a grief to me if I could solace it. . . ."

But no one could solace her. She must help herself. It took her ten days, until November 27, to resume the painful process of self-examination and analysis she had embarked upon. That was the eve of his thirty-fifth birthday, and she was reminded how happily she had gone all the way downtown the year before just to get him the cigars he liked, whereas now she could not even congratulate him. Then she recalled and recorded the memory of her solitary stay in Maine that summer, through the vain struggle against her passion, through the happy period of her certainty of his love, until his return with the devastating news of his engagement. She had covered seventeen more of the folded sheets when she stopped because of the agony of this recollection.

Since speaking to Mamma and Louis she felt she would have to go for help to someone outside the family, someone who did not love her as they did and hence would not accept her interpretation of his acts. She decided on his friend Dr. Marx, although it was hard to think of laying her heart bare even to so friendly an outsider. She put it off for a week, until the Marxes called on a Sunday and asked her to go walking with them the next day. By the time they set out for Morningside Park she was so distraught she could not speak and would have left them then had they not insisted she go on with them. Finally the dam in her gave way and she began to pour out her heart. . . .

Dr. Marx tried to comfort her but admitted that he had been

as shocked and puzzled as she; he had hoped there might be some reasonable explanation of his friend's behavior but could not imagine the nature of it; he had supposed until then that *she* had refused *him*. Two years ago he, Dr. Marx, had been expecting an announcement of their engagement and had even gone so far as to say to his friend before he left for Tannersville that he, Marx, expected to hear from him as soon as it happened. . . . Dr. Marx assured her that what the world had seen was enough to justify her expectations, even before she herself had nursed them. She talked again and again with the Marxes, going over the whole ground with them, begging them to give her, as *his* friends, their vision of him, and pleading with them to maintain their friendship for him. Sometimes they succeeded in restoring her self-respect; and they were fairer to him than others, although they could not see in him the ideal she saw. They utterly condemned his behavior, chiefly because he had given no accounting of it to his friends and to her. But they did not know him as she did: once he had set his face in a certain direction he never looked back. And this too, this unswerving strength, this conviction, she had loved in him.

At this time she was plagued about the still uncorrected proofs of a certain work she had done for him. She hated to think of leaving him to struggle through it alone without the help she could give him with all her detailed knowledge of it. She tore up two notes she wrote asking if he had received the proofs; but when he came up to her at synagogue early in December and hesitantly, as if fearful, bade her good Sabbath, she could not refrain from telling him to send her those proofs. He had not received them yet, he said, and looked relieved, but he would send them to her when they came. She further relented then and said she would send him some chapters of his legends book with a number of queries she needed to have answered.

Just then Mamma approached them, and he stepped toward her with his old assured manner of the man who is certain of a friendly reception; but, despite all Henrietta's pleadings, Mamma for the first time eyed him coldly, haughtily extending two fingers, with a look down her aristocratic nose as at something offensive. And he, with a wounded look, turned away and left them. That, Henrietta thought, ended everything between them—even the coolest of friendly feelings—and, in a sense, this was a solution; but to her it was dreadful, a calamitous ending.

He did not appear at synagogue the next Sabbath. For ten days she did nothing; did not even resume the task of catharsis she had begun, until she was pricked into it on December 15, when his niece, who was still typing for her, brought her word that he wanted the scrapbooks she had been making of his press clippings. No word of thanks for that long labor of love came with the request. After the girl had left with the books she sat down at her desk, resentful, and continued the history where she had left off over a fortnight before, from her first reaction to his announcement of the engagement, and covered eight more folded sheets.

At the end of that week, she continued with the observation that it was a year since they had gone together to Dr. Schechter's sixtieth birthday anniversary celebration at the Seminary. Now she could no longer attend such affairs for fear of having to face him before others and risk the loss of her self-control, as she had just that Sabbath, leaving the synagogue in the midst of the New Moon prayer with its reference to "shame and disgrace," to "joy and delight," and its plea to "fulfill the wishes of our hearts" which had reduced her to uncontrollable tears. She recalled then and recounted the reactions of others to her plight, and wrote how he had returned and resumed his visits and walks with her, acting exactly as he always had. Now it seemed to her that if his behavior was calculated, as Adele thought, then it was the most wonderful acting ever. Still she could not believe this was designedly done to deceive her into believing that before going abroad he had not loved her or known that she loved him—in short, that there had never been, for him, anything between them but an ordinary friendship. And now, her only answer to the question—What's to be done?—was this painful pursuit and discovery of the truth. So she went on writing what had happened until she came to where she had given his fiancée's letter to Mamma. And there she stopped, until December 21, on her forty-eighth birthday, when she resumed with the thought that in the two months since October 20 she had been so utterly and abjectly miserable that she could no longer distinguish degrees of misery.

Three days later she wrote that she could not finish this record because, instead of getting accustomed to the new order of her life, she was growing more and more puzzled and pained. Although she felt stronger physically, from day to day she seemed less strong spiritually. On this day she was overcome by the tragedy of it, that a friendship such as was theirs—aside from her love for him and his (and here she inserted a question mark)—for her—should be completely destroyed. And she was not too proud to put it in writing: that she still missed him every minute of the day and night, while he apparently went serenely on his way without thought of her. That very day she translated this sentence in his manuscript: "No matter how great one's grief is over the death of a dear one, at the end of a year one responds to consolation. But the disappearance of a living man leaves one inconsolable." And he, too, had departed alive from her life, leaving her inconsolable.

And now, having set down like a methodical physician the history of her case, what, she asked herself in writing, had she learned from this record of those events and her feelings, her happiness and bitterness, her joys and sorrows? Nothing new, it seemed—only that she had loved, and, alas, still loved passionately to the point of adoration; that he had been and remained, despite all that others might say of him, still her ideal; that she had lavished herself upon him with the reckless generosity of love, never counting the cost, never stopping to ask what the world was saying or thinking; that she had stripped herself bare of all reserve, and had been blissfully happy to do so; and wished that she could do it now and always.

She had given him her first love, and, coming so late in her life, it was a love chastened and strengthened by a rich experience of sorrow, a manifold experience of circumstance and action. She had not asked for marriage, for release from daily drudgery, she had asked only to serve him still more, asking in exchange only his companionship. And this strong, disinterested love of hers—what had it brought her? None of the "attentions" a girl expects—no flowers and candy, none of the gallantries and gifts other women take as trophies. Books he had brought her, mostly his own, his mother's *Teḥinnah,* and a couple of mementos from abroad—the Dutch inkwell and the Danish buckle. But the two things she treasured were the knotted veil he had tied for her on Riverside, and a small pasteboard box which had held the medicine he got her one Sabbath when he missed her at synagogue and hastened over to find she had not come because of a cold. How happy his concern had made her—his wide-eyed alarm!

But his supreme, cherished gift to her was his awakening of her womanhood. Out of her love for him had grown an awareness of the mystery of sex, of which she had been as ignorant as a girl of sixteen. She ransacked her memories—the bitter, the bittersweet, the wholly sweet—how he looked up references for her; took her watch to the jeweler's when it needed repairing; how he walked and talked with her, making her feel that he loved her, making her supremely happy, giving her everything—or nothing, now that she doubted the reality of that happiness which was either deception or self-deception. What remained real and ever present now was her tragic unhappiness, and her belief that he was quite unconscious of her feelings as she continued to work over his book, seven hours a day, six days a week, sobbing and grieving like that "poor thing," that forlorn woman crying aloud they had passed on the street last February, on their way to dinner at the Friedlaenders. She felt herself something to turn from with a shudder, a woman spurned, an *agunah*—a deserted wife, who can no longer be married to anyone.

Now she turned her consideration to the nature of *his* feeling for *her*. Had he loved her? She had to admit that she could not summon up much concrete evidence to support the belief that he had. Her signs and tokens, the things he did which made her happy, became questionable as the actions of a lover. She could not now say with certainty that he had loved her. Surely it could never have been anything like his love for the girl in Berlin, an immediate, spontaneous desire for marriage. With that girl he had not had to weigh, to calculate, to decide. At most, as Louis Levin had suggested, Henrietta had served to unlock his heart so that this girl could enter and take possession where she could not. And had he not the right to his preference and to act upon it? Thus she reasoned and wrote.

But if it was *not* love, what was that change in his way with her of about a year ago—when he spoke to her of himself and his concerns so unreservedly, looked at her so warmly, sought her out daily and openly? What did that mean if it was not the sign of love? When this change came he had been associating with her for three years, she was three years older than when they had met; and he had never been deceived about her age. And if not love, what did those daily visits mean, and those silent sessions together on Riverside?

No, she argued, it could not have been love; for if it was, he surely would have declared himself before he went off to Europe, he could not have left her in the misery he had seen when they parted at the post office. Or had he intended to decide when he returned whether to marry her or make her his life's companion—an intention abandoned when he saw that girl and his feeling for herself was obliterated. She could understand and accept that explanation. But what then had become of his sense of duty?—something strong in herself which she had thought he, too, must have or she could not have loved him. He had himself defined happiness in part as the "satisfaction of duty performed." Was it possible he had no sense of duty to her after all those years? Or was this new love so powerful that it erased all previous intentions and principles?—an effect she should very well understand in the light of what her love for him had done to some of her own intentions and convictions. In any case, she concluded, for her present understanding, the primary thing to determine now was not whether he had loved her and now loved someone else more, but whether he had known that she loved him. Was it possible that he had not? Until her talk with Dr. Marx she had thought it must be apparent to everyone in their world. But Dr. Marx had said that the general impression was that *he* was pursuing her, but that she was not giving him much encouragement. Was it not possible then that *he,* too, could have been misled by her behavior, her reticence?

There were many things she had done, it was true, of which he could not have been aware: that she was never without his letters in which she read, as in a prayer book, every day; and that she preserved every scrap of paper he ever addressed to her. Nor could she expect him to know that in the last three years she had arranged her life in every detail to meet his possible wishes. Nevertheless, could he not have perceived her constant compliance with his expressed wishes? He could not know that when he referred to the book of legends as "our" book, her heart almost jumped from her breast with joy; yet could he not read the light in *her* eyes?

But she found it difficult to pursue this primary consideration; it seemed to be leading nowhere—no answers came to her questions. But her mind and her pen kept straying back to that other question: Had he or had he not loved her? Did it not mean something that when they walked with others he deliberately left the others to walk by her side; why had he always gravitated to her? What did it mean when he was with her and Mamma at the shore, and a cool wind blew in from the sea, that he took her shawl from his pocket and insisted with a look that she put it on? Only with his eyes did he seem to be telling her his love, and she, being a woman, *had* to be more reticent than he. He could not know that when she was called to the telephone while he was in the apartment she would touch his hat on the rack as she passed it because she dared not touch his head. He did not know how avidly she collected the cases of happy marriages of men with older women, nor how many such cases he himself had contributed to her not inconsiderable list. He did not know how the spring sunshine, the budding trees, the colorful falling leaves of autumn, the rain, the stars, the new moon and full moon, the mute benches on Riverside Drive, the bricks and stones of every house on her street—how they all cried out his name to her. But was it possible for him not to perceive the intensity of her feeling for him, even if she kept him in ignorance of those acts and thoughts which would have made it plain? Her last letters alone must have revealed her adoration even if she never permitted herself an explicit avowal. And before that her eagerness to give him what he wanted, to serve his needs, must of itself have told him how she felt. When he admired a newly bound book on her desk, she said, "It is yours." And as she wrote, a host of such occasions came vividly to mind; and she was amazed that her memory, which she used to think was a poor one, had retained so many minute things. She realized now that what was inscribed not in the brain but on the heart was indelible, unforgettable.

For a number of years her brother-in-law, Joseph Jastrow, firmly established at the University of Wisconsin as one of the leaders in the burgeoning field of psychology, had been publishing papers and books on human behavior and the mysteries of the mind, among them a fat volume on *The Subconscious,* that dark storehouse, in which she now seemed to be delving. But nothing in all Joe's learned and witty works was a help to her. Nor, for all his information about human behavior, was she prompted to go to Joe for advice. Like Job she found neither help nor comfort in the conversation of her friends. Her salvation, she felt, lay in unburdening herself of her affliction while examining it, painful as was that process.

During the last two days of the year 1908 she resumed in writing the pursuit of the question of his knowledge of her great love for him. She had once heard him say that there is no love in modern times like that recorded by the ancients, and in his book on the legends he cited the love of barren Rachel who gave Jacob her handmaiden for a concubine, so that he might have sons. Now, though her own love for him seemed to be as great as any woman's possibly could be, it was true that she could not bear to see him find fulfillment with another woman; although it was not that which kept her from maintaining with him the friendly relation they had had, but the fear that the intensity of her love must drive her to wickedness if she did so. It was not love which had changed since ancient times but mores. What was noble of Rachel, who shared Jacob's love with another woman, would be evil for her, although her love, she believed, was the equal of Rachel's. And she could not believe he did not know how great that love was. It was surely plain in last summer's glowing letters to him if nowhere else.

She must assume now that he had never loved her in the least and, moreover, had had until her last letters no inkling of her love for him; that, first and last, it was for him a passionless friendship. But, if so, his behavior since his engagement and return remained inexplicable. Why in his last three letters had he referred to her as his "victim"? Why had he not upon his return, seeing her distress, sought to explain himself to her, and expressed at least his regret for her misapprehension of his feeling for her, and then asked for her continued friendship, instead of assuming it? That would not have been disloyal to his fiancée.

In the eyes of their world, he was being condemned for paying her "attentions" when he had no "intentions," for having "exploited" her, for being so "conceited" that although he was flattered by her feeling for him he thought she would suppress it and remain his useful "friend." All his behavior since his engagement was being interpreted as "calculated" to disarm her. But she refused these explanations—some of them undoubtedly prompted by academic jealousy—which were intended to console her and which were not, to her mind, consistent with the character, the ideal, she had known so intimately and loved. This ideal persisted, remained for her intact.

She continued to translate daily four thousand words of his book, while such thoughts kept plaguing her until she wrote them out. What had caused the marked change in his manner toward her a year ago? It was as if he had finally made up his mind that her devotion and the qualities of her mind and heart made up for her age; and this had broken down her reserve and encouraged her to reveal to him her innermost being after he went abroad. . . . True, she herself could be charged until then with a measure of hypocrisy —as when she had told him she was happy to help him with his works because it kept her in vital touch with Jewish thought, which was only part of the truth; the other, the major part, being that it kept her in touch with him. And finally, when she had suppressed her outraged feelings upon his announcement of his engagement and wished him happiness, was not that hypocrisy? But even that was, in part, the truth: she still wished him happiness and still wished she had had the strength to hide all her misery from him so as not to mar the happiness he had achieved. But she missed him every moment of every day of that beautiful fall. She dared not go out into the sunshine lest its brightness make her weep; she must wait until darkness had fallen on the wonderful world; while he, if he thought of her at all, must think her behavior was due only to wounded pride. She still wanted his good opinion, wished he could know how everything good was now sealed up in her—all the fine feelings and thoughts she could share only with him.

It occurred to her then that perhaps she would find the relief and peace she sought in a frank talk with him. But what could she hope to gain? The fundamental fact was that she had lost him; and he would remain lost to her no matter which of her doubts he clarified. The sole use she could make of such clarification would be to refute his detractors.

And what now was her loss? For ten years before they met, her life had been one of hard and unrewarding labor—Adele had once called it colorless. Then suddenly a light and a joy shone in upon it and she had come to look to the future buoyantly and gratefully, until the cup of happiness was dashed from her lips. . . .

So she wrote in the journal on the last evening of the year of her greatest happiness and her greatest sorrow, greater even than that sorrow she had thought the greatest six years ago, the death of her father—a sorrow so great she now felt that, although she might recover outwardly, her life was done. She would go on working hard because of the discipline she had learned; she would probably learn to eat and sleep normally again, to stop weeping, and to laugh again. Friends would cease remarking that something was wrong with her—it was nerves, she now told them, not a broken heart—but she would not be the same as before he came and roused her to womanly love, for which, for all its painful passion, she would remain everlastingly grateful to him. "God bless him and that other woman, and God help me!" she wrote, adding, "Dec. 31, 1908" on the forty-ninth of the folded sheets.

Not once in all those pages had she written his name. Like Jeremiah she might have cried, "I will not make mention of him, nor speak any more his name. But his word was in mine heart as a burning fire shut up in my bones, I weary myself to hold it in, but cannot. . . ."

On the fifth day of the new year 1909, a rainy Tuesday, recalling how many Tuesdays his coming to lunch had elated her, she began probing her wound, still unhealing and constantly painful. "It matters not whether the sun shines or the rain falls. It is he of whom I think and the thought is always pain. Pain, all these wonderfully fine days we have had, because in other days they would have meant walks on Riverside and happiness. Pain, a rainy day brings, because in other days he would have been at my side by my desk. . . ." She continued translating his book, and continued her probing, at once fearful that "If I write this way I am on the road to losing my ideal," and hopeful that "I will wake up one morning cured of my infatuation and my sorrow."

Two days later, after wakeful nights in which the physical pain of an abscess in the ear vied with the pain at her heart, she found herself becalmed. She could see his side clearly: he could not ignore her age and marry her; and to ask him to remain unmarried and her platonic companion was expecting the superhuman of flesh and blood. Yet she missed his companionship more than ever. "What shall I do to cure myself?" she wrote. And then asked herself why—two years before the debacle, when he was behaving in the masterful possessive way of the courting male—why had she not then got him to state his "intentions"—in one of the ways conventional women have of bringing such matters to a head. Her answer was, "It seems I am too much of a woman, a loving and trustful woman ever to be feminine"; and came to the conclusion that "Convention is historical, organized common sense, handed down for the safeguarding of those laboring under strong emotion."

Nevertheless, convention had not served Henrietta well in this instance. It had safeguarded her from the possibility of getting her heart's desire and she would have done far better to have heeded not convention but the ancient Hebraic tradition, so wisely pragmatic that it condones the transgression of convention in crucial cases—especially in the cases of well-meaning women when faced with the obstinate blindness of men. Time and time again this is exemplified in the Bible. Did not Rebekah resort to the deception of her blind husband Isaac in order to obtain the birthright, not for wild barbaric Esau but for gentle aspiring Jacob, who thus became the father of Israel? And did not Rachel, Jacob's wife, steal the gods of her father Laban in order to weaken him when he came angrily in pursuit of Jacob, and by deception concealed them from her father and thus saved the life of her beloved Jacob? The good ends justified the means of those women who had no other means. Perhaps had wise Mamma, like Naomi, counseled her daughter to ignore for once the decorous convention in which they had both been raised, instructed Henrietta as Naomi had instructed Ruth: ". . . anoint thee, and put thy raiment upon thee, and get thee down to the threshing floor; but make not thyself known unto the man, until he shall have done eating and drinking. . . ." Every year at *Shavuot,* the Feast of Weeks, she had heard the old story read in the synagogue, and yet . . .

The next day Henrietta recorded: "I have not shed a tear for twenty-four hours. Have I conquered myself?" and ascribed her continued calm to the absence of his book from her desk; she had got no copy from him for three days. Calmly, objectively, she proceeded with her probing, examining again his last three letters, which, in protesting too much, appeared now to indicate that until the end of August he had loved her and had known of her love for him, and had intended either to marry her or to maintain their platonic relation; and that then, under the influence of a more powerful emotion, he had determined to break off this relation and had written her those warning letters calling her his "victim." This realization, she wrote, "shatters my ideal. . . ." She seemed to be making some progress.

But the next day was Saturday. And "Saturday is the very worst day of the week now—because it was, with the exception of Tuesday, the happiest before. . . . All the calm of which I boasted a day or two ago vanished when the Sabbath approached and today I am as uncontrolled as ever." Perhaps also because she had got fresh copy for his book. So disturbed was she that she could not trust herself to go to the Seminary Synagogue, and decided to find another place of worship, for his sake as well as hers. She was swept now by alternate waves of resentment against him and sympathy for him, and with guilt for whatever embarrassment her lack of self-control might be causing him at what should be the happiest time of his life.

Her spirits were not raised by her attendance that evening at a feminist meeting where a "dramatic reading" presented "the life of a wronged woman" who found solace for her sadness in public work. Was it because she was not young; and because of having worked so long and so hard that she could not turn to work as a refuge? Joe Jastrow in his psychological writings talked of "sublimation": "Sublimation as a process in development, and sublimation as an instrument of mental hygiene, I accept completely." But could one will to sublimate?

There was no escape from her anguish; everything invoked it. Hearing someone say that even then, in mid-January, it was difficult to get transatlantic steamship reservations for June and July, made her think of him hastening to get a ship to take him abroad to his marriage, and filled her with bitter envy and hateful thoughts such as never before had arisen in her heart and mind.

Over a week later she was still wondering "why the shame, the humiliation and the pity of it" had overwhelmed her anew with all their original force. She was still hoping against hope that when she had finished translating this book of his she would recover. Mamma was suggesting that they move away; but actually she hadn't seen him for a month so that wouldn't make any difference; and it would mean depriving Mamma again, as well as herself, of their family of friends. If only she was filled with pride instead of love! If only she could forget! But she went on remembering. On January 20 she recorded "Today it is three months!" since his announcement. What had begun as therapy had turned to compulsive irritation.

That day she had a conversation she had been avoiding—with Dr. Schechter. He was gentle and sage. He advised her not to take flight, not to stay away from the Seminary Synagogue and not to leave the neighborhood, but to resume the friendly relations she had broken off. She must forget the suffering she had brought upon herself, because of her innocence of worldly matters, because she was too idealistic, because she had no knowledge of human nature. As though her love had anything to do with a knowledge of human nature! Dr. Schechter reminded her of *his* great scholarship—as if that were a mitigating circumstance. Finally, Dr. Schechter offered her the consolation that if any wrong had been done it was *he* not she who had done it. But it was not self-righteousness she wanted; it was *him*. And when Dr. Schechter urged her to finish his book and then undertake a work of her own, she could not refrain from asking whether intellectual pabulum could satisfy a heart hunger. She left Dr. Schechter thinking how happy she could have made *him,* and what a wonder he could have made of her life!

In Philadelphia that weekend she had to sit through a meeting of the Publication Committee in which was discussed the fact that the Society was in danger of devoting itself exclusively to *his* prolific works, a discussion which once would have filled her with pride instead of the pain she now suffered, shot through with irrepressible, disjointed memories—as of a talk they had one summer evening on Riverside sitting in the perfume-laden air and watching a yellow-lighted ferryboat glide across the darkening stream with unearthly beauty. "You know, I don't really know much about women," he had said; and now it occurred to her that perhaps he really did not know enough about women to have realized what he was doing to her.

Again and again, she had a sense of unreality about the whole thing; it was all too strange! Was it *she* to whom this was happening? Now even her spells of calm were unreal, unreliable, because the slightest association recalling a happier day would bring back the pain in full force. Returning from Philadelphia on the ferry brought back the last time he had ferried across with her and Mamma from a trip to Englewood. That night was clear, starry and perfect; and he had come around Mamma to stand beside her, his air of ownership unmistakable; and that was just six weeks before the fateful August 29. But, she wondered, was that, too, unreal—a phantasmagoria created by her love? Was the reality that, in his ignorance of women, he, the most clear-minded of men, innocently intrigued her to this painful pass? If so, her ideal must crumble; but now her probing revealed the plain fact that even the destruction, the death of her ideal would not mean the end of her love; it had discovered for her the truth of the ancient cliché: She loved him as he was—with all his faults.

On January 26 she resumed her self-probing with unemotional detachment: "I realize more and more the mediocrity of my character. My virtues are too small, my faults are too small, for full, deep-breathed living. The self-discipline that enabled me to control myself when the blow first fell counts against me; in another person it would have made for heroism, or at least serenity. In me, it merely prevented the outbreak that might have cleared the atmosphere; but it caused this lingering, paralyzing pain with its progressive deadening of all my energies, perceptions and interests. If I had cried out wildly when he told me the fact, when he said he had done the unexpected . . . the passion I would have displayed would have been irresponsible perhaps from a philosopher's point of view, but my moral and physical sanity and balance would not have been unhinged for so many months. It was either-or; and I did both. If I repressed myself at first, I should have kept my peace forever; if I had stormed and raged at once, the rupture would have been justified. I am a poor weak vessel, and my weakness is not amiable. If I could now only resign myself to my loveless fate, if every day did not bring me reminders of my unselfishness toward him . . . so that self-pity might cease!"

Having discovered the fact that the seemingly admirable self-control she had learned in childhood had become her undoing, and having frankly confessed her own shortcomings, she hoped for release from self-torment. But she had to work that day on the revision of his chapter on the legends of Joseph, that handsome, virtuous and brilliant young man, so avidly desired and pursued by Zuleika, his master's wife, who finally turned upon him in vengeful frustration. Instead of *his* standing beside her and discussing warmly with her each moot point in his manuscript, she had to erase his answers to the questions she had written upon it, and then make the suitable changes in lonesome drudgery! How could she hope for release from self-pity?

By the end of that day it seemed to her that even her probing had perversely turned into something else. She wrote: "I wish I could stop writing down my thoughts. It is no relief to me any more."

She felt like the psalmist who said:

> *Surely in vain have I cleansed my heart,*
> *And washed my hands in innocence.*

But three days later she began again: "I go back to this diary as if it were an opiate; but in reality nothing deadens my pain; and I have nothing new to write . . ." Yet a spate of pain-riddled recollections came, tinged now with suppressed resentment.

By the second of February she was so distressed by her inability to shake herself loose from the obsessive stream of hateful thought, that in desperation she decided to try talking with him after all. She wrote a short note, forthright but polite, asking him to come to see her on the following Thursday at eight. He promptly replied that he would do so, and came; and they talked for two hours and a half. The result was that she had her ideal back, and her pangs were redoubled.

It took her days to recall all they said to each other, but the net effect of his assertions was that he never had any feeling but friendship for her, and he never suspected that her feelings for him were anything else but friendly. When she reminded him of certain extravagant expressions she had addressed to him in her letters and conversation, he said he was aware that their friendship was extraordinary, and that so was her nature. All his acts which had been considered calculated by others he simply shrugged off; they were for him perfectly natural, friendly acts. He still considered her his best friend, and for his part he could resume their association just where they had left off. He was ready to admit now that he had done wrong in taking so much from her, in absorbing her, but it had never entered his mind that his behavior was open to misconstruction. Had *he* returned and found *her* engaged, he would have rejoiced if the man she chose had pleased him, and he would have expected the continuation of their association.

For her part, she spoke freely; told him frankly of all her feelings for him, and of her expressions of them. She recalled for him those actions of his which she had interpreted as expressions of his love for her. She told him what others had thought of their association—Mamma, Dr. Marx, and the rest. . . . He listened with interest but unperturbed as if panoplied, secure, in his rectitude and his happiness. Once he interrupted to say that if she cared to tell *all* the signs and tokens of her love he had no objection, but he questioned the need for that. For him her assertion that she loved him was enough; and she must believe that whatever he was, he was not a blackguard, who would willfully injure a woman privately and publicly. . . .

She asked what was she now to do? Should she resume their association knowing she still loved him? He answered that she must consider only herself, since she was the only sufferer.

He gave her plausible answers to all her questions. And to clinch the whole matter, he affirmed that as for the age question, it was ridiculous: it would not have entered his mind not to marry her on *that* account.

On leaving he said that he had the same feeling for her as ever. He was confident she was morally strong enough to "get over it." He did not fear to go on associating with her even with that painful feeling for him in her heart—he was sure of her.

But when he had gone she felt far from sure of herself: only that she must put the whole thing out of her mind and heart; must not talk about it any more, to anyone. And the best way to achieve that was to go on writing it out.

For days she recalled bit by bit her searching questions and his ready answers about specific things—like her tireless work for him, by which she had set such store as a mark of her love. To him it was but the sign of their extraordinary friendship. And he asked questions, too, in his own defense—like whether he seemed to her embarrassed by what he had done when he returned engaged. . . . His manner was not unkind, but neither was it comforting—not even with the tenderness of warm friendship; but that, she thought, might have been wisdom on his part, knowing that any tenderness then would only add to her misery.

Although no one else, Mamma, Adele, the Marxes, put any stock in his explanation, she did. She believed he had not loved her, and she *willed* to believe, despite all the testimony of her senses and good sense, that he had not known how she loved him. She told him, in that conversation, that he had saved her ideal and this she was determined to maintain. Now it only remained for her to find a *modus vivendi* without him; although, seeing him again early in February, at the funeral of a friend, all her pangs were renewed. And despite her decision not to talk about it any more she had to recount her conversation with him to those who loved her; and they assured her it was her good fortune that he had not married her. The talk did her good; it melted the ice round her heart; she slept well almost all of that night, and felt better the next morning than she had since the blow had fallen, and better able to comprehend *his* present difficult position and his attitude.

She saw him now as faultier and frailer than she once had, but she still loved him. She was going to try to believe that he had not realized the nature of her feeling for him; and now, at last, she would put him out of her heart, out of her thoughts, and out of her life, insofar as it was possible. "I shall set my face forward, and act naturally, as naturally as I can, and let circumstances do the rest . . . God help me to carry out this plan of action." And, having blotted that sentence with a thump to express finality, as a surgeon might mop up the last bit of blood, she thought she would not add anything for a long time.

But that afternoon, on the heels of one another, came crowding memories of what had seemed a tender attachment, contrasted with his cool detachment in their talk, when he explained his misunderstanding of her extraordinary behavior on the score that she was "an extraordinary woman." Now that argument seemed specious. "Does extraordinary mean to rise above human feeling?" she wrote. "It means to be intensely human, it means to raise ordinary feelings to an extraordinary plane. And in that respect I am extraordinary. My love for him was not an everyday affair. . . ."

Each day still yielded its collection of memories, flying back to be caught and held in the net of her mind, and then to be pinned down with her pen on paper, like dead butterflies, some bright, some somber. On a Tuesday, wanting to do something definitive on that once beloved day, she removed from her desk the Dutch inkwell he had brought her. But the removal of a physical reminder did not help cut him out of her memory. The days themselves were eloquent of him. On Wednesday, his day at home, it rained until late in the afternoon, when the sun came out; on such a day he would have found some excuse for going to look something up at the Seminary, would have come for her for a walk, stayed for supper, and the evening. . . . But all that was finished.

On the eve of the centennial of Lincoln's birthday Dr. Schechter gave a talk on Abraham Lincoln at the Seminary, and Henrietta attended it. It was almost forty-four years since little Henriettchen had listened to the sermon on Lincoln at Oheb Shalom Synagogue in Baltimore, her small heart filled with sorrow for the great man, and pride for Papa. Now she sat quivering with pain and shame in the presence of the man who had roused her to a love which had routed all thought of her father and his works from her mind. She heard Dr. Schechter quote from Lincoln's Inaugural: "We are not enemies but friends. We must not be enemies. Though passion may have strained, it must not break our bonds of affection. . . ." "Passion" was the word Lincoln had used for suffering—that man whose whole face had become a mask of sorrow, whose deep-set eyes were dark pools of pain. . . . "Oh, if there is a man out of hell that suffers more than I do, I pity him!" he had said after the defeat at Fredericksburg.

On Lincoln's Birthday, Henrietta wrote: "Today it is six years since I met him the first time; and since I have loved him. Yesterday something came to my knowledge that makes me believe, almost, that the tense of 'have loved' is not correct. I think the spell is broken. . . ."

She had found herself caught in a cross fire of ill will between him and an unfriendly colleague at the Seminary, whose wife spitefully reported to Henrietta a tactless remark he was said to have made the day after his talk with her, a remark which had been interpreted to mean he expected some reprisal from her for the hurt he had caused her. She wrote: "That ought to kill all feeling for him in me. If it does not, then love is an even more mysterious passion than I knew"; and, after reviewing the web of gossip in which she found herself tangled, she added, "I am completely bewildered by the revelation of human character this terrible experience has brought to me. . . ."

The experience was especially repugnant to her because in her childhood Papa had forbidden gossip for fear of transgression of the Commandment: "Thou shalt not bear false witness." Now she was torn by doubts of him and of herself. "I am left stripped of love and regard for an ideal—and from that I must try to recover. . . ." Then she reread what she had written that day, and added: "Am I dropping into self-righteousness? I speak of my doubt of all to whom I have spoken about this. . . . Am I blameless in the matter? . . . I search my heart, I cannot find untruth there . . . I want to steer clear of priggish self-righteousness . . . I hope that the consciousness I have of having acted truthfully and even nobly will restore my soul to tranquillity and enable me to behave with dignity henceforth."

But two days later this brave hope was disturbed by a talk with Dr. Schechter in which he advised her again to resume the normal routine of her life, including regular Sabbath attendance at the Seminary Synagogue, and he admonished her impressively that if she continued on her present way she would wreck two innocent lives —her own and that of the girl in Berlin.

Stung by the charge that *she* might cause the unhappiness of that other woman, her bedeviled heart broke loose and unburdened itself in writing of its long suppressed resentment of that "selfishness, self-sufficiency and arrogance" which had made it possible for him to ignore her love—a love that had asked for so little when it craved so much: "I have set down before that my mind rarely dwelt upon the thought of my marriage with him. I was happy as things were, and I was content to leave the future to him—content because I was happy and because I had unquestioning confidence in his rectitude and wisdom—subconscious confidence; I never said as much to myself. But occasionally the thought would come to my mind that he might want to marry me, and then I would pray God would put it into his heart to do so soon, that I might surely bear him children, and then my mind would wander further, and I would pray that if marriage came into his purpose so late that I could bear only once, God would let me bear a pair of twins—a boy and a girl—that nothing might mar the perfection of his human experiences. And how happy I would have been to be educator of his children! Such depths did he stir in me, and such depths must now settle back into dark quietude. Can they expect that to happen in a jiffy? It is true that I must consider him and the other one, but after all I am only a frail woman, I have never boasted of heroic qualities."

Nevertheless, the criticism of his colleagues, she wrote, "does not make me happy, does not even diminish my unhappiness. I would rather be wholly unhappy in my loss, and have the consciousness that the jewel I lost was exactly as precious as I always thought it. . . . My love for him dies so hard. . . ."

A few days of calm ended again in disturbance as a result of his failure to send her the further copy for his book which she had been waiting for. She was determined to finish her work on it and get it out of her hands by mid-July; but he had decided not to do the proofreading piecemeal as he had heretofore, but to wait until the volume had been completely printed. That, however, would extend her participation in the work for a longer time, which would be intolerable to her, and she had to write him that if he wished to proceed in that way he would have to get someone else to complete the work. He promptly sent her more copy but did not respond to her ultimatum about the time limit. However, he asked her permission to express his acknowledgment in the preface of the *Genizah* book of her "kind assistance without which this book would never have been published in English." It took her days and pages of painful heart searching to decide to say no to this—that "every memorial of that time of happiness turned to shame must be extirpated." Having dispatched her answer, she mourned that "I unlocked the store of his beautiful knowledge to the English-speaking world, and I myself had to bid him throw the key away."

She wrote of her decision to Mamma, who was in Baltimore at the time with Bertha, who was having her fourth child, a boy they named Jastrow. Mamma approved of this sign of her detachment from him; but when she considered asking for the removal of her name as translator from the title page of the first volume of his work on the legends, about to be published, sensible Mamma with the help of Louis Levin persuaded her to let her name stand.

On the following day, Henrietta got a proposal of marriage from a man she had known for some time, who spoke of his "lively admiration" for her, praised her abilities and her character. He thought she lacked only one thing, joy, and that he would give her. It amazed her with what *sang-froid,* even then, she received and rejected this proposal, just as she had the proposals of younger and happier days; although what he said was true—she lacked joy. She felt like a phantom; but there was only one man who could bring her to joyous life and he would have none of her; and the knowledge that she would be incapable now of giving any other man her wholehearted love made it impossible for her to consider such a proposal.

On the last Sabbath in February she ventured to go to the Seminary Synagogue. When he entered, her breathing became difficult, her head hammered. The preacher had chosen the Song of Songs as his text, interpreting it as the relation of Israel to God. Its bridal imagery tormented her until she wanted to cry out; but she held on to herself and grew calmer as the service ended. She determined to go again every week and force herself back into normal behavior. She must become again the person she had once been, self-controlled. "I am going to pull myself together," she wrote. "I am physically much stronger, in spite of the testimony of yesterday's breakdown at the synagogue. I can eat oranges again and peel them as I used to peel them for him day after day when he came here. . . . My hair has begun to wave again; all these months it was so lifeless that it hung down straight as an Indian's. Perhaps all these outward signs betoken a spiritual regeneration. If only he were not so hard toward me! . . ." He had not yet replied whether he would arrange it so she could finish the book by July; nor had he said anything about her refusal of his offer to acknowledge her assistance on the *Genizah* studies. "Possibly he thinks me as hard as I think him. Oh, how glad I would be to forgive, to be friends with him after a frank explanation. I need him! Does he think me ungenerous? . . . And that is the end of the matter—I do not understand him, I do not understand what happened, I do not understand the persistence of my love for him."

The week of *Purim,* that happy holiday in which a Jew is advised to drink wine to the point where he cannot distinguish between good Mordecai and evil Haman, hearing the *Megillah* read, the Book of Esther, was an unhappy reminder to her of their going downtown to hear it in an orthodox synagogue. She still had in her drawer of keepsakes, among her memorabilia of him, the penny *Megillah* he had bought her on that occasion; but she needed no reminder of how excited she was and how happy when they went afterward to eat poppy-seed cakes in that dingy little *kasher* restaurant, in an upstairs room. This year, after the reading in the Seminary Synagogue which she attended, he had left the altar and started up the aisle when he saw her coming along her row, and, realizing that they would meet, he turned back.

Sensible Mamma was insisting that she go abroad for a while, for rest from her labors and diversion from her troubles. So that weekend, when she went to Philadelphia to attend a Publication Committee meeting, she talked with Judge Sulzberger, President of the Board, about getting six months' leave, and about her decision to do no more work on *his* book after July, thus burning *that* bridge.

Spring was in the air, and she would wake mornings with an unknotted heart, telling herself that the spring would cure her, she would think of him now only as the man she had loved through no fault of hers and no fault of his. Then, one Sabbath in mid-March, they came face to face in the hall of the synagogue, nodded almost imperceptibly to each other and passed. He looked well and complacent. She went home and that evening wrote plainly that she must try to eliminate from her memory everything that was beautiful during the past five years of her life. "It is providential that time grows moss. If it would only grow over my keen memory."

A week later she was disturbed again by his cavalier treatment of her ultimatum about ending her work for him in July. Without referring to it, he wrote in a businesslike letter that he was going abroad in May and if he could not get his proofreading done by then it would have to wait until October.

It was almost mid-April before she returned to the journal to record the disintegration of her ideal which was taking place. When her father died, the loss of that ideal was an irreparable sorrow; but this seemed even more painful in that what was being destroyed was not a reality but her own illusion, her reliance on her own vision and feeling. She tried to find consolation in the conclusion that she must still be sane, since the insane are said not to suffer.

For Passover she went with Mamma to Baltimore where the family petted her, and Rachel came all the way from Wisconsin to help. The *seder* was not, of course, what it had been with Papa at the head of the table, but there were Bertha's four delightful children to revive the gaiety of a *seder* on Lombard Street.

Henrietta gave talks in Baltimore to the Federation of Charities and to the Council of Jewish Women, and she was extravagantly praised for her appearance and manner, her speaking voice, her language and ideas. Baltimore was proud of Miss Henrietta; and she let its adulation enter her tormented spirit like balm.

But the moment she stepped back into New York she knew it was self-deception; deep down she remained unchanged, she still craved satisfying reality, not childish consolation. She had sent him, with the corrected proof of the Joseph chapter, a request for the preface to that volume. In his reply on Saturday evening he indicated again that there would be a part of the work on this volume left until his return from abroad, which meant she would have to resume work on it after *her* return; and this prospect upset her so that Mamma, noticing her nervousness, got her to explain the cause, and then threatened to write him a letter demanding that he stop disturbing her. Determined little Mamma wrote out the letter and was only prevented from sending it, after something of a scene between them, by Henrietta's writing him plainly that it would destroy whatever benefit she might get from her vacation to have to resume working for him on her return.

She had got word from the Publication Society granting her six months' leave with pay and she and Mamma were planning the trip abroad, a trip to which she should be looking forward with delight, but which only reminded her of dreams she had had of going abroad with *him*. Now she was going abroad to be cured of him. It might calm her, dull her feeling; but she was incurable, she felt. "The wound may heal but the cicatrix will remain forever."

His reply to her letter was gentle and conciliatory. He would read the corrected proofs abroad if she would send them to his address in Amsterdam; but he ended by advising her to stop all work on his book now and leave it to someone else. "You certainly have no obligation on this matter to the Publication Society or to me." But although the work was torture, it was just as painful for her to contemplate giving it up to someone else.

She went out for a walk in the glorious April sunshine. A high wind was blowing, and the sight of a tree with greenish yellow blossoms brought back memories of a Friday afternoon in April just two years before—she figured it out—just eight days before he sailed. On just such a sunny, windy day when those same trees were in bloom, he had come for lunch; and after lunch she had to go to the milliner to order a new spring hat. Adele was going with her and Thomas would join them, and *he* asked to go along. They walked down Broadway to 81st Street and it was blowing so hard she had to comb her disheveled hair at the milliner's where she picked a straw hat to be trimmed with red roses. And the following Friday, while they were at work together, he asked had she got her new hat and would she wear it the next day when she went down to the steamer to see him off. "Is there anything," she wrote in the journal, "that does not bring back my loss to me?

Perhaps Europe with all its sights will remove him from my mind. And from my heart, too!" Anyway, by the time she returned he and his wife would be established in New York and the break would be complete and irretrievable.

Her brother-in-law Louis Levin brought little Harriet from Baltimore for a visit and they were out walking one day when he came toward them; to avoid meeting her face to face, he veered sharply and crossed the street. As he was to sail in a few days the thought that this might be her farewell vision of him made her unspeakably wretched.

There were still three months of thankless work on his books ahead of her. The literary press was making much of the fact that four of his books were being published that month—important contributions to Jewish literature in English, with no mention, however, of her contribution to that achievement.

Mamma and she were considering the possibility of going as far as Palestine on their trip abroad, despite the warning of some people that a visit to the Holy Land was a sure cure for Zionism. Mr. Schiff had come back from a trip to Jaffa and Jerusalem with a declaration that he would rather give $500,000 to get the Jews out of Palestine than one cent to add one more Jew to its present population. Henrietta, undeterred, talked with a Palestinian Jewess she met, who was conducting industrial training classes there, and who spoke of other women living full and interesting lives in the Jewish colonies. Listening to her made the meetings of American Zionist women seem pathetically unrealistic and ineffectual. The woman herself was happily married and she spoke of her hard-working husband in a way that roused Henrietta's envy. But she told of a young woman named Manya Wilbushewitz, a magnificent creature, a veritable Amazon in physique and with a forceful mind, who had "thrown herself away" by marrying a man named Schochat, a common laborer in one of the colonies, a man suffering from tuberculosis, ten years younger than herself, to whom she was devoted and submissive. No one in Palestine could understand this in Manya Schochat, whose doings there were becoming fabulous. "But," Henrietta wrote after this talk, "*I* can understand. . . . The world does not understand her and my kind—*he* certainly did not understand my kind."

Then, for the third time since her removal to New York, she

had to refuse a proposal of marriage. All three were widowers, upright but helpless men, who saw in her an admirable helpmate; and it was with wry wonder that she considered the fact that the one man who had attracted her with a thousand charms, and whose proposal would have made her unutterably happy, should now be so far removed from her in body and spirit. Nevertheless, she still could not repress fantasies of how they might be spending these fine May days together, although she knew by now that, for her, having to give him up meant having to give up marriage.

On May 10 she wrote: "Other women have suffered as I am suffering, and so far as I know they have not suffered so obviously—the world has not known so much about it, and they have not obtruded their suffering upon the cause of it as I have. Why? Am I more self-indulgent than others? I have not been so the rest of the years of my life."

He sailed on the twelfth of May. All of the day before, her mind was filled with memories of their farewells of other years. This time she had not even learned the name of his steamer, as if to prevent the possibility of being drawn to the dock. And when she knew he had sailed, a remarkable quiet descended upon her, a feeling that the irrevocable had come. "God bless him!" she wrote on that day.

And when others, after he left, impugned his motives in this marriage, while offering her consolation, she examined their statements, too, in the light of her own information and wrote: "No, he loves this particular young, beautiful, domestic, pretty, sprightly Berlin girl," although in moments of intense suffering she had herself been goaded to derogatory thoughts about the girl. Unhappy, however, she remained. "But I am strangely quiet—with the quiet of a churchyard inside of myself."

It was two weeks before she felt impelled to write in the journal again—on a June evening after her friend Elvira Solis had taken her for a drive in her auto and turned along Riverside. It was the evening when the lights in Palisades Park were first turned on for the summer season, and the lights of the Ferris wheel and the carrousel circled above the shimmering streamers of light in the river, where a lighted ferryboat glided across them. "Get over it?" she wrote. "Yes, I will—as a man lives on with a wound from which the missile . . . has never been removed; . . . and everything that happens . . . gives it a painful wrench. The air that comes in through the window now, soft as June can make it, yet has power enough to twist it until the pain makes me cry out aloud."

On June 3 she heard and recorded that his marriage had taken place on May 23 in London. But it was not until July 21, a year after the last time she had sadly but hopefully seen him off to Europe, that she was able to set down the talks she had had with her friends Mrs. Friedlaender and Mrs. Schechter a month before. They were serious talks in which the last vestiges of her ideal unworldly vision had finally been destroyed, and she took what consolation she could from their assurance that his association with her had been a saving grace for him. "He had become true to his better self," she wrote, "and not merely through me, but through that same better self! I have no right to condemn him . . . I must say *le tovah*—it is for the best. . . ."

The Board of the Jewish Publication Society had sent her a gift of $500 for use on her trip abroad, which made it possible to go as far as Palestine, and she was to sail with Mamma for Europe in ten days.

"Perhaps after all," she wrote, "I will recover my balance there. . . . I must forget him. . . ."

Then, recalling the letter of renunciation she had written just four years before, in reply to an imaginary letter of his, "Why did I ever recede from the position I took then?" she wondered. "Why did I ever forget my age? Oh, I am not all wrong—he made me forget it. . . . And now I sit here like the woman of that poem. . . ."

She had received a letter from her cousin Miriam, the daughter of Eduard Schaar, the uncle who had held her up to watch Lincoln's funeral in Baltimore, so long ago. Miriam wrote of her engagement to Dr. Schloessinger; and Henrietta had also heard of the marriage of Dr. Benderly, another old Baltimore friend.

"Happiness for all except me!" she wrote on the hundred and ninth folded page of note paper, and there stopped writing.

She added this to the pile of pages which had been gathering in the drawer of keepsakes, together with the pillbox he had brought her when she was ill, the veil he tied for her on Riverside

Drive that windy day, and the letter of renunciation. She shut the drawer.

On July 30, 1909, Henrietta and Mamma sailed on the SS *California* of the Anchor Line, leaving Adele and Thomas Seltzer to occupy the flat in their absence. As the sailing hour was nine o'clock on Saturday morning the two observant Jewesses had to go on board before nightfall on Friday, the eve of the Sabbath, and they celebrated that occasion in their stateroom by lighting candles in those two brass candlesticks which Mamma had got from her mother in Hungary, and which they had taken with them for use wherever the Sabbath would find them in the course of their travels. They had also to face the problem of adhering to the dietary laws, which meant that they must choose from the ship's menu only such dishes as were not prepared with forbidden non-*kasher* foods; but as the ship's menus were gargantuanly generous they found that no great hardship.

Indeed, from the moment she saw the water widening between the ship and the teeming shore, burdened with her sorrow, it was for Henrietta as if she were leaving all trouble behind. They glided past the Statue of Liberty and out to sea in beautiful weather, cool and refreshing after the oppressive heat of the city. A pleasant lethargy overcame Henrietta; she rested and ate and slept until the second day out, when passengers began greeting each other, and the sound of carefree laughter, of tramping feet, and sliding shuffleboards came from the sunny deck, punctuated every half-hour by the cheery clang of the ship's bell.

The ship sailed steadily over the glossy sea that turned deep blue, with tiny whitecaps furling from it. On the third day, from the steerage came gay Scottish music (the ship was bound for Glasgow), kilted dancers appeared on the lower deck, and the burr of their speech was a pleasant foretaste of foreign delights.

Henrietta, in her deck chair, divided the time between reading up on European history and Italian art, and some work she had brought with her; she was reading proof of a book on Philo, the first-century Jewish philosopher, by Norman Bentwich, the brother of Lilian Friedlaender who, with her husband, was visiting her family in England that summer. Henrietta looked forward to seeing the Friedlaenders there. But in her diary that day she wrote: "The vast unity of the sea has not yet brought serenity."

On Wednesday, August 4, there were all sorts of diverting sights —a spouting whale and a school of incredibly graceful, playing porpoises; small fishing smacks manned by hardy men risking for a bare livelihood the dangers of the vast and ruthless sea. A thick white fog suddenly closed in on the mournfully hooting ship for a few hours, and as suddenly vanished; an iceberg passed in glittering isolation. She still caught herself following uncontrollable flights of unhappy thought running in grooves worn smooth during the last nine months of their travel back and forth, back and forth. After reading *The Queen's Quair* by Maurice Hewlett she wrote in her diary: "Poor Mary Queen of Scots! So being a queen does not save one from the pangs I suffered, and she was young and beautiful! How is it that I never saw those things in literature before? I have wronged myself impossibly by my hard work. I estranged myself from men and from their writings; I had no time for either. I knew men only when they needed me, and books only when I was forced to need them. A one-sided attitude toward the whole world only because I gave myself no time for men, not because there was not more in me. I believe now that there was more in me than ever was brought out. I suppressed myself, and circumstances helped me to do it thoroughly."

With the help of gay, spry, gregarious little Mamma, who was already well acquainted on board, Henrietta was "dragged" from her deck chair into games of shuffleboard and quoits and *"mirabile dictu,* did not win the booby prize!" In her avoidance of games, too, she had been remiss. "And yet, am I a failure?" she wrote. "I must reply to fifty letters. . . . Would all those people have written me so lovingly if I were a total failure?"

Mamma told her that people, seeing her writing away industriously for hours, were wondering who she was. Someone had guessed she was Emma Goldman, the notorious anarchist, traveling incognito!

How wise was little Mamma who had made her do this. And yet, on the second Sabbath on board, a week after their departure, as the ship sailed through a thick blanket of fog, plaintively blowing its hoarse foghorn, in the midst of planning their trip through

Scotland and England, Henrietta heard *his* voice calmly saying, again and again, "You will get over this!" and that night "dreamed the whole wretched business over and over again, first one aspect and then another."

The passage being smooth, they made a record run, and Henrietta found herself thinking with reluctance of leaving the ship. The comfort and ease of its planless, effortless, uninvolved life had been a great relief.

Although it was evening when they arrived in Glasgow, it was still light enough to go sight-seeing in and around the city, and Mamma picked a bouquet of wild flowers which excited her more than the sights. Mamma was really quite remarkable for a woman in her seventieth year, and Henrietta recorded that "Mamma has been in a volcanic state ever since we left. She is indefatigable; but she insists upon first-class accommodations, and scolds madly any attendant that does not mistake her for a Vanderbilt."

On August 10, stopping in the town of Oban en route to Edinburgh, they celebrated Mamma's fiftieth wedding anniversary and remembered dear Papa. They delighted in the indescribable beauty of the Scotch countryside on the way to Edinburgh, a handsome city with history in every stone, where Henrietta insisted she could spend a month instead of the allotted day and a half. And yet, in the midst of the exciting kaleidoscope of strange streets teeming with people bent on business in the day and pleasure-bound at night, of castles and cathedrals, of museums full of paintings and sculpture, she wrote, "I missed *him* sorely . . . I still feel bottled and corked. I cannot speak out to anyone as I did to him—nor could he to anyone as to me; that I will believe to my dying day. . . ."

At York and Lincoln Henrietta was impressed by the magnificent cathedrals—the creation of a host of insignificant, forgotten individuals—as by any great work of nature. She felt that even an ordinary human being could not remain unchanged by the vision of the painstaking work of a thousand years of carving in wood and stone, of glorious stained glass. But in the castle keep at York, she and Mamma heard the guide recount how on the Sabbath before Passover in 1190 the Jews of York were besieged by a bloodthirsty mob and killed, one after another, when they would not surrender. The guide put the blame on the usurious Jews. And in the

Lincoln Jewtown they heard recounted the Ritual Murder case of Hugh of Lincoln in 1255 and the banishment of Jews from all their Jewtowns in England in 1290. In York the proscription had held until 1892! And the Oxford Dictionary, to that day, stubbornly and ridiculously defined "Jew, n. Person of Hebrew race; extortionate usurer; trader who drives hard bargains." "Why do they hate us so?" Henrietta still wondered.

They moved on to Cambridge where she was charmed by the constant chiming of bells from the university towers and the bicycles of students and faculty dashing about with their colorful robes flying behind them. It was sometimes observable that dignified academic attire covered the grubbiness of a not-too-fastidious scholar. They saw the house where Dr. Schechter had lived, before moving on to London.

London, vast and crowded, noisy and bewildering even in off-season August, made New York fade in comparison. They stayed at Miss Dobson's boardinghouse in Bedford Street, which would take the pen of a Dickens to describe, and in the round-robin letters she wrote to Rachel and Bertha and Adele she invited their malicious pleasure in imagining their finical old-maid sister eating at a noisy common dining table, reluctantly getting into a double bed of dubious cleanliness; and harassed by the care and transportation of their overabundant luggage. Miss Dobson herself, a sweet, slight woman, intelligent and pretty, set Henrietta wondering about her history—"Anything like mine?"

A letter from Mrs. Bentwich inviting them for the weekend in Carmelcourt, the Bentwich home at Birchington-on-the-Sea, proved a godsend. The weekend was well-nigh perfect, physically and spiritually. It was a spacious house set in beautiful gardens, and inhabited by a large family of talented and energetic individuals, very British and very Jewish, who welcomed Mamma and Henrietta warmly and entertained them royally. Their good friends the Friedlaenders being there too made them feel immediately at home. Norman Bentwich, the eldest son, to whom Henrietta delivered the corrected proof of his *Philo* book, was preparing to sail for New York, where he would visit Dr. Schechter, with whom he had studied at Cambridge; and he promised to call upon Adele and Thomas.

The Sabbath supper alone, on the Friday evening of their arrival, was a welcome delight which Henrietta and Mamma enjoyed unashamedly after their limited travelers' diet.

On the Sabbath morning, family services were held in the large library which contained an ark with a Torah scroll from which each of the children, down to seven-year-old Joseph, read a part of the portion for that day. After dinner, Henrietta talked with the Friedlaenders. They had attended *his* wedding in London and the talk naturally turned to the bride. She was described as a very attractive girl, who, young as she was, had been sensible enough to question whether so learned a man would want her for a wife. Henrietta, in her diary that night, wondered why she, so much older and presumably wiser, had not been as well prepared to question from the outset the intention of a man who sought her company. And she was prompted by Dr. Friedlaender's criticism of his hasty engagement to wonder if it was done to escape herself; but if that were so he could not have been unaware of her feeling for him. And there she pulled herself up short: "I refuse to go through the mazes of my old reasoning. . . . It was a misfortune and I am a victim." He and his bride were by this time on their way to New York.

In the guest room occupied by Mamma and Henrietta, she observed, inscribed with a diamond upon a window pane, the verse:

I slept and dreamt that life was beauty;
I woke and found that life was duty.

She learned it was done by an earlier suitor of lovely Lilian Friedlaender, whom she had had to reject because of his illness with tuberculosis; and Henrietta's sympathy went out to that unknown heartbroken man, who had also suffered rejection.

But the weekend was spent pleasurably, walking along the chalk cliffs by the sea, where they were told Dr. Schechter loved to stroll, driving out in the countryside, playing billiards with the family, meeting their interesting friends. Herbert Bentwich, the father, was a leader of *Ḥovevei Zion,* and there was much talk of Zionism and of the settlement in Palestine.

On Monday Henrietta and Mamma returned to London accompanied by Norman Bentwich on his way to America, and another guest, Dr. Hochman, who guided Henrietta about London, while Mamma treated a very severe cold. Westminster Abbey impressed Henrietta as much as it had twenty-eight years before when she went there with Papa: mobs of tourists, Baedeker in hand; the great building lost sight of in its crowd of tombs. After Carmelcourt, Miss Dobson's seemed very dingy, and the damp air of London was bad for Mamma; but despite constant rain, Henrietta visited the British Museum, a place she returned to whenever she had a minute. It made her tingle with the feeling that she was in her intellectual home. In England, her Anglo-Saxon education asserted itself so that she felt that even though the blood was not involved, the brain was also an element in spiritual relationship.

She visited Whitechapel, the Jewish settlement houses, the art galleries full of Rembrandts and Van Dycks, the Tate with its wealth of Landseers, Turners, Burne-Joneses, from which Henrietta came away with an increased regard for British painting. Still, at the end of the week, in the midst of the catalogue in her diary of painters and paintings she had been seeing, came the thought that this Sabbath was the anniversary of his meeting with the girl with whom at once he had fallen in love.

Proofs of his legends book, which then came for her correction, made her nervous and unhappy and convinced her she must end all work for him on her return, for, "I cannot stand the sight of his handwriting."

The next week on a trip to Oxford, "a perfect gem," in the Bodleian Library she met Mr. Cowley, to whom she had written so many letters in connection with *his* works.

Early in September they left London and crossed the Channel to Dieppe where her cousin Ignatz Schaar met them and took them to his home at St. Aubin-sur-Mer. Ignatz now had a charming wife and lovely children, and Henrietta envied their happy family life; but they were all assimilated to the point of apparently total unconsciousness of their being Jews, in contrast to the Bentwiches. Their Friday evening supper, with no reference to the Sabbath, seemed strange. Had they forgotten the Dreyfus case, too? They were Jews in name only; but that was enough for the anti-Semitic, even in America. The opening chapter of Edith Wharton's latest novel *The House of Mirth,* about high society in New York, introduced a character named Solomon Rosedal, "with that mixture of artistic sensibility and business astuteness which characterizes his race," and on the very next page another character "declared that he was the same little Jew who had been served up and rejected at the social board a dozen times within her memory." To the anti-Semite it didn't matter how little your Jewishness meant to you.

It was very pleasant at St. Aubin-sur-Mer. Henrietta lounged and walked by the ocean, and wrote her Jewish New Year letters, but none to *him,* recalling the heartfelt wishes she had sent last year just before going to the *Rosh Hashanah* services. Cousin Ignatz drove her to Rouen through the beautiful countryside with avenues of trees leading up to the chateaux on the hills. The cathedral with its exquisite glass was entrancing. On the train to Paris she wrote: "Finished legend proofs. Now only the page proof of a half chapter and I have done with him forever. How I suffered at St. Aubin thinking of him; as I did at Birchington! I need the distraction of a city. To think that I who was so self-sufficient in all crises, should arrive at the point of needing distraction. . . ."

They spent just the daylight hours of one day in Paris between their morning arrival and the night train to Vienna, but Mamma was herself again so they "did" the Louvre and the Tuileries, the Place de la Concorde, the Champs Élysées, and the Bois de Boulogne. Henrietta marveled how everything came back to her from that equally fleeting visit with Papa twenty-eight years ago. She and Mamma had a fine dinner in the Jewish quarter and stocked up with *kasher* food for the long train trip to Vienna.

But because of a connection missed at Munich they had to stop over there for nine hours. It was a holiday; the museums were closed, and they had only a little German currency. They went to a restaurant for lunch and then could not eat the poached eggs they ordered because it was served with non-*kasher* meat. A cab driver asked Henrietta if the United States was so thinly populated because there were so many spinsters in America, about which Europeans apparently had very curious ideas.

In Vienna they were met by an uncle and three aunts and royally received by a gathering host of other relatives, Szolds and Schaars, who took charge of them and made of the month they spent there a continuous round of entertainment and excursions. Here Henrietta felt the relationship of blood rather than brain, and it was interesting for her to observe features and traits in these men and women which were familiar to her because they had remained unchanged in her own small family in America. Mamma was carried off to tailors and dressmakers to get new clothes. They were taken sight-seeing all over the gay and beautiful city, from its galleries full of Rubens, Rembrandt, Van Dyck, Dürer, and Holbein to a risqué cabaret. There were lively family gatherings around sumptuous tables, with animated talk about Jews, Judaism, Zionism. They went to a fine synagogue for the *Rosh Hashanah* services with seraphic singing by the cantor and stirring blowing of the *shofar*—the ancient ram's horn—by a venerable Jew. It made Henrietta think that the charm of Papa's services at Oheb Shalom Synagogue in Baltimore was derived from Vienna. But she had no heart either to review the past year or to hope and pray for the coming year. "I dream of him and her, and see her go to the synagogue in the holidays in my place. . . ."

They were taken to Presburg to visit Schaar relatives—among them Tante Kathe, "the most beautiful old woman (she is over ninety) I have ever seen, Madonna-like and humorous at the same time." The women of Mamma's family were wonderful—wise, and gay, and indestructible.

They proceeded to Cziffer, Mamma's birthplace, full of her relatives and her memories, which were remarkably clear though it was fifty years since she had left for America with Papa. But Mamma was frankly indignant over the neglected condition of the family cemetery. She could not bear disorder; and in this Henrietta was very like her. This was a womanly passion—the making of order out of the disorder made by men and children, who were by nature quarrelsome, careless, and too preoccupied with their romantic aspirations to be orderly.

Then they went to Papa's country—to Nemiskert, his birthplace, where they were welcomed by many Szolds, at generous Hungarian meals. On the way back to Vienna, they stopped again at Presburg, where Henrietta rode up to the Schlossberg, remembering how she had gone there with Papa, and how she had found consolation for the indignities suffered by Jews in other times in the ruins of the might of their oppressors. But it had since become apparent to her that they were still hated; her question "Why do they hate us so?" had remained unanswered. Papa's sometime reliance, under the influence of Moses Mendelssohn, on Western enlightenment and democracy to dissolve that hatred now seemed utterly romantic.

Indeed it was becoming apparent to her that men, not women, were the romantics—men who with their fertile imaginations artfully create expressions of their willful spirits which become for them the realities. While women, the pragmatists, tried to make order out of their neglected, disorderly, real world. Papa had been wise in letting Mamma, with her passion for order, confine herself to the work of making it possible for him to pursue undistracted the creative work of his fertile mind; and perhaps he had not been so wise, perhaps he had erred, in making of his "Henriettchen" his collaborator. Perhaps there was a certain wisdom in that old orthodox Jewish prejudice—as there often is a certain wisdom in folklore, and even in superstitions—against women being learned in Torah. For men, when they married, did not seek collaborators in the creative work of their minds. Papa had not; and neither had *he*. Yet, as a result of Mamma's tutelage, she was as well versed in the pragmatic work of women, and was as passionately desirous of living a woman's life as any woman. At Presburg in 1909 she might well have wondered if Papa, inadvertently, had diverted her from that destiny with his scholarship; and she might have considered the irony of the fact that *he,* who had with *his* scholarship inadvertently brought her back to that road, would not accompany her upon it. Whatever else he had done to her, however, he had helped her to a pragmatic, unidealistic vision of men. But were *all* men blind, even the admirable ones, like the patriarch Isaac whom the woman Rebekah had to coerce into bringing about the desirable destiny? At Presburg this time Henrietta began to feel herself less her father's daughter than her mother's.

They returned to Vienna in time for *Yom Kippur.* At the synagogue, in one of the intermissions in the long day of solemn, incessant prayer, she was introduced to a woman who was related to Rabbi Hertz with whom Henrietta had corresponded when he was in South Africa. She told Henrietta of his sudden marriage

—not to the girl he had been courting for some time; and she said that the disappointed girl had found solace in another marriage. Henrietta spent much of the day not in penitence but in remembering how happy she had been on *Yom Kippur* the year before, thinking of *him,* when he was already involved with the girl in Berlin. Salvation for her would come not in marriage, she thought, nor from a mere trip abroad. . . .

She attended some meetings of the leaders of the Jewish community of Vienna to get an insight into their consideration and handling of modern Jewish problems, but she was ignored by them. Being a woman, and bearing no letters of introduction from American Jewish leaders, she was at a disadvantage. She wished her prominent friends in New York and Philadelphia had given her suitable credentials, as they undoubtedly would have, had she been a man.

Henrietta and Mamma left Vienna in October, escorted to the station by numerous relatives, and were welcomed in Budapest the next day by more relatives, who gave them a full day of sightseeing there. Two days later they were off for Constantinople.

Slowly the rugged country changed in appearance from Europe to the Orient. The atmosphere of the train itself changed. It filled up with Bulgarians and Armenians. It became untidy and uncomfortable. Their passports were examined at the Turkish frontier late at night in a frightful babble of incomprehensible languages where only baksheesh brought assistance. They arrived at their hotel in Constantinople in a depressing rain, through foul streets of dirty hovels, swarming with starving dogs, overloaded donkeys and ragged humanity. Even their hotel was unclean and they had to use insect powder. Outside the hotel a crowd of filthy beggars lay in wait to plague them like flies.

In these circumstances they were happy to make even a brief contact with their friends, Professor and Mrs. Richard Gottheil—he was on a sabbatical leave from Columbia University—who were on the way to Beirut, where it was arranged they would meet again.

They spent most of their time in the Jewish quarter. They went to several synagogues, and met a number of Jews who took them to visit the Jewish school and to see the city. It interested them as a congeries of Near Eastern nationalities among which, the Zionists there thought, the Jews would ultimately also be recognized as a national group. In the Sephardic Jewish quarter they saw poverty —filthy, miserable, squalid beyond description—which aroused Mamma's vociferous indignation. The Ashkenazi Jewish quarter of Galata was not as squalid, but it was corrupted. There was a community of brothel keepers, for whom the rabbis had procured from the government the privilege of having a synagogue of their own because no other synagogue would admit them. Henrietta observed the painted women sitting and smoking, and wondered that respectable men could be driven to such a recourse. On the Bosporus boat she sat for a while with veiled Turkish women and wished she could speak to them, to learn of their strange secretive lives.

She saw the more romantic aspects of the city of the Golden Horn on the Bosporus: its minarets, domes, towers and obelisks; vast St. Sophia with pigeons flying about inside it; pastel-colored houses clinging to the sides of the seven hills; the deep-blue waters of the harbor covered with great ships, with tiny caïques plying among them; the two-horned carriages making their way through the narrow streets swarming with laden donkeys and yellow dogs and carts pulled by buffalo; and multitudes of red-fezzed men, half-naked and unbelievably filthy. For a half hour on the Galata Bridge Henrietta watched the swarm of eunuchs, dervishes, priests and lepers. Armenians, Bulgarians, Greeks, Turks, Europeans of all nations, Negroes from Africa, all passing each other apparently in a pleasant tolerance of each other's habit, language and belief. Was it possible that these crude people had that *Menschenliebe* Papa had taught her? She tried vainly to describe it in a letter to her friend Judah Magnes in New York and ended with "now for the Palestine Lesson."

Through Dr. Magnes she had met in Constantinople Dr. Jacobson of the Anglo-Levantine Bank who knew and told her much about the Jewish colonies in Palestine and gave her letters of introduction to several colonists. He introduced her to other working Zionists, who took her to schools supported by the French *Alliance Israélite* and the German *Hilfsverein,* where future colonists were being prepared. The land of Israel was becoming something more than an ancient dream for Henrietta.

On October 29, the anniversary of the day *he* had come to her with that devastating news, she was on board the SS *Ismaila* bound for Beirut. In a newspaper sent her from home she read of the opening of the Seminary and, among the news of the faculty, that he had taken up residence with his bride on 143rd Street. In her diary she wrote: "A year has passed and I am on the Aegean, but neither change of time nor place makes a difference to my feelings . . . and my sorrow for him and for myself—for him that he proved unworthy of my ideal of him; for myself that I must go through life without his companionship." They sailed the bluest of blue seas, by mythological, mountainous shores and islands. They anchored off Mytilene's magnificent citadel while the caïques clustered about the ship taking passengers ashore. At the gleaming white crescent port of Smyrna they went ashore and saw again the squalid life of those picturesque Levantine places.

They stopped at Piraeus and went with a Cook's tour up to Athens, a refreshing contrast to Turkish cities. The glories of the Acropolis, the view from the Parthenon, brought visions of Socrates and St. Paul. The thoughts of *him* that intruded plagued her in the serene days they sailed across the Mediterranean to Alexandria, where there was a great to-do of going ashore in a rough sea. You had to jump from the ship's ladder to the arms of a dragoman in a bobbing boat. At Port Said they did not go ashore, it was so rough.

By then it irritated her that she could not banish him from her dreams, in which she forbade him to continue speaking to her as if nothing had changed; and he would look at her with that innocence in his eyes which said, "Nothing has happened between us." In an effort to exorcise him, she set down these dreams in her diary, along with the interesting conversations she had with a Greek priest she met on board.

The ship sailed north along the coast of Palestine, and they could see the southern desert and then the semitropical coastal strip of what had once been the land of the Philistines, with clusters of Arab houses like white sugar cubes piled on the hillsides. They anchored off Jaffa, a picturesque crowded town over thirty-five centuries old, with minarets and palm trees, and camels ambling through it. It was the city from which Jonah had set out to sea on his famous voyage; but they did not go ashore there, having decided to enter Palestine from the north and work their way down through the Holy Land. Henrietta wanted to see the country and the common people on the land with her own eyes before having her vision colored, as was Mr. Schiff's and other tourists', by the life in the cities, and by the opinions of the urban intellectuals she would surely meet in Jerusalem.

There were some Arab pilgrims on board, with children among them, whose remarkably dirty faces stirred Mamma to action: she bribed them with cookies and colorful pictures cut from magazines, so they would let their mothers wash their faces with the Castile soap she supplied them.

They landed in Beirut in a heavy rain and windstorm, and found they had missed by twenty-four hours the Gottheils who had gone on to Damascus; but their friends had left them useful directions about where to stay and whom to see in the Jewish community and at the American University, situated on a most beautiful campus between the sea, the mountains, and the city. There, Henrietta had to assure its President that even the success of the Zionist movement would not bring the Jews to the acceptance of Jesus, since it would mean their repudiation of the whole of the post-Christian development of Judaism. Perhaps therein lay the answer, in part, to that question: "Why do they hate us so?"

The train ride from Beirut to Damascus over the rugged stormy Lebanese mountains was turned into a nightmare by a washout and derailment of the engine; and the two women, burdened with their monstrous luggage, had to struggle from train to train in the night, in pouring rain, with the help of a French diplomat in their compartment. They arrived in Damascus before dawn and were relieved to find there the Gottheils, with whom they had breakfast.

They were plunged at once into the fantastic life of that ancient city, from its seething bazaars stocked with fabulous Oriental richness of textiles and metals, silks and gold and silver and rare inlaid wood, to the workshops where children labored under terrible conditions for ten cents a week. Weary Henrietta's sleep those two nights was deep and dreamless, interrupted only by the cry of the muezzin from a nearby mosque.

The train from Damascus left before dawn for Tiberias which would be their first stop in the Land of Israel. From the train window Henrietta watched a magnificent sunrise lighting the black basalt mountains, on the sides of which roamed flocks of black goats and sheep tended by robed and turbaned shepherds out of the Old Testament, crook in hand. In some places, especially along the banks of the Yarmuk River, the terraced slopes were cultivated. She and Mamma noted the variety of trees and blooming bushes and field flowers, some of which took them back to their botanical expeditions in Baltimore; for there were not only exotic tall date palms and silvery gnarled olive trees but the familiar crocus and narcissus. They saw Bedouin villages of black stone houses and black tents like caves, the men tall and fierce-looking, the women in black, wearing silver anklets and gold coin necklaces, and tattooed on their chins. By this time Henrietta was beginning to worry about the kind of Jews she might find in the colonies. The mixture of primitive peoples, languages and religions she had been seeing, the disregard of what the Occident looks upon as the elementary conventions of civilized social life, the unspeakable filth and disease, the riot of costume—all were colorful and interesting, to be sure, but she would hardly like to find her own people as an indistinguishable part of this backward Oriental mélange.

At Ramah on the Sea of Tiberias, the Lake of Galilee, they left the train and were lifted by Arabs into rowboats in which they were taken across the quiet water which is the source of the Jordan, to Tiberias. In that limpid air it looked ten miles away, but took two hours to reach. It was a huddle of black stone houses with narrow unclean streets dominated by a forbidding black stone castle. The hot springs which had brought the ailing to Tiberias since ancient times did not mitigate its cheerlessness. There was something depressing about the way its black stones absorbed the radiant golden sunshine. Its considerable Jewish population lived mostly on *ḥalukah*—charity received from abroad. The men were bearded, with the orthodox *peyot*—side curls dangling, and they wore the *kaftan*—the long coat of the orthodox. A Mr. Kahan of the *Alliance Israélite* school piloted them around the poverty-stricken Jewish quarter of ramshackle houses with sadly neglected children playing in the filthy streets, their eyes clustered with flies. Mamma wept to see small children blinded by trachoma. It was a rather discouraging introduction to the Holy Land. The Jewish community was indeed a sorry sight, but they did carry on the traditional learning; Torah was still learned in their schools. They were not as barbaric, even in their poverty, as the people Henrietta Szold had feared they might resemble. She and Mamma were taken to what were said to be the tombs of Maimonides and Talmudic rabbis, including that of Rabbi Akiba who joined with Bar Koḥba in the ill-fated Jewish resistance to the Romans in 132 A.D.

They found a letter awaiting them from Israel Shochat, the tubercular husband of the famous, heroic Manya, who was then in Europe collecting funds for their colony, Sejera. Mr. Shochat invited Henrietta and Mamma to visit Sejera. They went there by carriage, driving along the lake over rough stony roads among hills riddled with caves in which Rabbi Akiba's disciples were said to have hidden from the Romans. Wild oleander bloomed by the roadside and the remnants of ancient terracing were visible on the long neglected hillsides. But near Kinneret they came to land recently bought by ICA, the Jewish Colonization Association, for an agricultural colony. Its fields were well tilled and the place was alive with men and women at work, with their donkeys and geese. The colonists were experimenting with cotton, the fields of which were bright green, and with fruit trees which were pleasant to see set out in orderly rows.

That afternoon they arrived in the colony of Yemina where they were welcomed by a number of hard-working women. New houses and a school were being built but the place was still crude, with few amenities. The fields and cattle looked fine. There was a clean nursery for the young children; but the adults were too busy with the pressing problems of survival on limited resources to think of refinements. They had also had the misfortune of a fire which destroyed the stores of the Cooperative Society of the colonies in the area. Fortunately they had spring water from the mountains. They gave their guests tea, a spare supper, and cots in the administration building. It was a beautiful night, with clusters of stars, large and luminous, hanging low in the sky like lamps. And then the late moon rose, and something became clear which had puzzled Henrietta since childhood: why the psalmist had said that God would protect Israel so that the sun would not smite him by day, "nor the moon by night." How could the mild moon smite Israel? she used to wonder. But the light of this moon in the Land of Israel was so intense that one might fear it would smite you! Henrietta could not sleep for weariness and excitement. Dogs barked; roosters crowed.

Sunrise over the ancient somnolent land being revived by these inspired men and women was wonderful to behold. Mr. Shochat, who was overseer of workmen for the district and was organizing *Ha-Shomer,* a corps of watchmen to guard the colonies from the depredations of wandering Bedouins, had come on this business to Yemina and would take them on to Sejera in his wagon. "Until now," he told them, "we have had Arabs protect our fields. We paid them ten per cent of our profits, and then we were not sure that they were not stealing another ten per cent. And so now, as I am driving with you, I am organizing a company of Jewish *shomerim;* and they will take charge of the fields. The company is nearly completed. Some of the colonies have already engaged them. It is only a question if the other Galilean colonies will give their consent, and then we will have a militia of our own to protect our fields." Mr. Shochat was a gentle, refined young man, whose parents had sent him to the University of Halle to study agronomy. Fired by Zionism, he had run off to Palestine, and, being without funds, had worked as a common laborer. His wagon was springless, and the roads were rough. Sometimes Mamma and Henrietta would clutch each other for fear of being thrown out.

They passed the Arab village of Sarona. Some of the old houses were built of Roman stones. At its well, camels and sheep were watered and women came to fill their jars as in Biblical times, except that some carried tin cans. Henrietta and Mamma delighted in the sight of familiar things growing by the road—sage and fireweed and deep purple jack-in-the-pulpit; the sunny air was full of birds and their song. They stopped at Mesha, near Mount Tabor, which like Yemina, was an eight-year-old colony. The colonists were having trouble about their title to the land with the Arabs who had sold it to them. They had a school of three classes taught in Sephardic Hebrew, and the children looked healthier than those in Tiberias. There were some families of dark-skinned, gentle Yemenite Jews.

On the way from Mesha to Sejera they saw in the distance on a hill the ancient town of Safed, famed for its sages and Kabballists in Talmudic times. Sejera, ten years old, was a well-run colony, engaged in farming and poultry raising, the young women working everywhere along with the men. A stocky young man, David Ben-Gurion, had organized its workers' collective. Each household had a small garden plot in front of it and the village was somewhat more attractive-looking than the others. Henrietta was asked why Americans did not do more of a practical nature for the Zionist movement in Palestine. The colonists had hoped for more help after Dr. Magnes' enthusiastic visit two years before.

Mr. Shochat went on with them as their guide on the rough road over the hills toward Nazareth, through well-watered, fertile valleys with Arab villages, where life had not changed much through the centuries. Women were walking long distances to and from the wells with jars on their heads, or sitting on threshing floors fanning the grain, although there were camel trains on the road carrying grain to a steam mill at Nazareth. The Arabs still plowed with the ox and ass teamed together, which Moses forbade because the ox, which was so much stronger, overworked the ass; they even used teams of camel and donkey. It was tiring riding in Mr. Shochat's wagon but the advantage of his guidance with his knowledge of the colonies and their activities was invaluable. Besides, the men and women who took advantage of his passing to hitch rides for short distances gave them contact with a steady stream of representative individuals, lively, voluble, informative, and sometimes entertaining.

At the village of Mesha they were shown the tomb of Jonah. A sudden turn in the road brought them to Nazareth, a town of white houses on a hillside, seemingly full of artisans—millers, cutlers, carpenters. At Easter time, the only Jew there, the administrator of Galilean colonies, had to leave Nazareth for fear of molestation. Despite this, however, he preferred the luxury of a beautifully furnished house in Nazareth to sharing the hardships of life in one of the colonies under his guidance. Henrietta was shocked to learn that there was some despotism in the administration of the colonies—and it was not always benevolent. Beyond Nazareth came the Emek, the Valley of Jezreel, a superb vista of wide fertile fields spread like a green carpet between the hills of Samaria and Ephraim, with Mount Tabor rising nearby. Part of the land had been bought cheaply; then, for lack of funds, payments were stopped and the title lost. Later it had to be bought again for ten times the first cost because of the increased land value which had been created by the Jews themselves.

Then came the Carmel range of mountains, pitted with caves, the stones and the earth a coppery red. There were olive plantations, mulberry trees, vegetable gardens with rows of tomatoes and eggplants. The stony soil, seemingly arid when dry and neglected, burst into bountiful fertility under the husbandman's loving hand. It was as if the loose clods had only to be kept from rolling long enough for a handful of earth to gather and make a foothold for an olive tree, an investment for hundreds of years. And in this climate the sower trod on the heels of the harvester, once the gray stoniness had been washed by water. And over all spread the sunny sky, the limpid air, the wide prospect of mountain and valley. . . .

Haifa was a quiet Arab town of narrow, crooked, unnamed streets and a port on the blue sea. It did not even have the scavenger they had in Constantinople—the dog; and apparently there was no civic collection of garbage. There was a separate German colony with clean wide streets shaded by eucalyptus trees, neat houses set in gardens of flowers and vegetables and paths paved with sea shells, which showed what could be done with Western standards and means. They visited schools for boys and girls supported by the French *Alliance Israélite* where Hebrew, Arabic and French were taught. Here they found the children in better physical condition than elsewhere, especially their eyes, for there was a woman on the staff who made the care of the children her special concern. But here, too, Mamma cried out at the sight of blinded children in the streets, and said to Henrietta that her "Daughters of Zion," meeting in New York to debate the theories of Herzl, Ahad Ha-Am, and other exalted men, would be better occupied doing something about preventing the affliction of these innocent children.

They went up Mount Carmel, back of the city, where some prosperous Germans and Jesuit missionaries had villas with fine gardens, vineyards and almond orchards, and magnificent views of sea and mountains. They gathered bouquets of crocus, blooming in profusion, and of cyclamen with their beautifully marked velvety leaves. Henrietta loved to pick up a warm dry clod of the earth and crumble it in her hands, feeling its fertile richness. And standing there, looking down on the blue Mediterranean, she was thrilled by the thought that this was the place from which Elijah had looked down and seen the small cloud "like a man's hand" rise out of the sea, bringing the great rain that saved the children of Israel.

On the road south from Haifa they stopped at the cave in which Elijah was said to have hid from the wrath of King Ahab and his infamous Queen Jezebel whose implacable enemy he was. The large natural chamber with its antique tessellated floor and inscribed walls was a popular resort of the Arabs, too, of whom they met a large, gaily dressed party—men and women, boys and girls, on camels, horses and donkeys.

At Athlit, an Arab village, they saw Roman and Crusader ruins and, nearby, a small, two-year-old Jewish colony of ten people in miserable houses. It was evident that even their new houses were improperly constructed. Each house had two rooms, the smaller one of which was used as a granary, leaving only the one larger room for all functions of the family. The houses were ranged between the street and a wall of rock and, on the other side of the street, faced the stables. They were unsanitary and there was no room for expansion and improvement. The plans had been approved by an architect in Paris who had never seen the place. Nearby was a malaria-breeding marsh which still belonged to the Arabs who did nothing to clean up such pestholes.

The cliffs along the road were honeycombed with ancient caves apparently used as hideouts by smugglers of contraband. By the roadside Mamma and Henrietta found narcissus and grape hyacinth in bloom. Through a cleft in the rocks they approached Ziḥron Yaakob, a village founded by Roumanian Jews in 1882, where Baron de Rothschild planted extensive vineyards and built wine cellars. The road to the village was bordered by hedges of locust fencing the vineyards and the groves of bananas, oranges, almonds, olives and even apple trees. But the village shops were unkempt, the street lamps rickety, the inn rather primitive; and the doctor to whom they had an introduction was sick with malaria. However, his womenfolk, dignified German Jewesses, welcomed Henrietta and Mamma, inquired after mutual friends in New York, and directed them to the homes of some relatives of the Schechters and the Aaronsohn family. The latter were especially interesting intellectuals who were among the founders of the colony. They had two daughters, Sarah and Rivka, and three sons. Aaron, one of the sons and a vigorous young man, was the agronomist who had discovered wild wheat in Palestine and ran the Baron's agricultural station. Their house was spick-and-span, inside and out, with a beautiful garden.

But the village as a whole was depressing. It had a small public park which was closed and neglected; its waterworks were out of order. Workers' housing conditions were so bad they had much resultant illness; the hospital was unclean, inadequately equipped. The village administration was loath to make any improvements on the principle that "the colonists need no luxuries." Henrietta went about listening to everyone she met.

Among the colonists she saw an elderly man so startlingly like Papa she felt faint at sight of him; and the next morning, the Sabbath, she saw him again in the synagogue. The resemblance even in mannerism and gesture was incredible; but she hadn't the courage to speak to him and inquire if he might be related. The religious fervor of the Sabbath congregation was manifest; and when one stepped out of the synagogue there was the feeling that one was not precipitated into anything different, but into more Sabbath. It was expressed on every face, in every house, on every street. The Sabbath peace was everywhere; no one desecrated it. It was easy to keep the Sabbath here, therefore it was doubly holy. It was just as Papa would have liked to see it kept.

Talking to the colonists, although there was some complaint about the discouraging economic conditions, she found a remarkable enthusiasm for the future of Zionism. At the Schechters' while she partook of their home-grown olives, almonds, bread and wine, she heard of the hardships they had endured and the limitations of their present existence which netted them nothing beyond the barest subsistence—and yet they would not think of leaving even if they could. Their love of the land was like the attachment of an infatuated lover to the indifferent object of his affection. Although the land offered them only obstacles, they struggled for its possession with might and main, because they loved it—its air, its fields, its skies, its fruits, its very sun and moon, with unparalleled, pathetic devotion. At the end of the history of thirteen years of hardship there, one of them said: "But was there ever such a sky and such a moon as this?" And Henrietta, too, had the feeling that there never had been any place like it anywhere else in the world. The land was gliding into her heart; its gray stoniness seemed better than fat meadows elsewhere. It was as wondrously beautiful as the prophets and psalmists said. Its wide prospects had made it the land of great seers; its surprising sharp contrasts had made the Jew the enigmatic combination of qualities that still defied analysis.

A woman doctor at the hospital, who complained of its shortcomings, seemed happy to go on striving under such discouraging conditions. But this courageous optimism seemed, sometimes, to operate as a handicap. Henrietta, in a discussion with a group at the inn, asked why something wasn't done about tidying up the town, making it more attractive. She learned that on the occasions when the Baron came to inspect the wine-growing industry on which he spent millions, shortcomings were hidden from him. He was greeted with a band, and given glowing reports by people lined up about him so he couldn't see the miserable huts his money had built; hence he saw no reason for supporting improvements. Among his administrators, who were mostly away off in Haifa, there were said to be grafters. But, in answer to her criticism, someone asked, sarcastically, if she thought the incoming Jewish immigrants should be given a course in esthetics. Another said: "What right have you to live in America? If you are interested in Palestine, your place is here." All the same, they said, living was better, more comfortable, here in Ziḥron Yaakob than in most other colonies. For all the unkemptness of the village, its Sabbath air was indeed pleasant, with men, women and children going about in their clean white Sabbath dress.

In the afternoon, she was taken for a walk from the height on which Ziḥron Yaakob was situated, down to the colony of Nesly. The hillsides on the way looked hopelessly arid; yet wherever there was a natural terrace, olive trees had been planted and flourished; and in the valley, Nesly was a modern farm, a wonder, a jewel—set between Ziḥron Yaakob and the sea, gleaming in shades of luxuriant green—a costly jewel which still belonged to the Baron who had paid for it, reclaimed it from marshland. It had grape vines, eucalyptus, orange and olive trees which the colonists owned if the trees survived and paid for if they perished.

Accompanied by the woman doctor and one of the Schechter girls, Henrietta then climbed up a rocky mountain covered with wildflowers, to the agricultural station where there was a plantation of 12,000 orange trees, vines and olive slips and a eucalyptus forest—all of it reclaimed from a marsh. Slips were sold to colonists. The station, run by Aaron Aaronsohn, was in perfect order.

They returned at sunset, and that evening, in talks with the Aaronsohns, Schechters and others, she heard more charges against the administration. They gave labor contracts to Christians and Arabs rather than to Jews who wanted a higher standard of living and asked for higher wages. They were also morally loose, it was said; the schoolteachers they brought in were married off to young colonists after the administrators had tired of them. . . . All the same Henrietta by then had shaken off the depressing effect of Tiberias; she felt there in Ziḥron Yaakob both the indestructible old Jewish spirit and the strong new spirit of revival, misdirected as it apparently was.

They started south from Ziḥron Yaakob, early Sunday morning, Mr. Shochat driving, along a very rough road between hedges of fragrant mimosa and fields of blooming blackberries, and stopped at a poverty-stricken offshoot of that colony, where one teacher taught three classes of children in a wretched building. Mamma spent her time there teaching the women to darn. A rather large cemetery nearby, full of graves—there were more tombstones than people in the colony—was explained by the fact that the malaria victims from distant colonies came to the hospital at Ziḥron Yaakob to die and were buried there.

On the road to Ḥaderah Mr. Shochat described to Henrietta the

Abodah, a workers' group being set up which would make Jewish labor available where and when needed. The road ran among desolate sand dunes and marshes, and then suddenly there was a grove of fragrant eucalyptus, green meadows and an orange grove where a colony had been established by some *Ḥovevei Zion,* who had accomplished all this by drainage and irrigation. They were shown around proudly by a couple of happy, high-spirited young men, one of them a *ḥassid,* one of that cheerfully anti-ascetic sect of pious Jews whose adherents still wear the orthodox beards and side-curls. He was one of Mr. Shochat's watchmen.

Soon they came to Ḥaderah, a cluster of about thirty independent colonists established almost twenty years. They had had a hard fight against malaria which incapacitated and even killed many of them, but now they had a flourishing settlement beautifully situated between the Mediterranean and the mountains of Ephraim. The village had wide clean streets and a well-equipped school and kindergarten, but they had labor problems, which the immigration of Yemenite Jews was partly solving. The persecution those poor gentle people had suffered in their native land moved Mamma to tears. They loved learning; many of them arrived with a few rags of clothing and a box of books.

Henrietta slept little that starlit night which seemed to her the most beautiful she had ever witnessed, as she watched the moon rise from the ancient sea and pass over the ancient land. It was no longer an inner anguish that kept her awake—all that agony seemed far away in time and space; she was gripped now by another emotion, an excitement communicated to her by these heroically struggling colonists devoted to the Land of Israel, as she had once been moved in Baltimore by the spirit of her "Russians." How could one sleep in a land which cried out for so much!

And, besides, the accommodations they found at the so-called hotels on this trip were far from conducive to slumber even after days of weary riding in Mr. Shochat's wagon. But it took them to fourteen agricultural colonies which Henrietta got to know in a way she could not otherwise possibly have achieved; she was unspeakably tired but grateful.

They proceeded at six in the morning from the fruitful Valley of Sharon accompanied by the young *ḥassid,* who jumped off now and then to get Mamma a bunch of the many-colored wildflowers which grew everywhere. Mr. Shochat spoke of the remarkable adherence of Jewish farmers to Jewish learning—how they took their young children out to the fields with them and taught them Torah during the midday rest. No, Henrietta need not worry about Jews losing their culture and becoming barbarous, even under such crude conditions; but Mamma's keen blue eyes, delighted as she was by the landscape and the spirit of the people, found much to criticize candidly in those conditions which seemed to her unnecessarily, inexcusably crude. There was, for example, the food, which was uniformly bad, as if Jewish women in the Land of Israel had forgotten how to cook! Something should be done about *that.*

Petaḥ Tikvah, a town founded in 1883 by pioneers of the first *Aliyah*—the first "going up" into the Land of Israel after the Russian persecution—had with the help of Baron Edmond de Rothschild developed mainly citriculture, but besides orange groves it had bananas, olives, grape vines, and some grain. The town in its lack of plan and order resembled an old Russian Jewish village of the pale, although there were evidences of prosperity in some of the houses and gardens. It had an adequate school and kindergarten with a fine playground, and a Talmud Torah, a Hebrew school, run by an old friend of Dr. Marx of the Seminary; but the children looked undernourished. In the extensive orange groves a large number of Arab laborers were used, but they did not live in the community.

On the way to Jaffa they saw new settlements of independent colonists who had built their own homes, many with their own hands, and were starting orange groves. It had rained during the night and everyone was grateful for this dispensation. At Sarona they passed a German colony with beautifully kept fields, exquisite gardens and attractive houses; and again it was obvious that with means and knowledge wonders could be accomplished.

Jaffa, a largely Arab city, was like all Oriental towns, beautiful from a distance, in a setting of date palms and orange groves; but it proved on close inspection as crowded and malodorous as the others. Israel Shochat, to whom they were greatly indebted, left them there. In their hotel by the sea, they met a number of interesting people engaged in Zionist activity, the cultivated intellectuals Henrietta had put off meeting, among them Dr. Arthur Ruppin, formerly of Berlin, the representative of the Zionist Organization in Jaffa, engaged in land development and labor colonization. He knew of Henrietta's important work on the Year Book, and he gave her much information.

The next day, looking for a certain school, Henrietta came to a house which had a small American flag painted beside the name of the resident, Joseph Eisner—a name she had known in Baltimore. She went in to inquire and found it was indeed the same family. The inside of the house, clean and tidy, was a sight for sore eyes after most of the interiors she had been seeing.

She found a large and excellent modern girls' school, founded by the *Ḥovevei Zion*, where the girls got medical treatment for prevention and cure of trachoma, which was so prevalent, and which Mamma maintained was a disgraceful, unnecessary affliction, caused, as it was, by neglect—especially when it blinded young children. At this school, where a nurse came twice a day and a physician twice a week, there was no trachoma. Coming away from the school, and seeing more children with eyes wreathed around with flies, Mamma said emphatically to Henrietta, "Here is work for you."

They drove out to Mikveh Israel, near Jaffa, where there was an agricultural school, founded by the *Alliance Israélite* some thirty years before. It was a good school, where, curiously, because of its loyalty to French culture, there was a strong feeling against the Zionist Organization's activities; so divided could Jews become, even in the Land of Israel, as a result of their national attachments in the Diaspora. One of the problems of Jewish settlement in Palestine, Henrietta recognized, would be the multiplicity of overlapping activities of independent organizations, differently oriented. The drive back to Jaffa after dark was fearful, between the thick dark foliage of the orange groves, and through the dimly lighted streets of the city in which groups of Arabs sat smoking and eating before their squalid cafés.

Further travel was made more uncomfortable by the winter rains which now fell every day; but moving south into the long-settled, more prosperous area of Rishon le-Zion, where Baron de Rothschild had established extensive vineyards, it was pleasant to ride between well-kept fields hedged by fragrant mimosa, and find substantial houses set in gardens, on wide, paved streets. They visited the large wine cellars which were sending wine abroad, and the admirable schools, where Henrietta enjoyed speaking Hebrew with the children, who, however, were critical of her accent. Here, as at Ziḥron Yaakob, the colonists complained of their lack of independence. At Rehobot, further south, a similar old colony which had started with vineyards had changed to orange groves, there was a scarcity of Jewish labor, and mainly Arabs were employed. The Yemenite Jews who had come there presented a peculiar problem with their different mores. They were polygamous and preferred the Arab style of house—dark and cool—to the light modern ones; but they seemed a happy people.

Henrietta and Mamma drove to Ramleh to take the train to Jerusalem, passing through a wonderful old orchard of olive trees, the gnarled twisted trunks hollowed out like shells which still supported great gray-green masses of foliage. On the train they met a Mr. Dizengoff, a cheerful round-faced Jew who had organized a company, *Geulah,* for the purchase of land for Jewish settlement. He was the man whom Judah Magnes had heard in 1907, standing on a box among the sand dunes outside Jaffa, describing the new Jewish city to be built there. Mr. Dizengoff said the city had just been founded, it had a couple of streets, and it would be known, he announced with the utmost confidence, as Tel Aviv—the name of a city mentioned by Ezekiel. Through the window of the train as it wound and climbed, puffing and rattling, up the picturesque and stony Judean hills, he pointed out to Henrietta the Arab settlements with their terraced farms hanging on the hillsides, and a Jewish colony, Artuf, which was originally started by Christian missionaries for Bulgarian Jews, in the hope of converting them. The scheme failed, of course, and the Jews, with the help of Mr. Dizengoff's *Geulah,* bought the land for themselves.

Arriving at Jerusalem at noon Friday, November 12, they were greeted by Dr. Gottheil and Professor Schatz, who came mounted on donkeys. Professor Schatz, a sculptor, had founded a school of arts and crafts called *Bezalel.* After a refreshing dinner Henrietta and Mamma called upon Mrs. Gottheil, and they all rode up on the Mount of Olives from which she had her first view of the breath-taking panorama of Jerusalem—"the city which the Lord did choose out of all the tribes of Israel, to put his name there."

Across the Valley of Kidron stood the eternal city on its hill crowned with its massive crenelated walls. From the rectangular Temple area rose the dark Dome of the Rock—enclosing the Rock of Moriah on which burnt offerings were sacrificed in olden times, when Solomon's Temple and palace stood there. Now there was the Aksa Mosque, and between the Mosque and the Dome the tall dark spears of slender cypress trees surrounded a large fountain. Beyond the spacious Temple area were the thickly crowded flat-roofed houses of stone, each with its small dome; churches and monasteries lifted towers and spires alongside minarets, and in the Jewish quarter were domed synagogues. The two domes of the Holy Sepulcher and the minaret of the Mosque of Omar stood within a stone's throw of each other. The thick zigzagging walls seemed hardly to contain the jumble of buildings; and at each of the city gates the seething traffic of men and burdened animals was like that at the entrance of a beehive. By the Jaffa Gate rose the square-towered Citadel of David, who took the city from the Jebusites a thousand years B.C., made it the capital of united Israel and installed there the Ark of the Covenant of Moses. The timeless sun pouring down from the vast blue dome of sky illumined the time-worn mass of golden-hued stones quarried from these hills and builded by countless men. . . . "Jerusalem the golden . . . what radiance of glory . . ." sang a medieval poet; and so it still was to this day.

Beyond the ramparts of Jerusalem spread the Judean hills, stony and bare yet beautiful. The sun-bleached slopes of the Mount of Olives were still dotted with silvery trees, and there were still some vineyards, despite the fearful destruction Titus had launched upon the city from this very mountain where they stood, and the flocks of goats which now grazed relentlessly upon it.

On the way down they passed through the cemetery in which Jews had been buried since the time of the first Temple. All the tombstones were horizontal, with small stones left lying on them by visitors. Since the death of little Johanna in Lombard Street, Henrietta had found cemeteries depressing, and this one was even more so. It happened that a funeral was in progress; and its stark primitive simplicity was almost gruesome. There were no vehicles and no coffin. The body, wrapped in a coarse linen shroud which barely concealed the form, lay on a crude bier made of planks, carried by eight men who chanted psalms as they transported it to the grave, followed by the mourners. The Jews, whose toast is *Le-Ḥayim,* "To Life," have never glorified death; the psalms they chanted glorified God, the Creator of life.

The three women went down into the old city, threading the crowded, narrow crooked stepped streets, in which, long before Jesus, Isaiah had walked; and they went through the teeming, odorous bazaars to the 2,000-year-old Wailing Wall. The space before the great moss-grown stones was filled with a mélange of sight-seeing tourists in European dress, bearded orthodox worshipers in fur hats and plush *kaftans,* weeping, kerchiefed women lighting lamps in memory of the dead, Moroccan Jews in white robes and turbans, and slender Yemenite Jews in their colorful embroidered garb. In their stubborn, routine devotion, there was something at once grotesque and dignified, emotional and spiritual.

They returned to their hotel outside the wall by way of the Jaffa Gate where the traffic of men, donkeys, camels, and herds of goats and sheep was incessant. Shoeshine boys with brass-studded boxes polished the shoes of red-fezzed Arabs who carried strings of yellow prayer-beads. The new Jewish quarter was quiet with the peace of the Sabbath eve.

That evening Henrietta talked with Dr. Ruppin, who had come up from Jaffa with some teachers from the Girls' School maintained by the German *Hilfsverein* in Jerusalem. There was much to be learned before one could know how it might be possible to help in this confusing complex of needs and activities.

The next day began an incessant round of sight-seeing and visiting—all on foot since it was the Sabbath—from the Temple area, the site of events in the lives of Abraham, David, Solomon, and Jesus, to the modern Bezalel Art School with its Museum of Natural History. Sunday they visited schools at which handicrafts were being taught, and a hospital well run by German doctors, despite the shortage of funds. Henrietta, talking with the men and women running these institutions, discovered a new kind of optimism, a toughness of idealism which could bear the deplorable present condition so long as some improvement, however small, was being effected. They didn't mind being criticized by those disappointed ones who came seeking the realization of a dream, nor being considered ruthless for their preoccupation with what was immediately possible and useful. Thus Dr. Schatz made clear to her why it was more important in the present state of their economy to teach handicrafts than to dream, as most American Zionists did, of a modern industrial development in the Land of Israel. She also learned how difficult it was being made for the Jews to regain that land: how, after they had paid well for some area of stony, neglected soil, or marsh, their contracts were often repudiated or their use of it handicapped by unknown governmental restrictions. The Jews had to learn a toughness in the face of such disappointments, resorting to baksheesh if necessary to gain their ends. In their devotion to this land these lovers of Zion were indeed idealists. There was no explaining their persistent desire to serve and be married to so difficult and unresponsive a beloved; but in the attainment of that end they were pragmatists. Such pragmatism Henrietta, herself the idealistic lover, had not learned, alas, even from Rebekah and Rachel and Naomi and Ruth. . . . But in ten busy days in Jerusalem with Mamma, in November 1909, Henrietta developed a new devotion to an ideal which could only be served pragmatically.

It was difficult, however, to know where in this complex of sometimes conflicting devotees a lover of Zion could best serve. There were *Hilfsverein* schools which insisted on teaching in German, just as the *Alliance* schools taught in French, since their teachers, of course, came from Germany and France. But what was the use of German or French to youngsters who were being prepared for life in the land of Israel? It seemed a pity that Hebrew was not adopted as the general language of instruction. The attitude of both the *Alliance* and the *Hilfsverein* seemed like that of a philanthropic, condescending Lady Bountiful, who goes to the slum not to help it develop its own potentialities for its own progress, but to draw out and unfit for home use whatever native talent she finds. The graduates of two professional schools did not remain in Jerusalem because there was no work found for them. There were four hospitals in Jerusalem under different Jewish auspices, but there was no maternity ward, and infant mortality was 13 per cent. Some poor mothers had the choice between bearing their babies on heaps of rags in a basement or in one of the missionary hospitals where the price of the service was conversion. Even pragmatists, when uncoordinated, could be inefficient, and ultimately ineffectual. Nevertheless Henrietta found the spirit of Jerusalem Jews—warm, vital and hopeful, like that of her Baltimore "Russians"—most attractive to her.

She visited the large Evelina de Rothschild school run by Miss Landau, a fine English Jewess who had been a settlement worker. Here English was stressed, and Anglo-Saxon discipline inculcated upon children from all sorts of backgrounds, Ashkenazic and Sephardic, Yemenite and Kurdish. There was religious as well as secular instruction; workshops and needlework produced quantities of articles, especially lace, which the students sold. Miss Landau worked heroically, often with children who came to her covered with vermin. She had just managed to get funds for the enlargement of her inadequate building.

Henrietta talked with a teacher who thought Hebrew and Arabic should be the basic languages of instruction in primary grades, with all foreign languages taught later; and since the Jews would have to share the land with the Arabs, that sounded sensible. She talked with a nurse who complained of the inadequate antisepsis practiced in hospitals where physicians who demanded higher standards were dropped. She heard complaints of the primitive treatment of the insane. At dinner with the Gottheils she heard of a School of Technology being set up by the *Alliance,* and an experiment in the manufacture of silk which had failed. There was no end to the needs of that beloved land. Afterward she went with Dr. Gottheil to the Holy Sepulcher which, after she had admired the beauty of its pillars and capitals, struck her as a monument to human folly that had raised upon the death of gentle Jesus the dreadful structure of violent anti-Semitism. But was this really the answer to "Why do they hate us so?" She and Mamma made a tour of many synagogues, some impressive, others revoltingly unclean; they saw Solomon's quarries, and Jeremiah's cave . . . and after late supper with the Gottheils the two women returned to their hotel through the dark streets carrying a borrowed lantern.

But that did not deter them from starting out early the next morning on a round of orthodox Hebrew schools where children were studying Talmudic subjects such as Henrietta had studied at the Seminary in New York. In one school she saw a rope hanging in the middle of the room, with which children were punished: shades of Jonas Goldschmitt with his rattan on tingling finger tips in Baltimore long ago!

In a Sephardic synagogue they saw not a single woman, but it was filled with row on row of red-fezzed men; and Henrietta realized how the Jew, while giving part of himself to his environment, holds firmly to his own. They went to the synagogue of the Karaites, a sect dating from the ninth century of which there were but eight families in Jerusalem. In accordance with the psalmist's "Out of the depths I cry unto thee," they descended, shoeless, several steps into their synagogue, which was unlighted on the Sabbath eve and had rugs on the floor for seats; but all of it was clean and neat.

They visited churches, too, Abyssinian, Armenian, German, Catholic, Dominican . . . and then rode to Bethlehem over terraced and cultivated rocky gray hills, past Rachel's tomb, a small white-domed structure by the roadside where she was said to have died in childbirth; now it was the resort of barren women who came there to pray for Rachel's intercession in their behalf. And in Bethlehem was the memory of Ruth, the woman of Moab, who, instructed by Naomi, had gone down to glean in the field of Boaz and then lay down at his feet at night on the threshing floor, when his heart was merry, and induced him to marry her—thus becoming the forebear of David and Solomon and, according to the Christians, of Jesus, too. The Church of the Nativity, a dim, damp, cluttered building, divided among hostile Christian sects, was interesting architecturally. They visited a *Hilfsverein* school, and a touching and needy Institute for the Blind; and a big burly young Jew, who offered to show them something important, took them out for a drive in a carriage toward evening, and after groping around in moonlit darkness, showed them the cypress tree which Herzl planted when he was there one hopeful day in 1898 with Kaiser Wilhelm II whom he was trying to interest in his dream. A small group of Jewish colonists, settled in Bethlehem, urged Henrietta to raise money in America for some developments they had in mind.

Back in Jerusalem, she went with Dr. Gottheil for an uncomfortable but interesting donkey ride through the weirdly picturesque Valley of Kidron, the necropolis of ancient Israel, with its tombs of prophets, kings and princes. She felt sorry for the poor donkey, and for the barefoot boy who led it along the stony path.

Dr. Gottheil told her of the Turkish government's expressed intention to exact military service of the colonists. The Yemenite youths and those of other orthodox groups were distressed about the prospect of having to shave off their side-curls in the army; and Jewish women were weeping at the tomb of Rachel in behalf of their sons who would be taken away from them for armed service.

She attended a meeting of the leaders of the community concerned with the fact that there were many workers in Jerusalem, skilled and unskilled, who were without employment, while in the colonies large numbers of Arab fellaheen were being employed. The Arabs' low standard of living was having a bad influence upon the colonists, especially if they lived in or near the Jewish villages. Among the leaders was a Mr. Ben-Zvi who expressed the need for widespread labor organization in the land. Mr. Shochat's effort in the north appeared to be an independent local enterprise, unrelated to Jerusalem.

It was like being plunged into the turgid waters of a stirring sea of diverse activities, all of them interesting and needing immediate attention, as well as much study and consideration. But there was no more time; Henrietta and Mamma were booked to leave Jerusalem the following day. That evening a host of people came to say goodbye to them; some were real friends they had made, and some were importunate people who hoped Henrietta could further their causes and find for them in rich America the means desperately needed to continue the many-faceted work of revival they had hopefully started.

Much as she had been moved and involved by what they were so devotedly doing, she did not see this enterprise with the eyes of the blindly infatuated. Indeed, after looking and listening intently as she had been for four weeks, from Tiberias to Jerusalem, Henrietta wondered how it was possible that so many mistakes could be planted, wittingly and unwittingly, in such blessed soil.

Some of the colonies were monuments to a stupidity that seemed almost heartless and wicked; and some aspects of the towns were the result of plain governmental mismanagement—their filth was criminal, their disease unpardonable. Fortunately, having seen their like in Constantinople, Smyrna, Alexandria, Beirut and Damascus, she knew what the Oriental standard was or she would have despaired, but here European and American Jews must set the standard. And it was remarkable that European and American Jews, with their reputed acumen, could make such blunders. The land was as strewn with abortive experiments as the Mount of Olives with graves. And why? Because Jews, even when idealistic, were jealously individualistic where they should be collaborative; and they were impulsive to the point of irresponsibility. Administrators came and acted before studying the land and the people. Houses were built without regard to sanitation, let alone beauty. New colonies were being planted now, after thirty years' experience, where colonists must die of malaria. In the educational field, praiseworthy as was much of the work, the chauvinistic German *Hilfsverein* was adding to the chaos begun by the chauvinistic French *Alliance*. And in this chaotic effort, the American Zionists were perhaps the worst sinners: their support was haphazard, without plan, unorganized; and she meant to tell them so when she returned, citing chapter and verse. She had it all down in her diary. And she would not permit herself to be hushed as if she were just a tourist, or because she was a woman.

For the colonists themselves as people, for the men and women heroically struggling for the good life under such conditions, she had nothing but admiration. They were often misguided, but they were sterling spirits. Their self-abnegation was unparalleled. There was, for example, Professor Schatz, the founder and soul of Bezalel, who, in his fifties, had come there, learned Hebrew, and started to teach. His rather conventional school of arts and crafts would not by itself "bring the Messiah," but it was a sign of a coming cultural springtime in that long lost land. And there were many like him.

But she saw plainly what pangs that rebirth would entail—the heroic efforts to be endured and survived: the struggles with the nationalistic young Turks and other antagonists, aroused by undiplomatic and premature Zionist pronouncements; the tremendous debates within the divided Zionist ranks themselves; the surgery to be performed on what had already been accomplished; the cleaning of Augean stables in the cities—extirpating the filth and disease, disorder and ugliness bred of bad habits, at the thought of which the spirit of her mother's daughter rose up in her. There was women's work to be done. If ever she had been a light-hearted Zionist, she was that no more; but a Zionist she was, more than ever. She had fallen in love with the land, its history, its beauty, its potentiality as the only possible refuge of oppressed Jews in many places. The impressions of it she had got came too fast, were too vital and too varied—sentimental, social, economic, agricultural—to be set down yet in orderly array; and in disorder they would have no meaning at all. But of this much she was certain: It was a land worth working and fighting for, with word and pen and even (God forbid!) with the sword.

Dr. Gottheil saw Henrietta and Mamma off at the railroad station. The rugged old hills of Judah going down to Jaffa were more beautiful even than when they had come up, greener now from the winter rains. The ancient harbor of Jaffa was picturesquely bathed in the light of the setting sun as they went aboard the steamer and sailed for Port Said under the light of the rising moon.

They arrived early and went by train to Cairo, where nothing excited Henrietta, not even the Sphinx and the pyramids by moonlight; and although they were still to "do" Italy before setting their faces westward for home, she felt that all that must be anticlimactic after the gripping, revolutionizing experience in Palestine. She deplored not having had it earlier in her life, which would certainly have been shaped by it. Coming so late she feared it would resolve itself into nothing more than a stimulating memory, with little resultant action. Nevertheless it had done something drastic to her. On the steamer *Habsburg* which took them to Trieste, she wrote long letters to friends in New York and Philadelphia, trying to give them some slight idea of what she had experienced, and she realized, as she wrote, how far she had left behind the life she had had—all the work and the anguish, and how wise Mamma had been to take her away from it all.

A reference in a letter from Mrs. Schechter to the Hudson-Fulton

Celebration in New York, with a pageant of ships which she had watched from Riverside Drive, evoked in Henrietta only an eagerness to get back to the dear old ugly city with her new-found excitement. "I am strong," she wrote her friend, "and I have myself under control. But you will soon see for yourself."

On board the clean, comfortable, almost palatial *Habsburg,* she felt that she would not regret it if the ship did not go to Italy but sailed on until it reached the port of New York. Palestine had used her up; she felt apathetic to everything else. Among the passengers, she met two Englishmen who got to talking about British interests in Palestine. One of them, apparently not taking her for a Jewess, said he would rather see the Turks than the Jews in possession of the Holy Land, and that, anyway, the Jews wouldn't be able to hold it if they ever got it. When she told him she was Jewish, he apologized, most politely. "Why do they hate us so?" But, no matter. It was worth struggling for. The Jews would win out. All the same, she could not get even the ship's Jewish doctor interested in Zionism.

They took the train from Trieste to Venice in pouring rain. Yet Italy was pagan and joyous after the Spartan struggle and austerity of Jewish Palestine, although, after the warm, golden sunshine there, Italy in December was nipping cold, like New York. They shivered in the coffinlike black gondolas of Venice, but enjoyed, nevertheless, the radiant, barbaric splendor of St. Mark's, and the Titians, Tintorettos, and Bellinis were luminous even in the dim, dank churches. And after the tenseness of the experience in Palestine with its misery, its aspirations and its problems, which had demanded all her powers of attention, there was unexpected relief for Henrietta in the Christian-pagan atmosphere of Italy. Here there were no people to engage her emotions, only things to look at and enjoy uncritically. Mamma, much as she admired the beauty of Venice, thought it stupid to build a town where you could not take long walks or make a flower garden; but Henrietta, despite her expectation that nothing could interest her after Palestine, was enchanted with the noiseless, dustless city, with its countless domes and spires and campaniles, the gliding gondolas laden with greens from the country, the swish and splash of oars to the accompaniment of honey-tongued Italian, which she wished she could speak, and the gay, gentle folk who went about singing by day and by night.

She went to the old Ghetto, where Sara Sullam, of whom she had written so knowingly when she was too young to know better, had lived three hundred years ago. In the crowded, poverty-stricken, slumlike quarter she could not help "contrasting the meanness of my people with the *grandezza* of the others."

She and Mamma happened in on the pageantry of a High Mass at St. Mark's Cathedral on the Feast of the Madonna Immaculate. There was the wonderful basilica with its domes and vast aisles of marble and porphyry, its mosaics and treasures of gold and jewels. There were majestic music and an angelic choir; surpliced acolytes swinging fragrant censers; richly robed dignitaries, and the cardinal-archbishop in princely vestments, seated in his regal chair, attended with pomp and ceremony before the crowd of devout worshipers. And, seeing these symbols of a vast unseen power, Henrietta thought of her people, poor, powerless Jews, knocking at the door of humanity and begging for the right only to live and work hard in their long neglected, stony land, which had given Christianity the very reason for this sumptuous celebration. She almost lost there her Zionist courage and hope. She could not help contrasting "what *they* have with what *we* have. With them, might, glory, power, beauty, wealth; with us, dirt, poverty, and misery. We are rich only in hopes and ideals. The Christian will say that it is because the early Church had the same spiritual assets that she is now triumphant. But she had, besides, armies, and she did not shrink from cruelty. Venice, in all her magnificent beauty, is nothing but a thief, a brigand of the waterways. As she brought her patron saint, Mark, from Alexandria, so she rifled the East of its treasures, under the pretense of glorifying the Church and the tutelary apostle, she burned and murdered, and robbed and lied, and oppressed. Are the Jews prepared to do that? Can they do it if they will?"

But the more she saw of Italy the more she saw how pagan Christianity had become in the Renaissance, and the more she felt that the indomitable spirit of Judaism, which had withstood and survived the might of paganism in the past, would win out in this struggle, too. Thinking of it gave her the feeling she got looking out the train window at a magnificent peak in the Apennines, its base dark and immovable, its aspiring slopes obscured in cloud, its summit soaring triumphantly into brilliant sunlight.

From Venice, from Milan, from Florence, from Rome, from Naples, she wrote long eloquent letters to her family and friends at home, to her sisters, to Judah Magnes, Judge Sulzberger, Alice Seligsberg, the Schechters and others of the Seminary circle, telling them what she had seen and now foresaw: "Wherever a Jewish fragment exists—and where is the place at which it does not exist?—and is persecuted—and where does it exist without persecution?—the trend is toward the Holy Land. The Yemenite Jews are going there in a steady stream . . . and the Bokharans, and the Moghrebs, not to mention Roumanians, Russians and others. If the Jews of the world outside are not to be the mockery and laughingstock of the nations, the gathering of their people in their natural center must be welded into a homogeneous body. And that cannot be done by argument and debate, or by the *laissez-aller* policy. It requires sage and active planning and no small means either. . . ."

In Milan, a substantial modern city full of treasures, they deplored their ability to spend only hours instead of weeks in the Carthusian monastery stuffed with Renaissance art, which was paganly sensuous even when it was Christian. The martyrdom of a Saint Sebastian, bound to a tree, with darts sticking through him, was voluptuous. And there was da Vinci's "Last Supper," and "Last Suppers" by Rubens and Titian, all beautiful reminders of the indebtedness of even this half-pagan Christianity to so Jewish a tradition as the Passover *seder*.

One difficulty they encountered in Italy after Palestine was the food; they almost starved at times because even the macaroni, rice and vegetables had meat sauces, which were not *kasher*. Yet they spent three weeks in Florence, where there could be time for little eating, drinking or sleeping, only for looking, if one were to do even a quarter justice to all its wonders catalogued by Baedeker. Although both were eager now to get home "and talk our friends to death if they will listen," it was impossible to slight the magnificent riches of Florence: of sculpture in its arcaded squares, of paintings in the inexhaustible Pitti and Uffizi, of trips to Fiesole, San Miniato, Settignano, and Vallombrosa. Henrietta's one criticism of what they saw in Florence was the way babies were painted. "Among the Florentine paintings one never sees a real, natural baby. They have hydrocephalous heads on grown-up bodies. Perugino and Fra Filippo Lippi and Botticelli knew how to make fair Madonnas, but not one of them knew what a baby looked like. . . . It was only when their many-sided men forced them to study the antique in all its manifestations that Raphael and Andrea del Sarto painted real babies." But the white ceramic *bambini* of della Robbia were delightful.

She was also struck by the essential difference between the strong individualism of the Renaissance artist asserting himself, even in his religious art, and the self-effacement of the Gothic artist in the cathedrals, anonymously working for the greater glory of God. "The conscience of the north is self-abnegation and chasteness; the imagination of the south is self-assertion and fertility."

On the Sabbath they went to an elegant synagogue, a gemlike building set in a rose-and-palm garden. It seemed to Henrietta the only really beautiful synagogue they had seen in all their travel, and she attributed its beauty to the influence of its surroundings, giving point to the old Jewish saying: *Wie es sich Christelt, so Jüdelt es sich*—that the mores of Jews are strongly influenced by the mores of their Christian environment. At the synagogue they met the rabbi, who introduced them to a gentleman who said he had heard of Henrietta Szold from a mutual friend of theirs whom he had met the summer before last in Henningsdorf and again last summer in Berlin. The sudden reminder of *him,* like an unexpected blow on a forgotten wound, was so painful she declined the man's cordial invitation to his home. She wanted no more reminders.

Her forty-ninth birthday came that week in Florence. She spent the day visiting palaces, churches, galleries, and the house of Galileo, who had insisted that the world does move. . . . And four days later, on Christmas Day, came the seventieth birthday of Mamma—indomitable Mamma to whom she felt closer now than ever before. Henrietta spread an array of gifts on Mamma's bed before she awoke that morning—a fifteenth-century Sardinian plate which she had coveted when they saw it in a shop window on the Ponte Vecchio, and other lovely things of silver and tortoise shell, each one given in the name of one of Mamma's three other daughters and her four grandchildren.

Mamma was suffering again from a severe bronchial ailment brought on by fatigue and the chilling rains; so Henrietta, who had been asked by her friends in New York to attend as an American delegate the Ninth Zionist Congress being held in Hamburg, decided not to go, because it would mean subjecting Mamma to an additional wearisome journey, or leaving her alone and unwell in Florence. Besides, after seeing in Palestine what had come of all the cogitation of other Congresses, she did not feel too optimistic about the outcome of this one. She was not in the mood to listen to men talking abstractly about practical matters in a haze of tobacco smoke. "One can never tell what will come of an assemblage of men, not to mention Jews," she wrote home with playful acerbity. "I leave it to you to decide whether that last phrase means that I think them more or less than men." She was certainly entitled to a little bitterness about the unreliability of men in general and Jewish men in particular; and it was a good sign that she could be playful about it.

She spent Mamma's rainy birthday reading to her George Eliot's novel of Renaissance Italy, *Romola*, which Henrietta found "wonderful, psychologically, historically and artistically. Many of my feelings expressed as I never could express them—and my experiences. Only Romola was young when her life was truncated!" The life of George Eliot herself, whom she greatly admired, especially for a sympathy with the Jewish spirit remarkable in a gentile, and for her early approval of the Zionist aspiration, offered Henrietta food for thought. Cultivated and high-minded Mary Ann Evans (George Eliot's real name) had, like Henrietta, been educated to the point of erudition, and was attached to her ailing father until spinsterhood; but she had gone off and lived, unmarried, for some twenty-four years with George Henry Lewes, the brilliant essayist and biographer of Goethe, an unhappily married man. A passionate intellectual, George Eliot had not let her life be truncated by convention or even moral law.

Henrietta and Mamma saw the new year in, 1910, there in Florence, and left on January 3 for Rome, where they industriously enjoyed the regular tourist round—the Vatican, St. Peter's and the Sistine Chapel, all the glorious works of Michelangelo, the Capitol, the Forum, and the Coliseum; to which they added, of course, a synagogue. In Rome Henrietta was reinforced in her strong conservative feeling for the cultural importance of the past, especially to the Jew: "When the guidebooks send you to look for the houses Goethe and Keats and Shelley lived in, you feel we are still chewing the cud of the Renaissance . . . that is a symbol of human progress. It is always the past and again the past with us. Live as we will, we cannot banish the dead; and the most joyous thing I have ever seen, namely the Renaissance, is a resurrection—a resurrection that points to its empty tomb at every street corner in Rome." There she also saw depicted on the Arch of Titus, Jewish captives bearing the *menorah*—the seven-branched candelabrum and other fittings taken from the Temple which had stood in that place upon which she had looked down from the Mount of Olives. Was the Jewish renaissance and resurrection to be just a forlorn hope? Herzl, in his diary in 1897 predicted that the Jewish state would be a reality "certainly in fifty years." That would be in 1947. "If you will it—it is no fable," he had said. Would all the Zionist will in the world bring that prediction to pass?

On the tenth they were in Naples, and the visit to ancient Pompeii was made more vivid by the sight, at the base of Vesuvius, of some modern houses buried in lava up to their second stories by the eruption of 1906, an example of courageous but misguided humanity. That was the last of their strenuous sight-seeing, and they were happy to board the Cunarder *Saxonia* on the twelfth, taking with them a Miss McCall of New Orleans, the young daughter of a couple they had met at their hotel who asked them to chaperon the pretty American girl. She was engaged to a Mr. Freeman of Baltimore! Already they were enmeshed in the web of home.

Henrietta kept her diary of the voyage home in a leather-bound notebook entitled "My Ocean Trip" which had quotations of verse heading the pages, such as:

On Life's vast ocean, diversely we sail,
Reason the card, but passion is the gale.

—Pope

The ship sailed from Naples after dark, so they missed seeing Capri and Sorrento; but the sunset over smoldering Vesuvius was luridly beautiful. The very next day they ran into a gale, with electric flashes crackling along the masts and rigging, and a wind in the night that carried off hatches and ladders, and flooded the steerage, which was filled with Hungarian and Italian immigrants. The following day being calm, sunny and warm, the irrepressible immigrants in their colorful costumes came up on deck and danced to their own gay music. The women's faces, framed in their head-shawls, were like early Tuscan and Lombard Madonnas; and Henrietta deplored the fact that within a week after they landed in New York those men and women would become ashamed of their native color, beauty and gaiety, and discard them. And she began to have qualms about herself when she would get there. Would she, too, lose the good she had gained abroad? She was not sorry to hear that the ship would be delayed a day because of the storm.

She read and wrote. There was no one on board to interest her —not even Horace Fletcher of "Fletcherizing" fame, who preached that long mastication was the way to good health and salvation. He was accompanied by a lady who was said to be a marquise—"a lively, yellow-haired cocksure woman . . . the triumphant type that rides roughshod over others, and yet she is not without good nature. . . ." Henrietta, with her *Menschenliebe,* and her painfully gained knowledge of the heart of a woman, found it difficult wholly to condemn any woman in pursuit of happiness.

On January 25 they passed dear dowdy-looking Liberty with her lifted lamp, and docked; and Henrietta's heart was high again. For there on the pier were her beloved family and friends: not only Adele with Thomas, but Bertha who had come from Baltimore and Rachel from Madison; and Mrs. Schechter and Mrs. Marx.

The three sisters presented Mamma with an extraordinary memento of her seventieth birthday, which they had missed celebrating with her. They had taken apart a loose-leaf calendar for the year 1910, sent each page to a relative or friend of Mamma's in America and Europe asking for a suitable inscription and autograph. The collected and assembled calendar pages would serve to remind Mamma every day of that year how beloved she was, far and wide. And, while Henrietta and Mamma were busy reinstalling themselves in the flat on 123rd Street, Mathilde Schechter, with the help of other friends, set about organizing a dinner party to welcome home the two returned travelers.

And what a welcome it was! It was held in February 1910, the day after Lincoln's birthday, at the Hotel Premier, where, gathered around the great festive board were Rachel, Bertha, Adele, their husbands, and a host of good friends: the Schechters, the Marxes, the Friedlaenders, the Magneses, Sulzbergers and others from Philadelphia, Friedenwalds and others from Baltimore, Alice Seligsberg, Rose Sommerfeld, Sarah Kussy and others of Henrietta's wide circle of Zionist women. Bearded Solomon Schechter with twinkling blue eyes and nimble tongue was the witty toastmaster; handsome, sonorous-voiced Judah Magnes introduced the courses of the generous menu in which the dishes were appropriately dubbed for the occasion. There was "Zion Punch," and "Potatoes Jerusalem"; "Young Turks" were consumed; Papa was remembered with the "North River Shad à la Nemiskert." Bertha's husband, Louis Levin, and Adele's husband, Thomas Seltzer, read sonnets they had written for Mamma's seventieth birthday. It was, in a way, even more Mamma's celebration than Henrietta's; for had not Mamma saved Henrietta, and shown her the way to transcend the disorder men made? So there Mamma sat, serene, like a stout little queen, trimly contained in her well-corseted black Victorian basque; her hair, still wavy brown, parted in the middle, gathered up to a chignon and curling down over her broad brow; her bright, humorous blue eyes strong with intelligence, yet soft with compassion; her short nose proudly lifted, her generous mouth firm though bowed downward a little by the weight of sorrows survived. It was easy to see how much like her slight Henrietta, sitting beside her, had come to look, except for Papa's dark eyes.

Last of all, Henrietta was called upon to speak. She stood up and, when the rousing applause had subsided, she told them, with quiet eloquence, what she had seen and felt and thought in Palestine, and of the great work to be done there—the woman's work. . . .

PART THREE

Her Mother's Daughter

You knew my mother, therefore you know me.

—HENRIETTA SZOLD 1936 *

* In letter to Jessie Sampter

1910s: EMANCIPATION

ALTHOUGH she had resumed her arduous editorial work for the Jewish Publication Society—she was introducing Sholem Asch to American readers; she had the Year Book to get out—she went about speaking to group after group, from Harlem to Brooklyn and even across the river to Newark, to men and women, Zionist and non-Zionist, to any who would listen, not, as she had threatened, "talking them to death" but to a revival of interest in their lives as Jews. Her slight figure, her small voice, her gentle dark eyes, fiery only, like Papa's, when kindled by quivering indignation, somehow commanded and held their attention.

"When I stand before a gathering like this, fellow Zionists and fellow Jews, I am dominated chiefly by a sense of my responsibility toward you. I feel as Caleb and Joshua must have felt when they returned from the Vale of Eschol; for a trip to the Holy Land is not only a privilege, it entails obligations. You have a right to look at me questioningly and say to me, 'We demand an account of you; what have you seen? What have you to tell us?' Unlike Caleb and Joshua, I come empty-handed. I have not brought the grapes from Eschol. I do not bear a heavy weighted bough of oranges from Jaffa; I cannot scatter any of the wheat of Galilee among you. Even the narcissus and the crocuses that I gathered on top of Mount Carmel in the month of November, have withered. I have not a dry stony clod to crumble before you to show you wherein the fertility of the land consists; not even a handful of earth can I bring before you, full of its richness, its blackness, its wealth of small seedlings sprouting before the rain. I have not even the chaff that I saw flying in all parts of Galilee, driven before the wind. As the psalmist says: 'I come empty-handed; I come only with words.' You may consider them chaff.

"But I want to reassure you about the quality of my words, because I have good tidings to bring you, of the good and the beauty that I saw. I should like to take you with me on my trip through the Holy Land. . . ."

And this she did, taking them with her from Tiberias down to Jerusalem, so that they saw vividly the land caressed by its sea; its hills and its fields, its vineyards and groves, its deserts and waste places, its towns, its colonies, its people—their achievements and their failures, their heroism and their squalor, their devotion and their misery—". . . poverty such as our East Side has never held. . . ." She took them right into that distant place so they saw "boys with long dangling earlocks running to the synagogue . . . men carrying oilskins precisely as we know of them from the Bible pages. . . . We would mount a wagon and we would ride off through roads built by Jewish hands. The Arab does not build roads; he rides on donkeyback, camelback, or horseback. It was the Jew who brought the wagon and the roads to Palestine; and the roads are as good as mountain roads can be—that is, not very good."

She made them see the reviving life of the land: "We would be able to tell where a Jewish field began and where it ended, where an Arab field began and where it ended, because the hand of the Jew has made a very different impression upon the land from the hand of the Arab. Where the Arab works two inches deep, the Jew works a foot deep, and on a Jewish field there is no stone; but on an Arab field the old plow of ancient times must work its way between the stones. . . . The Jewish olive tree has learned to bear in seven years, while an Arabic tree waits twenty years, unless the Arab has learned from the Jewish settlers. . . . And one of the Jewish *shomerim*, their watchmen, comes riding along, bestriding his horse as though welded to the saddle, as though his ancestors had always ridden bareback, and not in a circus either. Palestinian Jews are muscular Jews. . . . Scarcely has the field been cleared of grain, and the sower already comes with the seed in his hands. . . .

"We go to Haifa, and get a little jealous, because we see the German colony there. That is beautiful, that is well planted, that has vegetable gardens, that has fine poultry, that has well-built houses. Why is it so different from our colonies? Some say that it is because the German government conducts these colonies. Some say it is because the Germans are better colonists than the Jews, and still—these German colonies buy their grapes from the Jews, press them in their own presses, and then send them out to the world as their own wine. . . . But in Haifa, although it is largely Arab, one also finds Jewish life. . . . That is the place at which a Technical Institute is about to be raised. That and Jerusalem should be the educational centers of the Jews. . . .

"In Jerusalem you meet some kindergarten children and you ask them, in Hebrew, with great difficulty if you are an American, where the Yemenites are to be found. And the little children look at you in wonderment and tell you, with their Sephardic accent: 'You look like a Jew, you act like a Jew, and you do not know Hebrew!' and then run ahead, telling you all about the flowers, and about their school, until you come to the Yemenites . . . some of them sick and miserable but most of them sturdy, baking the bricks for the houses they are going to build, the women baking bread in outdoor Arab ovens. . . .

"The Yemenites, from the extreme southern part of Arabia, have had to flee from persecution there. I doubt whether they know very much about Zionism, about the Federation of American Zionists, or the *Actions Comité*, but they did find their way to Palestine and to Jerusalem; and they are among the best colonists, the best workers in silver, the best carpet weavers, and are learned in Hebrew to boot. In Jerusalem, in their own *Bet ha-Midrash,* they study sitting Arab fashion, on the floor, one book for six; two at the head, two at the foot, and one on each side; and those at the head and those on each side of the book read with the same ease, the same alacrity, the same ardor as the two in front of the book. Think of what that means: in the first place, that though they have been separated for centuries from the body of the Jewish community, they have held fast to the literature of the Jews. It also means that for centuries they have never had as many books as they needed. They were too poor. You see them come to Palestine, day after day, because they were persecuted; you see them in rags, their children in rags, some of them naked, but carrying with them a box of *seforim*—books. They are the Jews who have the longest sidecurls. They are tubercular, rachitic. They have big, lustrous eyes, full of intelligence and feeling. They take their children with them on the road work, and, in the intervals of stone breaking, they teach their children themselves, because they do not trust the schools to teach them as they should. That is the material that comes to Zion whether we send them there, whether we provide for them there, whether we have a Zionist movement, whether we are active in it or not. . . ."

But then, having given them, like Caleb and Joshua, her optimistic report of the Promised Land, she said she was also inspired by the misgivings of the other ten men who had gone with Caleb and Joshua to spy out the land. "I shall not be afraid," she said, "to tell the truth"; and then described for them the giants of evil to be overcome in Zion—the creations of Turkish misrule and of Jewish mismanagement in the cities: "There is squalor; there is uncleanliness; there is narrow-minded charity instead of philanthropy; there is disorganization; there is petty strife; and there are the vices created by Zionists, by Western Jews. . . ." She told them, for example, of the miserable colony at Athlit: "Ought not the ten houses, of the description I have given you, to be abandoned? Is it necessary to carry out the plan of a colony where it will do more harm than good? . . . I have been told, you have been told, how things are so much better now than they used to be. The optimist's subterfuge! What I should like to see is a whole lot of pessimism among Jews in the Holy Land. I should like to see the women rise up in their might and make demands. I think such discontent would bring about a radical change. . . ."

But she did not stop at criticism. *Eshet ḥayil,* the woman of valor in Proverbs, was a doer—practical, constructive: "She considereth a field, and buyeth it; with the fruit of her hands she planteth a vineyard. . . ." Henrietta counseled them: ". . . colonization in the twentieth century must be a philanthropy—a philanthropic scheme, not a charity scheme. A philanthropist, a leader of his people, will lay out a big plan, in which the architect will not blunder, in which the engineer will engage his best talents, in which men of science must have a share. . . .

"Years ago the Jews were told that they must show the world that they are not parasites; they must go back to the land, back to the soil. We have still the idea of making as many farmers as possible out of the Jews. Why should Jews be asked to do the unnatural thing? You know that farms are being abandoned here, that farming is becoming an industrial enterprise. Men do not seek farm life now. It is true, also, that if Palestine is to be the seat of a Jewish commonwealth, it is absolutely necessary that there be an agricultural basis to it; therefore we must make it worth while to them to give us that agricultural basis, by which I mean that every plan must be worked out in detail; that the whole country must be taken into consideration; that administrators must not be permitted to come there and make changes, if they do not know the people and the land; not one iota of the plan must be changed unless it be approved by the best talent we know of, by scientific men. We must have commissions that will pass upon these changes. . . . The southern colonies thrive because they are putting their chief strength into the cultivation of oranges. That is not agriculture; that is an industry. . . . The northern, the Galilean colonies, are true agricultural colonies, and they are having the greatest uphill fight I have ever witnessed. . . . I cannot go into the labor question . . . a labor question exists: The Arab workman will work for one franc a day. The Jewish workman requires more, and he must have it. He works hard. . . ." She quoted George Eliot's Daniel Deronda who said: "Difficulties? I know there are difficulties. But let the spirit of sublime achievement move in the great among my people and the work will begin. Let our wise and wealthy show themselves heroes. . . ."

She criticized the wastefulness of unorganized activity: "Before I went to the East, I had always heard of the immobility of the East, that it never moves. To a certain extent that is true. It does not move forward very much; but it is extremely busy. It is like the ocean, which never breaks its bonds, but is never quiet—to and fro, up and down; but no one knows what his neighbor is doing. . . . But soon the Zionists will have organized a scheme of their own. . . . One thing they are doing for which I am thankful; they are buying up land with the National Fund. If only they did it more thoroughly, more quietly! The trouble with them is that hardly have they bought a piece of land than it is known all over the world. This is unnecessary. The Germans are buying up land all the time, but nobody knows anything about it. . . . They tell you in the newspapers that the Turkish officials are going to regulate immigration, they are not going to permit the consolidation of the Jews. They cannot prevent it! Jews will go there, and if the Jews of the Western lands will buy Palestine, the Turkish government cannot prevent them!"

She told them of the educational situation—of the schools established by the *Alliance Israélite*, the *Hilfsverein*, and the Odessa Zionist Committee which represented the *Ḥovevei Zion*; of the Evelina de Rothschild School, and the colonists' schools. She told how these last had broken loose from the tradition of the others, which was to educate children not for Palestine but "for export," by emphasizing foreign languages and skills for which there was little use in Palestine so that their young graduates had to go away, to Egypt or Europe or America, to find work for which they were fitted. "The colonist schools say, 'We are here for the people. Our people need two languages—Hebrew, because they are Jews, and Arabic, because they must live and speak with the Arab; all the rest of the time can be devoted to the real needs of their education. . . ." She told them of Dr. Schatz's *Bezalel*, museum and art school; how the talented children got their motifs in the museum and worked them into carpets, and filigree, and brass and copper inlay, and lithography. . . . "Professor Schatz has the same attitude toward his school as toward a factory. He believes that only he who works can succeed in Palestine. Every child who comes to his school has learned something, he feels a new power; and when he has felt it he exercises it and applies it to those things needed in the land itself. He will not carve beautiful sideboards and make chairs to send to Alexandria and Cairo, but he will make things for his own home. . . ."

She deplored the fact that there was as yet no respectable national library in Jerusalem, where foreign scholars could come to study all aspects of Jewish culture at its source; and she told them how ashamed she was when asked: "How is it we get so little money from American Jews? They are rich; they can help us"; and how she answered, "No, you are mistaken; the Jews of America are not rich. They have great burdens. One hundred thousand immigrants come to America every year. Those Jews who love Palestine are the very ones who have to bring their own relatives over. They have to send checks to Russia. From these, who contribute to the National Fund, you get help, not from those living in palaces." But to her American audiences she added, "It is true you have burdens, but Palestine must be greatly helped! We cannot excuse ourselves on the score of our burdens. . . . It is the home of Jewish Jews. It is our bounden duty to help them; it is our bounden duty to invite upon ourselves their cares. . . . We must think of it as the land to be conquered by Jewish culture. There, there is Jewish life! . . ." She convinced them with her logical reasoning; she moved them with her quietly passionate eloquence.

She found herself speaking most often to groups of women—of the Young Women's Hebrew Association and the Council of Jewish Women, of Hunter College and Barnard College, of Temple sisterhoods and mothers' societies. At Barnard, where there were nearly one hundred Jewish girls among the five hundred students, she ran into intense opposition to her suggestion of the formation of a Jewish study group, because of the students' fear of exciting prejudice by segregation. The main argument was that the Jewish girls at Barnard had just succeeded in achieving a respected position; one of them had won the class presidency; and a Jewish society would undo all the success of such individuals. Fine-looking, intelligent young women, they denied that they were ashamed of being Jews; nevertheless almost all were assimilationists. Such was the pressure of the melting pot, it made them want to discard their admirable inheritance—like those gay, colorful immigrants on the boat. Not for them was that ancient song: "If I forget thee, O Jerusalem, let my right hand forget her cunning . . ." But most of Henrietta's audiences listened intently.

To women, she spoke mostly of the condition and work of the women in the colonies, of the schools, and of the health of the children. "So far as the women are concerned . . . that is where the philanthropists have made their mistake. They have done nothing to spur on the women, given them no encouragement. . . . If we come to Palestine after two thousand years of Western instruction, why should we not find modern methods there—domestic as well as agricultural? Why should women be burdened with old-fashioned ovens? Why should it not be thought out by a council of men as interested in *that* work as in farming? . . . Let a few American women go to the colonies and do settlement work there. They can teach modern housework and other domestic industries, as they are taught here in the Clara de Hirsch Home, so that hand and head are developed. The chief thing that the settlement worker should do is to rouse a noble discontent among them. The women are too patient! If they had only risen up and demanded better sanitation and better living conditions! That is what I call a noble discontent, and that is what should be aroused in them by women from the West." Somewhat belatedly, as in other areas of her womanly development, Henrietta found herself closer to the militancy of modern women like her sister Adele and the Council of Jewish Women, an attitude she had once deplored.

After recounting what she had seen of the schools in Palestine run by different and competing authorities she said, "The men and women connected with these schools are the true Jewish missionaries. They live a life of self-abnegation. But I cannot refrain from saying that if the *Alliance,* and the *Hilfsverein* and the people who are managing the Evelina de Rothschild School were to join forces, in order to make the whole system consistent, strong, perfect, if they were to select a body of educators who could sit down in Palestine and work out a true system of education, a great deal more could be done than by wrangling for the supremacy of one school over another. . . ." As she had learned long ago with her "Russians" in Baltimore the need now for education in Palestine was a pragmatic one—a far cry from that ideal progressive system she had envisioned at Old Point Comfort for the children of prosperous America.

Above all, when speaking to women, she made them see the children in those schools in poor Palestine and the needs of those neglected ones over whom Mamma had wept. There was women's work to be done. . . . She began organizing groups of women to that end, study and discussion groups to begin with, and she got herself a tutor for lessons in conversational Hebrew. The groups called themselves "Hadassah," the Hebrew for Esther, the Jewish queen who had been instrumental in saving her people in a time of peril. In 1893 at the World's Fair, Henrietta had not joined the Council of Jewish Women because of its militant separateness from masculine authority. Now, perhaps in part because of her personal disillusion, she counted herself among "the suffragists," along with her sisters Adele and Rachel, and Dr. Schechter's daughter Ruth, who spoke in public for women's rights despite her father's opposition; and Henrietta was herself inciting women to "noble discontent" and organizing them for separate action. She had little patience now with women who did not sympathize with and support the aspirations of their own sex. At a dinner party, where her rich and exquisitely groomed hostess declared that the three million women working in factories in the United States had gone forth from their homes "only because they wanted to earn pin money for gewgaws" Henrietta could not contain herself and reproved her with an asperity quite like Mamma's when she was indignant.

Nevertheless she was very much involved in the Zionist and Jewish community activities of the men, who came to her for counsel and assistance. Judah Magnes, ardent Zionist and idealistic liberal rabbi of Temple Emanu-El, when he came into conflict with his wealthy, ultra-Reform and largely anti-Zionist congregation, discussed with Henrietta Szold the revolutionary sermon he delivered, which cost him his post. She was asked to attend a meeting of the Executive Committee of the Federation of American Zionists, of which her old Baltimore friend Harry Friedenwald was President. It turned into a three-hour wrangle between ambitious power-seeking men about their growing deficit, during which even charming Judah Magnes became overbearing toward their ineffectual secretary, whose predecessor he had been and whom he had proposed as his successor. The finances of the Federation were close to bankruptcy. Henrietta came away from the meeting long after midnight, appalled at the chaotic state of American Zionist affairs. Visitors from Palestine, whom she had met at various institutions there, called upon her for help in gathering the funds they needed, and incidentally let her see the web of cross purposes between the jealous personalities running them. And when Aaron Aaronsohn came to get support for an agricultural station at Athlit he immediately enlisted the invaluable help of Henrietta Szold. Her involvement in such activities did not serve to lessen her disillusionment about that ideal of manhood, and of Jewish men in particular, which her father had inculcated upon her young womanhood. They gave her an insight into the emotional rather than reasonable motivations of men, and into their petty personal politics, which played a part even in the most altruistic movements. "Looking back," she commented, "I find my Baltimore life purity and innocence. There probably was as much scheming and seething, only it seems never to have reached me."

The purity and innocence of her past life was further impressed upon her by a reading of Anatole France's *Thaïs* which fell into her hands at that time. After finishing that superb, ironic story of the damnation of a saintly monk by his passion for a courtesan he had set out to save, and did save, Henrietta wrote, "I wonder whether reading a book like that early . . . would have altered the course of my existence. Perhaps if I had understood it. I must have read such books again and again. They glanced off from my stupidity. I wonder why I did not understand. . . ."

But she had learned not to let her maturer understanding and critical vision of the shortcomings of men deter her from working with them for good ends; and her disillusion had not soured her vision of men or lessened her appreciation of a truly admirable man. She did not hesitate to tell Judah Magnes that he had been foolish to think, when he took the post at Emanu-El, that his "God-given qualities were meant for the conversion to democratic Judaism of a few members of the richest Jewish congregation in the world"; and while she admired his courage, and approved his attempted conservative reconstruction of Reform Judaism, she criticized the vagueness of his principles and plans, which she considered a serious fault in a leader. He was too eclectic; yet she felt sure he would have a great influence with his fine personality. She held meetings at her house for his group, interested in the development of a *Kehillah* for the Jewish community in the New York area, with subsidiaries in other Jewish communities. She became the secretary of its Education Committee, and with Israel Friedlaender and Samson Benderly of Baltimore made a survey of

Jewish education in New York. She also wrote letters and arranged meetings for Aaron Aaronsohn with people who could be helpful to him; and he telephoned and came frequently to discuss his progress with her. He had written many papers on agricultural and botanical subjects, the latter of special interest to Henrietta who had little time these days for her girlhood hobby. She undertook the function of secretary for his projected Agricultural Station, of which they got Julius Rosenwald to become president, and Cyrus Adler, Samuel Fels, Louis Marshall, and Julian Mack to become trustees.

Aaronsohn's success in getting financial support for his project from such wealthy outspoken anti-Zionists as Jacob Schiff, head of Kuhn, Loeb and Co., and Julius Rosenwald, President of Sears, Roebuck and Co., who were less interested in what his discoveries of wild wheat and dry farming might do for Palestinian than for American agriculture, inevitably roused the jealousy and suspicion of less successful American Zionist workers. They came to Henrietta Szold and tried to undermine her opinion of Aaronsohn. But after many searching conversations with him, her faith in his integrity and her admiration of his personal qualities were enhanced. Despite her disillusionment with men in general and Jewish men in particular, she found this vigorous young man of thirty-four, of high intelligence and a charming personality, not only "a strong specialist," a scientist, who made her mind feel vague and flabby, but "a whole man"—the new type of Jew, muscular as well as intelligent, which the Land of Israel would produce, a type appealing even to a woman in her fiftieth year. He enjoyed a good joke, sports, people. Energy burst from his blue eyes and his robust body. He spoke half a dozen languages, each one with the idiomatic freshness that made you think he knew no other. He told her of his projected investigations, one of which was to be an examination of the dunes in Palestine that now covered a stretch of land described by Josephus in the first century as having been so fruitful and beautiful that it was the resort of the wealthy in his time. Aaronsohn also told her of ideas he had for the general development of the country, aside from his own specialized field of interest; and he had in mind a particularly well-fitted man to head each project—for examples, a canning industry, and the coordination of the schools—the very idea she herself had brought from Palestine and was promulgating in her talks. He was not merely a talking but a working idealist; and his bent for organization was an important characteristic to her.

He told her also of himself, of his adventurous early years and of his present outlook on life. He was a man who was not afraid of hard work, nor was he fearful of sentiment. He had a high regard for women, of whom he counted several among his best friends, and often put a greater trust in them than in men. Henrietta felt impelled then to urge him to get married. He ought not to wait. A woman, she said, would be happy with him, his energy, his great plans, his idealism; and if he married he would have someone devoted and trustworthy with whom to communicate and share his hopes and preoccupations. When he went back to Palestine, she wrote in her diary, "I shall miss his stimulating presence—scholar, gentleman, man of the world."

She kept the diary during the first half year after her return from abroad, which was a trying time as well as a busy one. There was the ordeal of dreaded but inevitable meetings, at the Seminary Synagogue and at dinners and teas, with the man who was responsible for her painful disillusion and the woman who had got what she had so passionately desired. "She has undoubtedly the beautiful eyes he spoke of . . ." Henrietta wrote, grudgingly; for she discovered that she was not yet quite so strong and self-controlled as she had thought at the end of her travels. Nor did the knowledge of emotional processes affect one's ability to control them. Eighteen years before on her return from the trip abroad with her father she had written in an article for *The Messenger,* "We may long ago have ceased to feel the heartbreak which was inflicted by some great grief. Let us but visit the grave of our dead affections or blighted hopes or the scene of our distress, and it arises again in all its poignancy." So she avoided, as far as possible, any contact with the woman she still bitterly envied; and *he* solved her dilemma by acting, whenever they came face to face, as if she were quite invisible. However, in the course of her duties with the Jewish Publication Society she was obliged to discuss his publications at the editorial meetings in Philadelphia, to read the proofs of his prolific works, and to correspond with him about them; and she found even this impersonal intercourse too distressing. She broke two pairs of eyeglasses in one week over his work. She returned to him some proofs improperly corrected; and when he sent her a preface in German she returned it to him with a request for it in English; then wrote in her diary: "I hardly know myself when I do these things to him—I who used to spare him every vestige of drudgery. Is it malice on my part? Or is it truly a measure of self-protection, as I say to myself? I don't know. I suppose I might have translated that bit of a preface and not felt any more miserable than I do. . . ." And Mamma, seeing how distressed she was, threatened to go to him and tell him what he was doing to her. Henrietta undertook then to engage someone at her own expense to take over this part of her duties. "I shall spend that money," she recorded, "in the same spirit as I would pay for a hospital operation on some diseased organ of mine. I am sure of myself at last. . . ." She was completing the heroic self-therapy she had begun in her journal a year and a half before. She considered making it somewhat easier for herself, as well as for the other woman, by taking Mrs. Schechter's advice "to pull up stakes and go elsewhere. But that," she decided, "I will not do for Mamma's sake. . . ." Mamma's health had apparently been undermined by their strenuous trek and her bronchial trouble abroad, and to take her away from her friends would be cruel. Besides, in June he and his wife would be going abroad for five months, which should help matters.

Because her sister Rachel was spending that spring in the East for some serious surgical treatment, Professor Joseph Jastrow was frequently in New York, lecturing on psychological subjects, the subconscious, and the like, which were then receiving a good deal of popular interest, stimulated by some lectures given, while Henrietta was abroad, the previous fall at Clark University in Worcester, Massachusetts, by a Dr. Sigmund Freud from Vienna. While Joe approved of Dr. Freud's theory of the unconscious, he took exception—as did most psychologists abroad also—to the emphasis Freud placed on the part played by the sexual drive in psychological activity. Joe Jastrow, like many others at that time, found Freud's frank insistence on that emphasis so shocking that he ultimately wrote an anti-Freudian diatribe, a book called *The House That*

Freud Built. But it was remarkable that Henrietta, before she had ever heard of Freud, should have undertaken to rid herself of an obsessive emotional distress by the catharsis of psychoanalysis and self-expression which Freud practiced on himself and prescribed for others. She could not prevent the dreams and recurrent memories which still plagued her by night and by day; but she continued striving to exorcise the plague by writing them out in her diary, along with her observations of the troubled men and women who came to her for help, seeing in the distinguished, dignified Henrietta Szold, ironically enough, a tower of strength and wisdom.

The tales of one young woman who came and confided repeatedly in her about the abortive affairs she had had, together with the reading of several popular novels, prompted Henrietta to comment that tragedies like theirs "grow as thick in life as blackberries in August—so thick that the novelists know every twist and fold of their bruised beings, and I ought to be silent about my lot—it is too common. Instead of which I continue to be rebellious. . . ." Max Löbl, who was sister Sadie's fiancée when she died, came from a Western trip to tell her of his discontented life. He had not married. "Poor fellow! I know exactly what his soul looks like. He has nothing to live for," wrote Henrietta. Even Joe Jastrow, who professed to know so much about the psyche, came to her with his personal problems and anxieties. She could well understand Thoreau's dictum that "most men live lives of quiet desperation," and why some were driven to suicide; but, as for her, so long as a human being needed her, she could not say no to life. *Le Ḥayim* was the Jewish toast.

Her strenuous working days were constantly interrupted by callers. A melancholy author with three children, wanting her help with his book and in getting engagements for parlor readings, so distressed and unnerved her that she felt ineffectual in the address she had to deliver later that day to a Hadassah group. Nevertheless Dr. Friedlaender, who also spoke, likened her to Deborah, the militant heroine of ancient Israel. She had found his praise "too fulsome. How I dislike that sort of thing!" she confided to her diary. But they flocked to her—strangers who had heard of the renowned Henrietta Szold, or had heard her speak; friends who, like herself, had failed to find mates. There was the admirable social worker and teacher, Alice Seligsberg, who shared her idea "that women need a particular education, not less high education than men, but a different high education," if they were ever to achieve the self-respect which would make it possible for them to thank the Lord "who made me according to Thy will." There were Jessie Sampter, the gifted poet, and Nellie Straus, daughter of one of the first women physicians, both of whom she turned from an assimilated background to Zionist interest and activity.

Even her sister Adele now came to her for advice and assistance; for Adele found herself married to an ineffectual neurasthenic, whose publishing failures made it necessary for her to work as Mrs. Schiff's secretary. Being childless, Adele was devoted to birds and cats; she trained a sparrow, named Count Zeppelin, to come to her call, and was writing a book about cats. Nevertheless Henrietta still envied Adele the sick husband upon whom she could lavish some of her frustrated maternity; and she even envied lovely Rachel (who was also childless) the illness that elicited from Joe the tenderness with which he treated her. Henrietta's world was full of frustrated women; still she saw in marriage and children woman's greatest fulfillment. Her ideal woman was radiant sister Bertha in Baltimore, with her good husband Louis Levin and her bright children. It "flattered" Henrietta when they cuddled up to her as soon as she came for a visit. When she saw on the street in Baltimore those Quaker women whose apparent serenity had inspired her girlhood envy, she wondered now what turbulent emotions were concealed in those brown- or gray-clad bosoms, what wild thoughts under those demure bonnets. And after meeting a girl in New York who was planning to teach at Columbia, she wrote: "I wish I dared shout it out to every young girl not to turn away for a moment from her natural destination. Do I mean that women are not to be educated to be self-supporting and self-reliant? No! But they must also be taught not to lay too much stress upon mere intellectual efficiency. Their artificial vocation, for use in an emergency, is secondary to their real vocation. And how real the real one would have been for me, I know only now, when my heart hungers for love and for the opportunity of loving. I mean exclusive love and loving. . . ." And whenever she saw those who were achieving or had achieved this blessed state she was racked with excruciating, despicable jealousy. . . . "Why am I so particularly wretched and despondent today? Is it because I saw Florence Robison in her young radiant happiness over her engagement to Mr. Brodie? Or because I saw at the Seminary people together in their happiness?—the Marxes, the Davidsons, the Friedlaenders with little Herzl. . . ." When she saw how the happy marriage of one of her friends had in one year "made her less aggressive in manner, looks, and even dress"; when she went to Philadelphia and saw the happiness of her friends "the Malters in their dear little home," and they talked of the happiness of her cousin Miriam married to Dr. Schloessinger; when she saw the complete accord of the Marshalls, and the contentment of her girlhood Baltimore friend Racie in the beautiful home and the child she had with Cyrus Adler—"I cry out at Fate! I feel so deep a capacity in me for happiness and making happy, and I must seal myself up. The books and the wise people tell you to help others and you will forget yourself. Am I not putting my time into other people's work? Does that make me forget . . . ?" She was working so hard in fact that her eyes were painfully strained.

But though life was real it was not all earnest. The apartment on 123rd Street, like the house on Lombard Street, had become again, with Mamma's hospitality, a pleasant gathering place on Friday nights. All sorts of people were drawn to Henrietta, and she warmed them with her enthusiasms. Assimilationists became conscious of their Jewishness and, inevitably, Zionist workers. A distant cousin, Robert Szold, a young lawyer who came to call, found himself before long involved in Zionist affairs. Young educators and social workers, scholars and rabbis, found there a common stimulus.

At Passover, in April, Adele, who was living in the country, in Connecticut, came to help Henrietta with the preparations for the *seder,* bringing dogwood and apple blossoms, columbine, anemone, violets, filling the flat with the glory of spring; and Henrietta conducted the *seder* for ten of the family and friends, as Papa used to do. They sang and talked until late. With Joe and Rachel, who was slowly convalescing from a surgical wound, Henrietta enjoyed going to the Irving Place Theater where a troupe of German actors from Berchtesgaden, Bavaria, took her back to memories of her first theater play, *Uriel Acosta,* with the great Dawisohn.

In May she organized a large farewell dinner party at the Astor for the Schechters, who were going abroad, a gala event which everyone said was a brilliant success. It was a culinary triumph, followed by a feast of wit and eloquence served by such diverse talents as Magnes and Schiff, Friedlaender and Adler, presided over by Louis Marshall as toastmaster—except that, despite all her careful calculations, Henrietta discovered that, of some hundred and thirty guests, she had somehow seated the couple she least wanted to see at a table adjacent to her own. Him she could see reflected in a mirror; with her she was face to face. She was surprised at her own outward calm.

She was interested to hear the different Jewish attitudes expressed by several of the outstanding leaders of Jewry: Jacob Schiff, speaking on "American Israel," said that Jews in these times were influencing the Christian world toward Judaism, and he spoke scornfully of Jewish nationalism. The applause he got was thin; whereas Judah Magnes on "The Regeneration of Jews and Judaism" got an ovation; and Cyrus Adler dodged the issue by declaring he was not an "adjective Jew, just a plain simple Jew. . . ." As Mrs. Schiff put it, "My, this is exactly like a political meeting!" Israel Friedlaender smoothed the troubled waters with "a subtle, kindly and true characterization of Solomon Schechter as man and scholar."

By the summer after her return from abroad Henrietta was still quite undecided about what her future career would be. Life had taken on the semblance of an obstacle race. She had not succeeded in finding someone suitable to take over that part of her editorial work which she could not bear to continue, and she felt she would have to resign from the Publication Society. Letters from Aaron Aaronsohn and Manya Shochat kept her in touch with Palestine, but the obstacles to progress there were increasing, while the state of the Federation of American Zionists and the lack of headway made by the Hadassah groups gave very little promise of her finding a channel for effective, practical Zionist activity. Even her Hebrew teacher proved unsatisfactory.

Because of the popular success she was having with her talks on Palestine, she was being urged to make a career of lecturing—on Palestine in the United States, and, in German, on America in Europe. Despite the fact that her small, feminine voice was not resonant, and she was not an orator, she did move her audiences; non-Zionists like the Council of Jewish Women and even anti-Zionists like Mrs. Schiff, who heard her give a talk at the Sulzbergers', were impressed. In Baltimore, where she had once dreaded to rise from her seat to address an audience, she had a veritable triumph: "I felt the electric response I elicited from them as I stood before a sea of upturned, tense, familiar faces, some of them my teachers, most of them my contemporaries, but already many newcomers to whom I am only a name, and my dear father no more a living memory, only an almost hallowed tradition . . ." But Henrietta doubted if she could hold audiences who paid to hear her and were not predisposed in her favor. She was offered the job of making a study of Jewish education in America, the editorship of a Jewish Literary Encyclopedia, of a new Jewish magazine, and other positions. But she had begun to think that in working for others she had cheapened herself by undertaking menial jobs and had been undervalued and exploited. In this she had been unlike *eshet ḥayil*: "She perceiveth that her merchandise is good." She felt now like doing something quite independently. Why should not her own "works praise her in the gates"? What she would really like to do was to write—an ambition from which she had been sidetracked by others. She had amply demonstrated her talent; her prose had the lucid, well-ordered, quiet eloquence of her speech; and she had a varied accumulation of information, ideas and experiences. She began planning several books: on her travels abroad, on Palestine, on Jewish community life in the Baltimore of her childhood, on Western literature. . . . In mid-June she had actually begun a series of sketches for the travel book.

But in July, the Zionists holding their convention in Pittsburgh sent her a telegram asking her to become their honorary secretary—"honorary" meant without pay—and undertake putting their disordered house in order. She did not need the urging of friends like Israel Friedlaender who told her it would be the salvation of Zionism in America. She could no more resist that Zionist appeal than Mamma could resist getting those dirty children's faces washed with her precious Castile soap. So Henrietta, for all her resolutions about not giving herself cheaply and working for others, put aside her precious plan to write, and accepted, knowing full well the state of the household she would have to serve; but she was by then passionately devoted to the Zionist cause, ailing as it was, and she could not refuse this proposal which came from Harry Friedenwald, her Baltimore friend of the Lombard Street days.

Israel Friedlaender returned from Pittsburgh with an account of the hubbub at the convention which was not encouraging. "Zionism as an organization," Henrietta anxiously recorded, "is at too low an ebb"; but with Harry Friedenwald continuing as President, and Louis Lipsky, founder of the Zionist organ, *The Maccabean*, and herself, as members of a three-man Secretariat, improvement was expected. Lipsky, a long-experienced and dedicated Zionist, with a brilliant, incisive mind, wrote her a fine letter offering his fullest co-operation.

Henrietta refused all invitations to the country, and having seen most of her friends off to Europe, settled down to her duties: the Year Book, an Index for the Jewish Historical Society—eminently useful works, but drudgery. The heat in the city was frightful. The depressed young woman who had made Henrietta her confidante would come in the afternoon for a walk on Riverside Drive, where Henrietta tested her own fortitude by sitting on a bench she had sat on two years before. They engaged in speculations as to the extent to which our spiritual emotions are really only indirect manifestations of our purely physical desires, a notion which the recent lectures of Dr. Freud at Clark University had served to make popular, but which was of no apparent use to pragmatic Henrietta.

In a conference with Dr. Friedlaender about the Zionist office she got an appalling picture of what was to come: the Augean housecleaning to be done in the midst of clashing personalities. She was accustomed to drudgery, but she hated the thought of internal strife. The previous secretary was resigning before the end of his term, so she would have to take over before her term really began. "Everything I hear makes me realize that I have taken a huge burden upon myself and a hopeless task." She would not have time for any of the reading or writing she had been looking forward to. After a meeting with a Miss Ida G. she wrote: "She is a lady! I wish I could be one for a couple of years. I long for gracious living . . ." And critically observing Mamma in the course of some household difficulty, "And as I am exactly like her, I, too, am wearing myself out in detail work, in which I excel as she does. So it is fate with me!"

On July 14, 1910, she was inducted at the office of the Federation of American Zionists downtown on the East Side. Her first impression was of complete confusion. "People coming and going as if it were a café"—and using the phone for their personal business: "$17 extra on the phone bill" she noted. As it was one of her duties to keep track of the staff's working time, she democratically called to the attention of the officers as well as of the clerical help their laxness in keeping the office hours. "If you set a bad example how can I reprimand others?" she would say even to Mr. Lipsky. Her working day's program, beginning at sunrise was: Historical Society Index, Year Book, secretarial work for Publication Society, and for Agricultural Experimental Station, Zionist office, proofreading. "Will I stand it? I suppose I shall, but nothing else will be done, nothing worth while." And she lost her temper when the man who was supposed to assist her with the Year Book went abroad, leaving it at loose ends which she would have to repair: "I wish, oh I wish I could be confoundedly unconscientious. I hate myself for a prig when people dare to do it to me. They, of course, *must* go to Europe, they *must* go to Atlantic City; but Miss Szold is a fine beast of burden. Did I leave anything at sixes and sevens when I went to Europe? Did my going to Europe mean more labor for anyone else? Am I self-righteous? Do I see only the bag filled with others' faults that hangs in front? And not that other bag behind that contains my faults? I wonder; but in the meantime I hate myself and the life I have made for myself."

"My mind harks back," she wrote, "to the teaching days. They were happy! After all, there is nothing like association with the next generation either as mother or teacher . . . that is what I most enjoy . . . contact with the optimism and hope and trustfulness of the young."

As for that other life she might have made for herself, she arrived at an explanation for her failure to do so after talking with Mrs. Friedlaender and others of her married friends with children: "If only I had been thrown with so many young women in my own young womanhood days, and they had been so frank about their happiness, I might have learned the secret of a woman's life, her true life, and all might have been different. I am beginning to realize the fact that instinct was not there to teach me the cosmic secret. . . . But will I ever learn to thank God for having sent me the greater knowledge so late that it was only a heritage of pain? . . ."

Three days later, July 20, 1910, realizing that no further good would come of self-examination she stopped writing in the red-covered diary and gave herself unreservedly, in her fiftieth year, to the service of Zionism, that troubled cause, that ailing mate, that frail child, which was her undeniable destiny. She continued the editorial work which was her livelihood, which made it possible for her to spend uncompensated hours straightening up the disordered files in the musty Zionist office and untangling its finances; advising Aaron Aaronsohn and Manya Shochat in Palestine; and stirring her Hadassah groups to renewed life.

She spent eight months, often at night, working on the Zionist financial files. Horrified to find that many contributions to the Jewish National Fund had not even been acknowledged, she dug out the names and addresses of all such contributors, sent them receipts, and advised the head office of the Fund at The Hague of her findings.

In the spring of 1911 she went to Baltimore, had Dr. Friedenwald attend to her overstrained eyes, and entered a hospital for needed surgery, which forced her to spend the summer at Mt. Desert, Maine, in slow recuperation. She returned in the fall, healed and refreshed, to New York and her labors.

Early in 1912, she worked with Gertrude Goldsmith, who had attended the Tenth Zionist Congress at Basle, on a new plan to organize a Women's Zionist Organization in the United States; but she approached that more ambitious project with caution. When her plan was received with enthusiasm by her eager young colleague who cried, "Oh, Miss Szold, that will work very, very well!" Miss Szold replied: "No, Miss Goldsmith, it will *work*. That is all." With the help of a few friends—Mrs. Schechter, Mrs. Gottheil, Sophia Berger—they circulated a call to a meeting: "The undersigned in consultation with other women Zionists of the city have come to the conclusion that the time is ripe for a large organization of women Zionists. . . ."

The first united meeting of Hadassah was held in the vestry room of Temple Emanu-El on Saturday, February 24, 1912, at 8 P.M. Some forty women came. Henrietta Szold was elected President and Gertrude Goldsmith, secretary. By May, they were considering the possibility of undertaking various practical projects in Palestine—a visiting nursing service, a nursery, a maternity hospital, a training school for midwives. Israel Friedlaender supplied them with a motto from Jeremiah: *"Arukat Bat Ammi"*—"The healing of the daughter of my people." Victor Brenner, who designed the Lincoln penny, gave them an emblem: the six-pointed star of David, with "Hadassah," in Hebrew, superimposed on it and the motto above.

In December Henrietta heard from Judah Magnes, who was planning to visit Palestine again, that Mr. and Mrs. Nathan Straus (Mr. Straus was a generous philanthropist) were also going. She asked Miss Goldsmith to call upon Mrs. Straus and try to interest her in Hadassah and its plans.

At that time Henrietta was troubled by a letter from Louis Lipsky, critical of Hadassah for not having affiliated with the Federation, which would mean submitting to the direction of the men but having the benefit of their greater financial resources. As Hadassah was having some difficulty collecting adequate funds for its own projects, the second consideration was not negligible; as for the first, Henrietta who, back in 1893 at the World's Fair, had not seen fit to join the Council of Jewish Women, an autonomous women's organization, now felt rather differently about the need for women acting independently of men in certain areas. Hadassah continued to function as an autonomous "affiliate" of the Federation.

That Miss Szold was not, however, unduly depressed by the prospect of a sex war in Zionist ranks was evidenced in a playful talk she gave that month at a banquet tendered her by a group of women in Baltimore. It was in the *Ḥanukkah* holiday week, close to her fifty-second birthday, for Henrietta was born on the day of the lighting of the second candle. She began her talk by declaring that women could not possibly have a speechless banquet—something as naturally abhorrent to them as the concentrated food tablets which men were predicting for the distant scientific future, to which both such tasteless improvements should be relegated, she thought. Besides, women were too recently emerged from their "gabble-giggle-gabble stage of development" to be able to feast without talk. And, finally, women were too (she whispered it) "conservative" to change that custom. She whispered the word because this was the vaunted age of militant suffragettism. Nevertheless, she insisted, women *are* conservative; they are the preservers. For all their so-called militancy, it was not the suffragettes but the men who used force, who called out the police and the army to suppress them. Among the Jews, she pointed out, it is the woman who lights the peaceful Sabbath candles, thus maintaining an ancient tradition and shedding light, illuminating the world, "not by might, and not by power, but by spirit. . . ."

In January 1913 she called the third meeting of Hadassah in New York with a program in which Professor Gottheil talked on the Jewish colonies in Palestine, Herman Struck, the distinguished artist from Germany, spoke on Jewish art, and Aaron Aaronsohn, recently returned to America for further promotion of the Agricultural Station, told of his exciting work there. The spirited meeting ended with the singing of *"Hatikvah"*—"The Hope"—the hymn of the Zionist movement, written by Naphtali Herz Imber.

> *. . . Our hope is not yet lost—*
> *The hope of thousands of years:*
> *To be a free people in our land,*
> *In the land of Zion—in Jerusalem.*

Henrietta had followed up Miss Goldsmith's contact with Mrs. Straus by herself calling upon the Strauses, and was able to announce that she had got from them an offer to pay the travel expenses of a nurse to Palestine and her salary for four months, if Hadassah would undertake to maintain her thereafter. The reality of this prospect was so stirring that they were able to collect not only enough to engage Rose Kaplan as their first nurse, but enough additional funds in Chicago—where Jane Addams gave them the benefit of her professional guidance, and Eva Leon gathered the funds—to engage Rachel Landy, and send a team of two trained nurses. Henrietta saw to their preparation and equipment. On January 16 she and Mamma gave them a farewell party, and by March 24, the two nurses sent back a letter saying that they were leasing a house in *Mea Shearim,* the orthodox Jewish quarter of Jerusalem, in which they were installed and operating by mid-May.

On September 8 there was a meeting of Hadassah at which the nurses' report, with photographs, was submitted. Some 10,000 children had been treated for trachoma. They were also beginning the work of maternal instruction and realized that their struggle would be as much with ignorance as with disease. Mamma's tears had not been shed in vain.

Henrietta, realizing that funds for this work collected from Hadassah alone—it had then about 250 members—would be inadequate, planned public meetings. She got Miss Goldsmith to find some Hebrew songbooks and to organize a chorus of Hadassah members to sing at their meetings. On January 8, 1914, the meeting held at Beethoven Hall was crowded and successful.

"Miss Szold"—as everyone but her closest intimates called her—Miss Szold, that erstwhile "fine beast of burden," was discovering, belatedly as ever, her executive ability—the ability to get from others the devoted performance of details such as she had hitherto given to others, thus leaving her freer to exercise, in planning, that frustrated creative power which she had wished to put into writing. And women flocked to her now, not for her help but to help her in the woman's work to be done.

In February she was making plans for sending a third nurse to Palestine and for the establishment there of a training school for nurses, an expansion made possible by Nathan Straus's generous offer of further aid; and in April she was corresponding with Dr. Albert Ticho in Jerusalem about plans for a maternity hospital with a social service department.

That she happily managed all this while maintaining her editorial work was a psychological miracle. For the hitherto dreaded Year Book, she produced in 1914 a paper on "Recent Jewish Progress in Palestine" which ran to 158 pages, was reprinted as a separate book by the Jewish Publication Society, was reviewed at length by the *Nation* under "Literature," and was utilized as rich and reliable source material by the *Methodist Review* under "Archaeology and Biblical Research." In compact, lucid chapters it gave the history and development of Jewish life in Palestine since and despite the destruction of the Second Temple in 70 A.D., followed by a vivid description, supported by statistics, of Zionist activity and accomplishment there in every sphere and area, rural and urban. It ended with a prophetic vision of the time "when spiritual Jewish problems are grappled with tolerantly but earnestly, without the excommunications of the past or the indifference of the present; then the Jew's whole personality will be brought into full play, and for the first time in two thousand years he will, in one spot at least, fashion all the manifestations of his life in a Jewish mould." The *Nation* said, "It is likely to become . . . the most authoritative statement thus far made on the subject in any language. In English it has no peer. . . ." And Henrietta Szold had, incidentally, demonstrated how great a sacrifice she had made in giving up the literary life for the Zionist cause.

But she had neither the time nor the inclination now for any regrets. She was too busy planning meetings and programs with her staff of women friends and a corps of girls who acted as ushers, distributing and collecting Hadassah membership forms, and made house-to-house canvasses for funds. Lantern slides of Palestine views were obtained to give audiences a vivid picture of the Land of Israel, its cities and people, and the life of the Jewish colonists. . . .

But in June 1914, the outbreak of the First World War suddenly cut Western Zionists off from Palestine. The alignment of Turkey with Germany and Austria-Hungary against Russia, France, Great Britain and other allies, although the United States remained neutral, practically put an end to communication between American Zionists and the Jews in Palestine under Turkish rule. A group of Palestinians who moved to Alexandria served as a precarious liaison between them. Aaron Aaronsohn had advised that the two American nurses return to the United States. Brave Rose Kaplan, after serious surgical treatment in the United States, knowing she was doomed, returned to Alexandria, where she worked in the Jewish refugee camp until she died there. The refugees were Jewish nationals of allied countries who had to leave Palestine when Turkey declared war. Before leaving Jerusalem Miss Landy had arranged for Dr. Bertha Kagan to take over Hadassah's work there with the help of three probationers Miss Kaplan had trained, and with Dr. Ticho, an expert in trachoma, she set up a clinic in Jerusalem. Also, as a result of Miss Landy's report of critical conditions in Jaffa, arrangements were being made by Hadassah for medical service there.

The administration of the World Zionist Organization in Berlin was completely disorganized. Some of the members of its Actions Committee were serving in the Russian army, others in the German and Austrian. Two leaders were in London, two in Berlin, one in Copenhagen. Dr. Schmarya Levin, Russian writer and ex-member of the Russian Duma, a member of the World Zionist Executive who happened to come to the United States on the last trip of the *Kronprinzessin Cecilia* and was stranded here, organized a Provisional Executive Committee with headquarters in New York.

Henrietta Szold, though deeply distressed by this world catastrophe, was not deterred. The war would end, the Land of Israel and the children of Israel would survive this as they had survived so many wars, and Hadassah would still be needed. She had obtained funds for two more nurses, and prepared them for district visiting work at the New York Board of Health and at Lillian Wald's Nurses' Settlement; but the war prevented their going to Palestine. Miss Szold called a meeting of the New York chapter for November 30, the invitation stating that "owing to the war, there has developed so grave a crisis in Zionist affairs that it is very important for all interested in the cause to keep in close touch with the organized work of the movement. The emergency should be used as an opportunity."

At the meeting, Gertrude Goldsmith, now Mrs. Rosenblatt, reported on the Rochester Convention of the Zionist Federation, and Alice Seligsberg reported on work done by Hadassah for the $100,000 fund being raised by the Provisional Executive Committee; the women had rallied to the aid of the men in this crisis. Mrs. Gottheil reported on the state of Hadassah work in Palestine; Jessie Sampter reported on Hadassah work in America; and Henrietta Szold submitted the new constitution of the New York chapter of the Hadassah organization. Its avowed purpose: "to promote Jewish institutions and enterprises in Palestine, and to foster Zionist ideals in America."

To this end, she had extended the field of her speaking activity. She moved into Connecticut and Pennsylvania, spoke in Boston, Cleveland, Cincinnati, Chicago . . . where Hadassah chapters were established, in addition to those already in New York, Philadelphia and Baltimore. She also agreed to serve on the Zionist Provisional Executive Committee.

Louis D. Brandeis, the distinguished Boston lawyer, had been made its chairman, and Henrietta Szold became one of his good friends as well as his colleague on the Committee, which included Jacob de Haas, Rabbi Stephen Wise, Shmarya Levin, Louis Lipsky, and other important Zionists. Louis Brandeis was only four years her senior, and there were strong affinities in their natures and backgrounds, with one marked difference: like Herzl, Brandeis had come belatedly to Jewish consciousness and Zionism. For this he was indebted to his association in Boston with de Haas, a young journalist who had worked with Herzl since the first Zionist Congress, had been sent by Herzl on a mission to America, had remained in New York as secretary of the Federation of American Zionists in the administration of Professor Gottheil, its first president, and had then gone to Boston where he met Brandeis, and interested him in Zionism.

Louis Brandeis, like Henrietta Szold, was the American-born child of German-speaking immigrants who settled in the South—his parents came from Bohemia to Louisville, Kentucky. But his upbringing was, unlike hers, assimilationist; and his life had been entirely separated from Jewish interests until his Zionist indoctrination by de Haas. His emotional involvement was stimulated, as was Henrietta's, by contact with the Russian Jewish immigrants whom he met in the course of his legal services to the New York Ladies' Garment Industry for which he formulated a protocol agreement. He helped settle the great cloakmakers' strike in 1910, and laid the groundwork for mediation and arbitration in the largely Jewish clothing industries, a work to which he devoted himself for six years, out of his powerful sense of social justice. In Boston he was known as "the People's Attorney" because of his defense of the people's rights against the Boston traction interests, the gas trust, and the insurance companies. President Wilson called him "a friend of all just men and a lover of the right."

Like Henrietta Szold he had been greatly influenced by the democratic spirit of Abraham Lincoln; his uncle, Louis Dembitz, was one of the men who nominated Lincoln for the Presidency. Henrietta Szold called him "a combination of Isaiah and Amos," those prophets of Israel who were even more concerned with social than with individual morality. Brandeis combined the simplicity of the Judean shepherd, Amos, with the authority of the statesman, Isaiah of Jerusalem, the counselor of kings. Endowed, like Henrietta, with a highly developed sense of responsibility and an infinite capacity for taking pains, once his interest in Zionism was aroused, he informed himself thoroughly on every aspect of the subject and prepared himself for effective action in the cause.

He read Jewish history; he questioned all available Zionist leaders: Schmarya Levin, who could give him an analysis of Jewish and Zionist ideology; Nahum Sokolow, a deeply erudite Jew and Zionist; Louis Lipsky, who knew the innermost workings of American Zionism and its organization; Aaron Aaronsohn, when he came from Palestine, who could tell him what had happened there, and who was, like himself, not merely a talking but a working idealist; and Henrietta Szold, who was developing a new force in the movement—the women. With him, as with her, conviction called for action. As when preparing the brief for a case, Brandeis read and listened and questioned and tested the accuracy of all the evidence, and then set out to reorganize the movement in a way that was after Henrietta Szold's heart, by law and order, by planning, by seeking out and directing the best resources and the most effective people for the execution of the plan. And perceiving in Miss Szold a kindred spirit, and realizing her potential powers, he made her a member of his Executive Committee. "Members, money, discipline, that is preparedness," he said, a dictum which Henrietta Szold quoted in her talks. There is a Jewish saying to the effect that God sends the cure with the affliction. Just as the Dreyfus Affair brought Herzl to World Zionist leadership, the First World War brought Brandeis to American Zionist leadership. His fortunate advent in the war crisis put new life into the movement and heartened Henrietta in her special sphere of activity—the women's work.

The war crisis, however, created a personal spiritual dilemma for her which was intricately related to the dilemma of Zionism in Palestine as well as in the world at large, and particularly in the United States, whose neutrality Woodrow Wilson was trying to maintain. The genius of the Jew, because world Jewry transcends national boundaries, is to find himself in no man's land in an international crisis. This time, with Palestine Jewry held like a captive hostage by the Turks, and German and Austrian Jewry held by national allegiance in the German camp, some American Zionists, while the United States remained neutral, were in the difficult position of fearing to antagonize Germany and Turkey, which, if they won the war, might vindictively put an end to the whole Zionist achievement and hope in Palestine. On the other hand, there were those like Brandeis who, from the beginning of the war, sided with the Western Allies, expected them to win and, in that event, looked to Great Britain to rescue and preserve Zionist Palestine. In London, Chaim Weizmann, the chemist who had made a discovery important to British warfare, was offering this service in return for British support of the Zionist national aspiration in Palestine. In Washington, Brandeis explained Zionist goals to President Wilson, who was an avowed advocate of the self-determination of small nations, and engaged the interest of the British and French ambassadors. Germany was desperately trying, by propaganda and threats, to keep neutral the United States with its considerable population of immigrants from countries on both sides of the conflict, who were naturally divided in their sentiments and opinions as to the course this country should take.

The dilemma of Henrietta Szold in this complex situation was typical but intensified. As a Jew and a Zionist she was vitally concerned for the survival of Palestine Jewry, and as a nationalistic Zionist she devoutly hoped for the revival of Israel. Since earliest childhood she had been steeped in German culture; its language, literature and music—Goethe and Schiller, Beethoven and Bach—were precious to her, almost as profoundly inculcated as her Jewishness, and it was impossible for her suddenly to repudiate this important part of her spirit, like those jingoes who went about branding all Germans as Huns and damning everything German out of hand. And above all, encompassing both of these strong elements in her spirit, was the fact that she was an American, loving her native land and its institutions, its democracy, its Anglo-Saxon cultural inheritance, which had so moved her in Westminster Abbey, its technological achievement, and the spirit of its great leaders from George Washington and Abraham Lincoln to Woodrow Wilson, who was trying now to keep his country at peace. And peace—that *"Shalom!"* with which Jews always greeted each other, that peace which was the essence of the weekly Sabbath her father had considered one of God's greatest gifts to mankind—was so precious to Henrietta, and her abhorrence of war was so great, that she joined with the pacifists, who re-elected Wilson because "He kept us out of war." With Isaiah she prayed for the time when "they shall beat their swords into ploughshares," and she had a horror of seeing American men marching off to that bloody conflict to be killed or maimed, like those she had seen in her childhood on the streets of Baltimore. Her vision of the conflict in 1914 was that "there were under arms twenty-five million young men and they were being sent out to battle for what purpose? Twenty-five men in the world desired it, and they could do no other than what they were bidden to do by the twenty-five." She became a member of the People's Council of America for Democracy and Peace, which was led by Scott Nearing, the radical Socialist.

But the time came when to be a pacifist was to be pro-German, and if you spoke and wrote German in those days, you were especially suspect. Day by day it was becoming clearer that we would inevitably be drawn into the conflict on the side of the Allies. Then, being an American, you couldn't, of course, be pro-German; and, being a Jew and a Zionist, you would have to make it plain that you were wholeheartedly for the war which would bring defeat to Turkey. A victorious Great Britain would then open Palestine to the Jews for a National Home—that was the promise Weizmann was getting in London. And now it behooved all good Zionists everywhere to come to the aid of this eventual victory regardless of every other sentiment and consideration.

David Ben-Gurion of Sejera, one of the new Jews, strong as well as intelligent, was in the United States organizing a Jewish Legion to fight with the British, and he returned to Palestine as a soldier. Aaron Aaronsohn, who knew Palestine like the palm of his hand and was ostensibly in the service of the Turkish government, was actually in the British intelligence. He organized the so-called *Nili* spies in Palestine, despite the fact that he was thus endangering not only his own life but the lives of his beloved family—one of his sisters, Sarah, was working with him—and even of his neighbors in Zichron Yaakob, some of whom were, understandably, opposed to this dangerous activity. And Louis Brandeis decided that in this crisis it was imperative that every important Zionist leader unequivocally support the Allied cause. Pacifism gave aid and comfort to the enemy. He called in his friend and colleague Henrietta Szold and told her so; and she agreed to resign from Scott Nearing's organization and to say nothing more about peace, seeing, like Jeremiah in his time, that this was a time when men go about "crying Peace! Peace! and there is no peace."

With British shipping engaged in the war and German shipping blockaded, the United States, despite its ostensible neutrality, became the producer and carrier of munitions and supplies for the Allies on a gigantic scale. Germany, prevented from getting food for her starving civilians, was retaliating with unrestricted submarine warfare in which American seamen lost their lives. It was ridiculous to say we were not at war, or to hope we would not be—you had to take sides. Louis Brandeis clinched the argument against Zionists as "hyphenated Americans" when he said forthrightly: "Let no American imagine that Zionism is inconsistent with patriotism. Multiple loyalties are objectionable only if they are inconsistent. . . . Every American Jew who aids in advancing the Jewish settlement in Palestine, though he feels that neither he nor his descendants will ever live there, will likewise be a better man and a better American for doing so."

The terrible disorder of the world cut into two warring sides, with most of their relatives in the other camp, was a great grief to Mamma, who was ailing; and in 1915, toward the end of her seventy-fifth year, she fell seriously ill with a disease of the lungs, probably a development of the bronchial trouble she had had on the trip abroad. It was on her account that they moved from the house opposite the Seminary on 123rd Street, just as it was on her account that Henrietta had, until then, insisted on staying there. The air of the city was being increasingly befouled by fumes from the rapidly increasing number of automobiles, so they moved to a new apartment house on Pinehurst Avenue on the northern edge of the city, where the few buildings were set among green fields and woods and Mamma could have plenty of the clean fresh air and sunshine she needed.

Solomon Schechter died in November of that year, and this, together with their removal, marked the end of an era in the life of Henrietta Szold that for more than a decade had been based on the Seminary circle. The removal, and Henrietta's devoted attention to the needs of her mother whose illness was a painful one, necessitated her resignation from the Jewish Publication Society; but at the instigation of Justice Brandeis—President Wilson had appointed him to the Supreme Court—several friends headed by Federal Judge Julian W. Mack got up a fund that was placed at Henrietta's disposal in order that she might be free to continue to devote herself to the various volunteer services she was giving the Zionist cause and the Jewish community. For this freedom to serve her people she was profoundly grateful, especially to Judge Mack, who saw that the fund was maintained as long as she needed it.

She was recognized now as the most distinguished American Jewess, eminently fitted to speak not only to but for the Jewish community; and she was asked to lecture in February 1916 for the People's Institute at Cooper Union. It was the day after Lincoln's birthday, a cold snowy day in a world more madly torn even than Lincoln's world. President Wilson was exchanging notes with Germany about the sinking of the *Lusitania* in which 128 American lives were lost; and he was inspecting our coast defenses. The Germans made five assaults that day on a hill in Artois and were checked by a curtain of French fire, littering the field with dead men. And transcending the carnage, a scientist named Samuel Mott predicted that in the not far future it would be possible to fly to Europe in six hours by planes climbing to rarefied air strata where they could attain astonishing speed. Henrietta Szold, too, said nothing of the day's madness and spoke of a hope for the future; and when she rose to speak from the very platform upon which Abraham Lincoln had first appeared in New York, Henrietta could not but wish that her father were there to hear her. Her subject was "Zionism: A Progressive and Democratic Movement." She had carefully prepared the speech. It was consummately planned and organized, but she did not read it. She had filled thirteen pages with notations in her tiny script, and then condensed and composed them into a single-page résumé of nineteen topics in ordered sequence, from which she spoke extemporaneously. It was addressed, not to the Jews, but to the world. It was not an oration; it had none of Papa's flowery phrases, although it did hark back to the Bible now and then. It was a straightforward, vigorous and accurate statement of a complex human situation, which was both convincing and moving. She began without mincing words:

"The Jews have been a problem these many centuries; they are today. . . . Being a problem is not agreeable." She pointed out, however, that when the gentiles solved that problem by restricting the Jews to ghettos, where they found compensation for the hostility outside in a rich communal existence, the Jews were less conscious of being a problem than they became when ghetto gates were left open, during the period of emancipation following the French Revolution, and Jews slipped out into the larger, freer world. They then were made to realize painfully that they were still a problem, and began making attempts themselves at its solution.

This resulted in the division of Jews into three groups, each with a different solution, which Henrietta Szold set forth without criticism. There were those who insisted that the Jews are a religious brotherhood and nothing more; that the Jews, wherever they live, have only to become like their fellow nationals in every other respect and the prejudice against them will disappear. The ultra-Reform Jews, as an example, dispensed with the Jewish cult and its national reminiscence, transforming Judaism from a way of life into a philosophical system—a creed comparable to any Protestant creed, a theology. Then there were those Jews who advocated complete assimilation, a solution which is attractive because it seems to be consonant with the most liberal tendencies—with the idea of the brotherhood of all mankind. For the Jews to choose to disappear would make them the heralds as they had been the preachers of the brotherhood of man. So let us disappear as speedily as possible, said these Jews—an apparently simple solution but practically an impossible one as yet, because the natural, internal, adhesive forces of Judaism are reinforced by the hostile, external, repellent forces. Finally, there were those who maintained that the Jews, religious or not, constituted a people, needing only its land to make it a nation, a nation which owes its existence to historical, religious, and linguistic, that is to say, cultural, affinities. These nationalists refused to accept either the Reformist's reduction of Judaism to a mere theology or the assimilationist's geno-suicide. They were determined to live *qua* Jews.

But neither were these nationalist Jews undivided. There were among them the territorialists who, seeing the desperate need of persecuted Jews in countries like Russia and Roumania and Arabia, and the restrictions against their immigration into countries from South Africa to the United States, sought to settle the Jews on any strip of land where they would be permitted to set up a self-governed haven. These were philanthropists first, and then nationalists. Then there were the nationalists—whose great spokesman was Simon Dubnow, the Russian historian—who asked for the recognition of Jewish national rights in the countries where Jews were living in large compact masses, as in Russia, Roumania and Poland, in Austria and in Turkey. These were largely non-Zionists who were hoping, through an American Jewish Congress, to obtain from the next Peace Conference not only civil and political rights for the Jews in all nations, but national rights as well, on the ground that the right to live in a community must be recognized as inherent in the idea of liberty, a principle to which Henrietta Szold herself subscribed. But national rights, she submitted, even if safeguarded the world over, do not insure the opportunity for full national development; and the Zionists were those nationalist Jews who maintained that the Jewish problem, in all its bearings, can be solved only if the Jewish nation is reconstituted in Zion, the ancient home of the Jewish people. In the words of the Zionist platform, the Basle Program announced there by Herzl, Zionism aims to create a legally secured, politically assured home for the Jewish people in Palestine.

Having thus defined and distinguished the Zionist from all other Jews, Henrietta Szold detailed the achievements of Zionism to date in Palestine, and then discussed the opposition which the movement had met from Jews and non-Jews who called it reactionary and argued that the Jews, the only true cosmopolitans, should not withdraw from the world in which they had been dispersed but should merge with it and act as a leavening influence, thus bringing to pass the prophecy: "In thy seed shall all nations of the earth be blessed." In this argument, Henrietta Szold saw two fallacies: Zionism would not withdraw all Jews from the world;

many would not wish to go to Zion, which, as a matter of fact, could not hold them all, even if they did. And the Jewish spirit was not homogeneous but was a composite as complex and antithetical as the so-called Jewish race was physically. She described the manifold elements of that spirit: "a feminine heart, an alert mind, a facile fancy, a keen intellect, universal susceptibility, quick comprehension of the strange, practical sense, wit and seriousness, versatility and persistence, enthusiasm and caution, pathos and sobriety, pliability and defiance, subjectivity and objective devotion, pride and subservience, the liberality of the gentleman and the parsimony of the workman, the firmness of rock and the fluidity of water, the hardness of steel and the malleability of gold." Even the Lord had said they would be "a peculiar people." The cosmopolitanism of the Jews, she maintained, has been misunderstood. It is the result of a process of osmosis, a transfusion of elements from their environments, transformed by their peculiar inner chemistry: for example, the Code of Hammurabi into the Mosaic legislation. Even the Sabbath was not original with them, but what they made of it was. They were "a group of human beings with a long period of instructed consciousness adding consciously to its store—a matching of colors, a search for affinities, an appeasing of a hunger for the spiritual which could be appeased only by what that peculiar organism could assimilate. Once it had assimilated, it gave forth new stimuli; that is the true cosmopolitanism of the Jew. Such cosmopolitanism cannot be destroyed by nationalism. On the contrary, nationalism, the recognition of one's own nature and need, fosters it."

The non-Zionists maintained that Zionism was merely the outgrowth of anti-Semitism; they called Zionists cowards; urged them not to mind the pinpricks of discriminations, which are not to be considered persecution in the enlightened lands. Russia, they believed, was bound to improve after the war; and they taunted Russian Zionists with the prediction that a free and liberal, revolutionized Russia would be the death of Zionism. We Jews, they argued, were destined by our dispersion to become the mediators between the Orient and the Occident, and Zionism is a retreat from that high destiny, a negation of it.

But Zionism, Henrietta Szold maintained, is not negative; it is indeed the only positive, constructive Jewish movement—unlike Reform, which considers itself advanced and positive but is essentially negative, a sloughing off of values. Zionism, in its present organization, only apparently owes its inception to anti-Semitism; its essence goes back to Isaiah and Jeremiah and even further back to the great nation builder, Moses. The longing for the return to Zion runs like a red thread through Jewish history. It is inherent in the Messianism of Jewish prophecy. While other nations pessimistically celebrated their Golden Ages in the irrevocable, irretrievable past, Jewish Messianism optimistically believed in the perfectibility of humanity; it lined up the ancient Jewish philosophy with the most modern and advanced ideals of social progress. With the Jew all of life lay in the future, to be molded by him.

The Zionist discerned that the Jews, the first forward-looking people, had become, to their poets and scholars, the backward-looking people *par excellence*. So he resolved not to go "back to Zion" but to go "forward to Zion," to recapture the opportunity the prophets of his people had been aware of—the opportunity to fashion man's life anew on progressive lines. He is not satisfied with the static state of scattered Israel, holding on to its precious inheritance by the skin of its teeth, adding nothing, or else seeing it disintegrate under the influence of modern corrosive forces in the guise of emancipation, when not of brutal suppression. The poor Jewish masses suffer as much spiritual degradation from grinding modern industrialism as from hateful Russian pogroms. In the old ghetto, despite its spiritual inbreeding, they at least preserved their old values if they could not create new ones. Now, without a coherent cultural center, the forces of disintegration are more effective. If, somewhere, scope is given to the impulses that have their roots deep down in the nature of the individuals who have become associated voluntarily or by the forces of fate; if such people have experiences, even under handicaps, that express their hopes and visions, and can shape their activities freely, then only may we expect to have a race of creative men. In the case of the Jews, we may have again a race of creators of Jewish values. In the democracy of the future, Henrietta Szold repeated, ". . . the right to live in a community must be recognized as inherent in the idea of liberty." The Jew, the Zionist says, must have at least one place in the world where his work is Jewish, and even his play is Jewish. Only then can he become again a creative factor in world civilization.

She foresaw the Jews' future contribution as the development of civilized communal living. Christianity, she pointed out, had exalted the individual, had emphasized the importance of the salvation of the individual soul. Judaism's contribution, in terms of promoting communal living, had never been given a chance to play its part in world progress. Social righteousness was the theme of the ancient Jewish prophets. And she did not fear the taunt "reactionary," said Henrietta Szold, which would doubtless rise to many lips, asking: Why hark back to ancient ideals? Why not stand shoulder to shoulder with the progressive elements of today? She reminded them that latter-day Jewish radicals—Spinoza and Marx—each, ironically enough, at odds with and separated from the Jewish community of his time, were concerned, like Moses, with law and social righteousness. And the Zionist believes that he can help the world, as well as the Jews, only in his peculiar way—a way which has been recognized as good by distinguished, thoughtful non-Jews. There had been George Eliot, for example. And she read them from J. Ramsay MacDonald:

"Perhaps no code of national law and custom has observed the balance between group life and individual life more successfully than that of Israel. . . . The individual Jew, unlike the individual Hindu, was never merged in his race. He retained the rights of individuality. And so we have in the Mosaic Code and its amplifications the most careful safeguards against slavery and a deadening poverty. Every seventh year slaves are liberated; clothes taken in pawn must be restored at the end of the day; every seventh year is a fallow year for the fields when they become common property; the rights of the people to the soil are protected by legal and religious penalties. The code, it has been frequently argued, partook of some of the qualities of some modern legislation and was more complete on paper than in practice. But, be that as it may, here it is, an expression of the sense of justice and an indication of the economic ideals of the religious leaders of the people. . . . Whilst the organization of Israel could not withstand the world pressure of its time, its spiritual and moral characteristics have always remained as enticing ideals in the minds of men, and thereby provide not only proof that they are to find another opportunity of expression in society, but an earnest hope that world pressure will change so as to aid rather than stultify the opportunity."

This, said Henrietta Szold, is the hope and vision which remains in the heart of the Zionist Jew. Almost his first achievement for the Land of Israel was the establishment of the National Fund for the purchase by Jews of land to be held in perpetuity. The Fund was based on the law of social righteousness characteristic of Jewish law—the characteristic dominating all the paradoxes attributed to the Jew by friend and foe. Then, turning her eyes to the future, she prophesied: "With peculiar nationality guarded and permitted to develop, he will not lose in cosmopolitanism, but gain in force; and, more than ever, become the intermediary between the Orient and the Occident. His osmosis will not cease; it will again, stirred by the modern spirit which is annihilating time and space, become a reciprocal process: the creative life of this group in the East will stimulate the creative life of groups in the West. . . ."

Mamma in her wheel chair, reading reports of this talk, might well be proud of her daughter; and Henrietta's triumphant emancipation from her personal difficulty, as well as her devoted nursing, mitigated the suffering of Mamma's last months. She had had the pleasure of a last summer spent with her children and grandchildren in Maine, and also of attending the *bar mitzvah* of her grandson Benjamin; it was her last visit to Baltimore. For on August 6, conscious and conversing with Henrietta to the very end, Mamma breathed her last. Henrietta closed the dear blue eyes and took her to Baltimore to be buried alongside Papa, as Mamma had said she wished in her will. In June, she had added a letter in her will to her daughters wherein she expressed her great gratitude to Henrietta for her "sacrifices for me in this trying time of my illness. Night and day she is watching over me like a mother watches over her child. . . ." She ended with the benediction: "May the Lord bless you and keep you. May the Lord make his face to shine upon you and be gracious unto you. May the Lord lift up his countenance upon you and give you peace."

When Henrietta returned to the apartment on Pinehurst Avenue it was no longer home to her; she was tied to no place now; but the raging war, which engulfed America, too, in the spring of 1917, prevented her from going to the place where Mamma had shown her the way she should go—the woman's work to be done; so she embarked on extended lecture tours in behalf of Zionism and Hadassah.

In the previous June, the World Zionist Organization, meeting in Copenhagen, had cabled the American Zionists a plea for doctors, nurses and medical supplies desperately needed in war-torn Palestine. The Federation of American Zionists set a budget of $265,000 for a medical unit, of which Hadassah, with less than 2,000 members, undertook to raise $25,000; and Henrietta Szold's efforts on her speaking tours were directed largely toward that goal. Her travels took her in 1917 and 1918 west as far as Kansas and Texas and south into Alabama and Louisiana. No two lectures were exactly alike. On trains between cities, notes for the next talk were written, developing new ideas with which to freshen the older ones; and there were also the stirring wartime events to be considered. Early in 1917 came the Russian Revolution with its promise of better status for the Jews there; and in November 1917 came the Balfour Declaration, announcing that "the British Government favors the establishment in Palestine of a national home for the Jewish people, and will use their best efforts to facilitate the achievement of that object." She spoke in Kansas City in December just after Jerusalem was taken and occupied by the British forces under General Allenby. It was, coincidentally, during *Ḥanukkah,* on Henrietta's fifty-seventh birthday. She began her talk with the benediction *sheheḥiyanu*: "Blessed art thou, O Lord our God, King of the Universe, who has kept us alive to this time," a time of great rejoicing; but, she adjured them, their rejoicing must be solemn and sober, for now the work in Palestine must begin in earnest. There was so much to be done, so much was needed! "Men, money and discipline" as Brandeis said. . . .

She did not confine herself to Zionism in her talks, because when she came to Jewish communities far removed from cultural centers she sometimes found their Judaism so stultified that she felt, as she wrote from Texas, "Better assimilation than this!" In Dallas, speaking in a synagogue on the Sabbath, she pleaded that the Jewish homeland was needed for the renewal and development of Judaism, that although America was the Eldorado of the Jew, it would be the grave of Judaism without that source of renewed inspiration. In San Antonio, speaking to a group of businessmen on a Sunday, their only day of leisure, she appealed to them to support the pioneering of those Jews who had gone to Palestine much as *they* had come to Texas—not to say: The Zionists have made their bed, let them lie in it; but to aid those Jews who wanted to move into Palestine behind the victorious forces of England and restore the ancient nation. She reminded them that the Balfour Declaration offered only an opportunity and a promise of help for that achievement, which, she maintained, would affect the lives and spirits not only of those who settled there but of Jews all over the world.

In New Orleans, speaking from the pulpit of the Temple, she began with a sermon on the spirit of sacrifice to which mankind is moved in time of war, exhorting them not to be misled into thinking of sacrifice for its own sake as a virtue—sacrifice to be good must be made for a good cause—and led them to the consideration of the Zionist cause as one worthy of sacrifice. She told them of Sarah Aaronsohn, the sister of Aaron and a member of the *Nili* spies, who had been caught by the Turks and tortured, and had killed herself without disclosing any secrets.

In Birmingham she said: "We shall not understand these tumultuous times of ours, with all their bitterness and with all their exaltations, until turbulence has passed, and we can sit down calmly and contemplate the whole course of events. . . . With all the wealth of detail the modern newspaper bestows upon us, we know little of the essential meaning of what is happening. We repeat the slogans: the world made safe for democracy—freedom of the seas—self-determination of peoples. But how does one or another event or measure tend to bring about the ends these pithy expressions aim at? Are the slogans the result of events or are they shaping the events? Perhaps the wealth of details the cable, the wireless, and the telegraph pour out at our doors every morning are the cause of our confusion. We lose perspective. . . .

"Herein consists the task of the historian. He must find the perspective for us. He must trace out the road. The details he may not slight. On the contrary he must know them well. But unless he can array them for us in orderly fashion, they are like the scrap iron and junk that cumber the outskirts of your city. He must arrange them in patterns. . . . He must be the miner who digs the ore out of your rich Alabama rocks, and also the artist. There is a danger here. The historian is only a human being. He has his prejudices and his limitations. . . . So long as he tells what actually happened he is objective, insofar as any human being can be wholly objective. When he begins to tell us whys and wherefores, the connection between events, what is cause and what effect, he becomes subjective. Then he is looking at the facts through his own spectacles.

"I have come here tonight as such an historian. I am going to endeavor to pick out some of the threads of Jewish history and hold them up to your view. That is a subjective interpretation. My personality enters into it. . . . I tell you at once that my subjectivity, my spectacles, my instruments are Zionistic. I am going to give you the Zionistic conception of some of the facts of Jewish history." This she proceeded to do.

Back in New York in the spring of 1918, she addressed the newly organized Women's League of the United Synagogue—the union of Conservative synagogues which Dr. Schechter had organized in 1913. She took that occasion to consider the general subject of the "Organization of Jewish Women in America," either as auxiliaries of men's organizations, like the one she was addressing and others, or as autonomous women's groups, like the Council of Jewish Women and Hadassah. She considered the wide variety of their aims and activities to revive and activate the spirit of Judaism, and concluded that for women, "The home is the first line of defense, the synagogue only the second . . ." and asked them to consider "How much of our object can be realized by organized efforts—how much of it is and will remain the outflow of individual feeling? The individual feeling is the fundamental condition. How can it be fortified by organization?" She explained that the need for Hadassah as a separate organization rose from the need for special propaganda to win women to the political idea, and for providing women with a special, suitable, concrete purpose to keep them attached to the Zionist movement. Since, however, with the Balfour Declaration, the whole movement had become concrete, she now questioned the continued need for Hadassah's separate existence; and at the convention in Pittsburgh that summer of the Zionist Organization of America—as the Federation was then renamed—Hadassah became an integral part of the organization, and Henrietta Szold became Secretary for Education of the Zionist Organization. Hadassah, then six years old, had, thanks in good part to her efforts, grown to sixty-one chapters, and over five thousand members.

The American Zionist Medical Unit which the men and women together had undertaken to send to Palestine took more than two years of preparation and negotiation, requiring the consent of the British, French, American and Turkish governments, plus the raising of the required funds, which had increased to $500,000. Half of this was collected by Hadassah; and Henrietta Szold worked with Jacob de Haas on assembling the Unit, which finally got to Palestine in the early fall of 1918. It consisted of forty-four men and women—doctors, dentists, nurses, sanitary engineers and administrators. Its equipment and supplies, originally estimated at half a ton, weighed 400 tons. A shipload of food was also sent over on the steamer *Vulcan,* in charge of Bertha's husband, Louis Levin. With the Unit went Henrietta's friend Alice Seligsberg; and Sophia Berger, who had gone abroad for the Red Cross, joined the Unit in Palestine; but Henrietta had to stay and continue her efforts to raise funds for its support. The Unit went to work immediately on its arrival. In Tiberias, where cholera had broken out among the troops and civilians, followed by an influenza epidemic, a hospital was set up, and maintained there by Hadassah after the epidemic was got under control. In Jerusalem, the Rothschild Hospital's fifty beds were augmented to a hundred. Medical centers were set up in Jaffa, Haifa and Safed.

In July 1918, Chaim Weizmann had hopefully laid the foundation stone for the Hebrew University on Mount Scopus, Jerusalem, not far from where Henrietta had stood on the Mount of Olives for her first view of the city. In September, General Allenby drove the Turkish Army out of Palestine, with an army of Englishmen, Australians, Anglo-Indians, Arabs, and battalions of English and

American Jews. "Now," said Henrietta Szold, "Jews must conquer the land alone, in a different way, with the farmer's plow, the workman's tools, the businessman's industry, and the teacher's wisdom. That will be the greatest victory, because it will be the whole world's victory." In that victory she was preparing to play her part.

Meanwhile, until she could go to Palestine, she was serving not only as President of Hadassah but as Secretary for Education of the Zionist Organization of America. In the latter capacity, she addressed herself to the leaders of its junior organization, "Young Judaea": "This day Zionists are standing on the threshold of opportunity. . . . The new Jewish world will require many tomorrows for its achievement. And the tomorrows belong to the young, and the young belong to you, for you to mould and temper for great deeds. You direct the armies that will win the land of Israel for us in the real sense of making it ours. You equally direct the armies that will hold for us, in faith and loyalty, the Jewries established everywhere 'outside the land' during the long generations when we were waiting for the old home to receive us. Because the future is yours, it is a privilege to address a greeting to you—a salutation that is at the same time an exhortation. We rely on you to make it a radiant future. Our part in it? We are happy that our organization has reached such a place in the sun that we can safely pledge ourselves to hold out a strong helping hand to you."

In November 1918 the war was ended, and then came the Versailles Peace Conference. Intrepid Aaron Aaronsohn, on a flight from London to the Conference, where he was serving as an expert on Palestine on behalf of the Zionist Organization, was killed in a plane crash over the English Channel. The Turks had destroyed the Agricultural Station at Athlit, and all his accomplishment there would have to be done over again. Henrietta Szold wrote a memorial of him for the *Young Judaean* in June 1919, telling of his life, his work, his personality and his spirit. At the end, she said, "All who loved and admired him must pledge themselves anew to the service of the land that was his first and last thought. In addition to what we do for Zion because we love the Jewish land, we must do a bit more in order that Aaron Aaronsohn, who has no sepulcher, may have a monument." Moses, too, who had no sepulcher, had an everlasting monument in the land and the people of Israel. Better a living monument than a sepulcher in a cemetery. But it was shocking to think of that vigorous young man dead, and herself still alive, approaching her sixtieth year. Here she was, when most people thought of retiring from active life, planning to embark on a new and arduous career, pioneering in Palestine where life was not easy. And this despite the fact that her doctor, after an examination in the summer of 1919, told her of signs—murmurs and tremors—that said that childhood chorea *had* left its mark on her heart—something she had herself suspected for some time. She should be careful, said the doctor, she should rest, she was no longer young. . . . But that would not deter Henrietta, for did she not know far more than any doctor about that passionate heart—of what it could suffer and endure?

So she set about collecting the equipment for life in Palestine recommended by the Medical Unit: a heavy Norfolk suit for outdoors; rubber boots, waterproof shoes and shoe polish; corsets and corset-covers and woolen tights; a fountain pen and ink tablets; a first-aid kit with a liberal supply of cotton for filtering water; mosquito netting; a long list of drugs headed by quinine. . . . She also started packing the personal things she would take with her—Mamma's brass candlesticks, the gold brooch watch Papa gave her for graduation, the bed linens she and Mamma had embroidered with a large *S* and adorned with drawnwork and crocheted lace . . . and crating those things which were to be stored in the cellar of Bertha's house in Baltimore.

The staff at the Zionist office gave her a farewell party, at which one of the girls, got up as Miss Szold, wearing pince-nez and a felt hat held on by a black elastic under her Psyche knot, shook a censorious finger at Rabbi Stephen Wise for coming late and at Louis Lipsky for omitting a comma. It amused her immensely. Everyone, including her sisters, envied her the adventure; but, being younger than she, they did not realize that, although the prospect of serving a great cause was indeed gratifying, the process of plucking oneself up, rootlet by rootlet, is painful. For she loved her native land, with all its manifest faults, from Lombard Street and 123rd Street to Texas. With all its imperfections, it was great, wonderful and beautiful; its woodlands and fields, its cities and people, were rooted deep in her heart, as the Land of Israel was rooted deep in her spirit, by virtue not only of the many years of happy growth and honored achievement she had had in it, but of the very suffering, too. Buried in the large packing case of books and papers shipped to Baltimore were the contents of her drawer of keepsakes—the journal, the letter of renunciation and the poem, the knotted veil. . . .

1920s: WOMEN'S WORK

SHE EMBARKED on the great adventure by sailing for London on February 21, 1920, and thence to Naples in early March. In her eagerness to get started she had not waited for the clearance in Washington of the British visa for her entry into Palestine. It was delayed, it was said, because of her association with that radical pacifist organization early in the war. She hoped to be in Palestine for the Passover. Since childhood, at the end of every *seder* Henrietta had said by rote, "Next year in Jerusalem!" Now she would really be there! She expected to find her entry permit awaiting her in Naples.

She was accompanied on the trip to Italy by Miss Julia Aronson, a pretty and delightful companion, who was going to join the Medical Unit as its nutritionist, a post for which she had been well trained. At Naples, however, Henrietta Szold found no permit, and, tied up in the red tape of the British consulate, she could not proceed with Miss Aronson, but had to remain in Naples until a permit was obtained for her. There were other obstacles to her progress. Postwar Italy was in a state of chaos. General strikes were the order of the day. There was no telling, said the clerk at Cook's, just when there would be another sailing across the Mediterranean; it might not be for weeks. He advised her to go sight-seeing until her permit came and they could get her a passage.

After doing the sights around Naples, Pompeii and Capri,

she went to Florence, and picked up where she and Mamma had left off just ten years before in their exploration of the Renaissance. This Henrietta now did only half-heartedly—"I never did like solitaire as a game," she complained in her diary, "however much I may have liked my own company otherwise"—and she was eager to get on her way to the work ahead. But she spent that Passover not in Jerusalem but there in Florence, at a Sephardic-Jewish *pension* which did not offer even the consolation of serving those delicious *matzoh-klös* which Mamma used to make, because that German-Jewish Passover delicacy was unknown to Sephardic Jews. However, at the *seder* at the rabbi's house she met Mrs. Herbert Samuel, who, with her son Edwin, was awaiting the return of her husband from Jerusalem, where he had been sent by the British government in consideration of his possible appointment as High Commissioner. Henrietta Szold had met the Samuels on her stopover in London en route, so this meeting in Florence with people she knew was a pleasant relief. And when Herbert Samuel arrived, he gave her his impression of Palestine—that he felt most optimistic about the development of the Jewish National Home under a British mandate, except for the matter of Arab opposition, which he thought might present a serious problem. He also said he would do what he could in London to expedite her permit. He impressed her as being a highly cultivated, dignified and distinguished British gentleman, a philosopher as well as a statesman.

Marooned there in medieval Florence she felt as if she were living a mythological existence, cut off from the modern world; news of its events came to her only vaguely: of an important peace conference at San Remo; of a great railroad strike in the United States; that peace had finally been made with Germany; that there was some sort of a riot in Jerusalem—which troubled her, but made her none the less eager to get there.

On April 21, her permit having finally come, she was back in Naples haunting Cook's office, which did not yet know definitely when the SS *Umbria*, on which she was booked, would sail. The morning of April 25, leaning patiently against the counter at Cook's, she heard a familiar voice and looked around to find Professor Schatz, the head of Bezalel Art School in Jerusalem, buying a ticket for Vienna. He was with Dr. David Eder of London, who was bound for Jerusalem and would also be sailing on the *Umbria*. Cook's clerk interrupted their meeting with the news that the *Umbria* would sail at noon. Henrietta hurried to her hotel, collected her luggage and, after some difficulty finding a berth on board, met Dr. Eder. As the ship sailed across the Mediterranean that evening, she had a talk with him which was enlightening but alarming and disheartening.

Dr. Eder, a British psychologist and a friend of Chaim Weizmann, who had interested him in Zionism, was a member of the Zionist Commission which had been appointed by the British government and sent to Palestine to advise the military authorities there on implementing the Balfour Declaration, and to act as intermediary between them and the Jewish population, by which it had been enthusiastically welcomed. Dr. Eder was returning from a conference with Weizmann at San Remo, where the victorious Allies were working out the details of the Mandate for Palestine and deciding on the appointment of its first High Commissioner. At San Remo all was going well, said Dr. Eder, and he showed her the message he had just received from Weizmann: "Mandate incorporated Turk treaty. Boundary discussions proceeding favorably. Administrative appointment contemplated to take effect shortly." It was Dr. Eder's news of what had happened in Palestine while Henrietta was passing the time in Florence that came as a shock to her:

On Easter Sunday, April 3, which occurred in the Passover week, there had been a pogrom in Jerusalem. This was the culmination of an intrigue on the part of the British military authority in Palestine, designed to oust the French from Syria and give Britain sole control of the Eastern Mediterranean through an Arab Federation which would include Syria, Palestine, Hejaz and Iraq. A Jewish National Home in Palestine would interfere with this objective, which was pursued, without regard for the Balfour Declaration and the Mandate, by the seemingly autonomous Colonial Office, in whose hands Palestine had been left by the British government. King Faisal's revolt against the French was staged in Damascus, followed by an Arab riot in Jerusalem, which had been perfectly timed. It was only a coincidence that the day happened to be Easter Sunday, the day on which pogroms were so commonly staged in East European countries that Jews in the ghettos and pales used to stay indoors on that day. But it happened that year that Easter Sunday was also the day of *Nebi Moussa,* the Moslems' festival in honor of Moses, whom they also revered as a prophet. It was celebrated in fervent chanting and riotous dancing by the great crowds gathered in the streets of Jerusalem for the occasion. Propaganda of the wildest sort about what the Jews, whose numbers had greatly increased since the Mandate, would do to the Arabs if they got control of the land was circulated among the swarming people. Agitators addressed them urging them to do away with the Jews before they got into power, and encouraged the mob with the assurance: "The Government is with us!"

The Governor of Jerusalem, General Bols, and his Chief of Staff, Colonel Taylor, were commonly known to be anti-Semitic. All Jewish policemen had been relieved from duty that day in the Old City where the bulk of the Jews lived. The inflamed, howling mob was completely unopposed when it attacked the Jewish quarter within the walls, brandishing knives and clubs, to maim and murder and rape and pillage and burn. . . .

In another part of the city, Vladimir Jabotinsky, a stocky, pugnacious, forty-year-old ex-Russian, Jewish journalist, who had long been an aggressive Zionist leader active in the struggle for Jewish civil rights and self-defense, and had fought for Jerusalem in a Jewish battalion under Allenby, gathered a group of ex-Legionnaires and led them against the rioters, some of whom turned tail and ran for their lives when the armed Jews appeared. But by that time the Government had surrounded the Old City with a cordon of police and troops which prevented Jabotinsky's men from advancing to aid the defenseless Jews, who were thus given over to three days of murder, rape and looting before anything was done officially to stop the pogrom. Jabotinsky and his followers were arrested and thrown into jail, while some of the Arab agitators who were apprehended were accommodated in the Governor's compound. During and after the rioting all Jews were searched for arms and rendered defenseless, or arrested for protecting their homes and families. And Governor Bols complained that the Jews were very difficult to deal with: "They are not satisfied with military protection, but demand to take the law into their own hands." Jewish notables who tried to protest to the Governor were refused an audience, while official cars were used to bring the Arab leaders for interviews with him. In Jerusalem, sixty people had been killed and countless injured; homes, synagogues and stores were wrecked.

That this was part of a concerted plan was further evidenced by the fact that a month before, during an Arab demonstration in French Syria, Bedouins had attacked the little Jewish village of Tel-Hai, in upper Galilee. There, gallant Captain Trumpeldor, who, like Jabotinsky, had recruited Jewish soldiers to fight with the British for Palestine, was killed with five others, two of them women, and cried as he fell: "It is good to die for one's country!"

In a verminous jail in Jerusalem, Jabotinsky, the Jewish patriot and ex-officer of His Majesty's Army, was stripped of his honors, hastily tried and sentenced to fifteen years at hard labor. But this savage anti-Semitic stroke boomeranged: world-wide criticism of England, which was having its troubles in Ireland and India, too, and was in danger of losing the Palestine mandate to France as a result of this outrage, brought about the reprieve of the sentence. Jabotinsky was transferred to the prison at Acre for a Court of Inquiry, and General Bols was removed, to be replaced by General Storrs as Governor of Jerusalem. But the Jews of Palestine had lost faith and confidence in the British upon whom they had looked as their champions.

This was the state of affairs in the Land of Israel to which Dr. Eder introduced Henrietta Szold as they sailed across the Mediterranean. This was the condition of the Jewish National Home where she had so long looked forward to playing her woman's part, along with the Medical Unit, as a bringer of health and order. Dr. Eder assured her that the Unit had behaved during the catastrophe with the most commendable courage and effectiveness in treating the wounded. He advised her, however, of a situation within the Unit itself with which she should also be prepared to deal. Dr. Rubinow, its director, was having serious difficulty with some of the physicians, and he was preparing to quit.

On April 30 they disembarked at Alexandria, where Henrietta found a month-old letter of welcome from Dr. Rubinow. They stopped in Cairo for a day and left there the evening of May 3 on a train crowded with British soldiers and nurses. She sat opposite one of the nurses, a sweet wholesome young English girl, who, in Henrietta's own girlhood, couldn't possibly have embarked alone on such an adventure. Even ten years ago, the parents of that girl in Naples had thought she must be "chaperoned" on her trip to New York; and Henrietta thought of the effect the war had had on the independence of women. At Kantara, where they changed trains amid a confusion of people and baggage, they were met by a man Dr. Rubinow had sent to assist them the rest of the way. He still spoke very excitedly about the pogrom—"the excesses" he called it; but somehow his nervousness did not communicate itself to Henrietta Szold. Had not Job said ages ago: "Man is born to trouble as the sparks fly upward"? Terrible trouble there was, and more trouble there would surely be, so long as there were men intent on making disorder—on war and not peace. And had she not come there for the purpose of fighting the disorder men made? And what had she to lose—a woman in her sixtieth year? Vital Aaron Aaronsohn was at his prime, only forty-three, when he last risked his life; his sister even younger when she gave hers; and gallant Trumpeldor only forty when he lost his. As Queen Esther—Hadassah of old—had said in her time of danger: "And if I perish, I perish!" Henrietta even slept a little that night in a cramped upper berth; and in the morning there was the wonderful panorama of the Land of Israel unrolling beyond the train window: the yellow expanse of sun-scorched desert, and then high-heaped yellow sand dunes with glimpses of the shimmering blue sea beyond, and then the fertile land abloom with blue thistles and red poppies and a riot of other colors. At a train stop, Dr. Eder and an English officer in their compartment got off and gathered her a magnificent bouquet.

The officer, who was returning from leave, said he liked Jerusalem so much he wanted to stay there forever; and it occurred to her that this enthusiasm boded no good for the Jews; for if the civil administration of the Mandate remained in the hands of the military, who would behave like British colonial governors, there would be little freedom for Jewish national development. While it might in a sense be inaccurate to call the British military governing class anti-Semitic, or for that matter anti-Indian or anti-Irish, the colonial-minded Britisher did not need any personal antipathy to move him to the most ruthless means of suppressing any people who stood in the way of the British Empire. The pogrom had proved that.

When they detrained at Lydda in the broiling sun, amid a mountain of luggage and boxes surrounded by a mob of screeching Arabs, quiet bearded Jews, and insolent military officials, they found Dr. Rubinow waiting with two of Henrietta's friends—Alice Seligsberg, who was living in Jerusalem, and Nellie Straus, who had married a man named Mochenson and was living in Jaffa. Henrietta had to wait an hour for the clearance of her luggage, and it was patent that the arrogant British officer in charge was deliberately keeping Jews waiting for his service.

On the drive up to Jerusalem, they were further delayed by two tire punctures. Henrietta's tentative questions about the affairs of the Medical Unit got her nothing but ominous looks from Dr. Rubinow, who talked excitedly only about the pogrom and the part the Unit had played in it. He had no doubt of the guilt of the British military, who had encouraged Arab demonstrations, he said, even before the pogrom. The Unit had served very well indeed during the riots. The American uniform of the doctors had got them through the lines and, with their automobiles, they had managed to rescue the wounded and shocked and carry them off to the hospital, which was filled to overflowing. The staff had worked heroically, and they were still treating a number of the severely wounded.

Dr. Rubinow said he intended going to America as soon as possible to report the situation. He admitted he had had the trip in mind for some time; but the pogrom, the fact that his cables and letters had not been answered, and that the newspapers from the United States indicated that people there had no idea of what had really happened, had convinced him he had better go soon.

A government car coming down the road hailed theirs and stopped; in it was the new Governor, General Storrs, who got out and was introduced to Miss Szold, and talked most graciously with them. "Honeyed words," Dr. Rubinow commented with disgust when he was gone, intended to conciliate and pacify the Jews so that the British could continue to hold the Mandate and keep their military in the civil offices. What was needed, they all thought, was a clean sweep; and there was much criticism in Palestine, they said, of Weizmann's continued reliance on British promises. On that drive up to Jerusalem, Henrietta Szold's vision of the state of Zionist hopes in Palestine was luridly lighted; and she saw the sinister and sordid drama being played out against the beautiful Judean hills clothed now in such a glory of spring flowers that she wished her mother were there to see them as they were now, with the season so much further advanced than it had been ten years ago. Indomitable Mamma would not have been deterred, even by a pogrom.

Alice Seligsberg, who was happy in her work with orphans, had found Henrietta a pleasant place to stay, with the mother of Dr. Kagan, who was away in Europe for three months of rest and study. She had the use of two large rooms with mosquito netting on the windows, and a good little maid named Rachel Cohen. When Henrietta arrived tea was set, with a bouquet of roses from the nurses. Soon Alex Dushkin, Director of Education, came to call on her; and then Norman Bentwich, whom she had last seen ten years before when she and Mamma visited the Bentwiches in England. As a Jew and a British civil servant—he was the government's attorney general, with the rank of colonel—Norman Bentwich was now in a very difficult position. Deplorable as the situation was, to be sure, he objected to the use of the term "pogrom" for what had happened, despite the fact that it bore all the earmarks of the Russian prototype: feathers from ripped-up bedding flying through the streets, torn Torah scrolls from the synagogues in the gutters, and the *laissez-faire* attitude of the government—in this case, the British military.

The next morning Dr. Rubinow took Miss Szold to the office of the Zionist Commission where Dr. Eder welcomed her and introduced her to Menaḥem Ussishkin, a sturdy man, one of the earliest of the Russian Zionist leaders, who had been a delegate to the First Zionist Congress, had worked with Herzl and headed the *Ḥovevei Zion,* those "Lovers of Zion" who had made a Zionist of Henrietta in Baltimore. She spent the morning at the office getting an insight into the miserable financial situation of the Medical

Unit, which was deeply in debt to the Zionist Commission, mainly because of the failure of the American Zionists to make good their promised support, upon which the Unit had based its budget. Incidentally she got from Dr. Rubinow a picture of the inner problem of the Unit, of the intrigue against him of several of the doctors, especially the Americans, a rather melodramatic version of the old story of jealous, power-seeking individuals working at cross purposes in an altruistic co-operative endeavor. Doctors, it would appear, were unorganizable. Anyway, it was plain that organization was not Dr. Rubinow's forte; and the man was completely worn out by his frustrated efforts. Miss Szold, who had been sent by Hadassah not to run the Unit but to strengthen its relations with the Zionist Commission, settled down to the task of bolstering up the director of the Unit, holding it together, and keeping it functioning. She had her difficulties, too, with the Zionist Commission, for though she found Dr. Eder very sympathetic, Mr. Ussishkin was an authoritative gentleman of the old school who did not welcome suggestions from women.

She wrote in her diary: "What a pity that I can't live hard and write hard too. My wonder grows that statesmen, diplomats, men of affairs, even society women have managed to record their lives. It would have been not only interesting, it would have been instructive as a contemporaneous record of what happened to me, especially during the first days in Jerusalem and my reactions to the happenings. . . ." As it was, the happenings so engulfed her that it was three weeks after her arrival before she found time to return to her diary and sketch them from memory.

A month after her arrival, she set out to see what was happening outside Jerusalem, despite the warnings of the timid of the danger of Arab attacks; and not without reason. A few days earlier, there had been an attack on Mescha where two of the colonists were killed and most of their cattle carried off. The *Haganah*, "Self-Defense," a clandestine organization, had been formed to take the place of Israel Shochat's *Ha-Shomer*, "The Watchman"; and some girls of the organization had come to Dr. Rubinow with a request for syringes of poison for use against assailants or on themselves, as they might be required. He had refused them.

But, along with such desperate activities, there was heartening news of constructive progress: Pinḥas Rutenberg, a Russian engineer who had been active in the revolution and was Mayor of St. Petersburg under Kerensky, but was opposed to the Bolsheviks, had come to Palestine and got a concession from the Mandatory Government for a hydro-electric project on the Jordan. He was also organizing *Gedud Ha-Avodah,* a "Labor Battalion" which was joined by ex-members of *Ha-Shomer* and colonists of Kinneret near Tiberias, and he was training them in road building in Galilee, with the plan that each man so trained would move to some other area and gather and train another gang of road builders. How could one let the timid deter one from joining forces with such men and women—not merely talking but working idealists!

And now after her criticisms of what had been accomplished she was putting herself to the test. Would she be able to do any better? She set out for Galilee on June 8, accompanied by Dr. Rubinow and Julia Aronson, the Unit's nutritionist, who wanted to visit a number of the *kevutzot,* the co-operative agricultural colonies, and try to improve the quality of their diet—a most worthy and needed improvement. It was remarkable that the famous Jewish cuisine of Germany, Austria, Hungary and Russia had deteriorated in the Land of Israel, not merely for lack of the rich ingredients the colonists had had in their native lands, but because, as Mamma had observed, they had somehow lost the taste for and the knowledge of good Jewish cooking.

They left Jerusalem, not in a wagon this time, but in an old Ford which, though somewhat less uncomfortable, was also a less reliable means of transport—subject to frequent tire and engine trouble that sometimes threatened to leave them stranded in the open road in Arab areas far from a Jewish community. Henrietta saw no sign on the road of danger, however, except perhaps some scowling Bedouin; but neither was there any sign of friendliness. When she waved farewell to a group of Arabs who had stood watching the chauffeur tinker with his stalled engine, she got no answering gesture—not, she hoped, from hostility, but perhaps because they did not understand the salutation, especially from a woman. Children sometimes returned her smile and waved back. But nothing could lessen her delight in the beauty of the country as they wound their way between hills whose gray stony terraces were suffused with pinks and purples. Although the height of the spring was past, there was still a profusion of flowers—mallows and pinks and half a dozen kinds of thorn, yellow and blue. There were great patches of the blue thorn, as if a huge paint pot had been spilled—the whole plant, stem, leaf and flower of electric, ultramarine blue carpeting the hillsides, doubtless the despair of the farmer but a delight to her old botanist eyes. All along the way northward the brooks were full and busy. They disturbed a flock of white ibis drinking. Harvesting was in progress; in the sunny fields men and women at work made bright patches, and little donkeys and tall camels went jogging along the road with huge laden panniers of the golden grain. There was no sign of danger in the peaceful landscape.

But at Balfouryah, where they stopped for late lunch, the talk dispelled that semblance of peace. Dr. Rubinow proposed to remove the colony's doctor to Kinneret where he was very much needed, while the men at Balfouryah, a new colony, were so healthy they hardly needed a resident physician. Whereupon one of the colonists, who was indeed a robust specimen of young manhood, protested that they were expecting to be attacked any day and that there were bound to be casualties and, from what he had seen at other colonies which had been attacked, they would certainly need a doctor on hand. The doctor confessed to Miss Szold that he was himself undecided as to what he should do: as he put it, the physician and the man were at war in him. A highly trained surgeon, he was in danger of losing his skill in this isolated place where he had, in fact, little practice and no opportunity for professional development; he showed her the fine surgical instruments he had brought and the primitive operating room he must work in. On the other hand, the man in him said he should stay and serve his comrades as best he could in their hour of peril. His dilemma reinforced her regard for the selflessness of these people, which made the timid ones in Jerusalem seem incongruous. Timidity was out of place in this land. Timidity had served no one, even in Jerusalem. Here they had thrown up earthworks around their barracks and piled sandbags against their windows. "Be of good courage," was the repeated counsel of Moses to Joshua who was to take the Promised

Land. Only with courage, that pearl secreted by the murmuring, quivering heart, could one cope with danger; and only with patient persistence would one make progress.

Although the new colony of Balfouryah had been designed in America it repeated the fundamental mistake of others: the stables were too near the dwellings. And the cooking was atrocious, although they had a good modern stove and sink, which Nellie Straus had procured for them. Julia Aronson did what she could about the cooking, danger or no danger, in the little time they had there.

They made a hasty trip in the rattletrap Ford from Balfouryah to Tiberias to get under cover before dark. At Tiberias there were goats and cows at the entrance to the hotel, just as there had been ten years ago. But the terrace was now also occupied by Hindu troops. There was talk of a coming attack by thousands of Bedouins. There had been a raid on Safed the day before yesterday. Dr. Rubinow said he would ask the military for a gendarme to accompany them. They inspected the Hadassah hospital which had, just the day before, been equipped with electric lighting, but the system was ridiculously inadequate. Two nurses had been at work all the night before, making bandages for the expected attack. Henrietta went to sleep in the same room she once had shared with Mamma, but was wakened at 2:30 A.M. by the muezzin chanting in a long-drawn-out wail. In the midst of it a shot rang out and roused the sleeping town. Dogs howled; roosters crowed. Only the Hindu troops slept, stretched out on the terrace with their turbans unwound.

After breakfast they proceeded to Rosh Pinah accompanied by the guard Dr. Rubinow had obtained. Dr. Rubinow himself carried a loaded revolver. The lake and the mountain scenery, lit by the rising sun, was breath-taking. The road was full of armed Hindus but the only trouble they had was two tire punctures which extended the ride to Rosh Pinah from one and a half hours to three. There, over lemonade on a verandah, the talk was of British perfidy, but they also criticized the Zionists for not having paid some attention to finding a modus vivendi with the Arabs—some means of friendly *rapprochement.* As they talked, Henrietta had a wonderful view of peaceful snow-capped Mt. Hermon on the northern border of the land.

The Ford miraculously climbed the beautiful basalt hills to Safed. They looked barren but were said to be fine for fruit trees, which in spring filled the air with flowers. At Safed she found the hospital in a good building and the children's ward delightful. But the nurses complained to Miss Szold of the food, their quarters, their pay, their lack of leisure time, and their head nurse who was a strict disciplinarian. She spent an evening listening to them, and decided that only their complaints about living conditions were just. Hadassah had bitten off more than it could chew in Palestine at this time; its budget was inadequate properly to maintain the activities which had been set up. She visited the orphanage where fifty girls were starting a workshop for mending and making clothes, and over five hundred children were being fed in two small rooms. Their parents had died of typhus, and they had been found living alone, eating refuse. . . . Miss Szold had a meeting with the doctors in Safed at which they gave her a picture of the general medical situation, and she broached the possibility of introducing a socialized medical service. As a result she decided to call a general meeting of Palestine doctors in Jerusalem for the discussion of socialized medical service versus private practice. One of the doctors also gave her an insight into the general objection to Dr. Rubinow, which she weighed against her own good impression of him.

After Safed, they visited several colonies in the area. At one of them, in a teacher's home that was in filthy disorder, she saw a beautifully kept natural history collection, which was like a commentary on modern man's ability to make order in his science but not in his society.

In Haifa she observed that, unlike Tiberias and Jerusalem, which had improved in cleanliness since her first visit, this town was as filthy as ever—like an old Levantine city. She inspected the hospital, clinic and orphanage, and realized that twice as much money as was now being spent was needed merely for the maintenance of Hadassah's present activities there, without considering their possible extension. After visiting a kindergarten and the homes of several of the children, she questioned whether medical work in the schools could have any durable effect on children living in such unhygienic homes. Medical work could not be dissociated from economic welfare; it was only part of social service. The doctors she talked to were all dissatisfied with their present situation and approved of her calling a general medical meeting in Jerusalem.

She decided to visit Vladimir Jabotinsky in the prison at nearby Acre. The road there followed the exquisitely blue Mediterranean, and the prison was in the picturesque old fortress in the walls of which cannon balls fired by Napoleon were still imbedded. Before she could see Jabotinsky she talked with one of his followers who had been the pathologist in the Rothschild Hospital in Jerusalem and was also a botanist. They discussed the identity of a plant she had seen just outside the prison. He had a table piled with botanical specimens and books which his wife brought him; and sometimes he was permitted to go outside on botanical excursions. Indeed, the laxity of their guards suggested that the government would like them to take advantage of the opportunity to escape and thus disembarrass it of their problem. But Jabotinsky was determined to get his freedom not by escape, but by a formal reversal of the court-martial decision, and was considering a hunger strike to that end. He appeared to be pleased to see Henrietta Szold, and she found him a fascinating, vital personality; she could well understand his ability to attract young followers. He recalled having met her ten years before at someone's house in Constantinople. He was of the opinion that Jews must have their own defense garrison in Palestine; he argued that if Englishmen lost their lives defending "the dirty Jews" English mothers and others would create a strong sentiment against Jewish Palestine. Henrietta Szold, however, was of the opinion that the only real and lasting solution of the Arab-Jewish problem lay in a peaceful *rapprochement,* with the longest steps forward being taken by the Jews. Jabotinsky was rather bitter about having been "forgotten" by the Jews in their rejoicing over the recent announcement that Sir Herbert Samuel, a Jew, had been appointed the first High Commissioner for the British Mandate in Palestine; and Henrietta tried to assure him that he had not been forgotten and that his wrongs would be righted with the coming of Samuel, whose appointment looked like a warrant of Britain's good intentions.

After returning to Haifa, she went to Ziḥron Yaakob to spend the weekend with Nita Lange, a sister of Norman Bentwich and Lilian Friedlaender, whom she had also met during her visit with her mother to the Bentwiches in England ten years ago. Nita, married to well-to-do Michael Lange, had studied agriculture in England during the war and settled in Palestine on an estate outside Ziḥron Yaakob which she herself superintended—the house and gardens, the stables and the fields. Henrietta went into the village and inspected its drugstore as well as the hospital. Druggists were presenting a problem with their complaint that the dispensing of drugs by Hadassah's clinics was ruining them, taking the bread out of their mouths.

She called on Sam Aaronsohn, the brother of Aaron, and he went with her to call on his father, who still mourned for his lost son and daughter. He told Miss Szold of how he was being hounded by creditors of the Agricultural Station who believed the station had received a large indemnity from the government, whereas they were actually bankrupt. Sam Aaronsohn took her to the small garden house which had been Aaron's home, his office and bedroom, tastefully furnished, and another house which had contained his library and botanical collection, beautifully arranged. His brother had managed to gather about a fourth of Aaron's scattered possessions. His papers—notes, observations, and correspondence—were destroyed. Some of his books, publications and museum specimens had been traced as far as Constantinople, Aleppo, Damascus and Bagdad. His mycological collection of Palestine fungi appeared to be intact but had been disordered. His accounts were partly missing. Sam Aaronsohn took her to the Agricultural Station at Athlit. The plantation of vines and fruit trees, figs, carobs, etc., appeared to be in good condition, but the buildings were dilapidated and the water supply was being piped up to the British GHQ on Mt. Carmel. In the exhibition hall the flasks containing the wild wheat exhibit had been broken, and the cocoon collection littered the floor. Henrietta stood awhile in the desolate place, remembering Aaron Aaronsohn, vital, strong and sensitive, planning and working there; and, thinking of his end and the end of all his ambitions, she wondered: Would he have no memorial?

They started up the Judean hills under a sunset sky in which bands of rose-purple fleece floated against the blue background—a blue which was neither turquoise nor marine, which was indeed not exactly blue, mixed as it was with pearl-gray and soft pink.

From the sloping fields, yellow and green, came the white-robed Arabs following or seated upon their hay-laden donkeys or camels. Then the moon rose over the peaceful hills, round and large as a wagon wheel; and with it the cool fragrance of the summer evening.

Two auto stoppages on the way brought them into Jerusalem late on one of the chill June nights they had at that altitude; and she found a batch of accumulated mail which kept her up very late. The next day Sophia Berger arrived to take over the work of Alice Seligsberg who would have to return to America, and would be sorely missed by Henrietta. Separation from those she loved had become an inevitable part of the pattern of her life.

On June 15 she prepared, with the help of Dr. Rubinow, to take over the directorship of the Medical Unit which he was giving up, at least temporarily—an intricate matter necessitating her knowledge of the functions, personalities and ambitions of many individual employees, and the internal conflicts between doctors whose departments overlapped and who vied with each other for jurisdiction. The withdrawal of Dr. Rubinow had the effect of channeling all those conflicts upon her, and she soon wondered how he had stood it. It seemed as if every one of the Unit's four hundred employees came to her with demands which it would have taken many thousands of dollars to comply with, and with complaints that their past services had not been recognized or that there had been discrimination against them, accompanied by requests for privileges and threats of resignation. In contrast to the people they had come to serve, some of the doctors seemed to her totally without dignity or manhood, possessed by nothing but arrogant self-assertiveness; nothing like the doctor at Balfouryah. Her general meeting to discuss socialized medicine versus private practice resulted, after a long session, in nothing more than a resolution that a committee of the doctors and Hadassah work out a satisfactory scale of salaries. It was a disorderly meeting in which the clash of group interests and personalities was fully aired. The Zionists were soon to have a conference in London which would be the battleground for many such contending forces, and it seemed to Henrietta Szold that Zionism was as much in danger from internal as from external hostility.

She realized that with Dr. Rubinow gone, she, a lone woman in a strange land, would be confronted with the task of getting willful men to do what should be done. The Hebrew matriarchs—Sarah, Rebekah, Rachel—had had one or two willful men to deal with; she would have a whole crowd of them. Could she do it? On June 20, Dr. Rubinow was given a farewell dinner which was anything but festive. Henrietta, listening to the speeches in Hebrew, observed that the old language still needed much modern development to give it new life.

The departure of Dr. Rubinow was like a signal for each doctor to descend upon his successor with tales of the politics and intrigues that had plagued the Unit, of packed meetings and jockeying for power. Miss Szold, who had little relish for people who neglected their practical duties for political activities, soon had a number of vacancies to fill, which necessitated seeing a large number of applicants, as adequately trained men and women were not easily found there. So she learned to compromise with characters who were displeasing to her but had the ability to serve Hadassah—the cocky, self-assertive doctor who was overbearing to her, as well as the cowardly, underhanded one who went out and maligned her. ". . . I am myself inclined to be a logic chopper, and stand on principles that are unassailable theoretically. Here I have become more malleable. I am certain that we must keep our hold on the Unit, else the present work will collapse, and the same preliminary agonies will have to be undergone again." She learned how to do this just as she learned of necessity about the effectiveness of various types of X-ray machines and the qualifications of other equipment, human as well as mechanical, required by hospitals, clinics and laboratories; just as she learned to dictate in Hebrew pamphlets on hygiene, although she had had no medical training and her Hebrew had, until then, been scholarly, not colloquial. For despite her attempted renunciation of the title of Teacher, she was always moved by the teacher's primary motivation: learning. She loved learning: the Jewish passion.

There were, fortunately, a number of people in the Unit who were not thorns in her flesh. There was, for example, Alex Dushkin, a young man of great charm and intelligence, reliable and effective in his field—education—who brought her excellent reports on the schools in Palestine. And with Dr. Kagan she was able to make good progress in developing the Nurses' Training School, where it was her conviction that a major problem would be solved: Palestine would not have to depend on imported nurses, many of whom, for all their good intentions, were not really at home and satisfied there; but would have its own corps of indigenous and well-trained nurses, a corps which would ultimately be able to supply the growing needs of the land. "The whole of Palestine has been starved of medical aid. Everybody is in need of repairs. . . . In spite of all shortcomings, it is a big piece of work we are doing. But . . . why am *I* doing it?" It seemed ridiculous to her that at sixty, with no training for such work, she should be directing hospitals, a nurses' training school, laboratories, clinics, school hygiene, "and that I should be fighting forty-five doctors!"

To add to her troubles, streams of visitors from far and near called upon Miss Szold, burst into her office regardless of her announced visiting hours, and interrupted her work for a variety of reasons. Burton Holmes, the travelogue man, came "to capture picturesque Zionism for American consumption from lecture platforms and the cinema." Miss Szold's comment after arranging for his needs was "Eheu!" A young man employed by the clinic in Tiberias appeared one day with the news that the nurses there were poisoning the patients. He proved to be insane and had to be confined; but where, it was not easy to determine. The old couple who appeared in her door could not be turned away: they had come all the way from Haifa, where they had built their own little house and lived on the proceeds from a stocking machine and some hens which laid six eggs a day. They needed a loan of fifteen pounds, which Miss Szold gave them from a special fund she had got from Rabbi and Mrs. Stephen Wise for charitable purposes. . . . But there were times when, wearied beyond endurance, she found the arrogance of demands made upon her insupportable, when the land and its people seemed pitiless: "Demands beat down with the same intensity as the rays of the sun, and self-assertion is as inflexible as the stones of its hills." And she would give way to an anger which dismayed her office workers, and was reminiscent of Mamma's sputtering impatience with tormenting children. She would pound her small fist on the desk and stamp her small foot. It was said that she once threw an inkwell, but that was only what it felt like to someone when Miss Szold coldly told him that his unreasonable, importunate demand was quite out of the question; and then wrote in her diary that "there is no excuse for getting excited over the impetuosity and arrogance of these poor people." Self-admittedly, she was no saint. Jews have no canonized saints. Even great Moses gave way to impatience and anger—killed an Egyptian, struck the water-bearing rock with his rod, smashed the Tablets of the Law in rage at the wrongdoing of the children of Israel. But Jews have learned patience through the centuries—that a saintly patience can be cultivated, and, once achieved, it is actually easier, takes less energy and arouses less antagonism than anger, which wears you out, leaves you depleted and others more stiff-necked. So Miss Szold learned patience, and saved her energies for constructive effort, for the many things that must and could be accomplished. She took a bulging brief case home with her from the office, and slept little. Home-going revelers saw her light burning late at night; and, like *eshet ḥayil,* she rose also while it was yet night.

Yet weeks would go by before she could find the time to write home to her beloved sisters. The Friday-evening weariness, which always took her back to peaceful Sabbath eves in Lombard Street, to those strenuous weeks packed with teaching, was now close to exhaustion. Only her strict observance of the Sabbath made possible her recuperation and continuation week after week. It was sad to see the embroidery patterns and the crocheting needles for lace collars which she had brought for leisure moments and had not touched. But Sophia Berger found a small, cozy stone house they could share, set in a lovely garden with olive, almond and orange trees and flowers. There she could have not only the subtropical flowers and vines of Palestine which dripped from every balcony and spilled over every stone wall in summer, but, in the temperate climate of high Jerusalem, daisies and petunias, which reminded her of home. And there she could set out all the personal reminders: the family pictures—Papa and Mamma, Bertha and Rachel and Adele as children, long lost Sadie, Bertha's young children, and the few pieces of bric-a-brac she had brought with her. And Sophia proved the perfect housemate: energetic, sensible and efficient, and raised, like the Szold girls, to be thrifty and tidy, to save string and paper, bags and buttons . . . to fold her towels. They took turns at the cooking; and Henrietta realized that the inferiority of the Jewish cuisine in Palestine could be laid, in good part, to the difficulty of cooking on a kerosene stove, since that was the only available fuel, and without the convenience of refrigeration. Henrietta's room had six windows, two facing east toward the Mount of Olives, over which she saw the sun rise when she woke and rose up with it, dressed and breakfasted and set out for her office, a brisk twenty-minute walk.

Then there were Friday evenings when she and her friends from America, Sophia Berger and Jessie Sampter and Julia Aronson and Alex Dushkin, Dr. and Mrs. de Sola Pool, and a few others would get together and sing American folk songs. That unfeeling teacher of her childhood to the contrary, she loved singing, and dancing too, and though outwardly she looked like a sedately aging woman, inwardly she felt more youthful than the spinster of twenty years ago. She found a music teacher and took singing lessons. Finding the available ultra-orthodox synagogue services, in which women were completely segregated, not to her taste, she gathered a group who held their own services which were conducted along the conservative lines of her father's services in Oheb Shalom Synagogue in Baltimore. They were held at the home of Jessie Sampter, the poetess and Henrietta's dear friend, a strong spirit in a frail body which had been crippled by polio and was now threatened by tuberculosis.

Life for Henrietta Szold was difficult but certainly not dull. She was taking lessons in conversational Hebrew from an uxorious little man whose wife had been almost constantly pregnant during the seven years of their marriage, and was bearing their fifth child then. Mr. K. admired Miss Szold excessively, and he tendered her the compliment that were she a younger woman he would have found it impossible to continue to serve as her teacher. Miss Szold who in her sixtieth year took the trouble to keep herself comely—every day upon early rising there was the ritual of calisthenics and the meticulous grooming of her person—kept Mr. K.'s admiration within bounds by discussing with him the situation of his wife. He agreed with her that so frequent childbearing was hard on a woman; but he couldn't go against his nature; and when he saw his dear happy little children he did not think it wrong to bring them into existence. And Miss Szold admittedly had no advice to give Mr. K. in his dilemma; but later that month, on June 30, which proved a memorable day, she had an illuminating conversation with a quite different man on a relevant subject.

Mr. Korf, who appeared that day with an introduction from Justice Brandeis, was an American engineer who had been employed by the Nile Reclamation Service to study the control of the flood waters of the great river. Brandeis had interested him in the Zionist effort and suggested his visiting Palestine after Egypt to look into the similar though smaller project of harnessing the Jordan. Unfortunately, Pinḥas Rutenberg was in England with his plans at the time; but Mr. Korf found in Miss Szold an interesting listener. She enjoyed three hours of his stimulating conversation, for he was a philosopher as well as an engineer, and his interests ranged from the ideal of modern city life versus country life, which was being greatly affected by his reclamation work, to the change in modern sexual mores effected by contraception and sterilization —a control of population analogous to modern man's control of other natural resources, which opened vistas of a new world to come.

After they had lunched at the Rothschild Hospital, they walked together toward Miss Szold's office in the Hotel de France, but were stopped by a cordon of Sikh soldiers who were lined up along the crowded street for the passage of the new High Commissioner making his first formal public appearance. Miss Szold and Mr. Korf thereupon sat down on a convenient doorstep and continued their animated conversation on modern sex morality and its probable effect on the economic order, until an officer of the guard permitted them to pass through the cordon to the nearby hotel, where Mr. Korf left her. She worked in her office for a while, until, hearing a stir in the street, she stepped out on the balcony in time to see the Sikhs present arms while, to a clapping of hands, Sir Herbert Samuel rode by in an automobile accompanied by armored cars. It reminded her of Nehemiah who, in the fifth century B.C., was the Jewish Governor of Judah, sent by the Persian King Artaxerxes to remedy the deplorable state of Jerusalem. He fortified the walls of the city against its troublesome neighbors and devoted himself to social reforms: Sabbath observance, cancellation of the debts of the sorely oppressed poor, the payment of tithes for the maintenance of the Temple. . . . But somehow the thought of the present parallel was not as satisfying to Henrietta Szold as it should have been. Later she learned from Dr. Eder how the members of the Zionist Commission, who had waited upon the High Commissioner to welcome him, had been unceremoniously rebuffed by his military aides.

That evening Henrietta and a party of her friends took Mr. Korf for a walk by moonlight, threading their way through the narrow, shadowy stepped streets of the Old City, out St. Stephen's Gate and up the long hill to the Mount of Olives, where they looked down on fabulous Jerusalem magically bathed in the soft brilliance of the full moon and countless stars hanging low like lamps in the heavens. It was a jolly party, with songs and much spirited talk, Mr. Korf holding forth on his favorite topic of modern morality, on which he was writing a book, the proofs of which he hoped Miss Szold would read for him. Curious it was how scholarly men were still moved to ask Miss Szold to edit their books.

At her next Hebrew lesson she relayed some of Mr. Korf's views to Mr. K., who agreed that this was a matter basic to modern civilization which might lead to a new and higher morality in the future. And he invited Miss Szold to stand with Mr. Dushkin as godparents of his fifth child.

Miss Szold's interest in the changing mores and morality of women as part of their postwar emancipation was stimulated by her concern for the welfare of the young women among the pioneers and especially for the students at Hadassah's Nurses' Training School in Jerusalem. She was having a spirited correspondence on the subject with her sister Adele who took the "modern woman's" stand, and sent her a book called *Woman* by Magdelene Marx, one of the new frankly confessional books emancipated women were writing—about her refusal to accept old traditions, her unsatisfactory marriage, her extramarital love affair, the effect of the war. . . . Henrietta was greatly moved by the book, but saw in it a sort of "woman's Ecclesiastes" and not a warrant for the "untutored modernity" which was leading young women along "the false paths they are treading." She wanted freedom for women, but not "lawless freedom."

Mr. Korf departed. Sir Herbert Samuel settled down to his delicate task of soothing the nerves of the Jewish population, which took heart from reports that he kept his office religiously closed on the Sabbath and he had fastened on all the doorposts of the Governor's mansion the *mezuzah*—the small case containing a scroll on which is inscribed the injunction that the commands of the One God of Israel shall be written "upon the posts of thy house, and upon thy gates." But, surrounded as he was by anti-Semitic subordinates whom he would antagonize by seeming to favor the Jews, Sir Herbert might feel obliged to lean over backward in his dealings with Zionist aspirations. Miss Szold was one of ten women invited to attend the ceremonial occasion at Government House when the High Commissioner, in white with a broad purple sash, the dignified representative of a great power, delivered a message from the King of England to the people of Palestine, followed by his own outline of the government's policy. The hall was filled with representatives of various districts and institutions, races and creeds —a picturesque gathering of Sheikhs and Bedouins, church dignitaries, and military and civil officials. He told them that there would be no full civil government until after the terms of the Mandate were settled and accepted by the Supreme Council of the League of Nations. He spoke in English, and then stood waiting while what he said was delivered by interpreters in Arabic and in Hebrew. When his reference to the Jewish National Home was spoken in Arabic there was a perceptible stirring among the Sheikhs and Bedouins. He proclaimed an amnesty for all political prisoners, referring to Jabotinsky and his followers not by name but as "those in prison on account of the Passover excess." The same amnesty was extended to Arabs who had murdered and maimed and looted the Jews. Would Jabotinsky accept it? Henrietta Szold wondered as she went out into the beautiful courtyard where refreshments were served, and introductions and conversations carried on most "correctly" between the British, Arabs and Jews.

Miss Szold continued her task of trying to scale down the budget of Hadassah's projects to somewhere near its resources; but it couldn't be done. The only recourse was to scale down the projects. But how could you, when the needs were so desperate? Life was an obstacle race. Or, better put, life was a restless sea in which you had to swim about, spending and husbanding your energies as best you could, hoping for no final restful shore, and maintaining yourself not by trying to get out of the troubled and ruthless element but by submerging yourself in it; for only thus would it buoy you up.

Miss Szold met with a group of doctors to consider the need for expanded trachoma treatment. Miss Szold met with a group from Safed to solve the problems of their clinic. Miss Szold met with a group from the hospitals to consider the setting of hospital fees, and the related problem of their private practice fees. Of one of them, a dermatologist, she permitted herself to comment: "He's our thin-skinned specialist"; and then decided he was no specialist: they all were thin-skinned. Miss Szold went to discuss with the American Consul the matter of permits of entry for American nurses to teach at the Nurses' Training School. Shmarya Levin, who settled in Palestine, came to discuss with Miss Szold the various forces which would be assembling at the coming Zionist Conference in London where they would struggle for power: he thought there should be a large enough American delegation to offset the Russians and others. Miss Szold held a meeting of the Finance Committee of the Medical Unit and, after wrestling with the problems of money and personalities, decided: "Money, no matter from where it comes will sink to the bottom, leaving behind only moral degradation, unless the men that give it come along with it and do some hard-headed thinking and energetic acting on the spot."

But more money was desperately needed if the courageous immigrants who were coming in were to be kept there; for pioneering in Palestine could not support itself. It was not like pioneering in America. The land provided nothing—no lumber or crops, without investment. For lack of money the long awaited opportunity would be lost. "In one day forty persons come into my office and ask for work, while I am overworked. They want to work, and I want to work; circumstances won't let them, and they won't let me."

What was most disappointing was not to be able to concentrate on the one coherent work she had come there so eager to do—the woman's work, Hadassah's "healing of the daughter of my people." The necessity of taking over the directorship of the Unit, and the welter of distracting details in which she found herself swamped, had been quite unforeseen. It was like the distraction of Mamma from her *ordentlich* housekeeping by some unfortunate unforeseen detail which had to be attended to. Ten years ago, Henrietta had written, "And as I am exactly like her, I, too, am wearing myself out in detail work, in which I excel as she does. So it is fate with me!" Her head was full of such figures as how many bedsheets were stolen from the Safed Hospital in six months.

But she turned for help to the women, young and old, who flocked to her as they had in America. A pretty girl appeared one day asking to be taken on as a secretary. It was quite apparent that she was not as old as she said she was, she was not fifteen, really still a child, but so fervent was the wish of black-eyed, black-haired Emma Gomborow to work for Miss Szold, so vital and intelligent her youthful aspiration, that Henrietta could not refuse her. Emma became Miss Szold's personal secretary, but with the devotion of a daughter. Emma shopped as well as typed for her, and bullied her into caring for herself; and working hours meant nothing to Emma even when young Louis Ehrlich came courting her.

With the help of Mrs. Robert Kesselman, the wife of the Secretary of the Department of Immigration, who had been a member of Henrietta Szold's chapter of Hadassah in New York, Miss Szold resolutely set about the work of aiding young immigrant mothers and bringing together a number of women's organizations in Palestine for the purpose of combining their presently overlapping and ineffectual activities and channeling them toward other pressing basic needs of the land. Their meeting was a babel of languages—Hebrew, German, Ladino, Yiddish—which required much interpreting. The Bokharan women in their exquisitely embroidered garments understood nothing. How, one wondered, could one hope for a *rapprochement* between Arabs and Jews?

Fortunately for her, a Women's International Zionist Organization was formed at the London Conference, which would undertake the organization of women in Palestine as well as in other countries, excepting the United States which would be left to

Hadassah. Henrietta Szold was, of course, offered the presidency of WIZO, but sensibly declined it, and confined herself to the work in Palestine. She was learning to limit her activities; but whatever one did, there was bound to be difficulty.

In September she made a trip with an engineer to Haifa to see about the location of a hospital. On the morning of their departure the chauffeur was stricken with malaria. The engineer turned up too late for the train. They got another chauffeur and set out. A cold, which Miss Szold had felt coming on but had ignored, developed so that by the time they got to Ziḥron Yaakob she was so sick she had to stop there overnight. The next morning shortly after they started for Haifa something snapped in the car. It took a pair of mules seven hours to haul it the rest of the way to Haifa. Two British officers in a car gave her a lift part of the way; but it was against the rules to bring a woman into the city in a staff car, so she had to alight outside the hilly city and walk to the hotel. Malaria was scourging the beautiful north country; she was beset by calls for help—"Send a nurse here, a doctor there, medicine here, bed linens there, quinine. . . . You must! You don't dare refuse!" Her response, "No money," was met with, "Then America must send some." Beset as she was she saw clearly that medical care must be rendered automatically as part of the living arrangements of every group that arrived for settlement. She proposed to carry on an educational campaign in the rural districts on the subject of malaria. They went to a camp of road builders by auto; had two accidents on the way, had to finish the journey in a springless wagon drawn by mules. By the time they were ready to return, the auto was repaired. They got in, and five minutes later it telescoped into a wagon and was smashed. They had to return to Haifa in a wagon, towing the battered auto. "An auto here," Miss Szold concluded, "is no convenience, because there are no real chauffeurs."

"In spite of all, my health is not suffering," she advised her sisters in November. "This week for the first time I felt the strain—not of work but of a moral question badly handled. . . . Then for the first time my heart reverted to its state previous to the Boothbay Harbor days. So I stayed in bed all day today." Fortunately Dr. Rubinow was prevailed upon to return that month and resume the directorship of the Unit, which relieved her of part of the burden although she continued to help him as best she could. She had the satisfactory feeling that she was handing back to him a somewhat less turbulent Unit than he had left with her; it was somewhat better organized and was showing results—especially with the frightful malaria scourge which was beginning to relent. It was reassuring to her that at three score she had had the elasticity to tackle a totally new problem and been able to make progress, despite the difficult doctors. Like the ancient matriarchs she had got the men to do what needed to be done.

Now with the torrential winter rains, interspersed with spells of glorious sunshine heralded by rainbows arching over the hills of Jerusalem, the landscape was transformed; fields turned emerald green; the dry, stony hills burst into flower, a riot of color. Fruit trees were laden with oranges, apricots, peaches, pears, bananas, figs. But indoors the stone houses with stone floors were stone-cold and clammy. The only heaters were the miserable little kerosene stoves which gave off more smell than warmth—which you hardly felt a few inches away. Miss Szold took to wearing woolen bloomers and multiple sweaters and to writing while bundled up in an old fur coat. At night thick woolen pajamas and long woolen stockings hardly kept her comfortable; and her heart ached for the plucky immigrants still living in tent camps, eight to a tent, and eating Australian bully beef. Soaked with rain and bitten by vermin, they worked and sang, holding fast to their hope of Jewish independence. Her only consolation was the thought that they came from conditions in Europe which were barely better. She wished she could quit her administrative work and go cook for them at least; their lives were so wretched in the lovely land.

All she could do for them was improve their sanitary conveniences and supply them with malaria prophylaxis, and even for this she had inadequate funds. "The immigration medical work was thrust upon Hadassah," she reported bitterly, "but those who flung it at us forgot to throw the appropriation with it." Immigrants were being infected with malaria right in the government's quarantine station; and when this was called to an official's attention for correction he complained of "Jewish impertinence." Miss Szold replied that "after waiting two thousand years, Jews may be permitted a little impertinence." Besides malaria, there was dysentery and typhoid—and not even a government delousing station, although many immigrants came from typhus-infected areas.

And lurking behind all other anxieties was the Arab problem. What would happen in the spring?

One day a visitor came—an unexpected intruder who gave her an insight into the Arabic spirit, which was so intriguing she could not resist his plea, nor could her weariness at the end of a long hard Friday at the end of a long hard week prevent her from setting down a vignette of that visit:

> . . . in the midst of the day's routine, the clerk announced the Sheikh of the Mosque of Omar, who refused to tell his business, and insisted upon seeing me. As he spoke only Arabic, Mr. G., the cashier, acted as interpreter.
>
> Enter a dignified, spare Arab, with white folds around his turban. He walked right up to my desk and kissed my hand, and, through the interpreter, expressed his pleasure in waiting upon me. I responded in kind, and then asked what had brought him to me.
>
> He was the father of five daughters, and he and they were starving.
>
> I said that in a few days I would bring him help, my idea being that I'd find out what was the meaning of "Sheikh of the Mosque of Omar."
>
> No, that would not do. He and they were starving now.
>
> Very well, I'd give him something now, and give him more after a few days.
>
> No; once he asked of me, and would take; but never again would he ask, or take. And thereupon he kissed the hem of my garment.
>
> When he kissed my hand, I withdrew it in protest; but when he stooped, with inimitable dignity, to kiss the hem of my garment, I at once felt myself an Oriental of the Orient, and played my part as he played his. Thereupon I asked, why had he come just to me.
>
> He had heard of me, and he felt I would help him.
>
> Who had told him of me?

Bolt upright as he sat, he seemed to grow taller, and he threw back his head, and looking upward, with his hands crossed over his girdle, he solemnly uttered the one word: "A-l-la-h!"

After that I questioned no longer, but silently handed him a pound. I was sure he'd come again. I was sure he was a professional, but his consummate simplicity disarmed me. Besides, I was sufficiently influenced by the prevailing mood still hanging over Jerusalem since the pogrom days, to want to propitiate any Arab I met.

He rose at once, again kissed my hand while I protested I was an American, and was about to withdraw, when I stopped him and told him I too had a favor to ask: I had not yet seen the Mosque of Omar, would he show it to me? He wrote his name on my card, and it was agreed I'd come on a Sunday. His face was all aglow. He withdrew to the door, turned, raised his hand to his lips and his forehead, and disappeared.

Not for a moment had he been anything but my peer—not a trace of the suppliant.

It was indeed a pity she had not the time to write her own life, which was hard, but fascinating; and she was well equipped to do it—she had everything but the time. The more she did, the more she had to do. "A woman's work is never done." Like that irresistibly persistent Arab, the Arab-Jewish problem was pressing, and unless it was faced and solved, no Zionist achievement would be secure; all her own effort would be in vain.

In trying to clarify the situation between the Jewish colonists and the Arabs she drew a parallel between herself and the cousins she met when she went to Europe with her parents, who had long spoken to her of Europe as their homeland. Her European cousins had hardly understood her and her American background. The Jew, she reasoned, comes to Palestine in much the same way and meets his cousins, the Arabs, there. The Zionist Jew, cherishing his Bible, has long thought of Palestine as the homeland of his forefathers, but his Arab cousins hardly understand him or his modern background. The Arabs had a saying: "I had no shoes and complained until I met a man who had no feet." It expressed a resignation at odds with the aspiring, progressive spirit of the Jews. Suppose now that she had wished to return and settle in Europe in the place where her cousins lived. Would she try to drive them out and replace them, or would she bring to her cousins the progress America had made, and create with and for them a better life in the land they both loved? There, she realized, the analogy ended for the Zionist Jew who was persecuted and driven from the land of his adoption—as she had not been—and came to Palestine as the one place he could truly call home and feel at home because he had lived in its 3,500-year-old history as in a home. But that had meant living in the past, and now he wanted real living—living in the future. The past must be remembered only for the sake of the future. And for that reason, in Palestine, their first consideration—after their basic sustenance was established—was the care and education of the children; the children are the future. But individuals cannot control and mold life; only societies can; and to this end political and social organization is required. This was the fact recognized by Lord Balfour in his Declaration. And if the Zionists were to implement that Declaration in Palestine it would have to be done for the benefit of their Arab cousins as well as themselves. The Jews were being given not merely a Homeland but an opportunity for the practice of that universal righteousness preached by their prophets. Jews who wanted merely material gains had only to migrate to lands where by unscrupulous opportunism riches were to be garnered. In this ancient and holy land, hard work and thrift would bring them little material but much spiritual wealth. And this only if they could work and live in peace with the Arabs. Arabs and Jews had worked together in the Middle Ages. They could do so again. "A Semitic Confederation in Palestine," wrote Henrietta Szold at the end of her notes on the subject —"a little point in the great Arab Sea."

Her good friend Judah Magnes came that year with his family to settle in Palestine and devote himself to the development of the Hebrew University which was to rise on the cornerstone Chaim Weizmann had laid on Mount Scopus. As Magnes, too, was at heart a pacifist, Henrietta Szold found in him a dedicated colleague in her endeavor to find a solution to the serious problem of Arab-Jewish relations.

It was interesting to see how those who came there intent on changing the land were themselves quickly changed. She herself when she traveled about went dressed in a belted sports jacket over breeches with thick woolen stockings and high, heavy boots. The eminent Dr. Magnes was to be met on the streets of Jerusalem as he would never appear in public in New York, his shirt wide open at the neck, a tin pail in one hand, a full market basket in the other, his handsome face bronzed by the sun and alight with plans for the future. He became Dean of the new Hebrew University whose classes were being conducted in temporary quarters while the building was being erected on Mount Scopus with funds he was still gathering. In this effort, also, Henrietta helped him. Money was not easy to find, but she left no stone unturned. One day, scanning a London newspaper, she came across a rather unusual name which was that of one of her "Russians" of the night school in Baltimore, whom Papa and she had helped when he first arrived penniless. She wrote to the man in London. He proved to be the son of her former pupil, and he was now well-to-do. He sent her $25,000 for the Hebrew University: "Bread cast upon the waters . . ."

Judah Magnes was a welcome addition to the burgeoning cultural life of Jewish Palestine. Artists and writers and scholars were settling in Jerusalem and Tel Aviv, the new Jewish city which had magically sprouted from the sand dunes by the Mediterranean just as Mr. Dizengoff had confidently told her it would, on the train ten years ago. As Herzl had said: "If you will it, it is no fable." And in that fast growing city there was a fine artist named Rubin, born in Roumania and trained in Paris, wonderfully painting now the unutterable beauty of Palestine, its stony flowering hills, its silvery olive groves and the blossoming air of Safed in the spring, its sunburnt fishermen and its gray-bearded sages, its black goats and gray donkeys; a joyous Jewish art free of the morbid sadness of the Diaspora. Other artists came—Herman Struck from Germany. And Ḥayim Naḥman Bialik, the poet, came to settle and write his great poems in Hebrew; and Shmarya Levin was writing his fine prose, and S. Y. Agnon his lyric fiction, along with J. H. Brenner, the poet and short-story writer who had been there for years. And the Zionist philosopher Aḥad Ha-Am settled in Tel

Aviv, and was so greatly revered that when he fell ill, the street he lived in, named for him, was closed to traffic in the afternoons when he rested.

Norman Bentwich's talented sisters, Thelma the cellist and Margery the violinist, had come from England and were making and teaching music. Eliezer Ben-Yehuda, who had spent much of his life working for the revival of the language, was compiling a comprehensive Hebrew Dictionary and finding new words, derived from ancient and modern sources, which were giving the ancient language new life. When he died in the midst of his work, his wife, Deborah, carried it on. You heard Hebrew everywhere—in the chatter of children. Immigrants were changing their names to Hebrew ones and giving their children Hebrew names—a reversal of what had been happening for centuries in the Diaspora: Isaac which had been turned into the French Isidor and the English Irving was here returned to the Hebrew Isaac: Yitzḥak. Moses, which had been changed to Maurice and Milton, now became Moshe. Second names, too, were Hebraized: Gruen had become Ben-Gurion.

The circle of Henrietta Szold's colleagues and friends grew in size and variety far beyond that of the circle in New York, Baltimore and Philadelphia, to which she had been so strongly attached. On her sixtieth birthday a dinner party was given her at the Hotel de France attended by Sir Herbert and Lady Samuel. Her name was inscribed in the Golden Book of the Jewish National Fund. Her circle now spread from Jerusalem to Jaffa and Tel Aviv, to Haifa and Safed and Tiberias, and to all the colonies sprinkled like seed and flourishing between the growing cities. There was a constant traffic among them, swelled by a steady stream of newcomers from the immigrants from Europe and from among her old friends in America. Some were drawn by the call of pioneering, some came seeking a haven. Dr. Benderly came from Baltimore, his head full of plans for education. Lilian Friedlaender came from New York as a result of a terrible misfortune: her husband, Israel, who had gone on a postwar relief mission to the Ukraine, was murdered by robber bandits. Lilian and their six children went to live in Ziḥron Yaakob on the estate of her sister Nita Lange, who died suddenly just before they arrived.

But the troubles of individuals, her own and others', paled to insignificance in the lurid light of the conflagration that burst forth again with greater ferocity at the end of April 1921 on *Nebi Moussa,* which bade fair to signify annually for the Jews in Palestine what Easter had meant in Europe. The carefully laid tinder this time was the slander that all Jews are Bolsheviks, that the Zionists were flooding the country with Bolsheviks, obviously untrue since Bolshevism was frankly opposed to Zionism. The spark, applied this time in Jaffa, at the height of the riotous celebration, was the cry that the Jewish Bolsheviks were marching on the mosques—the misrepresentation of a May Day parade of Labor Zionists. The Commandant of Police was conveniently absent that day. Uniformed policemen led the howling mob, armed with rifles and bombs, with boat hooks wielded by waterfront ruffians. At the Zionist Immigration Depot they butchered thirteen newly arrived immigrants, and then swept through the town murdering and pillaging. They advanced into nearby Tel Aviv, where the Jews, many of them veterans of the war, formed in self-defense and held the attackers at bay. On May 5, the settlement of Petaḥ Tikvah was attacked by thousands of armed fellaheen from the surrounding Arab villages. The colony of Kfar Saba was destroyed; Reḥovot and Ḥederah were ravaged. Gardens and orchards and vineyards, the works of years, were ruined; houses and barns burned down; equipment and cattle carried off. . . . All Palestine believed that anti-Semitic British officials had incited the disturbances. The High Commissioner pacified the Arabs with the announcement that immigration had been suspended. The Haycroft Commission was appointed to investigate and fix responsibility for the outbreak—95 persons had been killed; 290 wounded.

This time Henrietta Szold was in the thick of it. She had spent a few pleasant days in Reḥovot, whence she had written her niece Sarah Levin, one of Bertha's daughters: ". . . Your description of a precipitate Maryland spring made me very homesick. In spite of my ravings over the botanical wonders of Palestine, I have had a real longing for the flowers of my childhood. For instance, Palestine is particularly rich in trefoils, medicagos, and all sorts of leguminosae, yet I felt a void all through these spring months, and why? Because there is no white clover exactly like ours. I am really ungrateful. No one ought to want more in the botanical line than Palestine offers. And you will wonder when I say that most interesting of all are the seeds of the wild flowers. They are all devised with a view to being disseminated far and wide by the goats and sheep, of which the country is full. All the seeds are fortified with hairs or spines or protuberances of some sort, for the purpose. . . . The animals here have been one of my chief sources of pleasure. . . . I have never seen so many kids, and lambs, and calves, and fillies, and, cutest of all, young donkeys. You should see all these young things scurry when our automobile dashes along. . . ."

On her way back to Jerusalem, she stopped in Jaffa for midday dinner at a Hungarian place whose cooking was precisely like Mamma's, the only place in all Palestine which made *matzoh-klös* just like hers. While waiting for dinner she went over to Tel Aviv to see Nellie Straus Mochenson, and on the way passed the May Day parade. When she returned and was seated at dinner with others, they told her the parade had been stopped by the police; and while they were eating, shots were heard. The men said they were only warning shots; but at two o'clock her automobile had not come for her. A man went to look for it; but did not return. Alarmed, she went out into the street and knew at once that a riot was on. She hurried to the hospital and saw the first victims. Outside was a line of waiting stretchers bearing dead and wounded; inside eighteen wounded were being treated; the wounds were from bullets, knives, clubs; the operating room was jammed. . . . She set to work, took charge of arrivals, and the crowd of relatives seeking their lost ones. The small hospital became a bloody shambles, the floors strewn with wounded, the yard with the dead, mostly Jews and a few Arabs. The overflow was sent to a nearby school building and the Immigrant Reception House. She telephoned Jerusalem for doctors, nurses and supplies. They had trouble on the way down and had to get help from the military to get through. In the morning she had to telephone Jerusalem for food; the shops in Jaffa remained closed—Jews and Arabs alike were terrified. Men who ventured out went armed with sticks bristling with nails. Rumor filled the fearful air with explanations of the cause of the riot: mostly that the May Day parade, which had no permit and marched from Jewish Tel Aviv into a mixed

Arab and Jewish quarter of Jaffa, had been halted by the police; there had been a scuffle, shots fired, and unarmed Jews fell. Some were said to have fled for shelter into an Arab's house, and, as luck would have it, burst into his harem, and the screaming women had brought on the violent attack of the men, which turned into a general massacre. . . .

But Miss Szold spoke to those who knew better, to wounded eyewitnesses like the mother and son, immigrants who had arrived in the land only two days before. They were in the Reception House when the uniformed police rushed in—with their identifying badges carefully removed—and with revolvers, clubs and knives set upon the helpless inmates. Others told her that early in the morning of May Day, hours before the parade, they had been warned by Arab friends that something was brewing against the Jews, they had better prepare for it. Miss Szold heard and saw enough to convince her that the massacre had been planned to deter the Zionists, to put an end to their aspiration to the Jewish Homeland which had been promised them. The May Day parade was used as a trigger. It would have happened anyway, even had there been no parade.

"Why do they hate us so?" Here as in Russia, a benighted peasantry was incited by sophisticated governmental powers to attack the Jews for some political reason. But why was it possible to rouse the peasants to this hostility—the Christians on their Easter, the Moslems on their *Nebi Moussa*—on days when they were celebrating a venerated leader each had avowedly got from the very people they were persecuting? Why would they vent their violent hatred not only upon the people to whom they were so indebted but upon the very Scriptures that were the inspiration of one and the origin of the other of these two holy leaders and which were basic to their own Scriptures? Their pogroms left the streets littered alike with bloody Jews and torn Torah scrolls. Psychologists like Joseph Jastrow and disciples of the famous Dr. Freud, much as they differed, were agreed on the possible ambivalence of the human heart. Hatred and love could abide there together at the same time and for the same object.

When Dr. Rubinow arrived from Jerusalem at noon the following day Miss Szold decided to go home. She drove out through the dead city, patrolled now by troops with machine guns and airplanes. On the road outside the city troops of armed Arabs roamed the countryside. She heard that they had been attacking isolated Jewish houses; that in one of them the poet Brenner had been killed together with the family he was visiting. At an Arab village on the way up to Jerusalem the villagers were celebrating, dancing to music. They jeered at the passing automobile. She supposed it was foolhardy to have made the trip then, but she felt she would be needed in Jerusalem.

And when she got there she saw what panic did to people. Outside the Zionist office a group of the clerks stood talking excitedly, too nervous to attend to their work, while all along the street Jewish merchants were putting up their iron-barred shutters. They looked pale with fright. She felt it was the wrong thing to do. Timidity, fear would provoke assault. Groups of Arabs stood in the street watching the Jews. She went down the street and persuaded some of the merchants to keep their shops open. She was told that a handbill had been circulated among the Arabs calling upon them to follow the example of their brave brethren in Jaffa. Then, feeling like her mother's indomitable daughter, she went to the office of the Zionist Commission to give them some advice. Neither Dr. Eder nor any of the other department heads was there. The young man to whom she spoke did not know her; he asked her business and said he would transmit it. It seemed to her, she told him, that a band of young men should be organized to go about the city and keep up the courage of the Jews, to prevent them from giving way to panic which would surely bring an attack triggered by some act of the fearful. In her vehemence she referred to the "chicken-hearted." The young man mildly asked, "Madam, how many pogroms have you been through?" None, she felt obliged to admit, not having personally suffered assault in Jaffa. "I have been through twelve," said the young man. And she was silenced; she had got her lesson.

But that did not alter her conviction that basic to all human relations was the need and desire for love, which, if practiced as the prophets preached, would bring peace and harmony instead of the fearful, hateful violence aroused by unscrupulous seekers of power. An Arab neighbor in Jerusalem brought her a bouquet of flowers and, for want of any other means of expressing its significance, sadly repeated the words, "Jaffa, Jaffa!"

The Jaffa riot was a terrible setback at a time when Zionism seemed at the point of making practical advances all over the country. Pinḥas Rutenberg had announced his plans for the electrification of Jaffa, Tel Aviv, and Petaḥ Tikvah. Moshe Novomeysky, a Russian chemist, was forming a company to extract the wealth of potash and bromine from the Dead Sea. A co-operative roadbuilder's community had been organized in Galilee. Jerusalem was becoming important enough to warrant an air service from Cairo. Jews were coming to settle from all over the world. One had walked all the way from Persia to Bombay to get to Palestine. A group of Canadian farmers had come from Winnipeg to settle on the Holy Land. A short ride from Jerusalem, at Kiryat Anavim, also known as Dilb, Henrietta had seen a hundred East European young men and women set up tents on a stony Judean hillside and set to work clearing the long abandoned terraces, carrying the stones in baskets down to the neglected road which they repaired, and refilling the stone holes with rich soil they brought up in the baskets from below. She had seen them in sickness and in health, planting trees and building concrete barns for their cattle and a nursery for their children, and only finally, a barracks for themselves. Because it was near Jerusalem she took hurried American tourists out to Dilb in the hope that, seeing what could be accomplished by youth with brawn, with purpose and working idealism, they would go home and get others to support such heroic efforts. The colony of Nahalal was founded in the Jezreel Valley by another group of *ḥalutzim*—pioneers—part of a movement among whose founders were David Ben-Gurion and Yitzḥak Ben-Zvi; their *moshav* was a new type of colony of individual farmers whose small holdings were arranged in a circle radiating from their community of houses, which they built themselves of stone they quarried. Hadassah sent nurses to care for their children while they worked, and doctors for their malaria victims. Hadassah had successfully fought an epidemic of influenza and typhoid that winter.

The High Commissioner had appointed a commission to handle the land problem—to determine what land was at the disposal of the government; and he convoked an assembly for the consideration of the political organization of Palestine Jewry, to which women delegates were admitted despite the objection of the orthodox. The position of Sir Herbert Samuel was admittedly a difficult one, placed as he was at the center of a web of contending forces within as well as without Palestine Jewry. Henrietta Szold did not agree with those who saw him either as timid and cowardly or as a traitor to his own people in his attempts to mollify the British military and the Arabs in order to maintain peace. When his son, Edwin Samuel, was married, the Sheikhs of Beersheba crowned the bridegroom in a romantic ceremony and the bride was presented with thirty Arabian horses.

An effort was being made to improve the efficiency of Zionist functioning in the land by a commission sent over by Chaim Weizmann, head of the World Zionist Organization, to study the reorganization of existing Zionist activities; Robert Szold, the cousin who used to come to the Szold Friday evenings in New York, was one of its members. Weizmann, speaking in New York, where he was joined by Albert Einstein, was most optimistic about the future of the Jewish National Home under the British Mandate. Winston Churchill, outspoken in favor of it, had come to Palestine that spring and planted a date palm on Mount Scopus near the cornerstone of the University which Weizmann had laid. It appeared that the British government was not to blame for the iniquities of its unruly offspring, the Colonial Office and its military representatives. Their inability to prevent a minor riot on Balfour Day in which five Jews were killed and twenty wounded, all in self-defense, prompted Henrietta Szold to question her status as a pacifist.

Yet, in that year 1921, when Jewish unity was most needed for progress, a schism within the Zionist Organization of America came to a climax at its convention in Cleveland. It had been plain for some time that the pragmatic American philosophy of Justice Brandeis' leadership with its emphasis on orderly planning and businesslike investment as distinguished from philanthropic fiscal resources, was in conflict with the more flexible if less orderly program of Weizmann, who had his strong adherents in the American organization. At the Cleveland convention, this faction opposed the Brandeis-Mack group and caused their resignation from the direction of the effort. This, however, did not diminish the Zionist sympathies and activities of Brandeis and his following, who organized the Palestine Development Council (which later became the Palestine Economic Corporation) for the building and development of colonies, while the Weizmann regime relied on the *Keren Hayesod,* the world-wide fund-raising agency, for the support of Zionist activities.

The controversy was naturally reflected in the affiliated organization of Hadassah, the Women's Zionist Organization of America, which by then numbered some 10,000 members, the majority of whose Central Committee members were Brandeis adherents. In the course of their parallel controversy, they sought to gain strength by sending for Henrietta Szold, a Brandeis adherent. Although she believed that the *Keren Hayesod* would be indispensable, she disapproved of certain details of its operation. She agreed with Hadassah that its own funds, which had heretofore been contributed to the treasury of the men's organization, must be kept apart, earmarked for medical services. Her presence and persuasive speech would without doubt have been a most influential reinforcement; but Brandeis advised Hadassah not to send for her, so important for Zionist progress did he consider her presence in Palestine at that critical time—not only for what she did there, but for what she was, for her spirit. So Henrietta Szold stayed in Palestine; and Hadassah disengaged itself from the men's controversy over ways and means and devoted itself independently to the pursuit of the specific projects which their Miss Szold was doing her best to bring to pass. In her message to Hadassah's convention at Pittsburgh in November 1921, its first independent convention, Miss Szold advised further concentration on those projects: ". . . for with concentration goes responsibility, with responsibility must go full knowledge of at least one subject; after full knowledge of one subject comes understanding of adjacent subjects, after more understanding greater devotion, and if devotion is true and honest, more work, better results. Such, to my belief, is the content of genuine enthusiasm."

And it was with the greatest enthusiasm that, in the following month, the graduation of the first class of the Hadassah Training School for Nurses, which had been postponed from Balfour Day because of the riot, was celebrated in Jerusalem. The invitations were in Hebrew, as were the parchment diplomas which Lady Samuel distributed to the twenty-two who had changed from the delft-blue uniform of students to the white of graduate nurses, with the blue Star of David on their folded white caps. There were addresses by Lady Samuel, Dr. Eder and Dr. Rubinow, with Dr. de Sola Pool, the Joint Distribution Committee's representative, standing by to translate from English into Hebrew—a circumstance which prompted certain fanatic Hebraists not to attend.

Miss Szold spoke of the ten years' persistent work by Hadassah women in America to bring this occasion to pass. "Praised be God who has kept us alive and maintained us and permitted us to reach this day." She stressed the importance of their being Palestinian nurses: "In all departments of endeavor, in the professions, in commerce, in the trades, the arts, the crafts, all who love Palestine and believe in its future want to see life in Palestine become sufficient unto itself. . . . You, my dear girls, the first fruits of the Nurses' Training School . . . are another evidence of our growing self-sufficiency." She emphasized the importance of their being indigenous even in their language: "We boast that ours is the only Nurses' Training School in the world in which Hebrew is the language of instruction," and praised their ability to do without textbooks, which had not been available in that language and were only now being translated, and to find words for the growing new vocabulary of their profession. "Not a moment too soon do these graduation exercises take place. *Now* you are needed—now when the young pioneers are beginning to grapple with the primitive problems of the new life . . . when the scattered labor groups may be expected soon to consolidate themselves into communities in which proper health standards must be raised and upheld, for babies and mothers, in the schools and the homes, at the bedsides of the sick and in the working quarters of the vigorous. In this portentous time the land wants you." In their diplomas they were not called Sisters of Mercy but "Ordained Nurses"—their ordination being the outcome of their intense training. "Proficiency is the mother of mercy . . . women, at once tender and strong, becoming trained nurses, will at the same time be Sisters of Mercy. Only such women, faced with the emergencies of which a nurse's life is compact, will be animated by the genuine devotion of the queen for whom our school is named, and will be ready like Esther to say at every turn, 'And if I perish, I perish!' " She bade them live and strive for the ideal "combination of the strong and the sweet, of intellect and sentiment, of knowledge and sympathy which is the finest flower of human culture." The class picture was taken. There was a garden party.

Before long, requests for Hadassah nurses were coming from all over the Near East—from Cairo and Bagdad and Aleppo. . . . To open the door of a Hadassah clinic and come from a teeming malodorous street of Jerusalem or Jaffa or Tiberias into the antiseptic air where Yemenite and Arab women waited with their babies for the ministrations of the quietly bustling, white-robed nurses, was to span many centuries of human progress at a step. Children knew that when you were sick you sent for "a Hadassah" —a term which needed no translation.

A graduate nurse sent for postgraduate work at the Henry Street Settlement in New York was reported to be as well trained as the product of any American nursing school. The treatment you got in the Hadassah Hospital in Jerusalem was the equal of what you would get in a first-class hospital in New York. The only difference would be that nurses and doctors spoke Hebrew; and on Friday toward sunset, a nurse would come into the women's ward bearing a tray of candles, one of which each woman would be permitted to light with the benediction for the Sabbath. Here, as Henrietta had dreamed, one could live Jewishly at all times. "If you will it, it is no fable."

That Hadassah's whole medical organization was important to Palestine and would become in time an indigenously supported institution seemed evident from the fact that since 1918, when the Unit came over and got no income from the Palestine community, such income had voluntarily been received and increased until it amounted to £15,000 in 1921. Indeed, the colonies now eagerly welcomed the coming of Hadassah's agent to arrange contracts for medical service for the year ahead, for which they were now willing to pay up to 80 per cent of the cost.

When Henrietta Szold went out to Palestine in 1920, it was with the idea that she would stay for a term of two years. In her third year, there was still no prospect of any relaxation of the demands upon her, which would permit her to return home even for a spell. On *Nebi Moussa*, that spring, there was no Arab demonstration, because the government, anxious to have the Mandate ratified that summer, policed all Arab gatherings, proving that the earlier pogroms could have been prevented; but that did not prevent the spread of the anti-Jewish animus, even to little children, whom she heard in the streets singing Arabic equivalents of that doggerel she had heard with astonishment over half a century ago on Pratt Street in Baltimore: "Take a piece of pork . . ." These children could not sing the same song, of course, because like the children they were reviling they ate no pork either. But the dreadful hatred they had been taught was the same. Nevertheless, that summer Hadassah received from a Moslem organization in Tiberias a letter expressing their appreciation of the medical treatment given Arabic children in the schools that year; and Henrietta Szold felt sure that education would bring further improvement in Arab-Jewish relations.

In April of that year there was a fine exhibition of arts and crafts in the ancient Citadel of David at the Jaffa Gate, cleaned of the cobwebs and debris of centuries, opened and attended by functionaries from the High Commissioner down; the invitations were in Hebrew, Arabic, and English. But by July, when the Mandate was signed and sealed, Arab objections to it were overt, and the British government was reinterpreting the Mandate so as to make concessions to the Arabs at the expense of Zionist expectations and aspirations. Trans-Jordan was cut off from the Jewish Homeland; and the Zionist leadership was too hungry for even half a loaf to put up any resistance. Even Sir Herbert Samuel played a part in the British policy of whittling down the Mandate; and it was difficult to rationalize his having permitted the notorious Effendi El Husseini, who had fled after his implication in the riot of 1920, to return as Mufti of Jerusalem, and then to become head of the Supreme Moslem Council. It seemed to Henrietta Szold that the Jewish rejoicing over their expectation of getting political power in their Homeland was overoptimistic: she foresaw that the careerists of the Colonial Office would endeavor, as long as possible, to hold to their snug berths in Palestine. On July 20, the twentieth anniversary of Papa's death, she wrote: "Not a day passes but his wisdom and *Menschenkenntnis* come back to my mind. . . . Nothing, nothing is like what he visioned." She became aware of a growing tendency by government officials to minimize or ignore the improvements in the land made by Jewish efforts—including Hadassah's medical services.

Meanwhile, the funds available for Hadassah's activities had become so critically inadequate—there was not sufficient income to pay even the current low salaries of the doctors and nurses—that she went to the Zionist Conference held at Carlsbad in the summer of 1922 to plead for support of the Medical Unit and its invaluable achievements. She was joined there by Mrs. Edward Jacobs of the National Board of Hadassah. But the Zionists were too preoccupied with the organization of the Jewish Agency, which was to act as the Jewish governing body in the National Home, to pay much attention to the women of Hadassah, who had recently had the hardihood to assert their independence of male guidance; and among the American delegates there were those who could not forget Miss Szold's adherence to the ousted Brandeis-Mack faction.

Undaunted, Miss Szold then decided to go to Paris and appeal for help to the vastly rich Baron de Rothschild, who had endowed the Rothschild Hospital in Jerusalem, and had for many years poured millions into his pet colonies. Altogether, it was a depressing trip that summer. At Carlsbad, pathetic Max Löbl had appeared, still mourning the loss of Sadie, still unmarried, and looking so shockingly aged that Henrietta wondered how *she* must appear to others, her hair grayer, her face more wrinkled, although, surprisingly, she did not *feel* any older inside than the last time she had seen him. On the way to Paris, she stopped in Berlin and Vienna and saw the dreadful aftermath of war for the defeated, especially in dismembered Austria, and in the spirit of her relatives, the Schaars, whose changes would have made Mamma very unhappy could she see them—baptisms and intermarriages and other vain efforts to escape the Jewish handicap. But then, even in America being a Jew could be a handicap—there was a scandal that summer about the *numerus clausus* at Harvard and other colleges.

In Paris, she bearded the old Baron in his palace, was received in his luxurious den at the end of a picture gallery lined with priceless Rembrandts, Rubens, Titians. Suavely but coldly, he said no; advised her to try one of the American Jewish millionaires—he named several—and bowed her out. As she went back along the gallery it occurred to her that if she snatched one of the smaller paintings which stood on easels, just one charming little Van Eyck, she could pay all the salaries and go on. . . . Out in the bustling Rue Ste. Honoré she stood disheartened and wondered if the distinguished Henrietta Szold, a woman of sixty-two, should have exposed herself to the humiliation of a rejected *schnorrer*—a beggar—even for the sake of the Jewish National Home. It was too much. She was tempted to take the next ship to America; she had a vision of relaxing at last in that old rocking chair in Baltimore, with dear Bertha and her children to love. . . . She cabled Dr. Rubinow in Jerusalem; and back came his decision. He was definitely and finally quitting in October. He *had* to. It was just as in the old days in New York, when other people *had* to go abroad or to Atlantic City in the hot summer, and "Miss Szold, that fine beast of burden," *had* to do, not what she would like to do, but what *had* to be done. She *wished* she could harden her fluttering heart and go home to rest in Baltimore; but Henrietta remembered Jeremiah: "Is there no balm in Gilead? Is there no physician there? Why then is not the health of the daughter of my people recovered?" How could she forsake this task!

The one saving grace of the trip had been the opportunity of getting "things" she needed desperately after over two years in a place where she had been deprived of the possibility of getting even shoelaces for her Oxford ties. She bought some clothes and returned, "to take hold of the helm of a sinking ship."

Eshet ḥayil: "A woman of valor who can find? . . ." In the days of her studies at the Seminary in New York, they had discussed the real meaning of the Hebrew word *ḥayil*. In the Authorized and in the Revised Versions it is translated: "A woman of virtue . . ." But the Hebrew word does not really have that narrow puritanical significance. It denotes energy and capacity and goodness. "A woman of *valor* . . ." And not merely in times of plenty as she is described in Proverbs: "All her household are clothed with scarlet . . . her clothing is fine linen and purple"—a romantic man's wishful picture of a woman.

She returned and resumed the struggle. She organized, in Haifa and Jaffa, women's societies for public welfare work similar to the one she had organized in Jerusalem. That had begun as a babel and was now an orderly, self-sustaining organization, effective in child welfare work under the direction of Bertha Landsman, an able, experienced nurse she had brought from America. Her triumph was that she no longer did anything for them but consult with their committees; but it had been like holding wild horses, or rather infants who want to run when they don't know how to crawl.

But, for want of funds, Dr. Rubinow was closing outlying hospitals and clinics. The Unit was practically bankrupt, its credit exhausted. In December Dr. Weizmann with Dr. Halpern, the Controller of the *Keren Hayesod,* came on a tour of inspection, but gave no hope of better times. Dr. Rubinow left for good. Miss Szold realized that the Unit ought to liquidate, but they hadn't even the money to let go. She couldn't pay off the salaries due or the tradesmen. It was appalling. "If the Unit and I survive the winter, it will be a miracle," she wrote to her sister Rachel, who was herself seriously ill and making a valiant fight for survival. The fact that the income from local voluntary contributions in part payment for medical services was increasing while all other resources were failing was an indication of the growing importance of those services and made Henrietta Szold work all the more desperately for their maintenance. The graduation of the second class of nurses in November, although only fourteen this time, was another triumph at a time when she had not been able to pay any salaries for several months. Generous Nathan Straus came to her rescue in December with a gift of $20,000, which tided the Unit over the winter.

But in March 1923 she received word that Rachel was so dangerously ill that Henrietta had best come home at once if she wished to see her sister alive. In a few days she had packed and sailed, leaving the Medical Unit in the hands of Judah Magnes.

Rachel Jastrow, who was being treated in New York, was staying with Adele, whose husband, Thomas Seltzer, was having legal difficulties over his publication of the works of D. H. Lawrence, and was also drawing upon Henrietta's resources for help. Rachel's doctor said there was little more that could be done for her than to keep from her the hopelessness of her case; but Henrietta went with her to stay at the seashore where Rachel seemed to improve.

Hadassah took advantage of Miss Szold's presence in America to call a mass meeting that filled the ballroom of the Hotel Pennsylvania. Three thousand women came to hear her speak on "Jewish Palestine in the Making"; five hundred of them couldn't get in. She took the occasion to thank the women of Hadassah for their loyal support in desperate times when, she admitted, courage failed her and only discipline had kept her going. . . . She gave them a long, unvarnished report of her tribulations, but would not admit defeat: she must spur them to increased support of the struggle. "Our hopes have not been in vain. We have made a beginning in that great adventure unparalleled almost in the history of mankind, for which there is no precedent according to which to formulate our plan of work. . . . We are making mistakes. We are crawling. We are not galloping. But the aim is before us. The goal . . . is clear to our vision. We shall reach it. . . . Fragments of Jewry are coming to Palestine from all over the world. . . . Every national contributes what he has brought from the land of his exile . . . variety presents a problem. . . . The essential Jew must emerge. That will be brought about by the school. The school alone will be our melting pot. . . ." Just as, at her graduation from the Western Female High School in Baltimore, young Henrietta had seen in the public schools the melting pot of American culture, so now she saw in the schools of the Land of Israel the melting pot in which the acquired differences of Jews in the Diaspora would be sloughed off and burned away, permitting the essential Jew to emerge. But that must take a couple of generations: "I have come back after three years believing that we are going to do what we set out to do: establish a center for the Jewish people in Palestine, radically, fundamentally different from any other Jewish center in the world. I have come back also believing that we, with our own fleshly eyes, will not see the consummation of our hope. We are the generation of the desert. We are permitted only to fructify the earth with our ideas, with our hopes, with our very bodies. We enjoy only the distinction of being the pioneers."

The process would be one of both revival and progress. She spoke of the movement among the women of Palestine to secure equal rights before the law. It was not merely a political movement, it was also and primarily a legal movement, and it was appealing to the rabbis to begin at once on the task of modifying old Jewish laws which discriminated against women. There was also the *Histadrut Nashim,* the Women's Federation, which was preparing women for political action in the time when the Jews of Palestine would have won the freedom to govern themselves; and this too was not merely a program of instruction in political action but also in social service. It was the expectation of Henrietta Szold that women would play decisive roles in the history of the revived Israel as they had in Biblical times. It is remarkable that for all the emancipation of modern women they do not appear in modern histories as frequently and importantly as they do in the Bible, in times when they had the status of chattels. For good or ill, beginning with Eve herself, and continuing with Sarah, Rebekah, Rachel and Leah, Miriam and Deborah . . . Hebrew women were represented as taking actions decisive in the history of men. Henrietta Szold was herself playing such a role, and she invited all Jewish women, young as well as old, to play such a role again, not only individually, but collectively, as Hadassah was doing. She encouraged the organization of Junior Hadassah—of girls who undertook as their project the gathering of funds for the purchase of land near Zichron Yaakob, for a children's village called Meir Shefaya, of which Sophia Berger took charge. Women's work.

She said that she looked not only to Zionists but to the whole world for the support of Jewish aspiration in Palestine: "The huge world to the East must learn from us the justice of our hope, and the huge Christian world must consent to support us, if only to right the wrongs it has inflicted upon us." To illustrate how progress was being made she gave them this homely example: "When I arrived in Palestine I saw something I had never seen before. No egg I opened filled the shell. There was only half an egg. In my third year in Palestine I always had a full egg. . . . Three years ago there were few in Palestine who knew how to raise chickens, and therefore the eggs were starved. Today poultry raising is known, the chickens are fed, the feed is raised, and the egg is good. Here you have a very trivial illustration of what has happened to develop the life in the land."

Incidentally, she took the opportunity of trying tactfully to patch the rift between Hadassah and the Zionist Organization of America over the *Keren Hayesod* by asserting that such a central fund-raising implement was still needed and by approving certain alterations which had been made in its organization. She pleaded at the same time that Hadassah be supported in its wish to continue autonomously in the specialized medical work and education —the women's work—which had been so successful and was still so important in Palestine. She foresaw, besides its further development of nurses' training and public health services, the establishment of a distinguished medical faculty for the new Hebrew University, and of a modern hospital in connection with it. Women work concretely, she said. She was willing to leave it to men, the true romantics, to dream greater dreams and evolve subtle and intricate ideologies to support them. . . .

Trying to make her small voice heard in a vast hall which could only be filled by the clarion tones of a Rabbi Stephen Wise, she felt at the end as if she had been braying for an hour and a half; but a thousand women waited to shake her hand; Hadassah's membership rolled up; and collections amounting to $26,000 came in. She got countless invitations; checks came for the Nurses' Training School. . . .

She brought Rachel to New York for X-ray treatment, to which she responded favorably and was kept alive; but Louis Levin, Bertha's husband, died suddenly that spring, leaving Bertha with five children to support; and Henrietta was concerned about helping her sister get translation and editorial work.

She also continued her efforts to make peace between the Zionist Organization of America and Hadassah; she went to talk to the men, but they kept rehashing the sins of the women against them, until "I made the condition that the past was not to be mentioned. I mean to live in the present, and hope for the future."

She spent the summer caring for Rachel during the series of X-ray treatments, talking for Hadassah, and trying to pacify the Zionist Organization. In September Joe Jastrow took Rachel back to Wisconsin apparently much improved; Hadassah's membership had increased to 15,000; and the Zionists returned from their Congress in Carlsbad with the promise of support for Hadassah.

Anxious about the continued progress of Rachel in Wisconsin and concerned for the welfare of Bertha and Adele, Henrietta was loath to leave the country, but she was persuaded by Hadassah to return to Palestine at least long enough to help break in the new Director they had engaged, and to initiate the developments they could now afford with the funds her activity had secured. Hadassah, with its increased membership, pledged $200,000 for the coming year. The Zionist Organization's two fiscal resources, the *Keren Hayesod* and the Joint Distribution Committee, had promised Hadassah an additional $200,000, and, with an expected income of possibly another $100,000 from the population of Palestine, Miss Szold returned with a prospective budget of almost half a million dollars, in happy contrast to what the situation was when she left. She returned to Palestine early in December 1923, just after the arrival of Dr. Tannenbaum, the new Director of the Medical Unit, who would relieve her of that onerous responsibility. On the way, she began to feel herself so much the foot-loose vagabond that "I doubt," she wrote her sisters, "whether I'll ever again settle down in a way becoming my age." The vision of herself in that rocking chair in Baltimore was remote. But then was not the hope of a peaceful life just a wishful human illusion? *"Le Ḥayim!"*—"To Life!" was the toast of the Jews; and whenever they met they greeted each other with *"Shalom!"*—"Peace," despite the pronouncement of Job long ago that "Man is born to trouble as the sparks fly upward."

She arrived at the end of a serious drought when cisterns had gone dry and water was so scarce and costly that a pail of it was used over and over for one purpose after another—you bathed in it first, and then scrubbed the floor, and finally watered the garden with it. But that had not deterred the *ḥalutzim*. They were as hopeful and aspiring and hard-working as ever; and she could see signs of the progress that had been made in the half year she was away. In Jerusalem there were new streets, more street lights, growing residential areas outside the Old City. Tel Aviv had grown to a city of 25,000, ten times what it was when she met Mr. Dizengoff on the train to Jerusalem less than four years ago. This was a world of determined aspiration—a far cry from the American Jazz Age she had glimpsed at home.

Miss Szold set to work with a clear vision, a definite program of what might be accomplished with the renewed resources: the improvement and expansion of hospital and other medical services; postgraduate courses for nurses in public health training and community welfare, beginning with infants and school children; and the co-operation of Hadassah with the Women's International Zionist Organization in orienting the women in Palestine for social welfare work. To the women of Hadassah in America she addressed a plea for the increase of their membership from 15,000 to 30,000 and the gathering of increased funds so that they need not depend on contributions from either the Joint Distribution Committee—a wartime relief organization which must ultimately be disbanded—or the *Keren Hayesod,* which should concentrate on immigration and the settlement of as many pioneers as possible. It was her hope that Hadassah would before long be able, with the increasing help only of the people of Palestine, to support the whole medical and social service. Ultimately, she envisioned the Jewish National Home taking over these functions; but that, of course, would take a long time.

In 1924, Technion, the engineering school in Haifa, the development of which had been delayed by the war, finally got going with Hebrew as its language of instruction, and not German as its German founders had insisted. In Palestine, the Jews were proving that they could create a modern Western culture in every aspect of their society.

In the meantime there was progress and peace in the land. In April of that year, just before Passover, Henrietta Szold got her wish to experience the life in a pioneer colony: she went to stay at Tel-Yosef, one of several large *kevutzot*—co-operative agricultural settlements developed in the fertile Jezreel Valley by the *Gdud Ha-Avodah,* the Labor Battalion. Tel-Yosef, named for heroic Joseph Trumpeldor who was killed at Tel Hai in 1920, consisted of two hundred and thirty men and women who lived a completely communal life in the belief that this was the most economical and efficient way to develop the land. A large co-operative group could have not only its own farmers and herdsmen but its own engineers and machinists, cooks, laundresses, beekeepers and any other needed experts. Community nurseries and kindergartens conducted by trained nurses and teachers relieved mothers of the care of children during working hours, and brought parents and children together in their hours of relaxation and pleasure toward evening and on the Sabbath. Henrietta Szold was impressed by the prevailing spirit of the community—of cheerful dedication, from early morning when men and women, roused by the clanging bell, went from the showers to breakfast in the common dining hall and then to work in the fields and barns, the shops and offices, until midday dinner, after which they rested, out of the noonday sun, returning to work until sunset. Then, cleaned up and dressed, they visited and played with their children; and after the evening meal they had rousing songs and dances or attended lectures. They were high-spirited but gentle; the men sweet though strong, the women strong and sweet. They lived like peasants but were eager for culture. The poet Bialik came for a visit while she was there, and they clustered around him to hear his words, like bees for honey. Theirs was a pleasant life, though simple and frugal; it was no life for the lazy or shiftless man who longed to be a parasite, or for the vain woman not content without personal finery. Their prime concern was for the future—the children. "The babies," Miss Szold reported to Hadassah, "show the effects of the enlightened treatment they receive. They would take the prizes in the baby parade at any American seaside resort. . . . The system of child care is pointed to by the defenders of the commune as an illustration of the value of their principles. No other sort of a community . . . can give the child such meticulous attention and at the same time set the mother free to be utilized by society to good advantage according to her knowledge and experience, while yet not separating her from her child. However that may be and whether or not one accepts all the institutions connected with this system of child caring, one cannot but admire the tenderness and foresight of men and women who at the same time are unsparing of themselves. They will go on all through the summer months working in the malarial climate. But the children are guarded. . . ." She saw how the work was equitably divided, how carefully accounts were kept, budgets adhered to and debts repaid. . . . She left them with the reinforced determination that the health and strength and spirits of such men and women must be maintained.

The train to Jerusalem was crowded, as were the roads, with men and women and children going up to the Old City for the Passover festival, as Jews had been doing for many centuries. Schoolboys and girls returning from their spring hikes wore crowns and garlands and girdles of the flowers they had gathered in the fields of Galilee in the season of the Song of Songs, which would be chanted in the synagogues on the Passover. Sturdy young *ḥalutzim,* some married and bringing their children, were going up to celebrate the *seder* with parents in Jerusalem. There were pilgrims of other faiths, too: Christians going to celebrate Easter, and Arabs for the fast of *Ramadan.* Although there was no sign of trouble that year, it was considered fortunate that *Nebi Moussa* would not come until two weeks after the Passover this time, when Jerusalem would be so full of Jews. At Lydda, the railroad junction, hordes of tourists from the ships at Jaffa and Haifa joined the throng crowding into the city, which was not yet prepared to receive so many of them. To be sure, there were some complaints on this score, but these were overwhelmed by the prevailing spirit of elation—the realization that the beginning of a great and long dreamed-of undertaking was being achieved; and it was Henrietta Szold's hope that when the tourists to whom she spoke returned home with the memory of what they had witnessed—of this happy revival of Jewish life and spirit—they would incite others to come to the support of that undertaking. The Reverend Harry Emerson Fosdick returned to New York singing the praises of Jewish Palestine.

She herself did not return to America until the following spring, to speak and gather members and funds for Hadassah, and to see her family. Rachel, who was still fighting a slowly losing battle with a brain tumor, spent that summer in Maine with the children of Bertha, who was contentedly working as the first female member of the school board in Baltimore. With Adele living in New York, Henrietta was able to spend refreshing times with them all between speaking tours. These left her so fatigued and exhausted that she went for a check-up to a doctor, who "insisted that all my organs function remarkably well for my age, but I am old—as old as Pershing, and should retire." She was almost sixty-four; but she didn't retire. She continued working for Hadassah right through that winter, talking, talking, talking to large gatherings in halls with bad acoustics, but collecting money for Palestine.

From Chicago she came away with a check for $15,000; and Hadassah's membership went up to 21,500.

"I don't understand what keeps my machinery oiled," she marveled, in the face of distracting troubles—the *Keren Hayesod* was again at odds with too-independent Hadassah; in Palestine, the new Director, at odds with the doctors, had resigned; and in Madison, Wisconsin, Rachel's condition was so bad in January 1926 that Henrietta went to stay with her while Joe Jastrow, himself in poor health, went on a lecture tour. Her own speaking commitments made it necessary for her to return to New York in February, so she brought Rachel with her to stay with Bertha in Baltimore and get treatment there.

Hadassah, having engaged Dr. I. M. Bluestone of New York's Mount Sinai Hospital, as Director for the Unit, now known as the Hadassah Medical Organization, was asking Miss Szold to return to Palestine with him to put the H.M.O. in order; and she was persuaded to do so by Rachel's assurance that she would not need Henrietta's help. She left Hadassah in the hands of a growing generation of disciples—women whom she had inspired with her spirit and practice, her vision of "the hard reality of our enterprise," and who, besides functioning as housewives and mothers or in careers, managed Hadassah with a zeal and acumen and practical common sense that refuted those modern men who still denied women the right to equality. Henrietta Szold had raised up a band of women of valor.

The voyage in March was a rough one and most of the passengers were seasick, but Henrietta was becoming a seasoned sailor—this was her seventh Atlantic crossing in seven years—and even the disembarkation at Jaffa into a wildly bobbing boat no longer dismayed her. Immediately upon her arrival in Jerusalem with Dr. Bluestone, they were involved in a strike of some hospital employees, which had tied up the X-ray department. She was glad she had returned with the new Director, who was rather disconcerted by a situation unlike anything he had experienced in America and who might have been prompted to turn away from it, had she not been there to sustain him and remind him of the importance of the difficult job he had undertaken. He proved to be an able and tactful administrator; and in April she went with him and the Assistant Director on a tour of Hadassah's medical facilities in the country. They traveled from Galilee, where the springtime was "a delight to the eye, ear and nose," to Tel Aviv, where they were having a typhoid epidemic among ten thousand immigrants still living in unsanitary barracks or hovels for lack of employment, or housing, or the funds to supply either, due to the severe depression which had set in that year. Tuberculosis was also increasing, and they had to send tubercular patients to Safed to make room for the typhoid patients. But there were not enough funds to care properly even for these. Miss Szold, to spur Hadassah to greater efforts, sent a report, with pictures, of what she had inspected: ". . . Note the toilets. . . . One of the toilets . . . serves 150 families. They are open. The flies swarm in, above, and around them. They are cleaned at irregular and infrequent intervals. They are rarely disinfected. . . ." There was a shortage of nurses. "Our nurses get married and have babies as fast as we graduate them," reported Miss Szold, for which she could hardly blame them. "We never have enough to go round in the hospital service, let alone the public health work . . . most successful mainly because it doesn't depend on buildings and equipment which are far from adequate to present needs."

But life in Palestine was not all disease and unemployment. She went to see the archaeological excavations in the Kidron Valley by Professor Nahum Slouschz, whose works she had translated for the Jewish Publication Society; and others north of Jerusalem by a professor from California who had figured out just where Samuel's famous gathering place, Mizpah, would be, and had come and dug out its walls and artifacts. She watched him unearth a perfect jar 5,000 years old. Jascha Heifetz came and gave a series of concerts for the benefit of a music school and concert hall to be built in Tel Aviv. His concert in Jerusalem, given in the crude cinema house, was attended by as fine an audience as could be seen at any of the world's great cultural centers. And the Ohel Players, a workingmen's drama group, was putting on plays in Hebrew which, for content and style, put to shame the Broadway theater whose current crown was *Abie's Irish Rose.*

Along with this modern cultural development went the renaissance of traditional Jewish mores which in the Diaspora were practiced only by the religious. The Sabbath from Friday evening to sundown on Saturday was observed by everyone, in the way Rabbi Szold would have liked: it was a pleasant, festive day of rest; there was no traffic of business in the streets where people, dressed in their best, peacefully strolled and visited. The old holidays were celebrated with renewed meaning. *Shavuot,* when the story of Ruth was read in the synagogues, was again the time for bringing in the first fruits by the colonists. *Ḥamishah Asar Bi-Shevat* was now Arbor Day on which children went out of the schools to plant real seedlings in the treeless land. And at *Purim,* when the story of Esther was read, gay carnival reigned in the land, celebrating the liberation of the Jews, precarious though it still was.

The country was at peace. Sir Herbert Samuel had been relieved as High Commissioner by Field Marshal Lord Plumer, an iron-willed man who made it clear to the Arabs and to his subordinates that he would brook no disturbance. At the same time an earnest attempt to make real peace between Arabs and Jews was started by Arthur Ruppin, head of the Zionist Executive's colonization department, who organized the *Berit Shalom,* the "Peace Covenant," a society devoted to this objective. It recommended the establishment of a binational state based on equality of rights of Arabs and Jews irrespective of their relative numbers. Henrietta Szold, of course, joined its forces, and her friend Judah Magnes, head of the Hebrew University, became its leader.

The dedication of the University's first modest buildings on Mount Scopus, adjoining the Mount of Olives, containing Judaic, biochemical and microbiological departments to begin with, had been attended by the world's academic élite from universities everywhere. The great occasion was marred only by a demonstration of the Christian-Moslem Committee against the presence of Lord Balfour, with a public prayer "for deliverance from Zionist aggression supported by British arms."

It was pleasant for Henrietta Szold to be welcomed back by many friends all over the country, from Sophia Berger who had met her at Jaffa with her fiancé, Mr. Mohl, who was in charge of building construction for the Palestine Economic Corporation, to Manya Shochat whom she saw on a trip to Haifa, a warm, strong woman after her own heart, "the embodiment of courage and selflessness, one of the most respected leaders of the Workingmen's

Party" who, nevertheless, rose above party politics and tactics. It was notable, particularly in Labor circles, that women were playing important roles in Palestine public life.

After plentiful winter rains there was a wonderful harvest that June; valleys of golden grain rippling in the sun, and hillsides swarming with flocks of grazing lambs and kids—Aaron Aaronsohn's living monument. In the fields, dozens of Ruths, swinging sickles, gleaned the grain. Laden wagons, camels, donkeys, men and women, moved along the roads with only wheels and legs visible under their burdens.

But Henrietta Szold and Sophia Berger and even Dr. Bluestone succumbed that summer to the sting of the sandfly. It afflicted Miss Szold with high fever just when she was helping the Director work out their budget in time for a coming Hadassah convention. This she accomplished despite a thumping head and an aching back; but she found reason to be grateful to the sandfly which finally put her to bed and gave her the opportunity to read the *Forsyte Saga* of Galsworthy, whose fine writing gave her exquisite pleasure and stirred old longings for the time to write. . . .

But she must attend the Zionist Conference to be held in London in July, in order to fight for her budget against political attacks within the organization, for "Palestine life is intensely political. The struggle between the parties is intensely sharp. Even the medical work is caught up in the whirlwind of party conflicts. . . ." She was content at least with the fact that Hadassah had made no mistake in the choice of Director Bluestone, in whose hands she could confidently leave the work. "He is an excellent administrator and a human being of fine fiber. . . . He has been accustomed to execute without restraint, and in our doctrinaire Jewish community here everything is regulated by laws, rules, regulations in which the protection of the individual is put ahead of the welfare of the community. He chafes under the restrictions, which are framed socially rather than medically. . . . His path is not going to be smooth here. He is not a partisan. He looks at his task from a purely professional point of view. And if Zionist politics stand in the way of professional achievement so much the worse for Zionist politics. It is good that he has a stiff upper lip and good vertebrae. He has conflicts ahead."

For her own part, Henrietta Szold had the requisite upper lip and vertebrae to go to London and stand up to Zionist politics and save her budget. She got the promises she wanted; and in between clamorous meetings she managed to enjoy London's sights and life as she always did when she went there. "In Jerusalem I am a Jew, in London I feel Anglo-Saxon. I feel at home here and I love it. I like the English in their habitat infinitely more than in the—to them—colonial atmosphere of Palestine. That is to say, I like them better as natives than when they are dealing with 'natives'. . . ."

Her enjoyment of London was cut short in August by word from Baltimore that Rachel was dying. She took the next ship for New York. In Baltimore, in September, lovely Rachel died, Rachel who used to sing and play so sweetly in the Lombard Street days. "Where is the consolation?" mourned Henrietta. "It all seems so futile!" Still, *"Le Ḥayim"*—"To Life!" say the Jews. . . .

Henrietta Szold did not return to Palestine until February of the following year, 1927. This was a year in which the United States, ruled by humorless, puritanical Calvin Coolidge, seemed bent on a late-Roman orgy, dancing before the debacle; it was the peak of the "Jazz Age." One hundred and fifty thousand people paid three million dollars to see Gene Tunney fight Jack Dempsey. Yet there were sober individuals who persisted in making some progress for humanity. Lindbergh flew to Paris. Miss Szold returned to Palestine with the backing of Hadassah which had grown to over 30,000 members. At the Zionist Congress in Basle that year, despite the opposition of Labor Zionists, she was elected a member of the Zionist Executive in Palestine, along with Harry Sacher, a distinguished English lawyer, and Colonel F. H. Kisch of the British Army. Miss Szold's responsibility on the Executive, which had taken over the functions of the Zionist Commission, was for education and health; and the Zionist Organization of America signalized its recognition of her as a leader, not merely of Hadassah but of the whole Zionist movement, by tendering her a great reception and dinner at the Hotel Astor in New York in November. It was attended by many men and women prominent in every field of American Jewish activity. Homage was paid Henrietta Szold by Louis Lipsky, President of the Zionist Organization of America, who told how she was "bringing order into the House of Zion"; by Stephen Wise, the most renowned rabbi in America; by Irma Lindheim, President of Hadassah; by distinguished scholars and literary lights—all testifying that she was a great woman. After a prolonged and rousing ovation Miss Szold responded. She waved away "the analysis of my character and supposed ability" and spoke of Zionism: "It is a movement that carries the generations along with it . . . we feel that spirit that carried our people from patriarchal simplicity, from primitive life into the complexity that surrounds a modern people. We feel that apostolic succession of ideals, philosophy and aspiration that carried us through the sophistication of the legislator, into the lyricism of the psalmist and into the democracy of the sociological vision of the prophet, and down through the ages of saints and sages. And we are rising above self-pity into self-emancipation . . ." —an achievement on which she was well qualified to speak by virtue of her own experience. And as if to remind her of that personal achievement, she was fêted at the Jewish Theological Seminary on 123rd Street.

In December she was back in Jerusalem, undertaking an enlarged responsibility; for, as a member of the Executive, she was concerned not merely with Hadassah's medical and educational services but with those of all agencies in the Jewish community. The *Histadrut,* the highly organized Workers' Federation, for example, was developing its own *Kupat Ḥolim,* its sick benefit fund and medical facilities for its members, and the *Mizraḥi,* the organized orthodox element of the population, had its own schools in which religious education was stressed. Both these factions generally found Miss Szold's liberal philosophy too tolerant, and hence did not welcome her supervision or suggestions. To add to her difficulties, there was the old handicap of insufficient funds, made more acute in the late '20s by the great world-wide depression which seriously affected fund raising, and made it increasingly difficult for the Zionist Organization to fulfill its promised support. In 1927 there was more emigration than immigration because of unemployment. By the spring of 1928 payments from the United States were $200,000 in arrears, and the salaries of teachers and office help were five months behind. The janitors struck. Colonel Kisch was in South Africa and Mr. Sacher in London, both trying to get blood out of stones, leaving Miss Szold alone in Palestine to work the miracle of the loaves and fishes. "But my fortitude loses out," she wrote Hadassah, "when day after day, hour after hour, I am besieged by applicants and supplicants with perfectly just claims, not to mention the bristling attacks made upon this Executive." With her colleagues away, she had more than one occasion to wish she were a man instead of a lone woman, vis-à-vis arrogant government officials.

Her niece Harriet Levin came from Baltimore, and Henrietta realized how lonely she had been in Palestine without her own flesh and blood. Harriet, a handsome, vivacious girl, added a note of gaiety to the ménage of the Misses Szold and Berger. She had studied stenography, and she took a job in the office of the Palestine Economic Corporation, but that did not prevent her from having a jolly time in Jerusalem. Yet no matter how late the party, when she came in, Aunt Henrietta would be hard at work on her endless budgets and her mountainous correspondence.

Many of those not inured to this kind of struggle, and who could escape to an easier existence—especially Americans and Germans who had memories of easier living—left Palestine to its dubious fate; or, having been drawn to the Holy Land by sentiment, turned back from it when they saw its desperate plight. Typical of such Jews was a young American, Irving Fineman, an engineer on the faculty of the University of Illinois, who had got it into his head to write a book, taken a leave of absence and gone to Paris to write it as many American writers did, and had then been prompted by his deeply inbred Jewish feeling to visit the Land of Israel before returning home.

He was no hasty, superficial tourist. He covered the country on foot and by local conveyances, from Galilee to Jerusalem, observing the wonderful variety of its landscapes and the paradoxical contrasts of its life. He had spent a night in the lonely habitation of a Jewish herdsman in the north who carried a rifle as well as a shepherd's crook, who had a library of social studies in his hut, and whose children played their games in an ancient burial cave with a mosaic marble floor. He had stayed at a *kevutzah* where the *ḥalutzim* had dug a deep well but had no pump to bring up the water because the money which had been promised them in

Jerusalem was not forthcoming; so they doggedly hauled water for drinking and bathing and irrigation in barrels and tins from a distant spring. He had seen the new Jewish city of Tel Aviv rising from its sand dunes, building a music school when it could not yet pave all its streets. He had stopped by the Jordan where Pinḥas Rutenberg was building the power dam for which he had finally scraped together enough money for a start; and there Mr. Fineman saw the first steam shovel to dig in the Holy Land, and he learned that the modern Hebrew word for electricity, *ḥashmal,* had been taken by Ben-Yehuda from Ezekiel's apocalyptic vision. And Mr. Rutenberg, who needed competent help, as everyone did in Palestine, and saw in this well-trained American engineer a precious implement to be kept in Palestine if possible, suggested that Mr. Fineman call upon Mr. Mohl in Jerusalem, who was in charge of building construction and also needed help. Perhaps between them they could afford to employ Mr. Fineman there, in the land which he was finding so fascinating that his planned trip of three weeks was stretching into months. In Jerusalem, Mr. Mohl, who had married Sophia Berger, took Mr. Fineman to see Miss Szold, hoping that her undaunted spirit would persuade the young engineer to join them in the great work for which he would be invaluable. And Mr. Fineman told Miss Szold how moved he was by everything he had seen, especially there in beautiful old "Jerusalem, the golden," where he had just come from a trip up Mount Scopus in a bus full of children chattering in Hebrew—one was telling the story of Chicken-licken!—and how, at the top, while talking to a white-jacketed biologist in the modern laboratory of the new Hebrew University, he had glanced out the window and his eyes had come to rest on distant Mount Nebo, over beyond Jordan, where Moses had stood so long ago and looked with longing to the Promised Land, where Mr. Fineman now stood. . . .

But as they talked, Mr. Fineman frankly wondered why a gray-haired, soft-spoken, genteel lady like Miss Szold, who obviously belonged at a gracious tea table in Baltimore or Philadelphia or New York, chose to stay in that wild and woolly place—or that brilliant German biologist on Mount Scopus, who hadn't got his salary for months, or those desperate Russian Jews in the *kevutzah,* who couldn't get the pump they needed, because in this Promised Land you couldn't depend on anyone's promise. Mr. Fineman was certainly enchanted with what he had seen, and he was certainly excited about the possibility of working for the Jewish National Home; but first he had to report back to his university in Illinois, and he had to see about that manuscript in his suitcase. . . .

Well, it won a handsome publisher's prize and launched him on a new career of writing, which Miss Szold had reason to envy him; and she never saw him again. The Promised Land, for all its fascination, did not exert on some Americans the undeniable hold it had on her. Even Dr. Bluestone finally found the rigors of working in Palestine too much for him, and he resigned. But Miss Szold, at sixty-eight, still had the requisite upper lip and vertebrae to hang on and continue making bricks without straw, while being scolded and scorned for what she could not do; and her faith in the Jews of Palestine never faltered: "I am more than ever confirmed in my view that, if the outside Jewry were to abandon Palestine, those already here would build it by themselves. It would be a slower process, that is all. . . ." This time, as new Medical Director, a Palestinian was chosen, Dr. Chaim Yassky. He stayed.

In August 1929 Henrietta Szold went to the Zionist Congress at Zurich, attended by devoted Emma Ehrlich, who bullied her into buying some decent clothes there. Her niece Harriet, who was on her way home, also accompanied her. Miss Szold was prepared for attacks on the administration of the Executive for its failure to work miracles in Palestine without money; and at the Congress she was set upon as the scapegoat by the orthodox *Mizraḥi* from the right and by the Labor Party from the left; but when offered a chance to avoid public humiliation by answering the charges before the Actions Committee, she stood up before the full Congress and, in soft-spoken German which everyone could understand, lectured them on her faith in the democratic public processes she had learned in America, and defended her administration so convincingly that the whole Congress applauded when she sat down.

It further expressed its confidence in Miss Szold by re-electing her to the Executive, and by making her a member of the enlarged Jewish Agency, which was then organized to include an equal number of influential non-Zionists, like Louis Marshall and

Felix Warburg in America, Léon Blum in France, and Lord Melchett in England. These men would greatly reinforce the Zionist resources, since the non-Zionists, who were interested in Palestine as a spiritual center and refuge for Jews and not as a political state, were generally people of means.

What had not been foreseen by the optimistic Zionists was that this much-heralded reinforcement of the failing Jewish powers in Palestine would be seized upon by the Arab malcontents and their British Colonial inciters to foment a pogrom at a time when the Zionist leaders were away, attending the Congress. The strict soldier, Lord Plumer, had been replaced as High Commissioner by Sir John Chancellor, a pompous man with an obvious contempt for Jews. And he, too, was conveniently away on a visit to London at the time of the outbreak. This time it was not at *Nebi Moussa* but at the Jewish *Yom Kippur,* the solemn Day of Atonement, when crowds of fasting Jews gathered before the remnant of the western wall of the ancient Temple, known as the Wailing Wall.

It was there that this conflagration burst forth, after the spreading of inflammatory fabrications like the notoriously false "Protocols of the Elders of Zion" and baseless rumors that the Jews, with the help of their rich new supporters, planned to tear down the Mosque of Omar and rebuild their Temple. The friction required to spark the conflagration was provided by a series of irritating incidents in the area before the Wailing Wall: stones and offal were thrown down on the Jewish worshipers; the Arabs began using the area as a passageway; the Jews set up a screen, which was removed by the military police in the midst of the *Yom Kippur* service. . . . With the old cry: "The Government is with us!" hundreds of rioters brandishing weapons swarmed into the Jewish quarter of *Mea Shearim* and, under the eyes of unconcerned police, started the slaughter and pillage and burning which spread and continued for a week all over Jerusalem and over the country, to villages and towns, to Jabneh and Ekron, Hebron and Safed; and everywhere the government and its police did nothing but disarm the Jews and prevent their resistance to the horrible holocaust—more horrible even than any of the other pogroms. . . .

Miss Szold returned from Zurich to this unspeakable shambles and set about helping to clean it up. What else could a woman do, in a world so disordered by willful men—destructive as willful children? There was some compensation, ironically, in the fact that she had more means to work with by virtue of that augmented Jewish Agency, and the reaction of world-wide sympathy for the Jews in the shocking outrage they had suffered, under the aegis of an altruistic British Labor Government headed by J. Ramsay MacDonald, whose pro-Zionist statements Henrietta Szold used to quote in her speeches.

The British Government's investigating commission added insult to injury by ignoring its mission to find and punish the guilty, and by reporting that Zionist activity, which was actually reviving the moribund land and raising its standard of living, was displacing the Arabs. The stunned Zionist leadership, still naïvely hoping for justice, did not revolt and take matters into its own hands but continued to appeal to and negotiate with the government, which temporized by appointing one commission after another to review each preceding report. In America, the women of Hadassah at their 1929 Convention, as if expressing their impatience with the pusillanimity of Zionist male leadership, had a great row with the Zionist Organization of America. It got into the papers, and the men sent appeals to Miss Szold in Palestine to call the women off.

With a membership of over 37,000 and an annual budget of $500,000, the women felt prepared to carry out independently their concrete program of medical service and education in Palestine. And in October 1930 Hadassah invited Miss Szold, who had done so much to bring about its present strength and achievement, to come to New York for a suitable celebration of her seventieth birthday.

The grateful homage lavished upon her in America was at first balm to her spirit, weary of the struggle in Palestine under constant criticism; but Henrietta had never enjoyed adulation, and the endless round of dinners and luncheons and teas and meetings at which she was expected to be "inspirational" soon wearied her too. Months after the birthday celebration she was still answering messages of congratulations and refusing invitations to speak which came to her in shoals. But she felt herself no longer needed by either Hadassah or the Zionist Organization of America, or able to serve as a link between them. In Palestine, the Hadassah Medical Organization was in the capable hands of Dr. Yassky. In America a corps of her disciples were conducting Hadassah's now complex and large-scale business with such statesmanlike grasp of policy and housewifely attention to detail as made it absurd to think of women as irresponsible, frivolous and flighty. This seemed like the propitious time to sink back into that old rocking chair of Papa's in Baltimore; perhaps even to "write"—her memoirs? Many urged her to do so, not realizing that for her that must inevitably include some unhappy, unpalatable but instructive truths about herself and others, buried in her memory and her diaries in those boxes stored in Bertha's cellar. She was saved from this dilemma by a cable from Palestine.

Despite all setbacks, one great political advance had been achieved by the *Yishuv,* the Jewish community of Palestine, in the Communities Ordinance, which permitted it to impose taxes on every registered Jew for the needs of the community. This was its first important step toward self-governing autonomy. The *Yishuv* called for the registration as a member of the *Keneset Israel,* the new political community of Israel, of every man and woman above the age of eighteen, who would then be entitled to vote for a choice of candidates nominated by the various parties for the General Assembly. Henrietta Szold, before she left Palestine, had participated in the activities preliminary to this organization of the community, especially in connection with defining the relation of the Hadassah Medical Organization and its institutions to the community's Board of Health; but here, too, she had encountered such opposition from the Labor Party that she had been obliged to resign from her position on the Executive. She had left Palestine, therefore, with a feeling that perhaps there, too, her usefulness had come to an end in the process of the achievement by the Jewish community of that independence, that autonomy, which had been one of her own primary objectives.

The cable which came to her then, in the spring of 1931, announcing that her bitterest critics, the Labor Party, had nominated and elected her to the *Vaad Leumi,* the National Council of the General Assembly of the *Keneset,* was a gratifying surprise, sweeter to her than all the encomiums which had been showered upon her. She could not resist that call, although it was hard to go. Bertha, now the matriarch of the Szolds, at whose house only Henrietta and Adele celebrated the Passover *seder* that year, was displeased by her decision; but in May Henrietta was on board the *Saturnia*, bound for Palestine—not for a life of ease and praise. In answer to a cable from Colonel Kisch urging her to come she wrote: "Telepathy made me see vividly between the lines of your cable the struggles which are calling forth all your powers of endurance. . . ." Miss Szold, like the prophets of old, well knew her Palestine and her Jews, a contentious and stiff-necked people, as Moses had learned long ago; but they needed and wanted her. And this, at seventy, was still the elixir of life for Henrietta Szold, the woman: to be needed and wanted. Explaining her decision to her sisters she said, ". . . my maternal heritage seems to be asserting itself as against the paternal strain. . . ."

1930s: "SAVE THE CHILD!"

HER WINDOWS in the Hotel Eden in Jerusalem overlooked a wide segment of the city, the old with its walled-in towers and spires and cupolas, and the new with its spreading blocks of golden-hued stone; the whole studded with the dark spears of cypress pointing to that vast dome of cerulean sky which, toward evening, enshrined the eternal city like a jewel of ineffable beauty.

But what a city of problems it was for Henrietta Szold—set in a land of problems! Full as the land was of stones, so full was it of problems. It was certainly no place to spend a quiet old age. She had thought that in the years of her service on the Zionist Executive she had learned all the difficulties of that troubled land. But her new position on the *Vaad Leumi* of the *Keneset Israel* revealed to her new facets and complexities rising from the juxtaposition of the old and new strains in Jewish life: the Biblical, the medieval, and the modern, cheek by jowl, demanded expression and acceptance.

The modern alone was divided into a spectrum of parties ranging from the left, intent on developing a socialist economy in which they hoped to indoctrinate the Arabs also, to the right, intent on establishing a nationalist Jewish state, extending into Transjordania. The members of the latter party, known as "Revisionists," under the aggressive leadership of Vladimir Jabotinsky, were in opposition to the Zionist Organization's nonaggressive attitude toward the Mandatory Government; and the British Colonial officials, seeing in the Revisionists a stumbling block in the path of their Arab colonial ambition, persecuted the Revisionist party and drove it underground where it resorted to terrorist tactics. There were times when the whole Zionist aspiration seemed foolhardy, not so much because of Arab hostility and British perfidy, as because of the inner Jewish conflicts which were well-nigh irreconcilable.

Miss Szold found herself involved as referee in conflicts some of which would have seemed comic if they were not so serious for the contestants. There was, for instance, the problem of football on the Sabbath. For the members of *Agudat Israel,* the extremely orthodox—who were virtually anti-Zionist because they considered the Land of Israel a sacred place and did not want it turned into a secular state—football on the Sabbath was sacrilegious. Since she was known to be an observant Jewess they expected Miss Szold to be on their side, and suggested she ask the government to send police to stop the games! Henrietta Szold envied them the simplicity of their rigid legalistic vision, but her progressive spirit was in sympathy with the Western Europeans and Americans who had been affected by democratic enlightenment, and with the young Russian-Jewish Labor Zionists who had been affected by the revolutionary spirit; so for all her conservatism she found herself far more in sympathy with the Sabbath breakers than with the Sabbath observers.

To further plague her there was the unanswerable question: What would her father, for all his liberalism, have said?—Papa, to whom the Sabbath itself was sacred, the gift of Divine love. He might, if he were there, object to her striking a match to light her kerosene heater as she now did on wintry Sabbaths, for she had come to equate overzealous Jewish orthodoxy with some tenets of orthodox Catholicism and fundamentalist Protestantism. As for the football, she compromised by deciding that the game might be played, but if tickets were sold they must be purchased before the Sabbath. This did not, of course, win unanimous approval; but then, being a judge in Israel had never been easy, even "in the days when the judges judged" and "there was no king in Israel and every man did what was right in his own eyes."

It was diverting to learn just how it came about that she had been nominated by the radical Labor party to the *Vaad Leumi*. In the struggle among the various parties for the nominations, the Laborites won more than their representative share, and to still the outcry from the others they had suggested Miss Szold, that "damned neutral"; and she was happy to observe that they were refraining from putting any party pressure upon her, or even identifying her as a Laborite. When a Major Campbell, who was appointed District Commissioner of Jerusalem, came to call on the *Vaad Leumi* he was introduced by the President, Mr. Ben-Zvi, to each of its members, who was incidentally identified as to his party affiliation. When Ben-Zvi came to Miss Szold, he said, "This is Miss Szold, and she is—she is—" whereupon Major Campbell laughed and understandingly added, "She is Miss Szold."

Miss Szold, sitting in a chair with a high straight back at her neatly ordered desk with its vases of flowers, by the wide-open window overlooking Jerusalem, charged herself mainly with the task of organizing the Central Bureau of the *Vaad Leumi* as a clearinghouse for the social service work being done in the whole of Palestine. To a meeting of the Advisory Council of her Department of Health and Social Service she said: ". . . the approach to our task should be that of the practical, intelligent housewife. She throws nothing away until its worthlessness is demonstrated. She improves and beautifies day after day. She adds to her household equipment insofar as means permit additions. Above all, she trains her household in the ways of economy, order and system, and links up her family with the world outside and its large interests." It was the doctrine of *eshet ḥayil.* She revealed to them the scope of her plan: ". . . the work our program contemplates falls into three large divisions. The first division is Social Case Work, the sort of relief-giving that eventuates, whenever possible, in the rehabilitation of families, victims of the untowardness caused by ill-health, consequent unemployment, or lack of adaptation to circumstances on account of hidden and revealed psychic factors. The second division comprises Child Care and the Care of the Young, including the fostering of organizations youth itself reaches out to. The third division is Health Care, for the physically handicapped, the chronic invalid, the tuberculous, the cripple, the convalescent patient who returns to his home after a period of hospitalization, the debilitated in need of rest and recreation, the malnourished and the nervous child, in short, the health work that cannot be done within hospital precincts. If organized and interorganized properly, these three divisions of Social Service can cover the whole range of mental and physical suffering. Within them there is place for widows' pensions, for employment suitable in the special cases in which health, strength, and family relations demand specific provisions; for loans on easy terms, vocational guidance, and mental hygiene. But, I repeat, success depends on the development of an effective co-operative system which at proper times and on proper occasions surmounts the organizational partitions between division and division, and puts Case Work, Child Care, and Health Care, the extra-institutional service, into dynamic relation with institutional opportunities, the two sorts of undertaking interacting upon each other and reciprocally influencing each other. Such co-operation will leave no gap between Health Work and Social Service and between Education and Social Service."

By midsummer of 1931 she was discussing the methods and purposes of the Central Bureau with various charitable and governmental agencies in the land—there were 445—which through their work had acquired a knowledge of the situations and needs in the fields of their activities. She was also writing to bureaus of social service and research in New York, Berlin and Vienna for information and forms—questionnaires, registry cards, etc.—used in this work. Just as when faced with the necessity of preparing herself for activity in the modern medical field, she now went about informing herself as thoroughly as possible for activity in the field of modern social service. She read omnivorously, not only for technical but for general information, in a way that was reminiscent of her girlhood in Lombard Street when she sat in Papa's study devouring one of his big volumes of *Weltgeschichte*.

"And now, having passed the psalmist's term of years, I dare go into another field in which to expertize is imperative," she wrote to her friend Alice Seligsberg in New York, to whom she turned for information in the specific area in which Miss Seligsberg had much experience: the social problems of the child. She got from her a set of her card files and a comprehensive bibliography for her own reading and for the more intelligent readers in the organizations in Palestine dealing with children. She wished they had the money to employ a trained expert in this area particularly, but for want of anyone else willing and able to tackle this imperative job, she felt obliged to do it herself. As it was, she hadn't the funds to buy even the many books Miss Seligsberg recommended and had to put that off until the *Keneset* could organize the 120 *Kehilot*—the local communities which would be taxed for support of the executive activities of the *Vaad Leumi*. But in the meantime she got what literature she could from the Children's Bureau of the U.S. Department of Labor on such subjects as "Foster Home Care for Dependent Children," "Minimum Standards for Child Welfare," "Handbook for Directors of Institutions for Dependent Children."

The Mandatory Government made little provision for this problem. There was one institution for psychopathic and defective children but it did no preventive work and provided no facilities for the child's leisure hours. There were no children's libraries and very few playgrounds. Miss Szold planned for the correction of these conditions and recommended that the Jewish community build suitable facilities and demand partial maintenance of them by the government.

One practical work she undertook in this area was the handling of the juvenile delinquent, because "He is so much less an offender than the people who want to reform him. They talk from start to finish in terms of reformatory institutions, when all that the little wretches need is larger opportunity for recreation and education of the hand. . . . They should be in the open; do agricultural work; learn trades, interspersed with plenty of play. . . . If I had the money . . ." When the Palestine Government in 1932 appointed a probation officer, a Britisher who couldn't understand the languages of his charges, she became his deputy for the Jewish cases—"juvenile offenders, who are very juvenile and not offenders at all, but sick, defective, undernourished, mentally and physically starved children. . . . One of the basic problems here is the remanding of children to a reformatory in which there are big boys charged with and convicted of murder. And the first punishment decreed by the court according to the statute book is—flogging!" It was interesting to discuss this work with her sister Bertha who, in connection with her work on the Baltimore School Board was attending conferences in the Juvenile Courts; and she enlisted the aid of her niece Harriet, who was also engaged in social service work in Baltimore.

Since Child Care inevitably led to Family Case Work, Miss Szold insisted that such services must be organized at least in the three large cities: Jerusalem, Jaffa-Tel Aviv, and Haifa, although she was warned that the *Keneset* had no resources for family relief and that relief work had best be left to charity. But she was of the opinion that "the organization of charity is the only approach we have yet found to justice," and she persisted in the planning of organized relief in the hope that in time the funds for its execution would be available. This meant finding individuals who could be trained and entrusted with the future performance of the tasks which were parts of her plans; and at every opportunity she appealed to women to organize the social services.

Sometimes she was overcome with the sense that her whole life was an unco-ordinated patchwork of which this was just another patch. The first was in medicine, of which she had known nothing; the second, education, in which in her youth she had been an intuitive amateur practitioner, and which had since developed, under John Dewey and others, a modern technique and philosophy she had not had the opportunity to study; and now this social service which was rapidly developing into a modern science. "Patchwork and bluff," it sometimes seemed she had been engaged in. "I ought to be ashamed of myself. I cling to the consoling thought that in all these adventures that lead me beyond my depths, I am guided by an organizing instinct, which, among other things, enables me to discern the other person who can be trusted to supply the substance while I keep my eye and instinct on the form." But she was well aware that she was often criticized for her reliance on certain mediocre or unprepossessing individuals. "My attitude is, there is no human being that cannot be used in one way or another. . . ."

People were drawn to her. Although sometimes they were not to her taste at all, if they could help she put them to work. She did not seek them out. She would sit at her desk, grimly determined to get this or that done, and do it herself if need be. Then people would come and say: Let me help you with this or that. What drew them to her, she thought, was a certain warmth of personality she had got from her father, although there were still times when people irked her so that she stormed and raged as Mamma used to do. Then Emma Ehrlich would stand by while she vented her anger, until Emma would say, "Now you're going to be nice," and she would be. Anyway, people came to her and she warmed them up so they wanted to work with her; and then—what was most remarkable—they would give her credit for whatever they did, not only there in Palestine but in America! Rose Jacobs, when she became President of Hadassah, would not let Henrietta Szold's name be taken off the letterhead. It became a source of embarrassment—this tendency of people to glorify her, to present her as a plaster saint which she wasn't, to give her credit for things she hadn't done, and even for things she had tried to avoid doing. She was being turned into a sort of public monument: tourists came to look at her. However, she thought, all that would come to an end in a year, or two years at most, when she had done all she could on the *Vaad Leumi* in organizing the social services for the *Keneset Israel,* the developing Jewish government. She would then return to America to retire and be coddled by her two remaining sisters, and would finally get to clearing out those boxes she had stored in Bertha's cellar, and the overflow in Adele's barn in Connecticut. . . .

Her unwavering faith in the destiny of the *Yishuv*—the growing Jewish community of Palestine—its continued progress toward a self-governing state, she expressed in what was for her a valedictory address in Tel Aviv to a record gathering for a sports meeting of the "Maccabeah" from Palestine and abroad, at which Mayor Dizengoff presided. She now saw the achievement of Israel's revival in terms of a work of creative art: "The distinctive task that sets it apart from and above every other *Yishuv* in the world is creation. Creation for finite man can be only a process of combining existing materials and elements into new forms. . . . In Palestine the eternal people . . . searches its storehouses for what is known to be there and for what has sunk into the oblivion of disuse. The hand, the eye, the whole body, the mind, the soul are trained anew to restore atrophied possessions to use. That is the essence of consciousness, of creation." She reminded them that "the soul that would be strong and sane and noble must be housed in a body that is vigorous and healthy and well-proportioned and upstanding"; that "normal humanity is not a disembodied spirit but an aspiring spirit encased in solid flesh and vivified by fast-coursing blood." She saluted them "as apostles of the normal." She envisioned them as having destroyed "the inner ghetto that continued to stand though the physical ghettos had crumbled." She recalled for the Jewish athletes the difference between Judaism and Hellenism, which "the Maccabean Jew had no choice but to reject . . . its beauty along with its poison," and she assigned them "the task worthy of the unshackled, to find the way of Jewish life in the Jewish land that shall be irradiated with the beauty of holiness. . . . The hallowed land is spread out before you in its bridal charm. It invites you to go forth and view it. . . . Drink in its inspiration. Learn from its beauty as well as from its ruggedness and its resistance, that the Jew worthy of living upon it must make himself a complete man, forgetting no part of his people's heritage and also rejecting nothing that is human. Note the health and buoyancy of its children. Listen to their Hebrew prattle, the new value they have inherited. See their young sturdy parents reveling in a renewed value, in the labor from which prejudice kept them throughout many centuries in almost every country of the civilized world. Make an inventory of the achievements on every field of endeavor during the years since the Balfour Declaration. Carry these sights and sounds and new memories back with you to your homes here and in the Diaspora." She addressed them, as if in farewell, "with the mandate of my generation to yours, of age to youth, of age that has completed its work and is ready to pass the torch of Judaism on to youth with willing hands. . . ."

This had been a time of unwonted relaxation and comparative tranquillity in the life of Henrietta Szold. The Passfield White Paper—the infamous product of the last British Commission—had resulted in a cessation of immigration which caused a lull in the work of active colonization. Because there was no tax money yet available to *do* anything with, Miss Szold could only sit at her desk and plan, and meet with people and prepare them to take over and realize her plans. And for this she need not get to the office at seven as she used to, and she could leave the office when everyone else did, and without a bulging brief case. She slept more, even taking a nap in the heat of the day, and had time for wonderful, varied reading from a new bookcase full of the books she had gathered there in the years she hadn't had time to read. She looked forward to long days of reading the many books she had stored in those boxes in Baltimore and New York in the years when "Miss Szold, that fine beast of burden," hadn't time for such self-indulgence. Her sister Bertha was coming on a trip to Palestine early in 1933, and Henrietta would return to America with Bertha, stopping on the way in Egypt and in Italy, which Bertha would enjoy as she and Mamma had. And it would be such a joy to show Palestine to her "twin," dear blue-eyed Betsy. . . .

This tranquil period proved to be but the calm before storm; she had been counting without the rise of the National Socialist party in Germany and the advent of Hitler. In 1932 with the appointment of a new High Commissioner, General Sir Arthur Wauchope, the doors of Palestine were reopened and German Jews began coming in droves, reminding Henrietta of the days when she went with Papa to meet the Russian Jews arriving at Locust Point. It was difficult for her to believe that this would be any more than another of those recurrent but brief periods of persecution in the long history of the Jews. She was even able for a while to agree with her friend Alice Seligsberg that this ill wind might blow some good to the Jews, as had other periods of persecution which had the effect of consolidating and reinforcing the Jewish spirit in times when disintegrating forces were at work. Many of the refugees from Germany had been so far removed from Judaism by assimilation that they were like visitors from another planet who would become reassimilated as Jews there in the Land of Israel. There was also the benefit to be derived by the *Yishuv* in Palestine from this influx of highly cultivated and well-trained products of the German educational system, which had produced a Rabbi Szold and had been considered the finest in the world since back in the '80s when her friends Harry Friedenwald and Morris Jastrow and other American students had gone to Heidelberg and Bonn and Berlin and Vienna for their postgraduate studies. On the other hand, these refugees were mostly not *ḥalutzim*, pioneers, ready to turn their hands, literally, to anything. Many of the highly trained doctors and lawyers and engineers found no niches in which they could function in this still underdeveloped society, and the only thing they could turn to was business. And many of them, accustomed as they were to the amenities of Western European life—electricity and appliances, machinery, hot and cold running water—created a sudden demand and booming business which was economically unsound.

Most of them needed assistance; and Miss Szold, of course, headed the drive for funds to help settle the incoming German Jews. The drive was impeded somewhat by an ironical turn of the wheel of history. Just as in the '80s the comfortably settled, *ordentlich* German Jews in America had looked with disfavor upon the disturbing hordes of incoming, uncouth Russian and Polish Jews fleeing from the pogroms, so now the East European Jews, precariously settled in Palestine, looked with disfavor upon the disturbing German Jews who would be needing maintenance and employment, which were already hard enough to obtain in this poor little land. It was now their turn to say of the Germans as the Germans used to say of the Russians, "Are these Jews!" But just as she had worked for her "Russians" fifty years before, so now Miss Szold worked hard for the Germans, and succeeded, despite the unfavorable circumstances, in gathering some $60,000 right there in that land which itself was so largely dependent on charity. With Ben-Zvi, President of the *Vaad Leumi,* and Ben-Gurion, one of its members, she discussed the problems she foresaw from her experience in Baltimore: the problems of supplying the refugees with shelter, clothing, food, employment and education. And she found it stirring to think that the ardor of a handful of idealists, having faith in the efficacy of the age-long nostalgia of the Jew for the Land of Israel as a regenerative force, had prepared the remedy before the ravages of the disease appeared.

Among this influx of German Jews she came across a Mrs. Warburg who turned out to be the granddaughter of a rabbi of Worms. Away back in 1859, he had been instrumental in getting Rabbi Szold the appointment to Oheb Shalom in Baltimore; and now the paths of their offspring had met in the Land of Israel, in this "gathering of the exiles."

Along with many of these German Jews, Henrietta Szold was still hoping this was only a temporary calamity which would end very soon with the downfall of Hitler. *They* felt this way mainly because they longed for the fleshpots of their German Egypt to which they would return in a trice when this trouble passed—Palestine was only a refuge, not a home, for them; and for her it was hard to believe in the total failure of that culture created by Lessing, Goethe, and Schiller. . . . "So much of my own education was impregnated with the German language and literature, and I loved it so dearly, that this phase of the catastrophe needs must harrow my feelings. But I believe I should not react otherwise if a culture remote from me, the Italian, the French, had been violated by such brutality. At bottom it is a question of faith in the perfectibility of man. As a Jew, can one afford not to cling to such faith? . . ."

Early in the spring of 1933 Bertha came, and it was a great delight for Henrietta to take her on jaunts all over the land—to Meron, the ancient village of the Kabballists, where everyone went on *Lag Ba-Omer* to visit the tomb of the second-century mystic sage Simeon bar Yoḥai; and up on Mount Scopus where, in the amphitheater of the Hebrew University, Handel's "Judah, the Maccabee" was sung by the high school children in Hebrew. . . . And it was like old times, botanizing in Druid Hill Park, when Bertha and Henrietta together spied wild black iris growing by the road and stopped the car to pick some. With Rose Jacobs, President of Hadassah, who had come from New York, and Sarah Kussy from Newark, who was in one of Henrietta's very first Hadassah groups, and with Emma Ehrlich to keep Henrietta from overexerting herself, they went on a Cook's tour to Petra, the fantastic dead city with its pagan high places all carved out of the pink desert rock. With Bertha, Henrietta did and saw many things she hadn't had time for those thirteen busy years in Palestine—until now when she was packing to leave for good. After all, she was going on seventy-three and it was very unlikely she would ever come back.

But Bertha went home without her. It was the plight of the Jewish children in Germany that kept Henrietta from going. She had had intimations of it before then. Recha Freier, the wife of a Berlin rabbi, seeing how shamefully Jewish children were being mistreated in the schools and were finding themselves barred from further studies and any employment when they graduated, had cast about for some refuge for those bedeviled and bewildered youngsters who saw no future for themselves in their native land. She hit upon the idea of gathering them in groups, preparing them for life in Palestine, and arranging for their settlement there. Her plan had been referred to Miss Szold, who realized and said promptly that it was impossible at that time: aside from the lack of funds, there were simply no facilities available for taking in children without their parents; the colonies were, as ever, living a hand-to-mouth existence; and on the beaches of Tel Aviv whole families of German refugees, who had had to leave their means and possessions behind when they fled, were sleeping in the open for lack of shelter. Realistic, practical Miss Szold disapproved of permitting children to come unless and until adequate provision could be made for their reception.

But in April 1933, when the Aryan Decree was issued in Berlin and a cruel boycott of Jews was overtly enforced, the plight of those Jewish children in Germany became absolutely hopeless. Recha Freier came to Palestine. A high-spirited, energetic woman with intense black eyes, as indomitable as Henrietta Szold herself, she convinced Miss Szold, whose things were almost all packed for her departure. From Recha Freier and from other women who came from Germany and, with admirable fortitude and dignity, told what Jews were suffering there, Henrietta got so clear a vision of the sinister fate in store for those children that she realized that even the most inadequate reception in Palestine would be a godsend to them—that it was a simple matter of life and death. Means and money would have to be found: the children must be saved. Henrietta unpacked and said she would stay for two more years, and Bertha sailed without her.

Miss Szold then set about planning ways and means to bring children out of Germany and enlisted whatever help she could find. In May, Chaim Arlosoroff of the Jewish Agency in Palestine, a man for whose spirit she had a high regard, went to Berlin to organize a large-scale migration of adult *ḥalutzim* and some of the youth. When he returned he took the High Commissioner to Ben Shemen to show him what was being done for children and to get his approval of the plan to bring in German youngsters of fifteen to seventeen, when additional facilities could be provided for them. That night, while walking with his wife on the beach at Tel Aviv, Arlosoroff was murdered by an unidentified assailant. Although he said before he died that the assassin was not a Jew, an attempt was made to fasten the crime upon the Revisionists (because Arlosoroff was a Labor Zionist) in a scandalous trial which rocked and divided the *Yishuv* for months.

Speaking at a memorial service for Chaim Arlosoroff, Henrietta Szold recalled how, long before she ever met him, she had read, in a little publication of his, the cool, sober expression of "a constructive Zionism springing not out of negative phenomena such as anti-Semitic manifestations, but out of the reassertions of the positive values of a living progressive Judaism" with its "message on the value of labor to the atrophied Jew," and that "the realization of the ideal of Jewish nationhood on Jewish soil was linked up with the solution of the Arab question." This spirit had appealed to her; and ten years later when she first met him in the overheated atmosphere of a Zionist Congress she was again impressed by the cool, sober voice of the man with its underlying conviction and emotion—a man after her own heart. "Here was the man whom one sought out for the discussion of problems." She recalled then the last time she had sought his counsel, just before he went to Berlin to make arrangements for bringing in the youth. She had gone to him because she was depressed by the bitter partisanship which was undermining the whole Zionist effort at a time when co-operation was most needed, and by the breakdown of self-discipline among young and old in the cities, where a real-estate and business boom was exploiting the needs of newcomers, and a profligate way of life was developing. And the death in Tel Aviv of Ḥayim Naḥman Bialik, poet, idealist and prophet, seemed to Henrietta Szold like a symbol of this evil trend. Arlosoroff had met her charges with the optimism of a psychologist and philosopher: "He took a long view of frailties, how the past produced them, how the future would heal them. . . ."

To her old friend Justice Brandeis, who wrote advising her to take upon herself the role of prophet, and castigate the people for their transgressions, she replied: "I can see myself doing nothing but what I have been doing all along—keeping steadily at the tasks my life here has set me and performing them as best I can. . . . Why shouldn't *you* speak to their consciences publicly?" "Thou shalt surely rebuke thy neighbor" is a Biblical precept; and "Would that all the people of the Lord were prophets," said Moses to Joshua; but Miss Szold had her work laid out for her.

She went on with her planning to save those children. In Berlin, Recha Freier and the *Jüdische Jugendhilfe,* a federation of German-Jewish youth organizations, would gather the children in groups, teach them Hebrew, and prepare them and their parents for the separation. Some of the parents could provide for their equipment and transportation; but for the more than half who could not, funds would have to be raised by committees organized in countries other than Germany. To each group a well-trained, reliable young man or woman, with whom they were familiar, would be assigned as *madriḥ,* teacher and leader, who would conduct them on the journey. In Palestine entry permits would have to be got for them from the British Mandatory Government, and places found for their settlement, and funds raised to provide for them. Miss Szold rode up and down the land seeking suitable colonies willing and able to receive them. In October she went to a conference called in London to consider the German-Jewish situation and its relief. She begged for money to save the children.

From the discussions in London she went to Berlin to grapple directly with the practical details of what Recha Freier and Arlosoroff had started and she must continue. Foolhardy it might be to go into that realm ruled by a madman, from which all Jews who could were taking flight; but how could she not go? She was needed. "If I perish, I perish!" And how much had a woman of seventy-three to lose?

What she saw and heard there quickly dispelled any wishful illusion that this was a transitory affliction. Berlin was no longer the pleasant civilized capital of the country of Lessing, Goethe and Schiller. It was a fearful and dreadful city blatantly placarded with brutish hatefulness. The once *gemütlich* Germans were unrecognizable. Their decent orderliness and self-control was gone like a cast-off garment. It was as if their malevolent ruler with the long forelock and little mustache had blown off the foam of civilization from their culture and given them to drink the dark intoxicating underlying draught of barbarism; and to this they had promptly regressed from that superficially Christian civilization to which they had been giving lip service. In the lobby of her hotel she saw the entire staff, down to the last chambermaid, porter and bootblack, herded before the loud-speaker out of which blared the rasping hateful voice of Hitler ranting at those who were fleeing the Reich. "The Jews, the Jews!" they cried in unison, in response to their hypnotic high priest.

Henrietta Szold met and spoke with earnest, anxious leaders of the Jewish community, with parents pathetically torn between the dread of parting with their children and the hope of saving them, and with youngsters pathetically eager for flight from their senselessly hostile world. Among those who were desperately trying to organize their flight she found much confusion, little understanding of the actual conditions in Palestine, and some working at cross-purposes. She could not resolve all their tangled problems but she was able to help them work out a better path toward their objective. It was decided to make the first try with a group of sixty-three boys and girls between the ages of fifteen and seventeen, under the leadership of a stalwart young man named Hanoch Rheinhold.

Miss Szold returned to Jerusalem to arrange for their placement. The colony of Ain Ḥarod had agreed to accept the first group but additional barracks would have to be built for them. Miss Szold went up to Ain Ḥarod, and when she saw that the buildings were not going up fast enough she stayed there to boss the job. In her gray woolen suit and her small felt hat set squarely on her smooth-brushed gray hair and held in place by the black elastic under the bun in back, she stood over the workers until they got it done.

On February 17, 1934, Miss Szold went up to Haifa to meet the SS *Martha Washington*; and when she saw those children come crowding down the gangway to set foot on their Promised Land, laden with their pathetic possessions, their rucksacks and bundles, their mandolins and accordions, hopefully smiling and waving as they came, Henrietta Szold knew that her life was no longer a patchwork. There on the dock at Haifa, in her seventy-fourth year, her life achieved a coherence, a value and a significance beyond anything she could have hoped or planned. It was as if all the channels of her so varied lifelong activities, and all of her Jewish inheritance, everything she had got from Papa and Mamma and had herself learned, merged there at the foot of that gangway for the sake of those children who were coming to her, to be healed and taught and cared for, and given a goodly life in the Land of Israel. Even her failure to marry and have children of her own was like part of a predestined plan whose climax was enacted there on the dock in a driving winter rain. If ever there were children in need of a mother, it was these innocent children, who had come to the land of their fathers seeking refuge from the incomprehensible persecution which was also part of their inheritance. Deep down in the bottom of her heart she had always wanted children, "many children." Well, here they were; they were hers. Adolescents all, the bane of parenthood, they would be a burden, a trial and a responsibility; but she welcomed them, each and every one, with all her warm heart and every fiber of her womanly spirit.

Hanoch Rheinhold, their *madriḥ,* introduced each one of them to her, and then she rode with them to Ain Harod, where they were welcomed by the colonists with singing and dancing, in which she joined hands with them in the joyous circle of the *hora.* At seventy-three Miss Szold could finally sing and dance without fear of criticism. Before leaving them she saw that the children were properly fed and installed in their brand-new quarters.

The arrangement with the colony was that the group was to stay there two years as apprentices, performing suitable work in the mornings, in the fields or barns, in vineyard or orange grove, in workshop or kitchen, and attending school in the afternoons, where they studied Hebrew, Bible and Jewish history, the geography of Palestine, and sciences related to their practical work, botany, physics and chemistry. They were to live together as a friendly group, in order that they would not be abruptly subjected to the tensions which might arise from their difference from their hosts who were strange to them, but they would take part in all of the colony's functions and activities and thus become adjusted in time to their new environment. They would have leisure time for excursions and sports with the other children of the colony. At the end of the two years they would be at liberty to determine their future careers as individuals or in groups, continuing in the host colony, or going elsewhere.

During the two-year period they were to be under the jurisdiction of Youth Aliyah—*Aliyah* meaning "going up" or immigration into the land. In this department of the Jewish Agency, Henrietta Szold became not merely the leading light, because she was the only one acceptable to all parties, but the indefatigable servant. Group after group arrived. A month later came a number of girls who were placed in a farm school in a suburb of Jerusalem. A few weeks after that came younger children who were installed in a Children's Home in Haifa, an institution which was patterned on similar institutions in Berlin. Then came a group of children from orthodox homes who had to be placed in a colony where orthodox observances were maintained. Miss Szold saw to everything. She made the preliminary arrangements in Germany, and then, with their hosts in Palestine, arranged for their housing, education, and occupation. She met each group as it arrived and saw it installed. She made ceaseless rounds of inspection to insure the proper care of each child and to consider and cope with the cases of those who became problems. No detail was now too irksome. No longer did she complain that "in my life details have confused the issue; they have not gone to make a harmonious whole." At last she was contentedly putting into practice her own dictum—learned from observing Mamma: "It is only in rearing children that minute service piled on minute service counts. . . . In a mother's life, ability to lose one's identity in details is the great thing for the future of mankind." As the mother of a large and fast-growing family she could give little thought to herself. Like *eshet ḥayil* she was again working early and late.

Yet it gave her little satisfaction to be hailed as the great "Mother in Israel." Motherhood, for all its profoundly desired satisfactions to the womanly spirit, was an arduous and self-sacrificing ordeal, sometimes tragic too, as she had learned from some of those mothers she used to envy. For children were tender creatures, sometimes too frail to survive the rigors of the trying life to which their young bodies and spirits were subjected, whether in infancy or adolescence. The son of her old friend Lilian Friedlaender—Daniel, a lovely lad and a sensitive, gifted pianist—had found this sorely troubled world too much for him and had taken his own life. And Henrietta Szold, who could remember the deaths of two infants her mother had borne after herself, and the deaths of little Johanna and of Sadie, the bride, both losses she had suffered with Mamma, was now engaged in rearing a host of children who had come out of such a hell on earth as was destroying the souls and bodies of grown men and women. For help in healing and fortifying the less robust young spirits among her children she resorted to practitioners of that new psychiatry which, ironically enough, was a German-Jewish revelation. Truly, as the Jews say: "God sends the remedy with the affliction." But she could hardly bear to listen to sentimental praises, however well meant, for doing what she could no more refuse to do than any mother, no matter how weary, could refuse to answer the cry of her suffering child.

The stories of some of her "cases" would tax the powers of a master of fiction to report adequately. There was the boy of thirteen, crippled by polio, who hobbled into her office. Beside his youth his handicap had made him ineligible for an entrance permit; Miss Szold was in the unenviable position of a mother who is permitted to rear only her perfect children. After an incredible trek to the Black Sea, he had stowed away on a freighter; had been discovered by the captain and turned over to the immigration authorities at Haifa; had eluded them while they were deciding what to do with him; and had come to Jerusalem and found his way to Miss Szold. At thirteen he was a full-fledged Zionist and spoke Hebrew. She put him in the Hadassah Hospital, where three orthopedic operations corrected his handicap. He proved to be not only bright and resourceful but gifted—with a talent for sculpture.

Her life was strenuous as ever but full and rich. One midsummer night she went up Mount Scopus to a concert in the amphitheater which had been built there. "It was full moon. . . . The night was magically beautiful, and the moonlight on the Moab hills bathed them in an atmosphere and colors that have no name. The program was exquisite dance music . . . Bach, Handel and Glück, through Beethoven and Mozart, down to Strauss. The orchestra entirely strings . . . a huge audience that sat spellbound. . . ." It was hard to return to the countless problems awaiting her. In the fall came the first loss by death of one of her children. She was furious with the doctor who had not notified her of the boy's illness until the last day. She could not bear to think of his mother in Hamburg, to whom she must break the news.

In October 1934 she was asked to lay the cornerstone of the new Rothschild-Hadassah-University Hospital which was to be built on Mount Scopus alongside the growing nine-year-old Hebrew University. There, before a gathering of Zionist and British Government dignitaries and world-renowned physicians, after a eulogistic introduction by her friend Judah Magnes, President of the University, Miss Szold wielded an energetic trowel for the rearing of a temple of healing and learning "on the spot from which Titus hurled his firebrands into the Temple area," and in sight of distant Mount Nebo from which Moses, the great teacher, had looked so hopefully upon this land. Miss Szold, too, was still hopeful. She delivered a concise summary of the history of Hadassah's struggle from the time Israel Friedlaender gave them their motto, "The healing of the daughter of my people"—"the tender words of the sternest and saddest of the prophets," to this momentous day. But it was not merely the healing of the body that concerned her: "The Jewish soul stands in need of the healing which wells up for it from the soil that produced the prophets." And to this aspiration she looked for no conclusion. "In the life of the spirit," she said, "there is no ending that is not a beginning . . ." and her hopeful eloquence was broadcast by that modern wonder, the wireless radio, so that fifteen hundred women of Hadassah heard her in Washington, D.C., where they were assembled for their twentieth convention. As she spoke she remembered their first convention in Rochester, when a single bench had seated all the delegates. But to her sisters she wrote: ". . . of course, one cannot help being impressed with one's own funeral." This morbid metaphor may have been suggested by the sight of the cemetery on nearby Mount of Olives. "That's what it was, to the 'Mother of Hadassah,' and the 'Founder of Hadassah,' and the 'Inspiration of Hadassah.' What were my thoughts? Should I confess them, such an estimate of the honors accorded her would hardly have been appropriate for the ears of the dignified audience on Mount Scopus. . . ."

Her thoughts had to do with the difficulty she had in getting from those dignified government officials the permits to rescue her children in Germany and from those dignified Zionist officials the money to provide for them if and when they got into the Promised Land. The waiting list was so long that some of those hopefully waiting their turn passed the seventeen-year age limit and could not be brought. Then, desperate and undaunted, some of them came anyway and got in by hook or crook, and if they got caught were returned by those dignified officials to the hell whence they had fled.

Miss Szold herself again undertook the descent into that hell in the fall of 1935, her seventy-fifth year. This time she took helpful Emma Ehrlich with her, and she fortunately was able to leave the running of Youth Aliyah in the capable hands of Hans Beyth, a young man who had come that spring from the *Jugendhilfe* to assist her. He was a handsome, vigorous, intelligent man with something of the charm of Aaron Aaronsohn, friendly and jolly, but of a more urbane type. He had been a successful banker in Germany, and became interested in Youth Aliyah there. He treated Miss Szold, of whom he obviously stood in great awe, with the utmost deference, yet with a courtly protective attentiveness which would warm the heart of any woman. From their very first meetings a pleasant relation was established that quickly grew into a staunch friendship on which she could rely, as she had been relying on Emma's these many years. Now she often worked for hours at her desk, flanked by these two devoted companions; and when Emma bullied her in her daughterly way, Hans would nudge Emma to remind her to be considerate of his *"guter Kamerad"* as he called Miss Szold. And his way of calming her was different from Emma's; he had only to put his strong hand over hers. He accompanied her on the many hard trips she took in all sorts of weather, when the hot *ḥamsin* blew and in chill winter rains, quietly doing all sorts of services to smooth her way. He would take her arm when there was rough or slippery walking to be done, saying *"Achtung, Achtung!"*—"Careful now!"—for his Hebrew was still sketchy, so they talked German to each other. He had been sent primarily to help with financial matters; but as the work of Youth Aliyah developed and its staff was increased he entered into every department of it and easily grasped and relieved her of many burdensome details. Like Emma, he was married; and he was the devoted father of young children; but Miss Szold knew that, as with Emma, no personal ties would conflict with the duties Hans shared with her. Like Louis Ehrlich, Lotte Beyth was a patient, understanding spouse. And Miss Szold knew when she left the office in the care of Hans Beyth that it would be well run, and she would receive full reports of his doings while she was away, addressed to *"Meine sehr liebe Miss Szold."*

First she went to the Zionist Congress at Lucerne in August to report on two years of Youth Aliyah. Over a thousand children had been brought in and settled in twenty-three colonies. A group of forty of the first graduates of Ain Ḥarod were forming a new colony of their own, and fifty-four more had just arrived to take their places. Colonies all over the country were offering to take children in, and were making room for them. She was roundly applauded, lauded by Chaim Weizmann, the President of the Congress, and given the signal honor of having a colony named for her in her lifetime: the new colony of graduates from Ain Ḥarod would be called Kfar Szold. She begged for more money. Thousands of children were still waiting in Germany; and there were tens of thousands equally hopeless in Poland.

From Lucerne Miss Szold went to Amsterdam to attend the first conference of the International Youth Aliyah, and laid before them her plans for increased activity. She begged for more money.

From Amsterdam she went to Berlin, which was celebrating the passage of the infamous Nuremberg Laws: All Jews were excluded from German citizenship, and prohibited from marital and extramarital relations with non-Jews; Jews were forbidden to employ Gentile domestics, or to hoist the German flag. A Jew was defined as a person with at least one Jewish grandparent. . . . As she descended from the train her travel-weary eyes were greeted by an immense sign: "JUDE, VERECKE!"—"Jew, Perish!" On every hand in the streets hung huge placards: "DIE JUDEN SIND UNSER UNGLÜCK!" "The Jews Are Our Misfortune!"; "MÄDCHEN UND FRAUEN, DIE JUDEN SIND EURE VERDERBER!"—"Girls and Women, the Jews Are Your Corrupters!"

Awaiting her were eight hundred men and women, packed into a small hall. Her heart sank as she thought of the task before her. They were the parents of her children. It was heartbreaking to look upon the hopeful faces of those desperate mothers and fathers who had put so much trust in her. What could she say to them, how ease the anxiety of each one of them, reassure them that what they had done was best for their children under these dire circumstances? She had been warned to be guarded in her speech, for spies were everywhere; she had to be careful to say nothing that might result in official opposition to future emigration. In her flawless German, which brought her closer to them and strengthened their trust in her, she told them how their children had been received, how they spent their days, working, studying, playing, what fine progress they were making. . . . She was interrupted by the noise in the street of tramping brown-shirted Nazis returning from a demonstration, singing the Horst Wessel song: ". . . *Wenn das Judenblut vom Messer spritzt* . . ."—"When Jewish blood spurts from the knife . . ." At the end of her talk, she offered to answer questions.

But they asked her questions she could not answer: Had she met this one's young Hans, that one's Gretchen, at such-and-such a colony? Some had brought pictures of their children so she might recognize them. What could she say to a mother who needed the reassurance not merely that Youth Aliyah was working well but that this woman's eyes had actually looked into the living eyes of that one child who was gone from her? Inspired, she said, Yes, she had surely met this one's Hans and that one's Gretchen, for, "I personally greet every child on arrival"; and she visited all the groups of children again and again and held meetings with them and discussed them with their teachers; but, she explained, only the problem children were brought to her special attention. And they were appeased; for "What mother's child is a problem child?"

In consultation with the leaders of Youth Aliyah in Berlin it was decided that to circumvent the possibility of any interference with their emigration before the children could be received in Palestine, groups of them would be sent for their preliminary training period to camps to be established in Holland and France, England and Scandinavia, instead of there in dangerous Germany.

The newspapers, foul with obscene cartoons of Jews, were blatantly publishing inciting photographs of their public mistreatment. One showed a Jew surrounded by tall Nazi soldiers, one of whom was plucking hairs from the Jew's gray beard. Among the cruel, bestial faces of the grinning soldiers the calm face of the Jew raised to his tormentors was radiant with the pride of divinely inspired humanity. Twenty-seven centuries ago—seven centuries before Jesus said, "Turn the other cheek"—the prophet Isaiah had described that face; had taught him how to behave:

> *I gave my back to the smiters,*
> *and my cheeks to them that plucked off the hairs.*
> *I hid not my face from shame and spitting.*
> *For the Lord will help me;*
> *therefore have I not been confounded:*
> *therefore have I set my face like a flint,*
> *and I know that I shall not be ashamed.*

The horrors of that hell in which she spent a month were mitigated for Henrietta Szold by the dignity, the indomitable courage of her people, their steadfast refusal to revile their persecutors and their determination to put all their energies into constructive efforts to save and preserve their youth. In the midst of the holocaust they had the grace even to "entertain" their honored visitor. They gave her teas and dinners, sent her flowers and sweets. . . .

From Berlin Miss Szold proceeded to America to raise the money urgently needed for Youth Aliyah's rapidly growing program outside and inside Palestine. Her seventy-fifth birthday was approaching, and this time she would willingly have turned it into a circus, she would jump through hoops for the benefit of Youth Aliyah. Every strand of her life was now woven into the single strong line she had to haul. Miss Szold, "that fine beast of burden," no longer chafed at her harness. In New York it fairly jingled. From the dock, upon her arrival, she was driven to a floodlighted newsreel studio; and her face and voice became so familiar to newspaper readers and moviegoers that a salesgirl recognized her when she was trying on a dress in which she might decently appear at a mass meeting and at the countless fund-raising functions arranged for her. They were sponsored by leading Zionists and non-Zionists, from Rabbi Stephen Wise to Mrs. Felix Warburg, by distinguished Jews and Christians, from Eddie Cantor to Eleanor Roosevelt. Fiorello La Guardia, handing her the key to the city in a glare of flashlights, said: "If I, the child of immigrant parents, am today Mayor of New York, giving you the freedom of the city, it is because of you. Half a century ago you initiated that instrument of American democracy, the evening school for the immigrant. . . ." Shades of Lombard Street, where she had quietly scurried around raising $141 for her "Russians"! Thousands of dollars rolled in, despite the depression. In an impassioned report to Hadassah she implored them not to depend upon the superficial reports of sentimental tourists on the situation in Palestine, but to inform themselves reliably, and she gave, as an example of misinformation, the little girl in her history class in the Misses Adams' School who thought the Minute Men were on all sides. Hadassah, now numbering 100,000 members, despite its costly commitment to the building and maintenance of the new hospital on Mount Scopus, voted to make Youth Aliyah one of its major projects, and pledged $30,000 a year for two years. Even her founding of Hadassah almost a quarter-century before now fitted into this pattern the fates had woven with Henrietta Szold as their shuttle.

Back she went to Palestine, early in February 1936, leaving behind the fertile field of funds she had cultivated for Youth Aliyah to be harvested by Hadassah, which gathered over $100,000.

She had given some thought to those boxes stored in New York, in Adele's barn in Connecticut and in Bertha's cellar in Baltimore, when, in her traveling about between speeches, sometimes three a day, she had picked up an old *New Yorker* and read an item which began, "Possessions breed like mice. A man forgets what a raft of irrelevant junk he has collected about him until he tries to move it . . ." and ended with the description of "a little old fellow with his worldly goods slung on his back in a burlap sack. In his face was written a strange peace." *Shalom*—peace was not yet for her, even at seventy-five. She clipped the item and added it to a collection of oddments, poetry, aphorisms she liked, in the black writing case she used on her travels, and did nothing about the boxes, although she was able to spend her birthday in Baltimore with Bertha's family which had flourished mightily. Three of Bertha's children had been married in the year before: Benjamin, who, with his wife, Sarah, had gone to one of the colonies in Palestine; Harriet, who was now Mrs. Terrell; and Jastrow, whose wife Alexandra gave birth to Bertha's first grandchild, Betsy, just three days after the "twin" birthday of Bertha and Henrietta. Before Henrietta sailed, Bertha gave her the portrait of herself as a child in a pink dress—shades of the actor Dawisohn whom she had charmed in her pink Sabbath dress!—for presentation to the new Nurses' Training School on Mount Scopus, which was also to bear her name.

The most gratifying gift of all was the news that Hadassah was planting a forest in her name on Mount Scopus. "You," she wrote them, "have bound me, not to stone, mortar, some human institution in Palestine, but indissolubly to the land itself . . . in my name you are restoring a piece of the land to fertility and beauty. I have thus been made part and parcel, as it were, of the land of our heroes and prophets and of our holiest aspirations . . . you have incorporated me into something fundamental, something which in human parlance may be called eternal."

On board the SS *Lafayette* she spent her time acknowledging hundreds of birthday greetings and reading some of the heartwarming pieces published about her in the New York *Times,* the *Nation.* . . .

She crossed the Mediterranean in the SS *Tel Aviv,* the first ship of a planned Jewish merchant marine. She observed the officers' "brave attempt at disciplining a heterogeneous group of Jews above and below decks," and was reminded of her own difficulties in the Medical Unit and the Nurses' Training School. "However, Hadassah succeeded. . . . Seamanship ought not to be more difficult of attainment . . . only at this stage I should not like a great storm to come up and danger to life be imminent, and put these raw sailors to the test."

She arrived safely and was received with acclaim in Jerusalem and Tel Aviv, where belated celebrations of her birthday were held. Mayor Dizengoff, not to be outdone by Mayor La Guardia, made her an honorary citizen of Tel Aviv. Members of the Social Service School put on a skit in which "The Case of Miss Szold" was diagnosed and found perplexing: she was reputed to be of good character yet was the mother of a thousand children; and she broke all trade-union rules as to working hours. . . . But the mood of relaxation was short-lived.

She had got back just in time for the worst yet of the spring Arab riots. This one had been preceded by months of blatant anti-Jewish expressions and demonstrations, learned and borrowed from the Nazis. The Arab press was referring to Jews as "the human sexual disease," "a gang of swindlers," and "a menace to all mankind." Arab terrorist organizations paraded; brown-clad "storm troopers" marched, shouting "Heil Hitler!" Late in March there was a meeting of influential Arabs in Safed to plan the uprising. Fifteen days before this openly ignited bomb burst, the Revisionist leader Jabotinsky tried to warn the High Commissioner, who treated his warning contemptuously; and Revisionists were arrested on suspicion of being connected with "a secret revolutionary organization." Most of the ringleaders of the Arab terrorists' openly planned civil disturbance were in the employ of the government; but the government did nothing to stop them, despite the "Seditious Offenses Ordinance" which provided severe penalties for conspiring "to raise discontent or disaffection amongst the inhabitants of Palestine; or to promote feelings of ill-will and hostility between the different sections of the population of Palestine."

In April, with the old cry, "The Government is with us!" the bomb burst in Jaffa where the streets ran again with Jewish blood; but this time the slaughter was better organized under the German influence. Nazi flags and pictures of Hitler were displayed in shop windows. Gramophones blared out calling on Arabs to destroy the Jews. The whole country was swept for months by murderous anarchy. The Arab High Committee called a general strike, patently intended to demoralize the whole economy, yet the government did nothing about this illegal, seditious act. Bandits roamed the country roads and the city streets, unhindered by the police.

Three American senators, Austin, Copeland, and Hastings, went to the Holy Land to find out what was happening there. They were not welcomed by the British officials, and were told not to visit the Jewish communities. They reported that "there are really two strikes going on in Palestine. One is conducted by Arab terrorists, who throw bombs and snipe at passersby in the streets and highways. The other is conducted silently by the Mandatory Government of Palestine against the proper administration of justice. The prolongation of the terror in the Holy Land is due . . . to a manifest sympathy for the vandals and assassins displayed by many officers who are sworn to uphold the law . . . creating a condition which could not but shock any American observer."

Refugees from the riots fled from one town to another. From

Beisan they fled to Tiberias, and the whole Jewish population of Hebron was encamped in Jerusalem. In the Old City groups of families huddled together for protection. Half of Jewish Jaffa poured into Tel Aviv, where a huge bomb was discovered buried in the sand of a playground.

Miss Szold, accompanied by Hans Beyth and driven by husky young Oscar Eckhaus, for years her tireless chauffeur, who kept a revolver carefully concealed under his seat—for Jewish conveyances were frequently searched for arms by the discriminating police—would drive up to Haifa to meet each group of incoming children. What else could she do? They could not be left in Germany, where they would surely be destroyed. And in the whole of the Christian world there was no other haven for them. Although even kindergartens and children's playgrounds had been dynamited, and although the buses that took the children from the dock in the Arab quarter of Haifa had to have the windows boarded against stones and snipers, there in the Land of Israel at least the children were wanted and loved and their lives would be fought for if necessary. When an attempt was made to set fire to the Baby Home in Jerusalem, she addressed an appeal in the name of the Jewish women to the "Arab mothers and women of Palestine . . . to influence your husbands and your sons to desist from courses of action . . . which we believe to be as abhorrent to you as they are to us. In the name of our common motherhood and womanhood . . ."

For her own part, she found herself possessed by a calm which was not so much courage as the lack of fear. "If I perish, I perish!" was not so much the philosophy of a heroine as of one who was living on borrowed time; and, curiously, it proved to be a kind of life-saving armor. She had long known that timidity invited attack. Now she learned that fearlessness warded it off. Once, when she was returning from Haifa on the highway up to Jerusalem where many attacks had occurred, the car was stopped by a crowd of Arabs from a nearby village, gathered in the road. When Oscar started to reach for his revolver Miss Szold told him not to take it out. She opened her window and stuck out her head, saw that the crowd was in festive attire, some among them bearing bouquets of flowers. Miss Szold smiled and asked what the occasion was.

She was told they were awaiting the passage of the Mufti—the infamous Husseini who had openly directed the riots while acting as a high official of the government. Miss Szold said how fine they all looked and how beautiful the flowers were, and asked if her car couldn't be let through before the Mufti came. They made way for her.

She learned that it was possible to go on with routine labors in the midst of warfare; that, indeed, it was the only way to keep sane. One night early in July, when she and Emma Ehrlich were still working long after dark, a noise broke out in the street which made her think of fireworks and "the glorious Fourth," until she realized that rifle bullets were rattling like hail against walls and shutters. All lights in the house went off until the firing stopped. Then the lights were turned on again and work was resumed. She was depressed by the imminent departure of Emma, who had been sister, daughter and friend to her, who had to go to America with her husband for six months.

In August two Jewish nurses on their way to the Jaffa Hospital to nurse Arab patients were murdered. Miss Szold addressed a protest to High Commissioner Sir Arthur Wauchope demanding preventive measures; but she knew that the restoration of quiet, if not peace, would be at some cost to the Jews. After six months of terror, during which two thousand attacks were made on Jewish communities, with seven hundred slain and thousands wounded, hundreds of thousands of precious trees uprooted, countless cattle destroyed, and property with a value of fifteen millions of dollars lost, the horror was brought to an end by the government's promise to "give the Arabs justice"; and another commission came from London to investigate.

Miss Szold testified before them, but she had no hope that they would bring a solution of the Arab-Jewish problem—"the acid test of our right to form a community in Palestine." It would have to be solved by the Jews and the Arabs themselves. The British, who had helped them into the land, were no help but a hindrance to them now. She was convinced that the administration "deliberately thwarted every effort made by the Jews to find a method of conciliation between Jew and Arab."

When asked if she still hoped for survival of the Jewish National

Home she said it was her belief that the Jewish community in Palestine was different from all others in the world: it was indestructible. "Deeply rooted as was the Jewish community in Germany it was all but destroyed. History has produced a second Spain." But although, added to all its other burdens, the *Yishuv* now had to undertake the costly business of self-defense, she had no doubt of its survival.

Meanwhile, in addition to the direction of Youth Aliyah, there was the growing task of social service which could no longer be left in the planning stage but had to be performed. In addition to some forty thousand immigrants from Germany, hordes were now coming from Central Europe—from Poland, Roumania, Lithuania, Czechoslovakia, and from the Near East—from Persia, Iraq, Syria, Morocco. . . . The problems involved were not only quantitative but qualitative—the handling and absorption of people ranging in civilization from the fifteenth to the twentieth centuries.

Three times a week she got to bed at two in the morning and rose at five; the rest of the week she got five hours' sleep, including the midday nap. All her waking hours she was working hard; her travels about the country were more difficult because of the need for convoys in dangerous areas. She couldn't help wondering sometimes when the breaking point would come. Well into 1936 she was distressed to discover she still had not acknowledged some two hundred and fifty birthday messages of the previous December. In September Mayor Dizengoff of Tel Aviv died, and his funeral attended by thousands was a solemn affair that depressed her when she remembered that he was three months younger than she. She hoped her funeral would not be at all like his.

The winter of 1936–7 was unusually severe. The frequent heavy rains increased the difficulties attendant upon the maintenance of refugee camps for those who had abandoned their homes during the riots, and of their resettlement elsewhere if they could not return. At one time there were over ten thousand such refugees from Jaffa in Tel Aviv alone. But by the end of that winter Miss Szold, who was chairman of the committee for the liquidation of refugee camps, was able to report completion of the task.

At this time she got from Judah Magnes a copy of a Memorandum he intended to publish, proposing certain bases for settlement of the Arab-Jewish difficulties, to be worked out in conferences between representatives of the British Mandatory Government, the Arabs, and the Jews. "Sweet reasonableness with nobility" was Miss Szold's characterization of his proposals; but she recommended that he withhold its publication, because she doubted if the Jews, who had suffered so much and were still suffering, were in the mood for sweet reasonableness, and she doubted if the British were yet willing to discharge the responsibilities they had assumed with the Mandate. In this latter judgment she was overwhelmingly justified by the Report of the Royal Commission that summer—the most blatantly anti-Jewish and pro-colonial of all the reports to date. It saw no prospect of Arab-Jewish reconciliation and co-operation and suggested a partition of Palestine that would give the Jews a coastal sliver of land, with immigration restrictions which would in effect end the Zionist aspiration for a National Home—in a Palestinian ghetto. It also gave Britain the permanent occupation of a corridor between the Jews and the Arabs, with economic controls which would in effect make Palestine a British colony.

Miss Szold, who by then had had much experience with man's inhumanity to man, could reflect wryly on the fact that the Royal Commission which produced this cynical report had rejected a suggestion in Parliament that a woman member be included, giving as its reason the argument that "such a move would be incompatible with Arab ideals." Even this sickening outcome did not prompt her to turn her energies to the prophetic castigation Justice Brandeis had recommended.

Miss Szold had her work laid out for her. There were the incoming children to be met, to be placed, to be taught; conferences to be held with their teachers and supervisors as to curriculums and programs of work and play, and health of mind and body. At the end of four years of Youth Aliyah she was able to report that of two thousand three hundred and thirty children rescued under such untoward conditions, only seven had been lost. All the same, it had not been easy for her to have to write to the mothers of even those few. But she had reason to feel that, as a mother, she had succeeded. Whenever she appeared, the children gathered around her and sat spellbound as she talked. . . .

But because of the desperate plight of the immigrants who came crowding into Palestine while its doors were still open, she continued to work with the social service organizations. No human problem was too sordid for her attention. When a report came from London, spread by some missionaries, that prostitution was rife in Palestine and that most of its Jewish doctors were specialists in venereal diseases, Miss Szold, in her seventy-seventh year, undertook a thoroughgoing investigation: obtained reports from the police and copies of surveys which the government had made; got testimony from reputable physicians; and herself made inquiries at various institutions and social services which had reliable statistics on the subject. The results of this investigation she summarized in a lengthy explicit report, describing the innocuous night life in the towns—it was practically over by 8:30 P.M.—and the sober behavior of the people even on nights of public celebration like *Purim*. She presented figures evidencing the incontrovertible fact that, despite the presence of numbers of British troops, the incidence of prostitution in Palestine was negligible in comparison with European cities like, for example, London. In an interview with one girl who was brought to her, Miss Szold had been impressed by the description of her sordid childhood in a crowded one-room home, and was moved by the satisfaction the girl now got from inhabiting a room with only one other person, from being treated with affection, and from the simple act of politeness bestowed upon her by a man who waited for her to enter a room before himself.

The apparently high incidence in Jerusalem of specialists in venereal diseases, although actually not abnormal, Miss Szold discovered to be due to the fact that the incidence of skin diseases in Palestine was indeed high and that dermatologists are usually also specialists in venereal disease. Miss Szold was not unaware, however, that in a pioneer society, and especially among certain radical groups, unconventional sexual mores were to be found. And although she deplored this, she maintained that such behavior could not properly be called "prostitution." She took the occasion, however, to plead for a "well-planned system of sex education" and the elimination of conditions which contributed in any degree whatsoever to these evils. Her report ended: "If I were asked to point out the most immediate need at the moment, I would venture to urge the establishment of Homes for Young Girls in Tel Aviv, Haifa and Jerusalem. They will be doubly effective in meeting the worst evils, prophylactically and remedially, if they are fortified by well-endowed family welfare work, which will, first and foremost, enable the family without means to secure decent housing at a moderate outlay. No one factor is so fruitful of evil as the overcrowded one-room dwelling, from which the boy flees to the street, its gangs, and its inducements to delinquency, and the young girl to the enticements of street life and the ease offered by the seducer."

In her continued efforts to raise the standards of social service in Palestine, to get the *Keneset Israel* to co-ordinate the independent charitable institutions and to get from the government greater contributions to the support of such communal activities, Miss Szold found a handicap in the difference in the demands of the two parts of the population—Arab and Jewish. The Arab schools were still providing education for only one fifth of the potential school-age population, while the Jews were sending all children to school. The equitable distribution of government funds between the two parts of the population with such disparate standards became in itself a knotty problem.

Despite her preoccupation with Youth Aliyah and social service, that summer when she attended the Zionist Congress in Zurich, which was concerned primarily with consideration of the partition proposal of the Royal Commission, Miss Szold was prompted to prepare a paper arguing against partition as a solution of the Arab-Jewish problem and for a binational state, despite Mr. Ben-Gurion's ruling against the discussion of that possibility. There was at the Congress a strong group in favor of accepting the partition proposal and then bargaining or fighting for more land and better terms. Miss Szold tried at first to accept this idea out of loyalty to the Zionist leadership but she could not.

Basic to her argument against it was her forty-seven-year-old conviction that Palestine must be not merely the refuge of the Jews from anti-Semitism but the refuge of Judaism—the place where Jewish law and ethics would be re-established as the Jewish rule and way of life. And it was her charge that not only had the

British Government failed to implement the Mandate entrusted to it but that the Jews had failed to utilize the opportunity afforded by the Mandate to demonstrate their Judaism in action. Although the Jews had amply demonstrated their vigorous creative ability in reviving the land and in the growth of their colonies and cities, they had neglected the opportunity to establish the reign of *Yosher v' Tzedek,* of "righteousness and justice" in achieving the conciliation of Arabs and Jews. This she wrote in the face of the ruthless Nazi persecution which was climaxing the repeated failure of Christian peoples to put into practice their long-avowed belief in the brotherhood of man. She was cognizant of the fact that the Jews in Palestine had taken nothing from the Arabs, had paid well for every *dunam* of neglected land they occupied and restored to life, and had, indeed, made available to the Arabs services and a standard of living they had heretofore never enjoyed. But that, she maintained, was not enough: "I charge my own people with not having done *all* that should have been done. . . . And now that we have been led to the crossroads I want to choose the road that will renew the opportunity. . . ." Partition, a separate state, even if the Zionists could wrest more land and better conditions from the offer than the Royal Commission suggested, was not the road to that opportunity. "We entered the land by means of the sword," wrote Miss Szold in August 1937; "the *Judenstaat* of the Royal Commission will compel us to keep the sword in our hands day after day, year after year. . . . I, too, believe that the land will be ours, but this is not the way to win it. The way to win it is not by might and not by cunning but by the spirit of the Lord, which is the way of conciliation. This *Judenstaat* that is offered to us means war. . . ."

But Miss Szold suppressed this impulse to play the prophet; she did not deliver the paper. She did not even finish it. She put it away in her writing case and took up the work that had been laid out for her, leaving the Congress to come to its own decision to reject the partition plan of the Royal Commission.

In October, approaching her seventy-seventh birthday, she dared go to Berlin for the third time, mainly to encourage the parents of one hundred and twelve boys and girls who were being prepared for at Emek-Ha-Yarden, a colony in the Valley of Jezreel.

The experience was harrowing. She found the older Jews resigned to a fearful fate—they would rot or die there in Germany. Their one cry was: Save the young! She spoke to a gathering composed of parents of children who would be leaving in a few days, these children themselves, and parents of many who had gone before. These last came crowding around her with their pictures and questions, and she was able to tell them of over seven hundred who had finished their courses and were well established as farmers and artisans all over the land, some of them organized in labor groups of their own, working eight hours a day and continuing their education in evening classes. They were working hard, mostly with their hands, building houses and roads, planting, picking and packing the fruit and the produce of the land, but they were intelligent and civilized as well as hardy young men and women, a new kind of Jew—neither the unearthly *luftmensch,* the impractical intellectual, nor the *am ha-aretz,* the ignorant man of the earth of the Diaspora.

From Berlin she returned to the Congress and then to Palestine, and then went to America again, to raise more money—there were the children coming from Poland too, now. But this time she was not in the mood for a circus. She reported on Youth Aliyah to Hadassah at its twenty-fifth annual convention in Atlantic City, and told the membership how the young men and women they had rescued were making themselves available for the starting of new colonies. In dangerous areas they gathered in the nearest established colony and there assembled portable parts of their basic buildings, fences, gates, and watchtowers. Then they set out at sunrise and, with the help of their neighbors, erected these buildings in one day, set up and manned their fences and watchtowers, and by nightfall were guarded against attack. She was also able to tell them of the progress made, despite all hazards, on their new hospital on Mount Scopus and the new Nurses' Training School. She could still speak of ". . . faith in progress, in the perfectibility of life and the bearers of life, in human virtue, in the values of idealism and aspiration. Such faith is the guarantee of continued achievement."

Early in 1938 she was back in Jerusalem concentrating on the direction of Youth Aliyah. In March, the annexation of Austria by

Hitler, and the Mandatory Government's announcement of unrestricted certificates for Youth Aliyah, spurred her to superhuman effort. She appealed to Hadassah, saying that they were restricted now only "by our own limitations; available places and available funds." Hadassah's response was to raise in six months three times its collection in the previous three months. Almost a thousand children were brought in during the first half year, not only from Germany but from Poland and Austria, from Czechoslovakia, Hungary and Yugoslavia.

Miss Szold was also concerned with the development of social services dealing with child welfare in the general community. There, it was her opinion, "the child must remain in the family unless the development of the child be endangered by reason of an abnormal situation in the family itself, of such a nature as cannot be normalized with material and spiritual means at the command of the Family Welfare Agency. In short, family is the strongest and primary basis for the development of the child into a useful citizen."

That summer, however, the breaking point came and her work was interrupted by illness, for the first time in many years. She entered the brand-new Hadassah Hospital on Mount Scopus, which had been opened with three hundred beds. "A tired heart," said Dr. Kleeberg after his examination. "A heart that has been beating for seventy-eight years," said Miss Szold, whom that quivering old heart had served so well. The doctor agreed and gave it a name, "cardio-vascular disturbance," and recommended she give it a rest. She continued to direct the work, but let Hans Beyth and Emma Ehrlich relieve her of strenuous efforts. By the fall her strength was restored; but, with the help of Hans and Emma, she cut her working day down to twelve hours. When she asked for funds to bring in twelve hundred more children, Hadassah set out again in October and raised three quarters of a million dollars in the following year; and in January 1939 Miss Szold resigned from the *Vaad Leumi* in order to confine herself to the direction of the expanding work of Youth Aliyah.

That month she went to the dedication of a new Youth Aliyah house at Meier Shefaya, the children's village sponsored by Junior Hadassah. The countryside revived by the winter rains was radiant with flowers—the fields with red and white anemones, the almond trees with clouds of pink blossoms, the hillsides with carpets of lavender. . . . The children, gathered in the courtyard to greet her, sang the *"Hatikvah"* as the flag was raised; and a girl from Germany, sunburned and sturdy, stepped out and spoke; and Henrietta Szold heard a restatement of her own dauntless faith: ". . . We all recall the burning of our threshing floor and the destruction of the wheat which was the fruit of our labor. But we remember, too, that we refused to be discouraged and began at once to plow and plant anew. We had faith that this time we would harvest what we had sowed. . . ." Her children, though not of her flesh and blood, had inherited her spirit. They presented her with heaps of flowers from their gardens, roses and violets, with grateful words and a prayer: "May your days be long, for your task is great and many await salvation through you." She responded by reminding them of others to whom they were indebted—to Recha Freier before her, and her colleagues there in Palestine, and those women overseas who made possible their salvation and that of thousands to come.

In those dreadful days of 1939, seeing a large part of mankind bound and throttled, enslaved by fear, seeing her people bleeding from thousands of wounds, it would have been less than human not to lament. "I believe in lamenting," she wrote, "if only lamentation does not hinder action, if only acute fellow feeling does not paralyze fellow aid." And, standing one day on Mount Carmel, above Haifa harbor, the Mount of the Prophet Elijah, she thought again of that cloud he saw rising out of the sea, "as small as a man's hand," which brought abundance of rain after dire drought; and she thought hopefully of small signs: of President Roosevelt's ringing rebukes to Germany and Italy; of the host of neighborly acts of Christians to Jews, at risk of liberty and life, reported by refugees; and of the almost divine self-restraint of the Jews in the face of savagery. . . . Then she said to herself: "Yes, the Jewish doctrine is true and right. Man is perfectible. Setbacks there have been; setbacks there will be. But what our prophets, our poets, our philosophers, what the good and the wise of all ages and peoples have preached, will emerge triumphantly. . . . Man's humanity may sink out of sight for a span. It is bound to assert itself. . . . This is my creed in these dark, terrible days. It does not banish sorrow and pain, but it keeps ajar the door of hope. . . . Also, my creed demands that I shall keep on steadily with the work that life has entrusted to me and do it to the best of my ability. The sorrier the time, the more poignant the anguish, the keener the need, the greater the challenge to wrestle with fate."

Despite her preoccupation with Youth Aliyah, however, in June 1939 she was persuaded to join with Louis Brandeis, Albert Einstein, the Marquis of Reading, James de Rothschild, Herbert Lehman, Felix Frankfurter, and Léon Blum to prepare and promulgate a Memorandum calling for a "New Deal" in Arab-Jewish relations in Palestine, looking to the solution of that problem which she had declared would be "the acid test of our right to form a Jewish community in Palestine"—upon the solution of which, she realized, would depend the fate of all those children she was saving from destruction. She contributed to the Memorandum the ideas in that unfinished paper she had not delivered at the Zionist Congress two years before. It criticized both the Mandatory Government and the Zionist movement for their failure to initiate any positive approach to the problem, and it proposed the appointment of a reputable Inquiry Commission to examine the problem thoroughly—survey the whole field of Arab-Jewish relations, and inquire into the prospects of an agreement between the two peoples which would reconcile their national aspirations and bring about peace and co-operation for the free development of both peoples. The Commission would recommend the terms of such an agreement, and examine the economic, political, constitutional, and financial questions involved, including the future constitution of Palestine as a binational state, and the prospect of its eventual entrance into a federation of the neighboring countries. The Memorandum went into detail as to its objectives and procedures. But, despite its distinguished sponsorship by some of the best minds available in the modern world, nothing came of it in that world which was ineluctably headed for Armageddon.

Miss Szold, accompanied by Hans Beyth with a pistol in his pocket, and driven by Oscar Eckhaus with a pistol under the car seat, rode up to Haifa, rain or shine, to meet every batch of incoming children; she welcomed each one of them, sang and danced and talked with them, and saw to it that each of them had as good a life as was possible in the mad world they had not made.

With the outbreak of the war in September it became desperately necessary to make every effort to bring out the children trapped in every territory and transport them to still neutral lands—Scandinavia, Belgium, Holland, Switzerland, and even to besieged Britain. That dreadful year was gladdened for Henrietta by the arrival in the spring of her two remaining sisters, Bertha and Adele—Bertha grown matronly, like Mamma, and Adele, sprightly, witty and brilliant as ever. They came in April, in time for the Passover *seder*, which they celebrated together with Bertha's son Benjamin who came with his wife Sarah from Kfar Syrkin. The three sisters reminisced about the *seders* in Lombard Street, presided over by Papa and Mamma; and Henrietta said that it was the family life in Lombard Street which had given her whatever sympathy and understanding she had; nothing after that had altered what she had learned there. Adele, an excellent writer, decided to write the biography of Henrietta Szold, and began collecting materials for it. So the three of them, at meals and on the Sabbath, the only times when Henrietta was available, would revel in reminiscences about the history of the Szolds, starting with the early times of which they had no recollections but the stories of Papa and Mamma—of how they had met and married and come to America, and their lives on Eutaw Street where Henrietta was born, and her own first memories there. She could remember when there were town criers; when people wore night caps and had slaves. There were discrepancies to be considered—for instance, the oft-repeated story that Henrietta had watched Lincoln's funeral while perched on Papa's shoulder. But how could that be, if Papa himself was in the funeral procession as he must have been, along with the most distinguished clergymen of Baltimore. The Sun papers the next day had said he was there: "The Reverend Rabbi Benjamin Szold." It must have been Uncle Eduard who lifted her up from among the voluminous skirts and the pantaloons; but time had given Henrietta what that little girl had wished for—the feeling that it was her dear Papa's shoulder on which she had perched. Time could be kind as well as ruthless. There was much of its ruthlessness buried in those boxes in Bertha's cellar and Adele's barn, of which neither she nor Adele made mention. Adele, who was ailing, returned home in November with her notes for the biography.

But Bertha stayed on through that winter and celebrated with Henrietta on December 21 their joint birthday, Henrietta's seventy-ninth, when gifts and messages came from the four corners of Palestine and of the world. The most precious of all were those from her children. They sent her plants and flowers from their gardens, cyclamen and lilies, roses and sweet peas and gladioli, and the seeds of the flowers they knew she loved to grow in pots on her balcony in Jerusalem. They sent albums of photographs of themselves with her, and expressions of their love for her. The girls sent jackets and scarves they had knitted and sewn for her, and the boys sent the artful work of their hands in wood and metal. They sent money they had earned to contribute to her good works.

"Together," she said to them, "we will strive to achieve what at one and the same time is national and universal, symbolic and actual, antagonistic to strife and destruction, and constructive of what makes for progress, justice and peace."

1940s: A WOMAN'S WORK IS NEVER DONE...

In February 1940, Bertha ended her long visit with Henrietta and returned home, where she found that Adele, who had preceded her, was seriously ill. And in mid-March, Adele Seltzer, the youngest of the Szold sisters, died, leaving some pages of the biography of Henrietta Szold which she had begun writing. For many months Henrietta was plagued by the thought that, preoccupied as she was with her children, she had not attended to her sister's ailment when she was there; and now she could not even attend her funeral. Henrietta, in her weekly letters to Bertha, mourned for Adele, who used to sit beside her at table in Lombard Street and demanded her attention, and would have only Henrietta care for her when she was ill.

Soon after, her dearest friend in America died—Alice Seligsberg, who had long been her confidante, her aide, and her critical conscience. Then in April came the death of Cyrus Adler, whose friendship had begun in Baltimore back in the Lombard Street days and continued all through the years in Philadelphia at the Jewish Publication Society and in New York at the Seminary. Death and the conflagration of war that was engulfing the world was isolating Henrietta there in Palestine. Although modern invention had shrunk land and sea for the purposes of high-speed warfare, peaceful communication was becoming well-nigh impossible. It took months for Bertha's letters to reach her, sometimes via Singapore. All mail was censored; and because many letters were lost in the ruthless submarine warfare, Henrietta numbered them so that lapses would be noticeable. She discouraged Bertha from undertaking the biography Adele had begun. "If possible, the war has deepened my opposition. Half a million men, they say, destroyed in the course of the May battle! What is a single life. . . ." She found comfort in telling Bertha what a wonderful year this was for flowers in Palestine—of the tiger lilies she had seen by the Dead Sea.

With communication so difficult it became necessary to set up a Hadassah Emergency Council in Palestine, empowered to take action when necessary and to plan for organization in the event that the war invaded Palestine itself. Again, as so often in history, the Jews there found themselves in the no man's land between contending forces. Rommel was at Alamein and there was the possibility of his advancing against the British in Palestine. Rose Jacobs of Hadassah, who was there, organized the Emergency Council, with Dr. Magnes as its chairman and Miss Szold as one of its most active members. A slip on a broken step and a painful fall confined her to her room in the Pension Romm on Rambam Street to which she had moved; and the first meetings of the Council in May 1940 were held there. Her list of unfinished business at the end of one of them was:

Public services (water, garbage)
Care of insane and tubercular
General relief survey
Medical supplies
Hadassah-University relations
Skim milk powder
Rosenberg schools
Report from Kindergarten League

At the same time, the Federation of Jewish Child Welfare Agencies was organized, which adopted the Declaration of Geneva promulgated by the *Union Internationale de Secours aux Enfants,* which begins: "1. The Child must be given the means requisite for its normal development . . ."

Despite the raging and spreading war—the occupation of Denmark and Norway trapped three hundred and sixty-six of her "certified" children there—children were still being brought in by circuitous routes, which presented a difficult added problem. In May she had twelve hundred certificates for children scattered from Lithuania to France and Italy whose passage to Palestine had yet to be effected; and, beside plans for their placement, now plans had to be made for their shelter or evacuation from one place to another in the event of bombardment. For a while she tried to get a younger woman to replace her in the direction of Youth Aliyah, but she failed. Daily the door of her room swung in and out without cease as one after another, members of committees or unfortunate individuals, came seeking her help. And she did not welcome the curious who still came to look at Miss Szold and took up her precious time and energy. Larry Adler, the harmonica player, who was born in Baltimore, appeared one day with Jack Benny, an American comedian—why, she couldn't imagine. They had been on a tour entertaining the soldiers; she could understand their wanting to see Jerusalem, and there was some excuse for Adler calling upon a fellow Baltimorean—but what had brought the comedian, whose gay world was so far removed from her serious one that she had never heard or seen him? But he made her laugh for an hour, and she loved laughter, and before he had gone she was grateful to him.

When her injured leg had healed sufficiently, Miss Szold, with Hans Beyth beside her, driving to Haifa to meet new arrivals, or off to visit some settlement, would lean back and close her eyes while Hans read her the unfinished mail. "Please go on, I'm not sleeping," she would say if he considerately stopped. And at meetings with the children, their leaders and their hosts, while reports and discussions went on and on, she would close her eyes and rest; but she listened and asked questions and spoke up when she could help solve their problems. More often now they were receiving children whose mental health had been undermined by their shattering experiences, and she wished she had studied psychiatry, and then wondered if that would have helped—there was so much controversy in that field, too. Those meetings she loved, weary though she might be; for they encouraged and refreshed her. On her return in the rainy season, she would have to scrape mud from her overshoes and her shoes, her stockings, her skirts and underwear, and Emma Ehrlich would scold her for not sparing herself.

But there was no doubt about the goodness and value of this work, however difficult. The problems were never tiresome, they were so varied—different in the *moshavim,* the small-holders' colonies, from those in the *kevutzot,* the collectives; different for children from different cultural backgrounds and speaking different languages—not alone German now but Bulgarian, Yugoslavian, Italian, Roumanian, Hungarian, Turkish, Greek; different again as the times changed, for the war created new problems. There was a group of Czechoslovakian boys who said they wanted to leave the settlement and join the army. The Haganah was organizing Jewish battalions to serve with the British forces, despite the infamous anti-Zionist White Paper. As Ben-Gurion put it for the Jews, "We will fight the war as though there were no White Paper, and the White Paper as though there were no war." But to Henrietta Szold, who had hated all war since childhood, the thought of her children engaged in that hateful, bloody business was intolerable. Shaking an admonitory finger, she told the boys to stick to their duty as pioneers in the Land of Israel; they would be better occupied in peaceful work and study than in fighting. She was not impressed by the argument that in their young lives they had hardly known what peace meant; that they had every reason to want to fight for the freedom of man against that Devil incarnate who had overwhelmed and enslaved their native land and was bent upon the destruction of the Jewish people. She found herself in opposition not only to the youth but, as in the First World War, to the Zionist leadership. She said: "War is destructive, both materially—in lives and property—and spiritually. War is an obstacle to the development of humanity. War brings hatred between nations and peoples. The immigrant youth has a duty, not to seek revenge or warlike adventure, but education for a good life in this land." The boys listened to her, with interest, with respect, and with affection; but they did not heed her, they went to war. Hundreds of others enlisted, too; and many of her girls went as nurses. All the same, if any of them came to Jerusalem she would receive them, in her office or her home, no matter how busy, or weary, or ailing she might be. Not only did they need her, she needed her children too.

Cut off from Bertha, the last of her family, despite all her friends there in Palestine, she sometimes felt very much alone. It cheered her when on occasions her nephew Benjamin Levin and his wife Sarah came from Kfar Syrkin and could visit her. It was good to see that too-sensitive little boy, who had recovered from the mishap in her home on 123rd Street, grown to industrious manhood on the land of Israel; but he and his wife were preoccupied with the pressing problems of a small-holders' settlement—of cattle, of goats and chickens and feed—and could spend little time with her. And yet, had she really wanted to "go home," as she still phrased it, she could have done so more than once. As late as May, Rose Jacobs had gone back; and even later others returned to America by roundabout routes—Bombay and the Cape of Good Hope. In the summer she wrote Bertha longingly of "Golden Bantam corn and fish with flavor and a walk through ferny woods." But the truth was that Henrietta Szold was rooted there and could not go; the children had done that to her.

On the road to Haifa there was a tree, an ancient sycamore, there was no telling how old it was, its trunk a great twisted shell supporting gnarled, wide-reaching branches. Whenever she could she would break her journey there, get Oscar to stop the car and let her sit there for a little and rest in the leafy shade of that lone old tree, so serene, so noble, for all the storms that had beaten and bent its burdened trunk and branches. It was rooted there in the land; and so was she.

And she felt as timeless. The news of the fall of France to the Germans reminded her of the Franco-Prussian war in 1870 when she was ten years old. It seemed to her but yesterday she had heard with such excitement of the defeat of the French at Sedan, so well she remembered it. And now Sedan was again in the news. Did men make no progress?

Living there, as if cut off in time and space, she needed to reach out to those across the sea. She wrote regularly to Bertha every Friday before sunset. For the women of Hadassah she made a recording—human wonder of this inhuman age—which would carry her small voice, together with the voices of some of her children, to their convention in October: ". . . The contact of kindred spirits sustains vision and knits the sinews of conviction. So, comrades in ideal and endeavor, I reach out to you . . . across expanses of space, and also across the weeks and months, fraught with who knows what added burdens. . . . I grasp your hand to steady myself . . . I have sore need of steadying myself. . . . Amid the smoke and din of titanic battle on land, on sea, and in the air, an urgent perspective disengages itself clearly to my eyes. The world will not again wear the aspect familiar before forces were unloosed intent on shattering cherished ideals. They will not, they shall not, achieve their sinister purpose. Even the grave reflection must be faced undaunted, that, in the very task of striking down malignity, we ourselves must resort to measures hitherto alien in our world of ideas and ideals. We are resolved, cost what it may, to preserve the essence of our faith and our philosophy, while adjusting ourselves to new ways demanded by the times and their events. . . . My voice and my words will be followed by the voices and the words of the youth whom you have plucked as brands from the burning, to become the builders of the future of Israel in the Land of Israel. You have prepared them as an advance guard marching into the new era. . . . From them gather courage and hope."

Her admonition about the necessity of resorting to measures hitherto alien to certain ideals was an expression of her personal realization, belated as ever, that there are times when purity of action, adherence to the *kasher,* the clean, becomes impossible. The government's limitation of immigration after the White Paper did not prevent the "illegal" entry of thousands of desperate Jews, fleeing for their lives from the spreading holocaust. They would disembark at night at hidden places, coming ashore in small boats or wading through dangerous surf holding their small children and their baggage above the waves. . . . The detention camps at Athlit and on the island of Mauritius were packed with those who were caught. Ships laden with refugees were being chased back from the shore of the Promised Land; and the *Patria,* a ship loaded with deportees, exploded and sank with the loss of hundreds in the harbor.

Sometimes, if there were children among the "illegals," Miss

Szold, by special pleading, could get them certificates of entry. But Henrietta Szold, who would not use "influence" to bring in a relative, found it difficult to sully the purity of her procedure even in the immigration of her children. When one group arrived from Roumania, she discovered that some of them were the eighteen-year-old brothers of younger boys for whom their certificates had been issued. The older boys had been substituted because they would have been drafted into the Roumanian Army. Miss Szold had to shut her eyes to this cheating, both because she could not send them back to the horror of war, and because the revelation of the deception would make the British immigration authorities even stricter than they were. On another occasion, her cable to Dan Gelbart, a *madriḥ* in Lithuania, instructing him to wait until she could get the additional certificates still needed for his group, went unheeded by him because he knew that they must leave then or never. He procured some forged certificates and brought them all in, whereupon Miss Szold sent Hans Beyth to tell him she did not wish to see him. When he came to see her nevertheless, she said that deceiving the government was alien to the basic integrity of her character and undermined her ability to command confidence. Everyone knew Miss Szold was reliable; she never told lies. Now she would have to go to the High Commissioner and tell him that Youth Aliyah had brought in "illegal" children, over age, with forged certificates. . . . But when he told her how truly desperate the situation had been she admitted, "In your position I would probably have done the same." At eighty, she was still learning from those younger than herself.

And it was to the *madriḥim,* the leaders and teachers of the thirty-five hundred children then still in training, that she turned "for moral strength to persist unflinchingly. I turn to you whose source of strength is your daily contact with the youth which is in our charge. I envy you," she told them. "Your duty lies defined before you. The darker the outlook, the more clearly you see your task—to teach, to train, to influence, to open up vistas into the past and into the future. It is for you to heal wounds inflicted by malign cruelty, to replace the wrenches of ties that bound a generation of children to fathers and mothers scattered to the furthest corners of the earth, to restore confidence in men and their works

. . . to encourage aspiration and direct it into channels of action towards culture and peace. . . ."

Shalom—in the midst of world-wide war she could still hope for peace. She now drew some hope for peace, at least there in Palestine, from an organization being formed for the solution of the perennial problem of Arab-Jewish relations. It was being set up by Judah Magnes, with Martin Buber the philosopher, who had come from Frankfort-am-Main, and Ernst Simon the educator, who had also come from Germany—both now on the faculty of the Hebrew University. Henrietta Szold saw it as "a problem that goes back to Isaac and Ishmael, to Jacob and Esau, and winds its labyrinthian way through the Middle Ages into our times and penetrates into every cultural cranny, religion, art, science, custom, politics, life in the whole. . . . Do we want a Jewish State or do we want Palestine as a home in which our people can develop freely and wholly in accordance with its history, its law, its cultural needs and aspirations? . . ." It did not discourage her to recall how many years ago in New York she had discussed that very problem of Arab-Jewish relations with Israel Friedlaender, who was an Arabic scholar, and whose widow, Lilian, her good friend of the Seminary days, now lived at Ziḥron Yaakob. Palestine had become in fact the center of the web of Jewish life, as of her own. All strands met there. One of the girls she had rescued proved to be a descendant of one of her father's best friends in Germany.

And now that she was so firmly rooted there in the Land of Israel, it was interesting to observe how all her life had become a coherent fabric—the past and the present so interwoven that she was constantly being reminded of the one by the other. One evening, leaving the office with Emma Ehrlich, she saw a woman coming toward them along the narrow sidewalk. Her recognition of the woman was so unexpected a shock that she clutched Emma's arm—it was *his* sister, who was living in Haifa. But Miss Szold did not explain her agitation to Emma when they had passed, because it seemed so absurd; it was all so long ago and far away.

She herself in that year undertook to complete one unfinished strand from the past which she had long neglected, and which had been on her conscience. She got together her father's unpublished manuscripts, had them beautifully bound—one of them a Commentary on *"Eshet Ḥayil"* written in soft pencil in the time of his final suffering—and together with his published Commentary on Job and his annotated Bible, presented them to the Hebrew University. There she hoped they might be studied by future students —perhaps her children—as it had been her intention to study and edit them when she went to the Seminary on 123rd Street and was distracted from that intention—so long ago and far away.

As for the future—one prepared for it as *ordentlich* as possible. One day she took Emma Ehrlich into her bedroom and showed her where she had stored the shroud she had got for herself, neatly folded in her wardrobe. "And no eulogies," she told Emma firmly. She still did not like cemeteries, and especially the coffinless funerals they had there in Palestine, like the one she had seen that first day on the Mount of Olives. But, there she was, rooted in the land; and anyway she still had some hard living to do. There were hundreds of children in Europe for whom she had got certificates but who were trapped by the war. Ways had to be found to get them out. . . .

On her eightieth birthday she addressed herself by radio to the schoolchildren of Palestine: "When I was as young as you who now are listening to my voice, the world existed without a telephone, without an automobile, without an airship, without a radio. Today, in my old age, when I have reached the years of strength, as King David called the age of eighty, a marvelous invention grants me the possibility of sending my voice to thousands of little children, big boys and girls, and youth scattered to all corners of this land.

"As you see, in the eighty years I have lived, many wonderful changes have taken place. But in one respect the world has not changed. Today, as long ago, good men and good women do noble acts; today, as long ago, wise men and wise women think great thoughts; today, as long ago, energetic men and energetic women work and achieve. . . . The soul does not change; it only learns to use new and better ways of communicating with other souls. . . . Youth and old age can meet as I am privileged to meet you today with my voice and my soul, and old age and youth can resolve together . . . to live nobly and wisely and energetically . . . as long as the breath of life is in us.

"This is my promise to you—this is the birthday gift I ask of you."

Hundreds of other birthday gifts and honors, of course, came to Miss Szold from all corners of Palestine and of the world. There was furniture fashioned for her in the colonies; paintings and statues from the artists; slippers and gloves and shawls and lace collars and cuffs; a bouquet of eighty roses, and all manner of flowering plants; a thousand greetings, ranging from people she had never heard of to Franklin Roosevelt and Albert Einstein; and money which, added to her accumulated gifts in the past, came to some $90,000 that she turned over to the National Council for the establishment of a National Children's Bureau. Streets were named for her. The Women's Centennial Congress cited Henrietta Szold as one of the hundred outstanding women of the past century. Katherine Lenroot, Chief of the U.S. Children's Bureau, broadcast a tribute to her on NBC, quoting: "Thou shalt raise up the foundations of many generations; and thou shalt be called the repairer of the breach, the restorer of paths to dwell in." Carrie Chapman Catt sent her a copy of her book, *Victory: How Women Won it: 1840–1940,* which took Henrietta back to the World's Fair in Chicago in 1893 when she refused to be a militant woman, and to spirited discussions with her sisters Rachel and Adele about feminism and women's rights, and to her organization of Hadassah: the Women's Zionist Organization, and to its conflicts with the men of the Z.O.A.—all long ago and far away. And here she was at eighty, doing just what Mamma had done—that woman's work which is never done, raising a lot of children. . . .

One of the most gratifying of her gifts was the establishment by Dr. and Mrs. Magnes of a prize for the best essay on Rabbi Szold's works by a student at the University; and Miss Szold—after Dr. Magnes had referred to her as her father's daughter—took that occasion, in referring to his published "Commentary on Job," to recall that "It was my mother who, out of her meager household allotments, saved the money—and the savings had to amount to a considerable sum—that paid for the book. There, too, lay a root of my being." They took her up on the roof of the University library on Mount Scopus where against the magnificent vista of the Land of Israel a photograph was taken of Miss Szold in her gray woolen suit and felt hat, looking tiny among the distinguished scholars—Judah Magnes, Martin Buber, and the rest who had gathered to do her honor—and the stalwart young students, the new Jews she was intent on raising. Then Miss Szold returned to her work.

In addition to continued efforts to bring children in from Lithuania, Bulgaria, Yugoslavia and Hungary, she was experimenting with an expansion of Youth Aliyah—taking children of immigrants in the cities for training and education in the agricultural colonies. Graduates of the first group of German children trained at Ain Ḥarod had established a flourishing colony, Alonim. It was now seven years since that first arrival, and in 1941, of the 6,200 children brought in, 3,800 had graduated into independent living. Miss Szold was conducting a critical survey of Youth Aliyah's accomplishment, to find out: "What has been achieved? What has been done to and with the youthful victims of slander and hate snatched from a Europe that threatened to swallow them alive or torture them to destruction and death? Have only their racked bodies been transplanted from soil to soil?" That would not be enough for Miss Szold.

During March and April she was confined to her room by illness, her weary body taxed by dysentery; but with good nursing care from the school she managed to continue working. At this time, added to her illness as a good reason for going "home" there was the consideration in the U.S. Congress of the "dual loyalty" of Americans long resident in Palestine. She joined with Judah Magnes in arguing against the loss of their citizenship by such expatriates, citing, for precedents, William Wetmore Story, the American sculptor who lived most of his life in Italy, and Robert Browning, who was buried in Westminster Abbey although he had written,

Open my heart and you will see
Graved inside of it, "Italy."

They argued that "If you open the heart of many of the American citizens in Palestine you will find graved inside of it: 'The Holy Land,'" which could be said of many Americans outside Palestine, Christians as well as Jews.

Louis Brandeis, who had long argued that "To be good Americans, we must be better Jews, and to be better Jews, we must become Zionists," died in the fall of that year; and Henrietta Szold went to Ein Ha-Shophet—"the Well of the Judge," a colony named for Justice Brandeis—to do her great friend honor. She recalled the meeting in New York in 1914 at which he was persuaded to undertake the Zionist leadership: "The spirit of a quiet, grave, yet dominating personality was infused into it. To be of it, was like standing on a mountaintop with invigorating breezes blowing about one and vistas and perspectives of hope and achievement revealing themselves. . . ." To those who asked: "Where are the leaders to come from to fill the places left vacant?" she recalled Ecclesiastes: "One generation passeth and another generation cometh but the earth abideth forever. . . ." "Leaders will continue to exist, rising from the masses or from the recesses from which Herzl and Brandeis emerged. Leadership will not be lacking," she said.

The roll call of death was gathering in the friends of Henrietta Szold, but she mitigated those losses with constructive works in their names. On her return to Jerusalem she recommended the establishment of a Brandeis Center of trade schools, one of them to be the Alice Seligsberg Vocational School for Girls, endowed with moneys she had gathered—an institution which, to her mind, would be an important prophylactic against the problem of delinquency among girls, which still concerned her. She saw in such schools "a veritable refuge for girls exposed to all sorts of dangers that are incidental to war," and she stressed not only their vocational education, domestic and industrial, but their inculcation of good taste—"a spiritual possession which the pupils . . . will carry with them into all the departments of their lives, into their homes, into the education of their children, into their pleasures. . . . The cultured woman is the better dressmaker, the better cook, the better companion. . . ." On her way back to Jerusalem she had stopped at Haifa to attend a social service meeting at which she discussed sex education for children.

For her eighty-first birthday the *Vaad Leumi* entrusted her with the planning of *Le-Maan Ha-Yeled Ve-Ha-Noar,* its Fund for Child and Youth Care, something she had long hoped for. She saw in it "the spirit of a great-hearted mother . . . a wise, protecting mother whose sole aim is to fulfill the aims of those who trust her." She drew up its plan of organization and program of action in dealing with the needs of the young of the whole community. She based her plan on two ancient rabbinical precepts: "Nothing, not even the work of building the Temple, may interfere with the studies of little schoolchildren"; and, "Only the breath of little schoolchildren mantains the world." To these she added the Talmudic injunction she had quoted long ago to the gathering of Maryland schoolteachers against permitting a "teacher to teach more than twenty pupils in a class." Her plan embraced not merely education but health and social service. It included kindergartens and baby stations and school hygiene, summer camps, playgrounds, clubs, university and vocational education, orphanages, correctional institutions, homes for defectives, for the crippled, children's villages. . . .

By that time Pearl Harbor and its consequences had made the possibility of her return "home" remote indeed, and she was like a stranded woman stubbornly engaged in properly raising her brood on an island surrounded by angry seas. Long ago, Goethe, the prophetic poet, in *Hermann und Dorothea,* which her father used to read to her, had described just such a world:

> *. . . all is in motion*
> *Now for a time on the earth, and everything seems to be failing;*
> *In the firmest of states the old fundamental laws are dissolving . . .*
> *All is in motion, as though the already shaped world into chaos*
> *Meant to resolves itself, backward into night. . . .*

Of what was being done to the spirits of children in the land of Goethe and Schiller and Lessing she had read reports: "Teachers of history are instructed to stress the importance of race purity and the menace to Germany of Jewish influence in politics, religion, art, literature and morals. Children studying ancient Rome are to be shown that it was the Jews, after their dispersion, who penetrated all quarters of the Roman Empire and caused its downfall. Medieval and modern history should be taught with special emphasis on the desperate struggles of the Spanish, Polish and German peoples against Jewish domination. And it should be pointed out to students that wherever revolution upsets the established order, from the French Revolution on down to the present days, Jews are found. No biology instruction should lack emphasis on the deterioration of a race through the mixture of alien blood, and children should thus learn why it is a prison offense in Germany for a Jew to live with a non-Jewish woman. Even in elementary art instruction, children will be encouraged to develop their perception of racial differences by including caricatures of Jewish faces in their drawings, and kindergarten picture books will have pages designed to instill in the child sentiments regarding Jews similar to those regarding dangerous wild beasts . . ." It was no great hardship to be cut off from a world in which this was permitted. What could she do in that world? Here she was part of the great and ancient Jewish aspiration. Here, even if the family of Jewry were all but annihilated, a saving fragment of it might survive, with its civilizing ethic of which the world was more in need now than ever.

The statistical results of Miss Szold's survey of what Youth Aliyah had accomplished with children in Palestine was reassuring: "These figures are not dry. To those willing to penetrate to their essential meaning they reveal . . . the vitality which resisted the parching power of Hitlerism. . . . They are significant, a mine of educational suggestion, the raw material inviting pedagogic and sociological investigation. These figures do not lie—they preach, they teach, they admonish, they stimulate. They form the fabric of hope and are a source of energy to leaders and those led by them."

And when she saw signs in the Jewish community of the resort to that angry violence which was overwhelming the world, she was moved in her eighty-second year to prophetic admonition of her people. Not that the Jews of Palestine had not sufficient provocation for anger and even violence: the limited immigration policy of the Mandatory Government was being enforced with a ruthless rigidity which became inhumane. The *Struma*, a ship dangerously overloaded with "illegal" immigrants from Roumania, was warned not to approach the shore of the Promised Land and was turned back from Istanbul. It foundered in the Black Sea, and some eight hundred desperate refugees were drowned, many of them relatives of settlers they had hoped to join, and parents of children who had been saved. . . . Nevertheless, Miss Szold spoke out against those in Palestine who resorted to underground reprisal, and to conflict with those who disapproved of their violence.

"These wards of our people, whose ties to parents and home we severed, were brought here by us to be trained as citizens and builders of the new-old land sanctified by the words and the lives of legislators and prophets as well as by our fervent faith in an honorable future. For their sake, for the sake of all our young men and women, whom we cherish, and the future we aspire to, I would adjure the leaders and the led to take solemn thought of what is happening under our eyes, and remove partisan strife and violence from our midst. Intolerance bids fair to prevail. Men who express views at variance with those of a presumed majority are exposed to bodily harm. Political scores are settled with bombs. License is tending to replace law among the people of the law. Liberty of conscience and freedom of speech threaten to slip from our guardianship. Our hallowed ethical standards are in danger of declining. These are evil things, of which our camp must be cleansed.

"We are calling upon our young men to battle to the finish against totalitarianism with its iniquitous star-chamber practices. We lay the task upon them to save from annihilation the precious bits of culture amassed since the remote days when our fathers were bidden to 'proclaim liberty throughout the land unto all the inhabitants thereof.' These young warrior-builders fulfilling our behest and the mothers of our future hosts of peace, freedom, and justice demand of us to be mindful of the teaching of our people's history: the Jew and his cause have persisted through the ages not by the might of the fist, not by the power of brute force, but by the spirit of divine law and love."

Yet, as she wrote this, it was becoming increasingly difficult for her to maintain a consistent position, even there on her island in Palestine, which was being invaded by the prevailing winds of angry violence. She had lost her youthful ability to arrive at decisive judgments and hold tenaciously to them, as she used to in the days when as "Sulamith" she expressed her unshakable opinions. She had to admit now that some of her young "builders" of the peaceful future must of necessity for the present become "warriors." And when, in September, among the soldiers of the Allies now to be seen on the streets of Jerusalem, she saw numbers of Americans, she published a "welcome to the defenders of the four freedoms who have come from the United States . . . I feel impelled," she said, "to stretch out my hand to them and press theirs in fellowship and gratitude. . . ." Twenty-two years of absence had not obliterated from her memory "the richly painted woods of Maine and the Adirondacks and the Blue Ridge at this season," nor had she ceased to hear the "rush of the mighty rivers of America, and the roar of its waterfalls. . . . Only yesterday you sighted the Statue of Liberty which I have not seen for a number of years. You and I, we know, and we shall know as long as we breathe, that the inscription it bears expresses the soul of our America. We know that when you and your comrades in arms of other nations together have won the peace of our aspirations, America will continue to say: 'Give me your tired, your poor . . .' " And then she reminded them, too, of Moses: "I would recall to your mind another inscription, this one on an historical American monument, the verse from Leviticus engraved on the Liberty Bell, preserved in Independence Hall in Philadelphia: 'Proclaim liberty throughout the land unto all the inhabitants thereof.' Is it not a thrilling thought, that you warriors for liberty coming from America stand on the soil on which the words were written that summarized their great struggle for the Fathers of our Republic? . . . From the East to which you have come for the purpose of restoring liberty to the world, issued the concept of liberty and spread to the West and to all the world. This is your consecration and your serious task, and eventually will be your order of merit."

Now Miss Szold was changing her mind. And even her friend Dr. Magnes was becoming impatient with her because she was no longer certain that the arguments of his group for a binational state would lead to an acceptable and viable solution of the Arab-Jewish problem. A friendly Arab who had collaborated with Magnes in publishing an Arabic paper was murdered. Henrietta Szold was inclined to put her "faith in the values inherent in negotiation as contrasted with decisions of the mighty, which eventuate in resort to force, if not at first, then at last." King David's "age of strength" had brought Miss Szold only one indestructible certitude: that her children must be reared on the civilized ideals of the great Jewish past, no matter how mad and chaotic the world was at present. Of this she was reassured every time she visited the children in the colonies.

In the fall of 1942 she went up to Matsuba near the northern border, in hilly stony country, with exquisite views on all sides, but little water. It was a two-year-old colony of a hundred of her children, graduates of Youth Aliyah. They had finished a well which was giving them just enough water for drinking and household purposes but not yet enough for irrigation. For this they had still to depend on the winter rains. Nevertheless they had raised vegetables and planted trees, carobs and olives and plums. They had herds of goats; they had native cows; and they raised chickens, though they could not yet produce the green fodder for their livestock and fowl. They had babies, too, eight lively children. One of the sturdy handsome young mothers held up her baby for Miss Szold to see—as beautiful an infant as those white *bambini* of della Robbia which had delighted her and Mamma in Florence. The crowing child reached out a chubby warm little hand and touched her face, and turned Miss Szold into a beaming, cooing grandmother.

At the frugal dinner they tendered her, two addresses were given. The first gave the history of the colony from its beginning when the Jewish Agency gingerly offered the group of seventy-five teenage pioneers, thirty girls among them, their unwatered mound of rocks in that predominantly Arab, hostile region. The area still open to Jewish settlement was being strictly limited by the government, and they would have had to wait several years before they could get better land. They had preferred not to wait and had started there at Matsuba with all its handicaps. For all their hardihood, Miss Szold was filled with doubts and forebodings. Indeed, only a few days before, some hundred and seventy of their two-year-old plum trees had been destroyed by marauding Bedouin. Then the second speaker arose to tell of their plans and hopes for the future. A tall, broad-shouldered young man, his whole appearance betokened pluck and tenacity. Everything he said expressed a spirit of trust, confidence and resolution that was infectious. He made her believe in the old saw: "Where there's a will there's a way." She said to herself that Matsuba justified not only Youth Aliyah but the whole Zionist undertaking. Nothing could stop them. They had set up a small weaving establishment which was bringing some income. And there was a fellow, Shmuel Cohen, a linguistic wonder, who spent all his spare time poring over every book he could lay hands on—in English, French, German, Russian, Italian—which told anything about mushroom culture. He was raising mushrooms in the caves that honeycombed the surrounding hills. He was sure that the sale of mushrooms would in time pay for the buildings and equipment Matsuba would need for all those coming grandchildren of Miss Szold. . . . How could she not have faith in such children? At Huleh Lake north of Galilee another group of them had drained a malarial swamp, and had cows pastured on their earthwork fortifications. Young men worked tractors; young women edited the colony's newspaper while raising a crop of her grandchildren. Down in the Negev, at the other end of the country, another group was diverting a stream of fresh water to wash the salt out of the sand of the desert and make it bloom—you could see the green growth they had brought to pass. She had written Bertha: "Blessed the plants which go on growing and blossoming. And blessed the babies who likewise grow without having to take thought of the morrow—or of the ultimate fate of the world . . ." "From Dan to Beersheba" her children were saying *"Le Ḥayim!"*—"To Life!" If only they could have *Shalom*—peace, on this one small island in a disrupted world!

She drew fresh hope from the fact that there were still some strong men in that world—like Franklin Roosevelt whom she greatly admired for his courage—who still saw the possibility of a peaceful unity of nations and were willing to work to that end. One of them, Wendell Willkie, undertook the dangerous mission, in the fall of 1942, of flying around that war-torn world to survey the prospect of making it "One World," to talk to the men of power and influence who might make it so, to Stalin and Chiang Kai-shek and General Montgomery and King Farouk. He arrived in Jerusalem on September 11 and, after seeing High Commissioner

Sir Harold MacMichael and U.S. Consul-General Lowell Pinkerton and Major General McConnel, commanding the British forces, and Moshe Shertok, head of the political department of the Jewish Agency, and Ruhi Bey Abdul Hadi, Arab member of the High Commissioner's Secretariat, and Dr. Ariel Altman, head of the Revisionists who claimed the whole country for the Jews, and Awni Bey Abdul Hadi, Arab nationalist leader who claimed the whole country for the Arabs, Mr. Willkie was brought to Miss Szold. It was late in the afternoon and Miss Szold was at home in the Pension Romm preparing for the High Holy Day—it was the eve of *Rosh Hashanah*, the Jewish New Year.

At the end of that long hard day of interviewing Britons and Arabs and Jews, Mr. Willkie confessed to Miss Szold that he had come to feel "that the only solution to this tangled problem must be as drastic as Solomon's," the site of whose palace they could see from where they sat. Facing her across her desk in the late sunlight slanting down over golden Jerusalem, that rugged Midwestern American, with candid eyes under a shock of unruly hair, confessed to Miss Szold "my confusion and my anxiety to find the answer." He asked her if she thought it true that certain foreign powers were deliberately stirring up trouble between the Jew and the Arab to help sustain their own control.

Miss Szold answered, "With a sad heart I must tell you it is true." Then she said, "Mr. Willkie, this problem has been with me for many years. I cannot live comfortably in America while it is unsolved. There is no other appropriate place in the world where the persecuted Jews of Europe can come. And no matter how much we may wish it, that persecution will not end in your lifetime or in mine. The Jews must have a national homeland. I am an ardent Zionist, but I do not believe that there is a necessary antagonism between the hopes of the Jews and the rights of the Arabs. I am urging my fellow Jews here in Jerusalem to do those simple things that break down the prejudices, the differences between people. I urge each of them to make friends with a few Arabs to demonstrate by their way of life that we are not coming as conquerors or destroyers, but as a part of the traditional life of the country, for us a sentimental and religious homeland."

The sun was setting behind the Judean hills, and azure twilight was darkening the windows. Miss Szold got up and brought her mother's candlesticks; she set them on her desk and lit the candles, saying the benediction for the New Year. Then, with the lights between them, she went on to tell Mr. Willkie of her belief in the possibilities of education, of what had already been accomplished in the agricultural colonies and in industry in the towns; she told him stories of her indomitable children. . . .

At the end, Mr. Willkie said that it was probably unrealistic to believe that such a complex question as the Arab-Jewish one, founded in ancient history and religion, and involved as it was with high international policy and politics, could be solved by good will and simple honesty; yet, sitting there with her, he wondered if she in her mature, selfless wisdom might not know more than all the ambitious politicians. Then he clasped her hand, and he flew off on his well-meaning way round the troubled world, leaving Miss Szold to celebrate that solemn time of self-searching which is inaugurated by the Jewish New Year. She went to the synagogue to pray "for peace, for cessation of the butchering of another generation of young men," but realized that "I have so far left behind my old attitude that I cannot content myself with the wish for peace—I have learnt in the interval between the two wars that it must be a just peace, a peace that solves the problem, if men are to live humanly, as becomes human beings."

During the past two years, despite her daily preoccupation with distracting duties, she had had frequent occasion to recall and reconsider much of her life. After the death of Adele, her sister Bertha had undertaken the task of transporting the things Henrietta had stored in Connecticut; and since storage space in her own home in Baltimore was limited, Bertha had to dispose of whatever in Henrietta's boxes seemed unimportant. In this connection she tried to get Henrietta's opinion about some of the things she turned up, and as a result their correspondence was filled with reminders of the past—"pillow cases with Mamma's handknit lace and the cross-stitched towels," the medals she got in school, Papa's snuffbox—reminders of those lively years in Lombard Street and of those difficult years in 123rd Street—all so long ago and far away. Henrietta deplored her inability to relieve Bertha of that task which she should herself have attended to on her several visits to America. For her failure to do so she now blamed Hadassah, which had always kept her so busy on those visits; but she confessed that a sort of "paralysis" had always overcome her at the thought of attending to it when she could. For she knew very well that she would be faced with the decision of whether to destroy certain papers—journals, diaries, a letter to which was attached a poem and a veil . . . writings in which she had poured out the depths of her suffering spirit; and although she wrote Bertha that there were things which she, if she were clearing out those boxes, would be prompted to burn, yet she did not instruct Bertha to do so. Because to the writer—and although she had not found the time to "write" she had been, in fact, a prodigious writer—every letter, every report, every address she composed had contained some expression of her essential spirit, and her collected "writings," since that childish fantasy about George Washington, would have run into many millions of words—to the writer, to the spirit of the artist, the destruction of any self-expression, however painful, is as sacrilegious as the destruction of life itself. You might just as well expect Rembrandt to destroy that self-portrait of his face ravaged by time and suffering. So it was in a sense a relief to Henrietta to have to leave the disposition of her things to Bertha. She did however continue to discourage Bertha from undertaking the writing of that biography which Adele had begun, and which Henrietta still thought her life did not warrant.

Her friends in Hadassah, however, convinced of the importance of the life of their distinguished Founder, Henrietta Szold, had decided to honor her and present her before a wider audience. They got the excellent writer Marvin Lowenthal to make a representative selection of her letters which, supplied with a running commentary, would be in effect an autobiography. A copy of the book reached Miss Szold in the summer of 1942, and it was not easy for her at first to open it and review her own utterances in the light of time; but it proved an absorbing experience, exciting and saddening, painful and gratifying. The dedication alone, to Judge Mack, wove a web of memories between past and present. It brought back vital Aaron Aaronsohn whom she had taken so hopefully to Judge Mack, who had helped him build his fine Agricultural Experimental Station at Athlit. Now there remained of it no more than two rows of dejected palms, as she had seen on a recent trip to the nearby camp full of "illegal" refugees. When she had overcome that first reluctance, she found the book fascinating, "dashed through it from cover to cover, practically at one Sabbath sitting." But there were lacking whole slices of her life—writings of hers which either had been withheld by Bertha or, for all she knew, had been destroyed; matters which "touched deep-lying springs" as she wrote her cousin Miriam Schloessinger who had been one of her confidantes in the days of anguish. To Mr. Lowenthal she wrote: "All in all, I am still of the opinion that I am not a subject meet for a biography. I lived through great times—stirring transformations, social convulsions, scientific and technical achievements of the highest order happened during my more than fourscore years. Is there an echo of all this in my letters? Do they indicate that I responded to the events under my eyes by searchings of the heart, by revolt or assent, from which readers might learn how to battle with life? As a matter of fact, I may disclose to you that there was actually much more of a spiritual reverberation than the letters indicate. But the deeper reactions did not find their way into creative expression, creative subjectively and objectively. The book was conceived in the affection of my Hadassah co-workers, and they will read it with satisfaction because it is the portrait of the associate they knew. But the thinking of the great host of Hadassah members will not be leavened. . . ." Writing to her friend Rose Jacobs she questioned "if the reading of the book will stimulate the great mass of Hadassah members to think and feel and order their lives consciously according to a principle derived from a description of my spiritual struggles." To her friend Tamar de Sola Pool she admitted her absorbed enjoyment of the book but insisted that "biography should be more than chronicle. It should stimulate thought, influence action, lead to introspection and creation."

If the perusal of her past toward the end of the year 1942 did not convince Miss Szold of having had any great influence on the women of Hadassah in America, there in Palestine that *Yom Kippur* she had little cause for repentance. It could be said of her as of *eshet ḥayil:* "Her children rise up and call her blessed." Surely she had been compensated many thousandfold for that love which had once been denied her; love was now lavished upon her. She did not regret her decision to stay there, although there were moments when she longed to see the end of the cruel war when she might return to America to stay for a short time at least with Bertha and her children, who were also bearing her grandchildren, one after another.

In the meantime she tried to influence not merely the women of Hadassah but the women of the world. In November she wrote "Save the Child!" an appeal in the name of the Jewish women of Palestine to the Jewish women of the world, and through them to all women in the free democratic countries, whether or not participants in the war: ". . . on behalf of the children in the areas of Europe held in the clutches of sadistic monsters in human shape. Our children are perishing, body and soul. They are being exterminated pitilessly, of malice aforethought. They must be saved.

"The Jewish women of the world have long been hearing the cry of the Jewish children in Germany and Czechoslovakia, in Poland and Roumania, in all countries trodden by the Nazi foot. In particular the Jewish women of Palestine can testify to the great and good things it has meant to have plucked them like brands from the burning. We here have seen with our own eyes what promise the rescued youth holds out to becoming restorers of the breaches, of renewing the cultural values destroyed in Berlin, Vienna, Prague, Warsaw, Cracow, and a score of other centers of learning and treasuries of the past. At this very moment, the hearts of the Jewish women of Palestine are torn between hope and apprehension while message after message reaches them from nine hundred children at Teheran, most of them parentless, who are waiting to complete the last lap of their toilsome, long journey from Poland through Russia and Persia to Palestine.

"I would have Jewish women everywhere appeal in this fashion in turn to the motherhood instinct of all women, the creative instinct that abhors destruction. The women of the world cannot but recognize that the cause of the Jewish child is their cause. Is it necessary to remind them that the horrors that envelop our days and nights at present began with the designs against the Jews? Perhaps if the world had not sat by silent and unconcerned when the torture of the German Jews was begun and the extermination of all Jews promised, there would not have been a Second World War claiming its millions of precious young lives. They should ponder that the devilish work beginning with Jewish children may easily extend, if it has not already extended, to the children of all races and nationalities. Ay, here is proof of the prognosis—the Jewish child refugees at Teheran are encamped with hundreds of Polish Christian child refugees! The women of the world should be asked: if we Jewish women need to assure ourselves of future bearers of the Jewish spirit and if we must train exponents of Jewish values, do not they, likewise, and we together with them, require builders of the new postwar order of the four freedoms we dream of?

"Women are the natural protectors of childhood. They are the guardians of the generations. If Nazi brutality is not swiftly deprived of its child victims by removing all endangered children from Nazi-occupied territories to all countries whose portals will be open to them, what will be the aspect of the next generation? Is not the plea to women to organize a movement to 'Save the Child for Civilization' the plea for a supreme peace effort? . . ."

The children at Teheran to whom she referred constituted the largest and most remarkable group yet to be rescued by Youth Aliyah; and she was then mainly preoccupied with preparations for their arrival and reception. Seven hundred and thirty of them were coming from Teheran where they were encamped after an unbelievable trek of three and one half years from all parts of Poland since the fall of Warsaw in 1939. They had wandered, like packs of hunted animals, through Russia and Persia to Samarkand and Uzbekistan, and finally to the port of Pahlevi on the Caspian Sea, where representatives of the Jewish Agency gathered and took them in hand and transported them to Teheran, whence they were to be brought to Palestine. This final stage was delayed by the Iraqi government which refused them transit visas; so a ship was secured which took them from a Persian port to Karachi and then to Port Suez, where it arrived on February 17, 1943.

Miss Szold had sent Hans Beyth there to meet them, while she completed the complex arrangements for their reception at Athlit Clearance Camp on the following day, and their distribution among the colonies. Their epic story stirred the whole Jewish community to co-operation. For their transportation from the railroad station the bus company offered a fleet of free buses, and the hospitals provided a fleet of ambulances for the sick. Miss Szold, who had been a stickler for the maintenance of the Immigration Department's health regulations, now said at one of the innumerable preparatory meetings, "I have always, during all the time I worked for Youth Aliyah, demanded a thorough examination. . . . But here, as regards these children, I say that we have to accept all of them. All of them are the children of Israel—our children—and just as a mother does not throw out a child of hers, be it sick or an invalid, so we have no right to deprive such children of the chance to come here. We have to take upon ourselves the difficulties of absorbing those children. . . ."

Their long-heralded arrival excited the whole country. The train on its way up from Egypt was stopped at every station by crowds bearing gifts and flowers and sweets for the children. The arrival of the train at Athlit was tumultuous. Out of every window waved hands holding the little white flags with the blue Star of David that they had been given. From the mob on the platform the names of families and Polish towns were shouted in the hope that some long-lost child might be found.

In all the tumult, Miss Szold went about supervising her aides in their effort to carry out their plan for the orderly handling of the children, despite the almost hysterical people on the platform. And when the children detrained she saw that they would present her with problems beyond any she had yet encountered. They were pathetic beyond description—they looked indeed like "the wretched refuse" whom Emma Lazarus welcomed in the poem engraved on the Statue of Liberty. Many of them were still dressed like ragamuffins, in remnants of clothing picked up God-knows-where in the world—broken pith helmets, cut-down adults' trousers and dresses. And, worse yet, many of them, driven for years from pillar to post in a hostile world, uncared for and unschooled, were not merely sick—and many had to be carried from the train—they were wild, frightened creatures who went to bed with their clothes on, clutching the bread they had been unable to devour.

"We have to take upon ourselves the difficulties of absorbing those children . . ." Miss Szold had said; and Miss Szold was not one to retreat from difficulties even in her eighty-third year, nor to let others do so. Yet there were times when she was reduced well-nigh to hysteria herself by the deviltry of literally dreadful children, driven to near-madness during their flight through a mad world. These were much worse off than the worst victims of the Nazis in Germany. Some broke windows and refused to work or study in the good homes to which they were sent, but which seemed to them now like prisons. Miss Szold's admonishing finger and gently reproving voice was sometimes met not with respectful attention but with shrugging or sullen disregard. "We have to take upon ourselves the difficulties . . ." Miss Szold had said to her aides, and they did. "It is for us who have hitherto been spared the extreme horrors of war to demonstrate that we are equal to the task of saving the remnants," she maintained.

Difficulties came not only from those terribly wounded children but from the interference of sentimental adults who tried to assuage their own souls, laden with the guilt of having made a world in which this could happen to children, by showering them with misguided attentions. Miss Szold finally had to plead in published notices that the public should not disrupt the well-organized efforts which were being made to deal with the problems. And the greatest difficulty of all arose from the insistence of some Orthodox leaders that these children, having come originally from areas in which Jews were predominantly Orthodox, should be raised in Orthodox colonies; this despite the fact that there were not enough Orthodox places available for those children, even if all of them had had and still wanted such upbringing, which, as Miss Szold took pains to determine in the procedure of placing them, many of them did not. Her persistence in handling this matter on the basis of reasonable and practical considerations for the best possible benefit of each child, rather than on the basis of the emotions of people who were not actually involved in the problem, inevitably subjected her to bitter partisan criticism. Intellectually, Miss Szold was not dismayed by such controversy; long ago, as young "Sulamith," she had herself taken a lively part with Papa in the Orthodox-Conservative-Reform controversy which had rent American Jewry; but now her children were at stake and her heart was weary. After all, she *was* going on eighty-three. In the summer she wrote Rose Jacobs of Hadassah: "I ought to tell you of my troubles, my long-drawn-out agony connected with the Teheran children and their religious education. I have had six months of poignant struggle, and the end is not in sight. I can't write about it. As soon as the most important arrears in my correspondence are made up, I shall write a full report. My strength has returned after a severe illness which laid me low when the seven hundred children were in camps seething with devastating propaganda. . . ." Miss Szold was not spared the agonies of child-bearing; she, who had so wanted children—"many of them"—suffered in good measure.

However, as she wrote a young Zionist in the Bronx who was greatly troubled by reports of this controversy in Palestine, "there were always differences of opinion among Jews. The most learned of them, Maimonides, had his opponents; the Pharisees and the Sadducees approached Jewish discussions from widely different points of view. There were basic distinctions between them and their attitudes. But always in all ages and epochs there evolved a system which we call Judaism, which Dr. Schechter, the renowned scholar, called 'Catholic Judaism,' meaning an all-embracing Judaism which gave a place to all Jews and to their Jewish living. Personally, I have always hoped that, especially when we attained a normal life as a people in Palestine, we should be able to find a method comparable to that of the old Sanhedrin which would make clear an accepted trend of development in Jewish matters. . . . My firm conviction is that the solution of what we call the Jewish problem, the external and the internal, can be achieved only through Zionism, the object of which is, indeed, to give us a self-dependent form of life in Palestine. If the objects of the present war are world-wide, if the Atlantic Charter is more than verbal, but can have its counterpart in the forms of living, then a Jewish State that established itself without the consent of the peers of the Jewish people, that is to say, the enlightened peoples of the earth, cannot hope to maintain itself for a day. We have to reckon with the United States, with Great Britain, with the Arab people, and with our own past as well. You will recall that one of our Prophets said: 'Not by might and not by force but by the spirit of the Lord.' The spirit of the Lord I interpret as proper co-ordination with the world we live in. One more word . . . seeing that you are young and I am old, that I have the right to say: 'Don't despair.' "

In August Miss Szold was welcoming another batch of over a hundred children collected at Teheran; and in September, wearing a wide straw hat against the hot sun, and accompanied by Hans Beyth and Norman Bentwich, she went on a tour of inspection of Youth Aliyah groups.

The celebration of her eighty-third birthday in December merged with the celebration in February 1944 of Youth Aliyah's tenth anniversary. Her first greetings on that occasion went to Recha Freier, "the author of the idea of transplanting youth from an environment of poisonous hate into an atmosphere of free creative endeavor." Then she greeted the ten thousand who had come "from Germany, Austria, Czechoslovakia, Poland, Roumania, Hungary, Bulgaria, Italy, Yugoslavia, Latvia, Yemen, Iraq, Greece and Turkey," of whom three thousand were still in training, and seven thousand were making their own way in every field of human endeavor, including some fifteen hundred in the armed forces. And finally she addressed the whole *Yishuv*: "Be ready and equipped to take to your homes and your hearts the thousands whom, by the grace of God, we may still be privileged to serve." She saw no end to what she was doing. In explanation of several months' delay in her reply to a birthday greeting she said, "Life runs ahead too swiftly for eighty-three to keep up with it." Commendation for the achievement of Youth Aliyah came to her from President and Mrs. Roosevelt, from Wendell Willkie, and from a host of others, far and near; but already she was concerned with well-planned preparation for the greater social service problems with which Palestine would have to deal "in the period facing us when victory and peace will doubtless bring us a large-scale immigration . . . the reconstruction duty we anticipate with awe and joy." This she said, although war was still raging in Europe and in the Pacific.

She dreamed now of a single reception center for the refugee children, a pleasant, peaceful place where they would have time to recover, spiritually as well as physically, and where the background of each could be studied and the needs of each one determined before final placement. She chose Alonim as the place, and Hadassah agreed to establish such a center, to be called Mosad Szold. For its charter she outlined the aims of the organization:

"To arouse and stimulate a sense of responsibility in all sections of the Jewish community for the welfare of children and youth,
to collect and publish information regarding all problems connected with children and youth,
to coordinate the activities of the various existing child and youth welfare institutions and organizations,
to ensure a proper approach to problems concerning youth in the field of education, health and social service,
to encourage the extension of existing organizations and to promote the creation of new enterprises,
to improve the legal status of children."

But all that spring her tired heart kept Miss Szold in a hospital bed, where she celebrated the Passover *seder,* although she still supervised her manifold works in the field and office through her unfailing aides, Hans Beyth and Emma Ehrlich. By June she was recovered enough to leave the hospital but not to make the trip to Haifa to welcome incoming children. In July she attended the sessions of a seminar for *madriḥim* at the University on Mount Scopus, but by the end of the month she was back in the hospital with what proved to be pneumonia. She was still there in September when the twenty-fourth class of the Nurses' Training School was graduated—the first one she could not attend. In the address she sent them she pointed out that "oddly enough, never . . . could I have conferred the sign and symbol of your dignity and your competence upon graduating as nurses with a keener perception of the meaning of the act than this year, during which I was an object of your devoted, instructed care. . . ." In their new white uniforms they paraded by under her window so that she might see them. And from that window it delighted her to look upon the profusion of flowers in the garden between the hospital and the Nurses' Training School.

In October she was improved enough to think she might accept the invitation of Lilian Friedlaender to recuperate in Ziḥron Yaakob. It would be pleasant to recall the old days with Lilian who had had her heart's desire, a beloved husband and children, but had suffered greatly, too. Henrietta remembered her so vividly as the handsome Bentwich girl Israel Friedlaender brought to New York from England; she still remembered the blue dress and toque she wore that day so long ago. But in November Henrietta was still too ill to leave, and was moved over to the Nurses' Home, where, under the direction of Dr. Kleeberg, a group of Hadassah's physicians waged an unremitting campaign against the disease with the best of known medical aids, and where the nurses attended her devotedly. One of them, one of the Teheran girls, came daily especially to give her silvery hair its hundred brush strokes, and more, for the pleasure of talking with Miss Szold when she was able to do so.

There were spells of slow hopeful improvement when she made plans to leave the hospital, followed by feverish relapses. There were times of great anguish, when she learned what her father had meant when he said that Job could not answer the question why even the most worthy of men must suffer; there were long lapses of painful darkness, when she felt herself abandoned by all those she had loved and lost—Papa and Mamma and her sisters, and she cried out for Bertha who could not come to her. But her love of life was unflagging, and she would fight her way back. Her good friends were there every day to help her continue to serve with her unfailing mind those works which were never done: Judah Magnes who became her general manager and liaison with Hadassah, Hans Beyth who ran Youth Aliyah and brought her some of the children when she could see them, and Emma Ehrlich who saw to everything else, including the voluminous correspondence she still maintained. It was remarkable how even in her most wretched physical state her mind went on functioning calmly, its expression as lucid and effective as ever. She could understand how Job, in the midst of suffering, might compose so magnificent an expression of man's dilemma. But what gave her most comfort was the realization that, with or without her, her work would go on.

After her eighty-fourth birthday, which she was too ill to observe in any way, there was a marked improvement in her condition; and on December 27 Dr. Weizmann, who had arrived in Jerusalem to repair the deteriorated relationship of the *Yishuv* and the Mandatory Government, came to call on her. It happened that Dr. Magnes had just been to see her and was still in the next room. Knowing that the two men were greatly at odds because of Weizmann's strong opposition to the binational state which Magnes advocated, Miss Szold sent the nurse for Dr. Magnes. When he came to her bedside she took his hand and said: "I have just told Dr. Weizmann that of all the services he has rendered to Zionism throughout his life, I think that his coming here at this time is the greatest of all because of his attitude to England. There is another thing that is on my heart, and this gives me great joy, and that is to see the two of you together." Thereupon, Dr. Weizmann took her other hand, and she could see that both men were much moved. On the way out, Weizmann said to Magnes, "We must never quarrel." And Magnes said, "No; that seems to be"—and he used a Hebrew phrase—"an injunction from on high."

Later in the day she had a pleasant visit from her nephew Benjamin Levin and his wife Sarah. Benjamin was serving with the armed forces in Egypt, and he told her that instead of pictures of girls in their barracks, the Palestine soldiers had pictures of Zionist heroes—Herzl and Weizmann—and one woman: Henrietta Szold was their only pin-up girl. The visit cheered her. She loved good humor—it was for her "the quality which harmonizes contrasts, conciliates contradictions, uncovers the likenesses hidden in antagonisms." Humor dictated harmony.

Her improvement was maintained until February 12. Curious it was that a number of milestones in her life should have been connected with Abraham Lincoln, whose funeral she had watched so long ago. On the morning of the day after his birthday, feeling too tired to sit up, she leaned back and closed her eyes as she so often had on long journeys. But this time the pang at her heart left her too weak to open them again. All day her good friends came and went at her bedside—the doctors and nurses, Judah Magnes from meetings with Chaim Weizmann, Hans Beyth from receiving twenty-five children from Turkey, dear indefatigable Emma. . . . It was thirty-five years to the day since she and Mamma had been welcomed by their friends in New York after that voyage to the Land of Israel when she had first found her woman's work. . . . Yehudah Halevi, in his *Kuzari,* one of the books she had found on Papa's deathbed, said: "The servant of God does not withdraw himself from secular contact lest he be a burden to the world and the world to him; he does not hate life which is one of God's bounties granted to him, as it is said: 'The number of thy days I will fulfill' (Exodus 23:26); 'Thou mayest prolong thy days' (Deuteronomy 22:7). On the contrary he loves this world and a long life. . . ." It was true. She had not withdrawn herself from the burdens of the world, and she had prolonged her days; she had loved this world and her long life; she had been a good servant of God to whom Halevi sang—Papa used to sing it, too—

Lord, where shall I find Thee?
High and hidden is Thy place!
And where shall I not find Thee?
The world is full of Thy glory!

All her life, true to her given name, Ḥaya, she had said: *Le Ḥayim!* —To Life! But now her weary quivering heart was quite worn out. With the setting of the sun, when darkness had fallen upon Jerusalem, it stopped; and, relinquishing life, she found peace—*Shalom!*

Was This *Death?*

We are permitted . . . to fructify the earth with our ideas, with our hopes, with our very bodies.

—HENRIETTA SZOLD 1923 *

I have been made part and parcel as it were of the land of our heroes and prophets and of our holiest aspirations. From the point of view of nature and from the point of view of history, you have incorporated me with something fundamental, something which in human parlance may be called eternal.

—HENRIETTA SZOLD 1935 †

* From an address, "Jewish Palestine in the Making," delivered in New York

† From a letter to Bertha Schoolman

IN THE MORNING, Emma and the nurses readied her for the last of her many journeys, prepared the frail body for burial, from well-brushed hair to those slender ankles of which she had been justly vain. They wrapped her in the shroud she had provided and, covered by a blue embroidered pall, she was placed on a bier and carried down to the central hall of the Nurses' Home. There on a low platform, lighted by candles, she rested, so that those who wished might come and pay her their last respects.

The news had spread rapidly over the little country, and thousands came, "from Dan to Beersheba," from the towns and the colonies, though the day was wintry and overcast with gusts of fitful rain. All day they climbed Mount Scopus—throngs of men and women, sorrowful and grieving, from all walks of life, her friends and colleagues, her children, some bearing their own children—and silently circled the bier to look upon her for the last time. Her face was gaunt, but beautifully carved by life, the great eyes hooded as if still brooding upon the need and suffering of others, the mobile lips slightly parted as if still ready to utter hopeful and healing words of wisdom.

In the afternoon the bier was taken up and carried along the narrow winding road from Mount Scopus to the Mount of Olives, and hundreds formed a long procession behind it, a stream of humanity, moving between the tall roadside cypresses bowing like black plumes in the blustery wind from the lowering heavens. Children were held up on the shoulders of those she had brought to liberty, so that they might look upon and remember her passing, just as she, when a child, had looked upon and remembered the passing of a great liberator.

In the cemetery on the Mount of Olives, when the open bier was being carried to the graveside, just as she had seen it done that first day thirty-five years before, the steep stony ground was wet and slippery with rain, and Hans Beyth, among the pallbearers, was heard saying, "*Achtung, achtung*!" until they set the bier down safely by the grave. Then Simon Kresz, fifteen years old, who had come two years before from Poland via Teheran, stood beside her like a son and said the mourner's *kaddish*, the Hebrew "consecration," which makes no mention of death, but extols the Creator of life, with the prayer, "May he speedily and soon establish his reign of universal justice, peace, and holiness. . . . " As the bier was lowered into the grave, the dark clouds parted and a shaft of golden sunlight—a burst of warm, life-giving sunshine—illumined the Holy Land and the golden city below.

They filled the grave and left her there within sight of Mount Nebo whence Moses had last looked into this Promised Land. They left her there on the Mount of Olives whence she had first looked down upon the Eternal City.

Was *this* death?

"In the life of the spirit there is no ending that is not a beginning. . . ."

This was but the beginning of immortality.

The Search for Henrietta Szold

Only he who can take in details and store them in his memory and later transform them into some sort of a whole is the poet, the artist, the humanist, the scientific yet imaginative critic . . .

—HENRIETTA SZOLD 1910 *

Herein consists the task of the historian. He must find the perspective for us. He must trace out the road. The details he may not slight. On the contrary he must know them well. But unless he can array them for us in orderly fashion, they are like the scrap iron and junk that cumber the outskirts of your city. He must arrange them in patterns. He must fashion for us the soul of man.

—HENRIETTA SZOLD 1918 †

* From her diary in Rome
† From an address in Birmingham, Alabama

HENRIETTA SZOLD well understood the problem of the biographer, which is both artistic and scientific, since biography, a form of history, should be both moving and truthful. The writer of this book undertook to solve that problem by casting it, like fiction, in the form of a narrative. Thus he hoped to engage the emotion as well as the intelligence of the reader, who might then experience vicariously, as one does in a novel, the rich and painful and triumphant life depicted. For it does you no good being told *about* greatness; you have to experience it. This narrative, unlike fiction, however, was composed of information obtained from sources as reliable as possible; and early in its composition the writer became aware of the circumspection with which the biographer must gather his materials. There was, for example, the generally accepted story that Henrietta, when she was five years old, watched the passing of Lincoln's funeral through Baltimore while perched on her Papa's shoulder; and it is quite possible—memory often being wishful—that she herself was responsible for that story. But the writer, while consulting the files of the Baltimore *Sun* in the Pratt Library, looking for details of the funeral, discovered that Rabbi Szold was in the funeral procession and could not, therefore, have been standing by the window of his house with his Henriettchen on his shoulder. Hence the writer would not be surprised, indeed he would be pleased, to have called to his attention still undiscovered errors of fact in this narrative; but he feels reasonably certain that nowhere has he misrepresented the spirit of his subject, since his representation of that spirit is everywhere based on her own manifold, explicit and lucid expressions of it. Among her other exceptional attributes was the ability, rare in the writing of women, to say just what it is like to be a woman.

The writer hopes that, by the end of the book, the reader will agree that Henrietta Szold was great; that he will make the distinction recommended by Freud "between greatness of achievement and greatness of personality" and, conceding her both, will agree that the secret of the greatness of that personality lay primarily in her courage—a courage that is not merely bravado, which makes one dare to do what others dare not, but the greater courage to persist in doing when others would stop, that courage which, when in her last years she herself was beset by great trials, still prompted her to counsel a man much younger than herself not to despair. For with this courage to persist, each struggle, however desperate, in the life of Henrietta Szold was turned into fruitful action. Theodor Herzl was once profoundly impressed by the observation of an old man of the sea, a fisherman, who said, "The most remarkable of all things is when a man never gives up." In Henrietta Szold, as in Herzl, we have a prime example of that most remarkable thing. And out of that strength, as Samson said, "came forth sweetness."

In his search for Henrietta Szold, the author of this book, after his researches in Baltimore where she spent the first half of her life, followed her to New York where she spent the next quarter of it. There he was pleased to find that, although the house she lived in was gone, the adjacent duplicate of it still remained, and he was able to come out of it, as she had from hers so many times, and walk with her, either west to Riverside Drive or east to Morningside Park. But, having learned circumspection, he asked: Was Grant's Tomb on the Drive then? (It was.) And did the statue of Carl Schurz stand then by the entrance to the park where she went one stormy night in great distress? (It did not.)

Finally he went to the Land of Israel where she spent the last and most important quarter of her life. And there for months he lived a curious dual life between hours in the Zionist Archives, absorbed in the heartbreaking day-to-day struggle of Henrietta Szold to bring renewed life to the ancient land, and hours in the heartwarming company of the lively men and women and children who are now making a good life in that land. And one day—just thirty years after he had ridden up Mount Scopus in a bus full of children chattering Hebrew—he found himself riding up Scopus again, this time with a convoy of the Israeli military police who occupy the area on top of the Mount, which is now an Israeli enclave surrounded by Jordan territory. This time the writer, who wanted to see the place where Henrietta spent her last days and died, rode up in a sealed, armored car, guarded by United Nations soldiers until it arrived at the top.

The Hadassah Hospital, the Nurses' Training School, and the University, buildings whose foundations Henrietta Szold helped lay, are still there; but they were partly shattered by gunfire during the siege of Jerusalem; and, being inaccessible, they are now untenanted. But the spirit of Henrietta Szold lives in the Land of Israel. Looking down on Jewish Jerusalem, you can see on other hills the more stately mansions for the soul of Israel reared by her indomitable children—the fine new campus of the Hebrew University and the magnificent new Hadassah Medical Center. And among the young police up there on Mount Scopus, one of the posthumous sons of Henrietta Szold (some hundred thousand children have been brought in by Youth Aliyah since her death), when asked by the writer if he liked living in Israel, assured the writer that he did—"because being a Jew here is different from being a Jew anywhere else in the world." When asked *how* it was different, the boy answered: "It straightens your spine."

Henrietta Szold was spared the final bitter struggle of her children, against great odds, for even the ungenerous portion of the partitioned land which had been vouchsafed them. But had she witnessed it she would have been justly proud of the persistent determination they seem to have inherited from her. It is true that, although undeniably right in principle in her hatred of solution by violence, history has proved her wrong, together with men like Judah Magnes and Martin Buber who hoped for a binational state of Jews and Arabs living in harmony. (In the year after her death, her colleague Hans Beyth, on his way back from receiving some refugee children at Haifa, was killed by an Arab ambush.) And the pragmatists like Weizmann and Ben-Gurion, to whom the stubborn pacifism of influential Miss Szold was something of a nuisance at times, have proved to be right. History has said it: No other solution was possible.

But Miss Szold was wrong in good company—not only Magnes and Buber, but Isaiah and Micah, whose hopeful prophecy, "They shall beat their swords into ploughshares," has yet to come to pass. We do not discard such unpragmatic ideals, and with good reason;

they serve as a reminder of our potentialities and a measure of our progress and shortcomings; and it might be well for Israel today to review the hopes and expectations of such a prophet as was Henrietta Szold, in order to learn if the new nation is indeed progressing toward its potentialities—toward being not merely just another chauvinistic nation and a haven for persecuted Jews, but the place where, as she believed, the Jewish spirit will flourish and justify its long struggle to survive.

The writer could not visit the grave of Henrietta Szold because the Mount of Olives is now in Jordan territory. It is possible that, as is said, the grave can no longer be located—that, as with Moses on Mount Nebo, no one can now say where her sepulcher is. But the great need no sepulchers, they leave living monuments.

In the seventeenth century, Pascal said of man that he is "the glory and the shame of creation." In the twentieth century man has amply demonstrated his right to the latter characterization. Henrietta Szold was spared by a couple of months the full revelation of the monstrous depths of Germany's reversion to barbarism—its crematoriums where the parents of many of her children were destroyed together with countless children she could not save. And she was spared by a half year her own beloved America's resort to the wanton destruction, with the most terrible weapon of all time, of two enemy cities full of innocent parents and children.

But those of us who are moved to shame for humankind by such inhuman behavior can find reassurance, and hope for man, in the knowledge of rare spirits among us who are veritably "the glory . . . of creation." In the two years the writer has been engaged in learning the life of Henrietta Szold, he has experienced a strengthening, a reinforcement of his own spirit. It is his hope that he has succeeded in instilling in this book enough of the essence of that impassioned soul—its strength as well as its sweetness—to influence similarly the spirits of its readers. Such a result would be, in the eyes of Henrietta Szold, his only justification for writing her biography, for revealing not only her success but her suffering, without which that success would be insignificant.

For his own invaluable experience in getting to know Henrietta Szold, the writer is primarily indebted to Hadassah: the Women's Zionist Organization of America. He is deeply indebted to the nieces and nephews of Henrietta Szold—to Mr. and Mrs. I. B. Terrell, Mr. and Mrs. Jastrow Levin, Mr. and Mrs. Benjamin Levin, Mr. and Mrs. Benjamin Cooper, and Mr. and Mrs. Myron Milbouer, who made available to him private papers of Henrietta Szold without which his insight into her character and life experience would have been seriously limited. He is indebted to the Baltimore Hebrew College and to the Zionist Archives in Jerusalem for access to their rich collections of Henrietta Szold papers and for the generous use of their facilities for research, and to Emma Ehrlich of Jerusalem, who has for years devoted herself to the collection and preservation of the papers of Henrietta Szold. He is further indebted to Mrs. Ehrlich for personal recollections of Henrietta Szold with whom she was closely associated during most of Miss Szold's life in Palestine. To other colleagues and friends in Israel and America too numerous to name, the writer is also indebted for many memories of her which have enlivened this chronicle. And to Mrs. Robert Szold of Hadassah, the writer is immeasurably indebted for her determination that he undertake and pursue this project at a time when he was loath to do so, when, with a persistence which the women of Hadassah appear to have inherited from their Founder, she prevailed upon him to write this book, and availed him of every possible aid to that end.

IRVING FINEMAN

Baltimore,
New York, Jerusalem,
and Shaftsbury, Vermont,
December 1958 to December 1960

INDEX

ABOUT THE AUTHOR

Born in New York City, Irving Fineman is a graduate of the Massachusetts Institute of Technology and Harvard University. He practiced civil engineering, served as an engineer officer in the U.S. Navy, and taught mechanics at the University of Illinois until his first novel, This Pure Young Man, *won the Longmans Green Prize and started him on a writing career. He has since taught literature at Bennington College, written for motion pictures, had two plays produced, and published short stories, poems, and six novels, including* Hear, Ye Sons *and* Doctor Addams. *Mr. Fineman lives on a farm in Shaftsbury, Vermont.*